D0438673

The Policy Challenge
of Ethnic Diversity

Patrick R. Ireland

The Policy Challenge of Ethnic Diversity

Immigrant Politics in France and Switzerland

Harvard University Press
Cambridge, Massachusetts
London, England   1994

Copyright © 1994 by the President and Fellows of Harvard College
All rights reserved
Printed in the United States of America

This book is printed on acid-free paper, and its binding materials
have been chosen for strength and durability.

Library of Congress Cataloging-in-Publication Data

Ireland, Patrick R. (Patrick Richard), 1961–
    The policy challenge of ethnic diversity : immigrant politics in
France and Switzerland / Patrick R. Ireland.
        p.   cm.
    Includes bibliographical references (p.   ) and index.
    ISBN 0-674-68375-7
    1. Ethnicity—Political aspects—France—History.   2. Ethnicity—
Political aspects—Switzerland—History.   3. Immigrants—France—
Political activity.   4. Immigrants—Switzerland—Political activity.
5. Immigrants—Government policy—France.   6. Immigrants—
Government policy—Switzerland.   7. Political participation.
I. Title.
DC34.I74   1994
305.8′00944—dc20   93-28583
                                                            CIP

Preface

The roots of this study lie in the orchards of western Michigan. Living in a county in which unemployment rates hovered above 20 percent during the late 1970s, high school students like me with plans to attend college had few moneymaking alternatives to picking cherries, apples, and blueberries. Such summer jobs brought me into contact with families of migrant workers from Latin America, who perform such backbreaking labor not to pay for tuition but to survive.

Professor Peter A. Hall at Harvard University encouraged me to combine my interest in foreign laborers with a long-standing fascination with European politics. Immigration was becoming a hot topic in the mid-1980s. Following the lead of Mark J. Miller, social scientists had begun to take notice of the increasingly active political role that foreign workers and their children and grandchildren were playing across Western Europe. Yet I was disturbed by the inchoate nature of existing explanations for the evolution of immigrant politics in the "host" societies that imported labor after World War II. The literature has offered little empirical evidence to justify the general assumption that either ethnic background or social class status accounts for the immigrants' choice of political strategies and the policy responses they elicit. Work with immigrant communities in the Midwest and Boston, as well as preliminary research in Europe, led me to suspect that institutional factors have been far more important in structuring immigrant participation and ethnic relations.

It soon became clear that the questions about immigrant political incorporation that interested me could not be answered by means of the quantitative methods typically employed in immigration studies. Instead of advising me to change my questions, Professor Hall convinced me that careful use of the comparative method could produce an effective nonquantitative study that did answer them. Offering unflagging support from the beginning of this project, he has carried me through some desperately dry spells. His patience and friendship stand as proof that mentors, though somewhat hard to come by in this day of the entrepreneurial professoriate, do indeed still exist.

I have also had the great good fortune to profit from the expertise and advice of Professor Stanley Hoffmann. Not many novice scholars have the opportunity to work with one of their heroes. Fewer still, I wager, would find that person so unselfishly supportive and so gracious in counsel.

Others have been generous as well. Professor George Ross at Brandeis University provided extensive comments on several drafts of the manuscript. Abby Collins, Alice Holmes Cooper, Robert Fishman, Diane and Anna Kent, Anna Popiel, Ceillaigh Reddy, and other scholars and staff at Harvard's Center for European Studies gave me valuable input during my years of study there. Since then many people have helped with comments or moral support or both: Michael Barzelay, P. J. Brosmith, Kathleen Carberry, Thomas Faist, Barry Hughes, Steven Kelman, Tricia Kennett, Maureen Moakley, John Mollenkopf, Leslie Nord, Martin Schain, Marya Schechtman, Mary Ellen Sutherland, Pamela Tomkinson, Paul Weithman, Lisa Wilson, Aristide Zolberg, and my students at Connecticut College and at the Graduate School of International Studies at the University of Denver.

A Krupp Foundation Dissertation Fellowship enabled me to spend a year doing research in France and Switzerland in 1986–87. Unable to accept more than one such grant, I regretfully declined a Bourse Chateaubriand offered by the French government for the same period. Even so, the Services du Conseiller Culturel of the Embassy of France kindly facilitated contacts for me in Paris. In 1990 a grant from the American Political Science Association made follow-up research possible. Connecticut College and the University of Denver also have provided travel money and logistical support. Carol Taylor at the Faculty Computer Lab at Denver helped out in the critical final phases of preparing the manuscript.

I cannot hope to list all the people who have offered assistance and kindness during my stays in Europe. However, certain individuals deserve special mention here: Sophie Body-Gendrot, Riva Kastoryano, Gilles Kepel, Rémy Leveau, A. Moustapha Diop, and Catherine Wihtol de Wenden-Didier at the Centre National de la Recherche Scientifique and Centre d'Etudes et de Recherches Internationales in Paris; Jean Leca at the Institut d'Etudes Politiques de Paris; staff members at the Centre d'Information et d'Etudes sur les Migrations Internationales, the Fondation pour la Vie Associative, and the Institut de Recherches sur les Sociétés Contemporaines in Paris; Thierry Delattre at the municipal archives in Roubaix; Pascal Gaillard at the municipal archives in La Courneuve; Georges Abou-Sada and Jean-Paul Tricart at the Observatoire des Migrations Internationales dans la Région Nord–Pas-de-Calais and the Catholic University in Lille; Denis Maillat at the University of Neuchâtel; Rosita Fibbi at the University of Lausanne; Gérard de Rham at the Institut d'Etudes Sociales in Geneva; and Hans-Joachim Hoffmann-Nowotny at the University of Zurich.

Special thanks go to those public officials, religious and associational leaders, and political party and trade union activists who so graciously shared their time and insights with a naive American researcher. My mother, late father, sisters, and brother offered constant encouragement throughout the writing of this book.

As a social scientist I have worked extremely hard to be objective in this study, and some observers might find my analysis dispassionate or even uncaring. For me, however, directly concerned as I am about the functioning of liberal democracy, the immigrants themselves are the real heroes of this book. Their difficult lot has provided its raison d'être; and their dignity, congeniality, and sense of humor never fail to inspire. The pages that follow are dedicated to them.

Denver, Colorado
October 1993

Contents

Abbreviations
and Acronyms

AAE   Amicale des Algériens en Europe (Fraternal Association of Algerians in Europe)

ACLI   Associazioni Cristiane dei Lavoratori Italiani (Christian Association of Italian Workers)

ACO   Action Catholique Ouvrière (Catholic Workers' Action)

ADRI   Agence pour le Développement des Relations Interculturelles (Agency for the Development of Intercultural Relations)

ANAG   Bundesgesetz über Aufenthalt und Niederlassung für Ausländer (Federal Law of Abode and Settlement of Foreigners)

ANGI   Association de la Nouvelle Génération Immigrée (Association of the New Immigrant Generation)

AOP   Association des Originaires du Portugal (Association of Portuguese Natives)

APFEEF   Asociación de Padres de Familia Españoles Emigrados en Francia (Association of Parents of Emigrated Spanish Families in France)

APU   Atelier Populaire Urbain (Popular Urban Workshop)

ARLI   Associazione Recreativa e Lavoratori Italiana (Italian Recreational and Workers' Association)

ATAF   Association des Travailleurs Algériens en France (Association of Algerian Workers in France)

ATEES   Asociación de Trabajadores Emigrantes Españoles en Suiza (Association of Emigrant Spanish Workers in Switzerland)

ATP   Associação dos Trabahaldores Portugueses (Association of Portuguese Workers)

BC   *Bulletin communal* (Ville de Roubaix)

BM   *Bulletin municipal* (Ville de La Courneuve)

CAIF   Conseil des Associations Immigrées en France (Council of Immigrant Associations in France)

CASS   Comité pour l'Abolition du Statut du Saisonnier (Committee for the Abolition of the Seasonal Workers' Statute)

CCAE   Comitado de Coordinación de las Asociaciones Españoles (Coordination Committee of Spanish Associations)

CCI   Comitato Cittadino Italiano (Italian Citizen Committee)

CCPF   Conselho da Comunidade Portuguesa em França (Council of the Portuguese Community in France)

CEDEP   Colectivo de Estudos e Dinamização da Emigração Portuguesa (Center for the Study and Dynamics of the Portuguese Emigration)

CEM   Commission Extra-Municipale aux Etrangers (Extramunicipal Commission for Foreigners)

CFDT   Confédération Française Démocratique du Travail (Democratic French Labor Confederation)

CFE/EKA   Commission Fédérale Consultative pour le Problème des Etrangers/Eidgenössische Konsultativkommission für das Ausländerproblem (Federal Consultative Commission for the Foreigners Problem)

CGT   Confédération Générale du Travail (General Labor Confederation)

CNI   Comitato Nazionale d'Intesa (National Committee for Understanding)

CNTSE   Communauté Neuchâteloise de Travail Suisses-Etrangers (Neuchâtel Swiss-Foreigners Work Community)

COASIT   Comitato Consolare di Assistenza agli Italiani (Consular Committee for Assistance to Italians)

CSC/CGB   Confédération des Syndicats Chrétiens de la Suisse/ Christlicher Gewerkschaftsbund der Schweiz (Federation of Swiss Christian Unions)

CSL   Confédération des Syndicats Libres (Confederation of Free Unions)

CTA   Comité des Travailleurs Algériens (Committee of Algerian Workers)

DL   *Der Limmattaler*

FAEEF   Federación de Asociaciones de Españoles Emigrados en Francia (Federation of Spanish Associations in France)

FAS   Fonds d'Action Sociale (Social Action Fund)

FASTI   Fédération des Associations de Soutien aux Travailleurs Immigrés (Federation of Support Associations for Immigrant Workers)

FCLIS   Federazione delle Colonie Libere Italiane in Svizzera (Federation of Italian Free Colonies in Switzerland)

FEN   Fédération de l'Education Nationale (National Education Federation)

FLN   Front de Libération Nationale (National LIberation Front/ Algeria)

FN   Front National (National Front)

FOBB/GBH   Fédération des Ouvriers du Bâtiment et du Bois/ Gewerkschaft Bau und Holz (Construction Workers' Union Federation)

FONDA   Fondation pour la Vie Associative (Foundation for Associational Activity)

FTMH/SMUV   Fédération des Travailleurs de la Métallurgie et de l'Horlogerie/Schweizerischer Metall- und Uhrenarbeitnehmerverband (Metal- and Clockworkers' Union Federation)

GB   *Geschäftsbericht* (Stadt Schlieren)

HCI   Haut Conseil à l'Intégration (High Council for Integration)

HLM   *Habitations à loyer modéré* (low-income public housing projects)

IGSA   Communauté des Centres d'Information et de Contact Suisses-Etrangers/Interessengemeinschaft der Beratungs- und Kontaktstellen Schweizer-Ausländer (Community of Information and Contact Centers)

JA   *Actualités 93/Le Journal d'Aubervilliers*

JALB   Jeunes Arabes de Lyon et Sa Banlieue (Arab Youth of Lyons and Its Suburbs)

JOC   Jeunesse Ouvrière Chrétienne (Young Christian Workers)

LI   *L'Impartial*

MAAA   Mouvement pour d'Autres Actions Artistiques (Movement for Alternative Artistic Actions)

MRAP   Mouvement contre le Racisme et l'Anti-Sémitisme et pour l'Amitié entre les Peuples (Movement against Racism and Anti-Semitism and for Friendship between Peoples)

MTA   Mouvement des Travailleurs Arabes (Arab Workers' Movement)

MTI   Maison des Travailleurs Immigrés (Immigrant Workers' House)

NA   L'Action National/Nationale Aktion gegen die Überfremdung von Volk und Heimat (National Action against Overforeignization of the People and the Homeland)

NE   *Le Nord-éclair* (Lille)

ONI   Office National d'Immigration (National Office of Immigration)

PCE   Partido Communista Español (Spanish Communist Party)

PCF   Parti Communiste Français (French Communist Party)

PCI   Partito Communista Italiano (Italian Communist Party)

POF   Parti Ouvrier Français (French Workers' Party)

POP   Parti Ouvrier et Populaire (Popular Workers' Party)

PS	Parti Socialiste Français (French Socialist Party)
PSN	Parti Socialiste Neuchâtelois (Socialist Party of Neuchâtel)
PSO/SAP	Parti Socialiste Ouvrier/Sozialistische Arbeiterpartei (Socialist Workers' Party)
PSS/SPS	Parti Socialiste Suisse/Sozialistische Partei der Schweiz (Swiss Socialist Party)
PSU	Parti Socialiste Unifié (Unified Socialist Party)
PV	Procès-verbaux (Ville de La Chaux-de-Fonds, Conseil Général)
RAR	Roubaix aux Roubaisiens (Roubaix for the Roubaisians)
RPR	Rassemblement pour la République (Rally for the Republic)
SONACOTRA	Société Nationale de Construction de Logements pour les Travailleurs (National Society for the Construction of Worker Housing)
UCTT	Union Culturelle des Travailleurs Turcs (Cultural Union of Turkish Workers)
UDF	Union pour la Démocratie Française (Union for French Democracy)
USS/SGB	Union Syndicale Suisse/Schweizerischer Gewerkschaftsbund (Swiss Socialist Union)
UTT	Union des Travailleurs Turcs (Union of Turkish Workers)
VN	La Voix du Nord (Lille)

The Policy Challenge
of Ethnic Diversity

Introduction

The Puzzle

European politics is in many respects becoming the politics of ethnicity. Not since World War II have ethnic tensions and conflict caused such alarm on the continent and so dominated the political agenda. The collapse of authoritarian regimes in Eastern Europe, Soviet-propped and otherwise, has set loose tribal hostilities that Communism had repressed. The crumbling of the Communist bloc has driven large numbers of Eastern and Central Europeans to seek their fortunes in the West.

Many Western European countries also contain ethnic, religious, linguistic, and national minorities, most of whom cluster in relatively homogeneous geographic areas. Some of them have produced movements struggling for greater rights or even for self-determination: Catholics in Ulster, Scottish and Welsh nationalists in the United Kingdom, Basques and Catalans in Spain, Corsicans and Bretons in France, South Tyroleans in Italy, and Flemings in Belgium.

Still, by comparison with the non-Western world these nations have traditionally managed ethnic relations quite successfully and peacefully (see Heisler 1990). Larger countries with unitary states, like France and Britain, have typically stressed the homogeneity of their societies and have for centuries made it part of their public policy to create and maintain it. Smaller nations, like Switzerland and the Benelux countries, are culturally and linguistically divided but seek to maintain what they regard as a delicate balance along highly traditional lines established by the religious and nation-building conflicts of the nineteenth century. The development of the comprehensive welfare state in most of Western Europe after World War II, usually linking individuals (and not groups) to the state in accordance with "universalistic criteria of equity and inclusion," further mitigated many of the "objective conditions that might otherwise stimulate the politicization of ethnicity" (Heisler and Schmitter Heisler 1990, p. 16).

The times have changed, however. Like it or not, Western Europeans today live in societies that have become truly multicultural. Europe now faces a different, more challenging and troubling brand of ethnic politics. Since well before the demise of the Iron Curtain, the European Community has encouraged people's transnational mobility. Of far greater consequence, though, has been the importation of immigrant laborers into these nations since World War II.[1]

The nations of Europe had, of course, experienced migratory flows before 1945, with immigrants arriving largely from neighboring countries: Italians went to France and Switzerland, for example, and Poles to Germany and France, Finns to Sweden, and Irish to Britain. They often faced resentment and hostility, but for the most part such movements involved only short-term migration. Those people who did settle permanently in the receiving societies underwent a thorough, often painful, process of individual assimilation. They adopted the language, loyalties, and customs of their new country. The same was true of the Jews from Eastern and Central Europe and the refugees from religious persecution, civil wars, and revolutions who fled westward before World War II (see Safran 1986; Leveau and Schnapper 1987).

Postwar immigration into Western Europe has been a very different phenomenon. Immediately or shortly after 1945, rapid economic growth and shortages of workers across Western Europe spurred both private- and public-sector programs for recruiting foreign labor. By the mid-1950s the in-migration involved workers not only from peripheral areas of Europe but also from the Third World, including overseas possessions and former colonies. According to one estimate, "Something like 30 million people entered Western Europe as workers or workers' dependants in the post-war period, making this one of the greatest migratory movements in human history" (Castles, Booth, and Wallace 1984, p. 1).

For a long time neither the foreign workers, their countries of origin, nor their "hosts" saw their presence as permanent. Concerned primarily with meeting their industries' demand for cheap labor, Western European authorities implemented no coherent, coordinated policies for coping with the social and political effects of the mass recruitment of immigrant workers (see Miller 1986). The situation reached a crucial turning point in the 1970s, when oil shocks precipitated a rapid economic deterioration in the labor-importing countries. Organized anti-immigrant reactions developed, and ethnic relations soured—and not just for the immigrants (Peters and Heisler 1983).

All the host societies prohibited additional immigration during this period of rising unemployment. Their task has since become to integrate the variegated immigrant communities that postwar migration has created. For instead of disappearing, the putatively temporary foreign workers have constituted, in Professor Lawrence Mead's terms, "an ethnically and behaviorally distinct underclass" (quoted in *New York Times*, Oct. 29, 1991).

Ethnic pluralism, more than traditional forms of social conflict, is coming to define contemporary European politics (see Dittrich and Radtke 1990). The immigrants have become more or less permanent residents with legitimate needs and demands on the host societies. In the process, several profound, thorny practical and theoretical issues have arisen. What specific demands have immigrants made on Western European political systems, and how have they mobilized to have them met? How do groups such as foreign workers, regarded as marginal to a political system, actually relate to it? Have the immigrants found meaningful, effective ways of participating in host-society politics?

If they have not merely been temporary guests, the canons of democracy would seem to dictate some degree of participation for these residents and taxpayers in host-society political systems. From the perspective of these polities, the complicated process of coping with this new ethnic diversity presents a major political challenge for the future. As long-contained blood feuds and submerged prejudices revive and boil over, hostility toward foreigners—and toward non-Europeans in particular—has escalated across the continent. By examining the experiences of Western European liberal democracies with immigrants, we can better understand the implications of this challenge and assess possible ways of meeting it. How does a democracy deal with members of society whom it does not view as citizens? What role in host-society politics have European governments, worried as they are about upsetting existing political arrangements, accorded the immigrants?

Such are the central questions addressed in this book. Researchers have yet to provide cogent answers to them. Unlike in the "classic" immigration countries—the United States, Canada, and Australia—there exists in Europe no tradition of nonindigenous groups' enjoying the status of minorities with specific rights. Postwar immigrants, moreover, were not party to the earlier conflicts of nation-building, nor did they participate in the formation of European welfare states. In more cases than not, foreign workers in Western Europe have not been allowed to vote or hold public office.

Such a lack of formal political rights and other political resources at first led scholars, like host-society public officials, to see foreign workers as largely unorganized and largely apolitical components of the economy (see Girod 1972). Political scientist Mark J. Miller (1981) has termed this assumption that foreign workers were "visitors" who neither wanted nor needed active incorporation into the polity the "quiescence thesis."

This book, echoing and expanding on Miller's work, stresses that contrary to such conventional suppositions, the immigrants have not settled for a passive political role as the object of immigration policies and host-society political discourse. Over time it became evident to most foreign workers that an early return to the homeland was unlikely. The increasingly familial nature and slower turnover of their communities reduced both their interest in homeland politics and their willingness to accept their lot in the host societies. Since the outburst of protests across Europe in the late 1960s and early 1970s, foreign workers have exhibited noteworthy readiness to complain about their living, working, and legal conditions. They have supported a vibrant autonomous political life to fulfill their emotional, social, and welfare needs. And in contrast to the earlier, absorbed waves of immigrants, these more recent arrivals have given rise to an identifiable "second generation" with its own, often quite different political demands and organizational traits.

Catherine Wihtol de Wenden (1978 and 1988), Mark J. Miller (1981 and 1982), Stephen Castles and Godula Kosack (1985), Tomas Hammar (1985), Czarina Wilpert (1988), Zig Layton-Henry (1990), and other pioneers in the field have provided us with impressive amounts of data and valuable insights into the relationship between immigrants and politics in postwar Europe. But we do not yet have any rigorous, analytical accounts of how immigrant political activity has developed since 1945 and how host-society authorities' positions have developed in interaction with it. This is a critical omission: writing of the cycle of protest in Italy in the 1960s and 1970s, Sidney Tarrow has argued that "unless we trace the forms of activity people use, how these reflect their demands, and their interaction with opponents and elites, we cannot understand either the magnitude or the dynamics of change in politics and society" (1989, pp. 7–8). At one basic level, then, this book presents a broad, comparative study of the evolution of immigrant politics and immigration policies in two key receiving countries, France and Switzerland.

Three Perspectives

The factors that have caused immigrants to involve themselves in politics in France, Switzerland, and other Western European host societies seem clear in immigration scholarship: the shift from temporary to permanent settlement, the intensification of discrimination and racism/xenophobia, and governments' failure to improve the immigrants' socioeconomic situation and advance their sociopolitical integration (see Cordeiro and Dias 1985; Piore 1979, pp. 109–111).

Little consensus exists, however, on why the immigrants have participated in the ways that they have and what institutional responses they have elicited. No effort has emerged to test propositions empirically or to provide a broader theoretical context or a weighting of the variables that might explain the emergence and nature of ethnic politics in Western Europe. Scholars to date have supplied only a loose set of approaches. These explanations, still rather undeveloped and tentative, parallel the theories developed to explain minority political incorporation in North America, Britain, the Netherlands, and Australia. Social scientists have divided those theories into three broad categories, emphasizing social-class characteristics, ethnic and/or racial socialization processes, and institutional channeling in the host society (Welch and Studlar 1985). A similar, three-part typology of perspectives applies to the evolution of immigrant politics.

THE CLASS THEORY

Scholars like Castles and Kosack (1974 and 1985); Daniel Lawrence (1974); Annie Phizacklea (1980); Robert Miles (1982); Miles and Phizacklea (1977 and 1984); John Rex (1979); Stephen Castles, Heather Booth, and Tina Wallace (1984); and Castles et al. (1990) have held that, ultimately, the immigrants' common class identity determines the nature of their participation. Among the first to shatter the myth of immigrant political quiescence, they have argued that the capitalist system's need for cheap labor, which inspired immigration, has culminated in the creation of ethnic/racial subproletariats. In the host societies of Western Europe, migrants of all nationalities have worked overwhelmingly in unskilled, hazardous positions that the native population scorns (Schmitter/Heisler 1983; Bonacich and Modell 1980).

Yet race and ethnicity, the argument continues, have become the modalities in which immigrants experience class relations in Western Europe. Employers and the state have used racism as part of their strategies of crisis management and have split the working class into foreign and autochthonous components. This makes it easier to impose on both the costs of industrial reconstruction. The strategies of business and the state determine whether ethnic and class consciousness are in conflict or reinforce each other, as well as which political tactics are necessary.

Also important is the willingness or reluctance of host-society working-class movements—trade unions, left-wing political parties, and other associations—to offer solidarity with foreign workers. Such institutions, in this view, constitute both the arenas within which the desired proletarian solidarity occurs *and* a possible stimulus or a barrier to it. Across the West, racism and economic forces have isolated immigrant workers in the workplace and concentrated them and their families residentially; this segregation has been a precondition for ethnic community development (Castles and Kosack 1974; Ben Tahar 1979, p. 185; Miles and Phizacklea 1984, p. 171).

Neo-Marxists generally see all forms of immigrant political participation—especially antiracist movements but also ethnic-based organization—as part of a process whereby indigenous and foreign workers have been coming to realize and act on their common class interests. Since these social scientists find the origins of immigrant politics in the structural tensions and contradictions of advanced capitalist society, they see such efforts to improve conditions and fight racism as converging in nature and objective in all the host societies (see Cerny 1982; Castles, Booth, and Wallace 1984). Those crossnational divergences that remain, consequently, would have to reflect above all else varying maturity levels of the migratory process and of the working-class movements in the different host societies.

Part of a "broader anti-imperialist struggle" not confined to one particular country, ethnic politics here becomes one conflictual dimension of a complex and contradictory process of class formation. And in the long run, ethnic politics should dissolve into the more fundamental politics of class conflict. The entire process will have both strengthened and expanded it to include genuine solidarity with workers' struggles in the immigrants' homelands (Castles, Booth, and Wallace 1984, p. 226; Castles and Kosack 1985, pp. 228–229).

THE ETHNICITY/RACE THEORY

Analysts like Robert Moore (1975), Nancy Foner (1979), John Rex and Sally Tomlinson (1979), Mark J. Miller (1981 and 1982), Martin O. Heisler and Barbara Schmitter Heisler (1990), and Alain Touraine (1990) start from a different perspective. They make an implicit or explicit assumption that the immigrants' ethnic identity is of fundamental importance and that ethnic politics will endure, at least for the foreseeable future (compare Rath 1991). In contrast to Robert E. Park (1925) and the Chicago School of sociology—as well as those following in their footsteps (for example, Warner and Srole 1945; Gans 1962)—these students of postwar immigration into Western Europe generally reject the American assimilationist model: they have determined that characteristics of the immigrant groups themselves and the timing of their immigration have obviated any "multistage process of adaptation by immigrants to their new societies, ideally moving through ethnically differentiated groups, or enclaves, of immigrants toward acculturation and assimilation" (Heisler and Schmitter Heisler 1986, p. 14). In some studies a multiethnic racial identity (Rex and Moore 1967; Rex and Tomlinson 1979; Ben-Tovin and Gabriel 1982; Banton 1985; and Moulin 1985) or common religious identity (Dumont 1986; Hoppe and Arends 1986; Safran 1986; Balibar and Wallerstein 1988; Etienne 1989; and see Courtois and Kepel 1987) plays a comparably independent, durable role in determining the nature of immigrants' political mobilization (see Royce 1982; Thompson 1983; Richmond 1988).

It is natural, in this optic, that immigrants should organize and articulate their political interests along ethnic or racial lines. The argument here is that each ethnic (or racial or religious) group's own distinctive mode of political participation has developed from group socialization processes and in response to discrimination (compare Barth 1969 with Spicer 1971). Most often, this is seen as occurring in combination with the effects of a "homeland hangover," the persistence of patterns of participation that immigrants developed in their society of origin.[2] Participation oriented toward the countries of origin, which proceeds along the lines of nationality (that is, ethnicity), would represent a logical extension of this phenomenon.

Reflecting organizational characteristics developed both before and after emigration, therefore, each of the ethnic groups constituting a given host society's foreign population should exhibit a unique participatory pattern. The immigrants' particular participatory strategies depend on the organizational proclivities of each national group and on its interaction with those of other immigrant groups and the host society. Hence, the ethnicity theory predicts that immigrants of the same nationality or regional background in different host societies will adopt roughly similar forms of participation. This result is especially likely in light of the comparable socioeconomic conditions that virtually all foreign workers in Western Europe endure. Moreover, levels of anti-immigrant sentiment have been similar across the host societies (see Hoffmann-Nowotny 1973), and non-Europeans have borne the brunt of it everywhere.

THE INSTITUTIONAL CHANNELING THEORY

The class and ethnicity/race approaches have been predominant in studies of immigrant political behavior. Yet there is a third general perspective on immigrant politics, for which I will argue in the following pages. It emphasizes the influence of host-society institutional structures on immigrant political mobilization.

This approach has two strains. A number of journalists and public officials, first, have suggested that certain immigrant communities, especially the Portuguese and Muslims of all nationalities, have withdrawn voluntarily from host-society political life in the face of institutional indifference or hostility. Fredrik Barth (1969) has called such a withdrawal "isolation"; Richard D. Shingles (1987) has referred to it in the American context as the "total separation strategy." The following chapters will show that the immigrants, with the exception of some Islamic groups, have normally not subscribed to this tactic.

Another collection of scholars has ascribed immigrant behavior to the legal conditions and political institutions that have "both shaped and limited the migrants' choice possibilities" (Katznelson 1973, p. 42; see also Cordeiro 1985a). Milton J. Esman, for instance, has wondered whether the political strategies of migrants in the United States have been "critically affected by . . . the political opportunities they encounter, the relative openness of the polity to [their] political organization" (1985, p. 438). Researchers like Theodore Lowi (1964); Gaynor Cohen (1982); John L. P. Thompson (1983); Jakubowicz, Morrissey, and Palser (1984); Steven P. Erie (1985); and Patrick R. Ireland (1989) have noted that certain kinds of immigration policies and administrative practices seem particularly likely to spark certain kinds of ethnic and immigrant group activity. Stressing the importance of immigrants' organizational and other ties to their homelands, Barbara Schmitter Heisler has argued that "existing organizational structures and public activities are independent variables contributing to the . . . relative absence of linkages between host country institutions and immigrant groups" (1980, pp. 182–183).

At a more general level, Sidney Verba, Jae-On Kim, and Norman Nie (1978) have dealt explicitly with the "differential intervening effect of group-based processes" (p. 19) in their challenge to the powerful prevailing assumption that increasing levels of socioeconomic and other resources allow for directly concomitant increases in the political involvement of individuals and groups. They have found that institutions like political parties can variously weaken or reinforce the effects of differences in resources, thereby producing great crossnational variation in the magnitude of the association between them and participation patterns (Ross 1988). Verba, Kim, and Nie argue that institutional arrangements and actors can act as conduits that funnel that participation straight into policymaking circles, exert little sway over it, or effect a "lockout" of outsider groups (1978, p. 64). Still, these scholars do not specify which arrangements and institutions produce which participatory effects.

Similarly, in the recently burgeoning literature on citizenship, several important works have pointed to the key impact that policies and laws governing citizenship and naturalization can have on the integration of immigrants and the nature of ethnic relations in modern industrial societies (see Bolzman, Fibbi, and Garcia 1987; Castles 1992; Brubaker 1989 and 1992; Soysal 1994). As elegant and convincing as these arguments are—and this book will demonstrate the importance of such institutional factors—they remain far too theoretical and abstract. Their proponents have marshaled surprisingly little empirical evidence to support their conclusions.

These and other aspects of what I have termed the institutional channeling theory, therefore, have not been fully developed or applied to the immigrants. Several urgent questions are still awaiting answers: What types and levels of immigrant political activity do specific kinds of institutional frameworks engender? Are most of these effects intended or unintended? Is there any connection between the participatory forms the immigrants adopt and the level and type of impact that they are able to win?

These are issues that I investigate here. Making the institutional contexts that immigrants confront an independent institutional variable in their own right, I examine the ways in which the different frameworks and the very different "linking" processes embedded in them structure the participation of immigrant groups in Western Europe. The political opportunity structure includes the immigrants' legal situation; their social and political rights; and host-society citizenship laws, naturalization procedures, and policies (and nonpolicies) in such areas as education, housing, the labor market, and social assistance that shape conditions and immigrants' responses. Furthermore, indigenous trade unions, political parties, and religious and humanitarian "solidarity groups" have acted as institutional gatekeepers, controlling access to the avenues of political participation available to the immigrants.[3] The pattern of interactions between immigrants and these and other institutions has differed across the various host societies.

It is important to challenge prima facie assumptions that immigrant organizing must take place along either purely ethnic or purely class lines. Ethnic-based participation, after all, seems to be more an effect than a cause. Students of immigration since Nathan Glazer (1954) have noted that dominant groups—the majority—"create" minorities by ascribing to them certain characteristics that serve to justify their assignment to particular societal roles (see also Glazer and Moynihan 1963). The first national identity that many immigrants have experienced develops in the host society. It is not surprising, therefore, that they would form informal and formal cultural groups based on a common ethnic background.

Yet immigrants need not organize *politically* along ethnic lines. When they do, I will argue, it is primarily because host-society institutions have nurtured ethnicity through their policies and practices. This encouragement includes institutional discrimination and bilateral treaties and other arrangements with the governments of the labor-exporting countries.

For similar reasons, class-based political organizing does not appear inevitable either. I will show that foreign workers in similar industrial sectors but in different institutional settings often adopt strikingly divergent participatory strategies. As Jane Jenson remarks, even "whether the organisation of the working class *qua* class occurs is a profoundly *political* outcome" (1985, p. 16; see Katznelson 1981). Just as political is the decision that a nation's domestic labor supplies are not sufficient and that imported labor is needed in the first place (Freeman 1986; Coleman 1992).

Methodology

NATIONAL-LEVEL COMPARISON

Rigorous but flexible and open-eyed comparative analysis is essential to gauging the relative ability of class, ethnic/racial, and institutional factors to account for the evolution of immigrant politics. To test the relative explanatory power of these independent variables, I have chosen two countries and four cities that offer considerable variation in each, as well as in the nature and impact of immigrant political participation (my dependent variables).

France and Switzerland are ideal choices: the effects of immigrant political behavior in both are intrinsically important and amenable to comparative analysis (see Lijphart 1971). Because conditions there allow for effective control of a number of intervening factors, I have been able to disregard these for the purposes of testing the usefulness of my three competing explanations.

In addition to being representative democracies with highly developed, capitalist economies, France and Switzerland have had immigration experiences similar in several important respects. With foreign populations of 3.5 million and 1.2 million, respectively, France and Switzerland stand as two of Europe's leading recipients of immigration. In France worries about low population growth since the Napoleonic era have made the demographic rationale for immigration as important as the demand for cheap labor. Long known for exporting mercenaries, Switzerland, by contrast, has never considered itself to be an immigration country—even though it has had a far higher ratio of foreigners to its total resident population than France since World War II (see Table 1). Significant immigration into both nations began during the second half of the nineteenth century, unlike the case of Germany, where, with the exception of laborers from Prussian-occupied Polish regions who settled in the industrializing *Ruhrgebiet* after German unification in the late 1800s, the "guestworker" phenomenon did not truly begin until the 1960s with the aggressive recruitment of workers from Southern Europe and Turkey (see Bendix 1990; Johnson and Czepek 1992).[4]

Most critically for my argument, France and Switzerland make it possible to test the explanatory power of ethnicity/race, class, and institutional channeling. First, although the composition of the foreign-origin population varies in the two nations, two groups sharing key structural characteristics are present in both: Spaniards and Turks (see Tables 2

Table 1 Foreign population in France and Switzerland since World War II

	France		Switzerland	
Year	No.[a]	% of total population	No.	% of total population
1950	—		285,446	6.1
1954	1,765,298	4.1	—	
1960	—		584,739	10.8
1965	2,683,490	5.5	—	
1970	—		1,080,076	17.2
1975	3,442,415	6.5	—	
1980	—		944,974	14.8
1982	3,680,100	6.8	—	
1990	3,580,000	6.3	—	
1991	—		1,190,991	17.4

Sources: Costa-Lascoux (1989), p. 19; Martin and Miller (1982), p. 11; and Bundesamt für Statistik, *Statistisches Jahrbuch der Schweiz* (Zurich: Verlag Neue Zürcher Zeitung, 1993), p. 75.

a. Does not include naturalizations.

Table 2 Foreign residents in France by nationality, 1962–1981

Nationality	1962 000s	1962 % of total population	1969 000s	1969 % of total population	1981 000s	1981 % of total population
Algeria	351	16.2	608	19.1	817	19.3
Italy	629	29.0	612	19.3	452	10.7
Morocco	33	1.5	143	4.5	444	10.5
Portugal	50	2.3	480	15.1	859	20.3
Spain	442	20.4	617	19.4	413	9.8
Tunisia	27	1.2	89	2.8	193	4.6
Turkey	—	—	9	0.2	118	2.8
Yugoslavia	21	1.0	52	1.6	68	1.6
Other	617	28.4	567	18.0	860	20.4
Total	2,170	100	3,177	100	4,224	100

Sources: Ministère du Travail, *Les étrangers au recensement général de 1975* (Paris: La Documentation Française, 1977), pp. 43, 51–53, 66–69; and Castles, Booth, and Wallace (1984), p. 55.

and 3). France has had a somewhat longer history of seasonal, long-term economic, and political immigration of Spaniards than Switzerland, but these two countries are the only ones in Western Europe to have received all three types of Spanish immigrants, and they have done so in roughly comparable proportions. In terms of their regional and occupational backgrounds, the Spanish communities in the two host societies are comparable for my purposes (see Minces 1973; Sorel 1974; Parra Luna 1978; Puyol Antolín 1979; González-Anleo 1981).

Turks, for their part, are a "new" immigrant community in both France and Switzerland, one not resulting from the traditional flows of migration (namely, from Iberia, Algeria, Italy, Belgium, and Poland to France; from Italy and Spain to Switzerland). For that reason they can help illuminate the effects produced by changes in the immigrant populations' ethnic and religious backgrounds and in host-society institutional contexts since the years when Southern Europeans began arriving. Turks have entered both host nations in similar proportions, since the German labor market became saturated in the late 1960s

Table 3 Foreign residents in Switzerland by nationality, 1960–1991

Nationality	1960		1969		1981		1991	
	000s	% of total population	000s	% of total population	000s	% of total population	000s	% of total population
Austria	38	6.5	43	4.4	31	3.4	29	2.4
France	31	5.3	50	5.1	46	5.1	52	4.3
Greece	—	—	—	—	9	1.0	8	0.6
Italy	346	59.1	532	54.7	417	45.8	380	31.9
Portugal	—	—	—	—	13	1.4	102	8.5
Spain	14	2.4	98	10.1	100	11.0	116	9.7
Turkey	1	0.2	12	1.2	43	4.7	71	5.9
West Germany	93	15.9	116	11.9	85	9.4	86	7.2
Yugoslavia	1	0.2	21	2.2	49	5.4	173	14.5
Others	61	10.4	100	10.3	177	12.8	174	14.8
Total	585	100	972	100	910	100	1,191	100

Sources: Die Volkswirtschaft, April 1970 and March 1982; Bundesamt für Statistik, Statistisches Jahrbuch der Schweiz (Zurich: Verlag Neue Zürcher Zeitung, 1993), p. 75.

(Kastoryano 1986, pp. 16, 30–34). Though usually labeled "economic," the Turkish immigration has also included many officially recognized and illegal political refugees fleeing the series of authoritarian governments and military coups in Ankara (Ralle 1981, pp. 47–51; Nicod 1983; Evrensel 1984).

Though not as readily comparable as the Turks and Spaniards, several other national groups living in France and Switzerland offer rich possibilities for meaningful comparisons and insights into the evolution of ethnic politics in both countries. The political participation of the most prominent immigrant community in each, for instance, has influenced that of other immigrants in important, interesting ways. Certainly, this study could not leave out the substantial Algerian community in France (Bourdieu and Sayad 1964; Ath-Messaoud and Gillette 1976, chap. 2; Grillo 1985; Hifi 1985).

The same holds true for Italians in Switzerland, who as late as 1981 accounted for almost half of the foreign population. The Italians have in many ways defined the entire immigration issue for the Swiss (see Pittau and Ulivi 1986), and they were also among the first immigrants to France. Indeed, they have had a noticeable presence in both nations since the mid-nineteenth century (Avagliano 1976, pp. 16–20, 359–383; Di Meo 1986).

The Portuguese, finally, provide the possibility of comparing the same national group under contrasting conditions. Their presence in France has been far more extensive and significant than in Switzerland. To many French, "immigrants" means "Algerians," but the Portuguese are actually more numerous (Grillo 1985, p. 13). They have in fact arrived in France since the 1500s, although it was not until after 1960 that large-scale migratory movements began. France's more serious economic troubles led to the diversion of a share of this immigration to Switzerland after the mid-1970s. The immigrants in both host societies have come mostly from the same regions, but Switzerland has received a larger contingent of former peasants with experience as workers in Lisbon and Porto. And entire villages have not transported themselves from Portugal to the countryside in Switzerland, as they have in France (Gonçalves 1971; Anido and Freire 1978; Baklanoff 1978; Poinard 1979; Arroteia 1981).

It is a fairly straightforward matter to examine the different immigrant communities and assess their political behavior across the cases. In effect, it is possible to hold ethnicity constant when comparing the nations along certain dimensions. The similarities and differences among the participatory patterns characterizing Spaniards, Turks, Portuguese, Italians, and Algerians in France and Switzerland shed light on just how important ethnic factors are in generating these patterns themselves.

The factor of social class arises next. It has become a cliché that immigrant workers perform tasks that native workers disdain. Across Europe, "there is no denying that the distribution pattern of foreign manpower amply confirms the allegation" (Thomas 1982, p. 130). Despite the recent emergence of a small immigrant petite-bourgeoisie in all host societies, their foreign populations have overwhelmingly remained members of the French and Swiss working classes. The nonworking families of immigrant workers have formed a growing share of the total noncitizen population since 1974, which has yielded lower rates of employment activity (see Miles and Phizacklea 1984, pp. 162–163; Wihtol de Wenden 1990).

There have been some detectable differences in the socioprofessional position of immigrant workers from North Africa/Turkey and Southern Europe (Thomas 1982, pp. 69–70; Grillo 1985, pp. 373–378). In terms of the general economic sectors in which they have been employed, however, there has been no significant variance: around three-quarters of economically active immigrants of all nationalities are still manual laborers of some kind (see Table 4). Recruitment patterns and the influence of familial and kinship networks have had more to do with which specific industrial sectors immigrant workers have entered than any previous experience; the vast majority of the foreigners have been of rural, agricultural backgrounds. In both France and Switzerland several industries have availed themselves of immigrant labor particularly heavily: construction, civil and agricultural engineering, clockmaking, metalworking, iron and steel, mining, textiles/clothing, and domestic services. Seasonal workers have been drawn to the agricultural sector and to the tourist industry. The latter have been particularly conspicuous in Switzerland (Thomas 1982, pp. 68–72; Schain 1985, p. 5).

According to the neo-Marxist assumptions of the class theory, the immigrants' participation reflects their socioeconomic status in the final analysis. With most immigrants belonging to the working class, that approach would predict a crossnational convergence in the organizational patterns of different immigrant nationalities in France and Swit-

Table 4 Percentage of foreign work force in France and Switzerland by socioprofessional category, 1970–1990

	Switzerland				France		
Year	Workers	Employees	Employers and self-employed	Others	Skilled workers	Unskilled workers	Others
1970	80.0	18.0	2.0	<1.0	—	—	—
1975	78.0	20.0	+2.0	<1.0	22.9	49.0	18.1
1982	69.0	24.0	4.0	3.0	—	—	—
1982–1985	—	—	—	—	+35.0	+35.0	<30.0

Sources: Ministère du Travail, *Les étrangers au recensement général de 1975* (Paris: La Documentation Française, 1977), p. 53; *Die Volkswirtschaft*, Feb. 1975; André Lebon, "Chronique statistique," *Revue européene des migrations internationales* 1 (Dec. 1983), pp. 187–203; Martino Russo, "Toujours moins différents, toujours plus incertains," *Piazza*, no. 7 (July 1985), pp. 3–4; and *Le Monde*, Feb. 21, 1989, p. 17.

zerland. Ethnic mobilization should be giving way to the fundamentally class-based sources of immigrant politics.

My findings will suggest that such a view is too sanguine. Most of the immigrants are indeed workers, but their political behavior has differed markedly and persistently across the cases. Institutional ethnic and racial discrimination and the variable, intervening effects of the host-society labor movement have worked against a unified class identity. Instead, Charles Sabel's "ambiguities of class" are visible (1982, pp. 191–193): institutional contexts seem to have produced durable variations among workers of different ethnic/national backgrounds in different localities and sectors. Trade unions and political parties in both France and Switzerland have linked together socioeconomic and local issues (Gallie 1978, p. 273).

Since I am able to control for and to isolate both class and ethnic factors, the analysis here hinges on the dynamic, interactive relationship between the immigrants and indigenous institutions in the two host societies. In order to illustrate its effects most clearly, I have picked cases that present the widest possible institutional variation. The selection of France and Switzerland is especially apt for the purpose of testing the explanatory power of institutional channeling. France's large, centralized state has for centuries defended a painstakingly constructed, monistic national political community characterized by only limited associational activity (Grémion 1980). Switzerland, in contrast, is small and extremely decentralized. It has institutionalized and jealously guarded "patterns of consociational conflict resolution amid a multicultural national context" (Zimmermann 1989, p. 182), balancing cultural, linguistic, and religious cleavages that France experiences to a much less serious degree. At no level does one find a degree of administrative cohesion approaching that in France.

The two nations also offer up polar models of incorporating immigrants into Western European polities. Like such other former imperial powers as Britain, the Netherlands, and Sweden, France has proved more open toward the immigrants' sociopolitical integration. For example, its demographic needs and republican values have compelled it to see the conferral of citizenship upon a foreigner "as a means to facilitate his or her integration into the society" (Rogers 1986, p. 41). Switzerland, like Germany, views naturalization "as the culmination of an integration and acculturation process" (ibid.; see also Brubaker 1989 and 1992). At the federal level the Swiss have tried to implement a "rotation model" of immigration. They have persisted in viewing foreign workers and their children mostly as foreign nationals. Intriguing for theories of ethnic relations and immigrant sociopolitical incorporation, Switzerland has proved to be more closed than France even though a great majority of its foreign population consists of Europeans.

LOCAL-LEVEL COMPARISON

Have differing institutional structures thus produced contrasting patterns in the participation of immigrant groups in the two countries? Or have ethnic, racial, or class factors had greater effect? In order to respond to those questions, it is necessary to undertake, parallel to the national-level comparison, a comparison of four carefully selected case cities: Roubaix and La Courneuve in France, and La Chaux-de-Fonds and Schlieren in Switzerland. This strategy derives from a particularly effective approach in comparative politics that involves the combination of intranation and internation comparisons (see Linz and de Miguel 1970).

For in order to gain a complete understanding of the political aspects of immigration, one has to examine local-level developments. In 1982 the resident foreign populations of France and Switzerland amounted to 8 percent and 14.6 percent, respectively, of their total populations. The concentration of immigrants, however, has varied widely from town to town and region to region. Hence, the real and imagined problems they generate, as well as many of the policies developed to deal with them, all converge in certain areas (see Wihtol de Wenden 1978 and 1988; Freeman 1979; Schain 1982 and 1985; Rath and Saggar 1987; Body-Gendrot 1988).

An appropriate local-level comparison must screen out two factors that observers of immigrant politics almost always include as intervening variables: the relative size of cities and the share of immigrants in their population. Devising a comparative study that clearly spells out and isolates independent and dependent variables, Hans-Joachim Hoffmann-Nowotny and Karl-Otto Hondrich (1982) have examined the institutional determinants of the concentration and segregation of immigrants in four cities in West Germany and Switzerland. I have followed their lead and construct a web of paired comparisons between two crossnational pairs of cities of relatively (as opposed to absolutely) equal size in France and Switzerland. (The smaller scale of Swiss cities precludes comparison of entities exactly the same size.)

Roubaix, La Chaux-de-Fonds, La Courneuve, and Schlieren are well suited for the evaluation undertaken here. Their resident populations contain similar percentages of immigrants (see Tables 5 and 6).[5] As at the national level, four key national communities—Spaniards, Portuguese, Italians, and Turks—are present in each city, and Roubaix and La Courneuve are home to numerous Algerians (see Tables 7–10). The Spanish and Turkish immigrants at the local level share important structural characteristics: size, "age" and origins of the immigration, and socioeconomic status.[6]

As with the variable of ethnicity, furthermore, social-class factors can also be controlled and tested across the local cases. All four cities are heavily industrial. Irrespective of national origins, an overwhelming proportion of the immigrants in each are members of the French and

Table 5 Immigrants in La Courneuve and Roubaix, France, 1975–1987

Year	Total population	Immigrants		
		No.	% of total population	Composition
La Courneuve				
1975	38,021	7,300	19.2	Algerians, Portuguese, Italians, Spaniards, Moroccans, Tunisians
1982	34,455	7,580	22.0 ⎫	Algerians, Portuguese, Spaniards, Italians,
1987[a]	33,500	8,375	25.0 ⎭	Moroccans, Tunisians, Turks
Roubaix				
1975	109,230	21,493	19.7	Algerians, Portuguese, Italians, Belgians, Spaniards, Poles, Moroccans
1982	101,852	21,162	20.8 ⎫	Algerians, Portuguese, Italians, Moroccans, Spaniards,
1987[a]	100,000	23,500	23.5 ⎭	Belgians, Tunisians, Poles, Turks

Sources: Guillon, Rudder-Paurd, and Simon (1977), pp. 20, 96, 106–109, maps 10–13; Ville de Roubaix (1985), pp. 4–8; *Le Monde,* March 14, 1991, p. 9; and municipal archives, La Courneuve and Roubaix.

a. Estimates from figures provided by municipal archives.

Table 6 Immigrants in Schlieren and La Chaux-de-Fonds, Switzerland, 1970–1987

Year	Total population	Immigrants		
		Total	% of total population	Composition
Schlieren				
1970	11,869	2,959	24.9	Italians, West Germans, Spaniards, Yugoslavs, French, Turks
1980	12,891	3,246	25.2 ⎫	Italians, West Germans, Yugoslavs, Spaniards,
1986	12,744	3,291	25.8 ⎭	Turks, French, Portuguese
La Chaux-de-Fonds				
1970	42,347	9,000	21.3	Italians, French, Spaniards, West Germans, Yugoslavs
1980	37,234	7,054	18.9 ⎫	Italians, Spaniards, French, Yugoslavs, West Germans,
1987	36,282	7,336	20.2 ⎭	Turks, Portuguese

Sources: Bundesamt für Statistik, *Statistisches Jahrbuch der Schweiz* (Basel: Birkhauser Verlag, 1985), pp. 17, 37; *Annuaire statistique du Canton de Neuchâtel* (Neuchâtel: Service Cantonal de Statistique, 1974), p. 52; Statistische Mitteilungen des Kantons Zürich (1985), pp. 22, 56; and (1978), pp. 30–31; *Statische Berichte des Kartons Zürich* (Nov. 1986), pp. 72–73; *Le Courrier Neuchâtelois* (Neuchâtel, Feb. 11, 1987), p. 23; and *Neue Zürcher Zeitung*, July 21, 1992, p. 15.

Swiss working classes. Foreign workers occupy the lowest rungs on each local socioeconomic ladder.[7]

The final independent variable is the local institutional context. As national-level cases France and Switzerland represent something of the yin and yang of host-society institutional responses to the immigrants, so, too, my two pairs of cities cover the full range of institutional contexts in which immigrant political participation has developed in the two nations, even as they permit selected controls of the other explanatory variables.

Each of these cities, then, has presented immigrants with either a very open or a very closed political opportunity structure. Roubaix has been among the limited number of *communes* in France to set up a for-

Table 7 Percentage of immigrants in Roubaix by nationality, 1975 and 1982

	1975	1982
Algerians	44.9	43.0
Portuguese	21.5	22.5
Italians	14.4	11.3
Belgians	4.4	2.8
Spaniards	3.5	2.0
Poles	3.4	2.2
Moroccans	2.7	5.7
Turks	—	0.5
Others	5.2	10.0

Source: Ville de Roubaix (1985), p. 8.

Table 8 Percentage of immigrants in La Courneuve by nationality, 1975 and 1982

	1975	1982
Algerians	39.1	52.0
Portuguese	17.4	16.3
Italians	9.5	5.0
Spaniards	5.7	6.9
Turks	—	0.5

Source: Municipal archives, La Courneuve.

mal consultative body for its noncitizen population. La Chaux-de-Fonds has established a similar institution, and the city lies within a canton (Neuchâtel) that has since 1849 allowed noncitizens meeting certain residency requirements to vote in local elections (Débely 1986).

The contrast with "closed" La Courneuve and Schlieren could not

Table 9 Percentage of immigrants in La Chaux-de-Fonds by
nationality, 1960–1982

	1960	1979	1982
Italians	66.0	53.8	52.6
Spaniards	8.0	28.3	17.4
Portuguese	—	> 1.0	> 1.0
Turks	—	> 1.0	> 1.0

Sources: Ville de La Chaux-de-Fonds, *Rapport du Conseil Général* (1982), pp. 390–396,
406, 472–473, 504–505; and personal communication from Gérard Stehlin, Police
des Habitants, La Chaux-de-Fonds.

Table 10 Percentage of immigrants in Schlieren by nationality,
1970 and 1982

	1970	1982
Italians	52.2	50.1
Other Europeans	17.8	
Spaniards		6.8
Portuguese		1.9
Non-Europeans	2.2	
Turks		6.3

Sources: Statistische Mitteilungen des Kantons Zürich (1978), pp. 46–47, 56–57; and
(1985), pp. 72–73.

be starker. Their municipal governments have introduced no special
structures for the voicing of immigrants' demands and opinions. Noninstitutionalized consultation has been the sole source of contact between them and the local administration (Communist in La Courneuve
and consociational in Schlieren).

Together, these national and local cases permit generalizations about
the evolution of immigrant politics that go beyond the cases themselves. Comparing across them reveals patterns of crossnational similarities and differences in immigrant political behavior. These unfolding

patterns go a long way toward determining which factors explain its contours and implications in all the Western European host societies.

PARTICIPATORY FORMS

The following chapters address the central questions: What forms has the immigrants' political participation taken, and why? Why has immigrant politics evolved in certain directions and not in others?

There are a number of reasonable scenarios. The immigrants' actions could well involve mainly individual efforts, for example. Such strategies could aim for assimilation and personal socioprofessional advance, or they could voice upset. James C. Scott (1985) has argued from a microperspective that the poor and disenfranchised act rationally but necessarily in terms of their limited political, economic, and symbolic resources and opportunities. His Malaysian peasants employ the "weapons of the weak": they display their discontent primarily through individualized actions and social networks—work slowdowns, arson, boycotts, petty pilferage, gossiping, and occasional acts of violence—that operate without formal organization and outside the normal boundaries of institutionalized politics.

However, such "garden-variety resistance" is not the only form of political action available to "subordinate classes" (Scott 1985, p. 241). Macropolitical forms of immigrant activity could predominate instead. In their cross-national study of participation Verba, Kim, and Nie have argued that organization is in fact the weapon of "lower-status groups," which need group-based processes of political mobilization to counteract the greater motivation and resources of "upper-status people" (1978, pp. 14–15).

In fact my research demonstrates that immigrant participation has taken place both at the micropolitical level and also, quite extensively, at the group level. But although I take careful note of individual strategies, whether "assimilationist" or militant, the more common but also more striking forms of collective immigrant political activity have been of equal, if not greater, relevance.

And what of the contention, made by Frances Fox Piven and Richard A. Cloward (1979), Claus Offe (1985), and Scott, that autonomous, conflictual participation best characterizes and best serves marginal groups? Other recent work on collective behavior has made the opposing argument that social movements are never isolated from other organized interests in advanced industrial societies, nor are their action repertoires always devoid of conventional tactics (see Dalton and Kuechler 1990). Since the majority of the immigrants remain noncitizens, moreover, the question arises whether their political demands primarily concern governments in their homelands or those in the Western European host societies.

Immigrant participation, in a word, can adopt several distinct forms with different likely implications for social relations and politics. The class, ethnicity/race, and institutional channeling theories all focus on "structural possibilities" for participation more than on actual numbers of participants.[8] In examining immigrant political participation across the cases, it is not difficult to ascertain whether it takes forms that are based primarily on class or ethnic identity. In order to facilitate the far trickier task of determining the impact of institutions on them, I have divided these forms into three general types that relate to the specific political opportunity structures that immigrants face.

First of all, immigrants can direct their political activity not toward the host societies but toward their countries of origin. In fact this *homeland-oriented participation* has received encouragement from governments there, many of which have set up networks of consular services and other official organizations throughout Western Europe. Homeland opposition parties and movements have forged an organizational presence there as well. The home countries' organizational structures have varied among themselves and across host societies in terms of their actual degree of "institutional completeness" (Schmitter/Heisler 1983, pp. 315–316).

One might well expect such differences to have an effect on the immigrants' political mobilization. The real or perceived inadequacies of homeland diplomatic representation can cause emigrants to turn their interests to the governments of the countries in which they reside. By the same token, the breadth and inclusiveness of social welfare programs in the host societies with respect to foreign workers and their dependents can influence the institutional presence of their homelands there, and thereby the immigrants' homeland-directed participation. This form, which occurs necessarily (if not exclusively) along national and ethnic lines, may ultimately also target the policies of the nations in which they are currently resident.

A second form of political activity by immigrants, *institutional participation,* explicitly and directly targets the host society and proceeds along the channels it accords them and accepts in a positive fashion. This participatory form corresponds to Herbert P. Kitschelt's (1986) "assimilative strategies." Over time governments have widened and restricted these institutional channels, which may favor class- and/or ethnic-based participation. Such channels carry immigrants into political parties, trade unions, and other host-society institutions that can greatly influence the nature of their participation. Local-level variation can be significant.

Third, *confrontational participation* involves political activity that occurs outside legally available and favored channels. Such participation includes but is not limited to illegal actions and to the public demonstrations and acts of civil disobedience that E. N. Müller (1979) has termed "aggressive" or "unconventional" behavior. Nor need it always be autonomous: indigenous institutions and social actors can mobilize immigrants to abandon institutional routes of political access and opt for confrontational forms. Of course, what constitutes an "in-channel" mode of participation in one host society may well constitute "out-of-channel" activity in another. The immigrants' political-legal status and the general rules of the political game in a given host society determine which forms of participation are confrontational and which are institutional, as well as whether they organize on the basis of social class or ethnicity.

As in any study of very recent social phenomena, measuring the various forms of participation can prove problematic. Ideally, one would like to have reliable common measures of institutional effects, overall participatory strength, and the popularity of each of the likely political forms. However, the large number of strategies that the immigrants have embraced and the high turnover of immigrant activists and leaders preclude a precise assessment.

It thus becomes necessary to settle for a more qualitative measure, which is quite effective when employed in the context of a thoughtfully constructed comparative study. I have gauged the relative frequency with which immigrants have made use of the various forms of political participation through reference to the rich descriptive literature and archival material available; analysis of the publications of political parties, trade unions, and immigrant groups; and codable political activities found in national and local newspapers.[9] I also conducted some sixty open-ended interviews in 1986–87 and 1990 with national- and local-level immigrant associational leaders, political party and union militants, and activists in religious and other voluntary "solidarity" groups sympathetic to the immigrants' concerns, as well as with the municipal officials responsible for relations with the immigrant communities over the past decade and a half.

Especially since the immigration stoppages of the early 1970s, the character of immigrant political activity has evolved. The extent and direction of that change—up through the late 1980s in the four cities, through the early 1990s at the national level—is an important part of the story here, and the diachronic dimension of my comparative study serves to strengthen its findings. The attitudes and conduct of the immigrants and Western European officials have developed in interaction with each other. We can observe how institutions learn from their experience and what adjustments they make, along with the ways in which institutional processes influence preferences, resources, and the rules of the game (March and Olsen 1989, p. 56).

When it had become apparent by the 1970s that the foreign workers and their families were not going to return "home" or remain politically passive, host-society authorities granted them greater political rights. The foreign workers have made use of the different kinds of opportunities opened in each host-society institutional context. Second-generation immigrants have worked within institutional frameworks that can differ significantly from those acting on their parents, and they have undergone a very different socialization process. The foreign workers' children have accordingly developed their own distinctive forms of political activity and pose new types of challenges for the host societies. To varying degrees in both France and Switzerland, racist reactions against the immigrants' presence and their political activity have limited authorities' policy options even further.

Broader Implications

This analysis, centered on the complicated, synergistic relationship between host-society institutions and immigrant behavior in France and Switzerland, both draws from and contributes to several political science literatures in which the political role of marginal social groups has animated heated debate. Insofar as this study attempts to determine the bases, levels, and forms of immigrant political activity, to take apart the "machinery of participation" (Gallie 1978), it resembles the work of scholars like Samuel P. Huntington and Joan Nelson (1976); Verba, Kim, and Nie (1978); Piven and Cloward (1979); and Scott (1985).[10]

Like them I treat political participation as the dependent variable, rather than as a causal factor influencing other trends.

Similarly, the growing research on social movements offers several useful ways of slicing into and responding to the central puzzles here.[11] Some recent studies have pictured social movements as expressions of collective identity, based on cultural, ethnic, and psychological factors; others have stressed their fundamentally structural origins (compare Inglehart 1977; Offe 1985; and Messina 1987). "Individual [socioeconomic] mobility" and "group organization," moreover, have often appeared as alternative routes to political participation (Huntington and Nelson 1976, chap. 4). The data presented here provide further evidence that institutional factors can help create or prevent collective social identity and movements among lower-status populations.

This book, in short, stands at the juncture of many lines of current social science thought and debate. But it also connects with wider intellectual and policy controversies over profound, ongoing changes in Western European political systems. After all, one of the central claims here is that the immigrants, those allegedly least autonomous and influential of Western European social actors, have taken an increasingly active and undeniably political role in the last two decades.

Few of the numerous challenges confronting the industrialized nations of Western Europe appear more intractable than those associated with the presence of politically assertive immigrant minority communities. In addition to being an investigation into how two European nations have coped with ethnic diversity, therefore, this is also a study about how liberal democracy copes with such diversity. What does it mean for such a polity when large numbers of its residents, workers, and taxpayers cannot participate fully in political decisionmaking?

So far there has been no empirical appraisal of the implications of postwar immigrants and their political role for the functioning of liberal democracy. Indeed, although there are many studies of the avenues, determinants, and effects of political participation in such polities, there are far fewer of the political behavior of the most disadvantaged groups. Comparative, crossnational analyses especially are at a premium. How do outsider groups go about articulating their demands on a democratic political system? Can they make themselves heard and win a response from it, and if so, what type of impact can they effect? Such issues go to the heart of our notions of what a democracy is and who participates. By looking at the politics of immigrants, we can learn a great deal about how effectively and fairly the institutions we associate with liberal democracy in Europe cope with the social needs and political aspirations of even those most marginal to society.

Plan of the Book

This book presents both an overview and specific analyses of the evolution of immigrant politics—the political activities of immigrants, as well as the responses of politicians and policymakers. Embedded in that discussion is a test of the class, ethnic/race, and institutional channeling explanations for the forms of immigrant political participation, providing a heretofore nonexistent theoretical framework within which to understand its development and contours.

The focus is on the period since World War II, with special emphasis on the years between 1974 and the early 1990s, which have been pivotal for immigration in Western Europe. In suspending new arrivals in the 1970s, the host societies signaled an end to certain illusions and announced their intention to improve the socioeconomic conditions of their resident noncitizen populations. Integration became the watchword, and officials effectively acknowledged the permanent nature of foreign workers' (and their families') presence. This sea change in policy influenced the political attitudes of the immigrants themselves.

This sharp historical discontinuity is reflected in the organization of chapters here. Chapters 1 through 3 cover the French cases. Chapter 1 surveys French immigration policy and the immigrants' political activity before 1974, focusing on the foreign-worker activism and the xenophobia of the nineteenth and early twentieth centuries, as well as the telling differences between the Western European immigration experience then and today. Chapter 2 chronicles changes at the national level since the mid-1970s, explaining how contingents of supposedly temporary foreign workers gave rise to politically assertive minority communities. Chapter 3 follows the same line of analysis for the two French cities of La Courneuve and Roubaix. The spotlight falls on the complex relationship between the political opportunities open to immigrants and the various forms of political activity that they have adopted. Though focusing on the post-1974 period, it shows how experiences with immigration before World War II and before the oil crises of the 1970s shaped the institutional context in which the foreign-origin population has acted. Chapters 4 through 6 apply the same approach to Switzerland, ending with the cities of Schlieren and La Chaux-de-Fonds. With each case country and city I add a new layer of cross- and intranational comparison. Although my intention is to develop meaningful generalizations about which factors determine the ways in which foreign workers and their families relate to and penetrate Western European political systems, I take care not to massage the rich empirical material out of all recognition, especially at the local level. Each city has an interesting and important story to tell about immigrant politics and immigration policy in modern Europe. Learning and now telling such stories is one of the great joys of conducting this kind of research. The final chapter knots together the threads of my argument and considers the wider implications of immigration for Western European polities and for the functioning of democracy.

1

France before 1974

Unlike many of its neighbors, France has a long history of immigration. The roots of the ethnic diversity that challenges it today lie in much earlier developments and policies. From the start, the actions (and inaction) of French governments and other institutions helped to determine the size, composition, and sociopolitical role of the nation's foreign population. They discriminated among the various national groups even as they pushed all immigrant workers into menial, backbreaking occupations.

Yet the long process of immigrant settlement and the French institutional response to it changed the nature of the foreign presence in the country. It once overwhelmingly involved people from elsewhere in Europe, who would either leave after a short while or undergo complete assimilation into French society. After World War II, however, economic forces and the effects of earlier policy choices eventually transformed a much more ethnically diverse foreign-origin population into true minority communities. A structurally essential component of French society, they could lay claim to rights guaranteed by the republic and republican values. France, in effect, *created* an ethnic minorities problem with far-reaching effects on its political system.

An intricate pas de deux, usually lacking in grace, has played out between French authorities and the immigrants. It has shifted the level of the entire immigration debate from the push-pull calculus of postwar labor policy to today's more contentious politics of a multiethnic society. And more than their ethnic background or social-class status, that institutional dance has determined the level and forms of the immigrants' political participation.

The Foreign Presence before World War II

As France began to industrialize in the second half of the nineteenth century, its working class underwent a rapid restructuring. The old trades were declining, and new industries like iron and steel, mining, and chemicals were sucking unskilled labor into Paris' suburbs, Lorraine, and the Nord-Pas-de-Calais. Forming the bulk of this new working class were migrants from rural areas not only in France (Brittany and Auvergne) but also outside the country (Italy, Poland, Belgium, Germany, Spain, and Switzerland) (see Noiriel 1980 and 1988; Fourcaut 1986).

For a long time, public decisionmakers in France were concerned merely with monitoring immigration movements. There was often police control of foreigners, but labor itself was not subject to legal regulation. Only after World War I did uncontrolled immigration—*l'immigration sauvage*—attain such dimensions that it sparked difficulties and real misgivings. From 1919 through the mid-1920s governments and employers began to relate immigration to the needs of industry and agriculture. They explicitly favored the immigration of white Europeans. Employers' associations joined forces to recruit them, while national authorities entered into bilateral agreements with major labor exporters like Poland, Italy, Yugoslavia, and Czechoslovakia (Cross 1983, pp. 37–40; Hifi 1985, p. 87). In addition to the influx resulting from those treaties, unorganized movements of agricultural and industrial laborers continued from neighboring countries. From the mid-1920s, moreover, France also accepted Jews from Eastern Europe and Russia, as well as a colorful collection of political refugees: Armenians, White Russians, Italian antifascists, and Spanish Republicans (Wihtol de Wenden 1988, p. 37).

France's high wartime casualties, combined with the assimilationist Jacobin tradition and long-standing worries that slow population growth retarded the nation's economic modernization (Brubaker 1992), led public officials to accept that some of those workers and refugees would remain in the country and to stress the importance of blending them into French society. Naturalization laws were designed "to make Frenchmen out of foreigners" (Mauco 1932, chap. 3). For foreign-born children, France's centralized, secular school system and, later, the army acted as agents of political socialization (Millet 1938; see also Weber 1976).

Public opinion and policymakers alike tended to construct a veritable hierarchy of foreign groups, ranking them through discriminatory practices and attitudes according to nationality and perceived cultural proximity (Mauco 1932, p. 269; Schor 1985a, p. 222). Such layering fostered an ethnic-based identity that was often lacking among arriving immigrants, who identified at first mostly with their home villages and their extended families. French employers further encouraged their ethnic identity through the provision of company housing and the promotion of athletic clubs—both organized by nationality.

French government policy also aimed at maintaining foreign workers' identification with their homelands. Most of these workers took it on faith that they would someday return to their countries of origin anyway. Naturally enough, then, when they began to organize at the end of the nineteenth century, they did so along the lines of nationality and directed much of their political interest toward the regimes in power in their homelands. French authorities insisted that immigrants observe strict political neutrality in France and refrain from all confrontational protest activity. The "revolutionary contagion" that had begun with the Bolshevik Revolution, many feared, might spread to the country's foreigners (Bonnet 1976, part 2).

The immigrants' own organizations met with suspicion at first. Mistrust of corporations of all kinds had been a legacy of the French Revolution, codified in the Allarde and Le Chapelier laws of 1791. After a century of struggle, the Law of 21 March 1884 finally legalized trade unions. It recognized the right of foreign workers to join them, although it stipulated that administrators and directors be French (Millet 1938, p. 62). Legislation in 1901 eliminated the remaining restrictions on the right of individuals, immigrants included, to join and form associations. Theirs were on equal footing with the French in needing only to deposit a "declaration of formation" at the prefecture.

Even before that legal change, each of the major immigrant communities—most notably the Poles and Italians—had forged its own ethnic associational identity. The organizations that foreigners or colonial subjects created involved themselves mostly with providing assistance to new arrivals and keeping alive the culture of the homeland (Cordeiro 1985b, p. 4). In fact homeland consular officials, religious organizations associated with the Catholic church, opposition political parties, and trade unions influenced or controlled many of them.[1] Islamic "brotherhoods" *(târiqa)* and pro-independence Algerian organizations of various political stripes also mobilized in metropolitan France throughout this period. Many of those on the left blended ethnic and class identities (Ath-Messaoud and Gillette 1976; Leveau and Wihtol de Wenden 1985).

The nascent French labor movement failed at first to integrate foreign workers into its ranks. Open fights broke out between French and foreign workers, especially Italians (Dupeux 1980, pp. 171–172; Mouriaux 1982, pp. 161–162; compare also Blanc 1901). They occasionally exhibited noteworthy labor militancy: Italian workers, for example, touched off massive strikes that hit the steel industry in Lorraine in 1905 (Rochefort 1963). Despite the legality of their involvement in such strikes, many ended in arrests and expulsions. And many French trade unionists continued to denounce them as strike and wage breakers or even as spies (Gani 1972).[2]

Unemployment in the 1930s exacerbated popular xenophobia. France's foreign population had reached some 3 million by 1931, 7.7 percent of the total population (very similar to their share in the mid-1970s). A 1932 law barred foreigners from certain occupations and instituted quotas in others.[3] By the mid-1930s governments were executing large numbers of deportations. Whereas the influx of political refugees swelled, these tough measures resulted in a sharp reduction in foreign workers and thereby imparted great elasticity to the labor market (Talha 1974; Zolberg 1978).

Simultaneously, however, notions of working-class solidarity were taking hold. The French Communist Party (Parti Communiste Français—PCF) developed a collective response to the economic crisis of the period and took charge of organizing the new working class. It insisted on solidarity between French and foreign workers. Wrapping its members in a web of personal and professional organizations and activities, the PCF, together with French trade unions, created an encapsulated society by means of which immigrant workers—particularly Italians, Poles, and, later, Spaniards—assimilated, gradually and certainly not without conflict, into French society (Schor 1985a, chap. 3; Courtois and Kepel 1987; Body-Gendrot 1989).[4]

Immigrants, many of whom specifically demanded more political rights, participated alongside their French comrades in the wave of strikes and demonstrations that ushered in the Popular Front in 1936.[5] Yet after an initial flurry of policy decisions in their favor, the foreigners wound up serving mostly as fodder in political battles between the right and the left and between the Communist and non-Communist left. The squabbles only fed xenophobia among the rank and file. By 1937 the Communists themselves, having accepted the reformist position of the trade unions, adopted the slogan "France for the French!" (Wihtol de Wenden 1988, p. 68). In the end, the brief experiment in governance by the left brought bitter disappointment and few lasting improvements for foreigners (Schor 1985a, chap. 4).

Their political space constricted sharply under Edouard Daladier's National Union government. Adding to a wide array of new restrictions, he issued a decree in April 1939 that forced "foreign" associations to obtain preliminary authorization from the minister of the interior.[6] Born of the fear that Fascist Italy and Nazi Germany might use such associations to undermine the French government, the 1939 decree was to remain in force long after France's liberation in 1944 (Morange 1981).

By the eve of World War II, in fact, the legal framework that would determine immigrants' relationship with the French political system until the mid-1970s was largely in place. The Vichy regime brought even greater harshness toward foreigners—and disaster for foreign and French Jews. But although immigrants demonstrated their willingness to defend France during the war—many were active in the Resistance, and over 40,000 fought with the Free French Forces (Wihtol de Wenden 1988, pp. 79–83)—the war years did not permanently alter the French approach toward immigration.

From Foreign Workers to Immigrants after 1945

What was different after World War II was the very nature of labor immigration into France.[7] With a demographic gap created by over a million wartime casualties, France needed immigrants. Officials wanted a stable, ethnically balanced inflow of workers who could be assimilated (see Bayet 1945).

General de Gaulle strove for a more consistent and coordinated immigration policy. An expansive, reformed Nationality Code (Code de la Nationalité) in October 1945 helped determine who belonged in the postwar national community. Though emphasizing blood ties and descent *(jus sanguinis)*, French citizenship laws continued to set great store by birth and residence in France as well (Brubaker 1992).

The new push for coherence also resulted in the *ordonnance* of November 2, 1945, which still regulates the residence and employment of foreigners in France. The law required any noncitizen seeking employment in the country to obtain both a work permit and one of a progressive series of residency permits.[8] It established a government monopoly over immigration with the creation of the National Office of Immigration (Office National d'Immigration—ONI).[9]

The immigrants themselves were to play a purely economic role and stay out of domestic political struggles. Public authorities and public opinion alike expected them to assimilate into French society if they hoped to become full political participants (see Rose 1969). The *ordonnance* made officials' task easier in this respect by asserting the administration's right to expel any foreigner menacing the "public order." This concept was never explicitly defined in legal terms, yet it gave rise to the principle that foreigners stood under an obligation to observe political neutrality. The government would occasionally forbid immigrants from joining a French political party or from expressing themselves at political meetings and demonstrations.

Nevertheless, immigrants at least theoretically enjoyed certain basic liberties that often proved superior to those available in their homelands: the same rights as citizens to seek judicial relief, freedom of expression, the right to join trade unions, and limited freedom of association. Those rights would evolve in the decades to follow. French governments responded not only to domestic and international political and economic pressures but also to the changing sociopolitical role of the foreign population itself.

For the time being, immigration was to be a matter for technocrats, analyzed in terms of costs and benefits and intentionally kept off the political agenda (Freeman 1979, p. 70). But by the mid-1950s the postwar economic recovery was sharpening demand for unskilled labor. For the first time, labor immigration into France took the form of the massive importation of an ever more diverse range of national groups: in addition to the Italians (the most numerous as late as 1959), waves of Iberians, Serbs, Algerians, Moroccans, Tunisians, sub-Saharan Africans, and Turks broke over each other in quick succession in the 1960s and early 1970s.[10] More and more of the newcomers were rural, uneducated, unskilled workers (see Wihtol de Wenden 1988, chap. 3). Each new national group contributed to the premature "sedimentation" process of the immigrant communities that had preceded it.

This diversification of the sources of immigrant labor was in part an

intentional effort by French authorities to introduce selectivity and economic competition among the various ethnic groups and thereby depoliticize their presence (Talha 1974). The ONI contributed to this policy
by renewing previously signed bilateral accords and forging new ones
as France competed in the 1950s and 1960s with the rest of Western
Europe for cheap labor from the south.

Each nationality's situation varied with its alleged ability to assimilate into French society and with the political weight of the sending
country. The focus of the agreements was on labor recruitment, but
they generally also included vaguely worded provisions dealing with
the host society's role in recruitment, family reunification, housing,
and equality of treatment. As Philip L. Martin and Mark J. Miller have
remarked, "the deficiencies and inequalities that characterized bilateral
labor accords are at least partially responsible for the disfavored status
of many foreign workers and their dependents at present" (1982,
p. 43).

By the same token, these accords furnished sending-country governments with formal channels that helped them maintain ties with their
expatriates and that led workers to look first toward homeland officials
whenever a grievance arose. Bilateral accords thus fitted well with an
official strategy to stress that postwar immigration was a temporary
movement. As "guests," foreign workers would have no claim on the
political institutions of the host society, only on those in their homelands (Schmitter Heisler 1985, pp. 474–477).[11]

Foreign-worker political opposition to homeland governments after
World War II took several forms. Anti-junta Greeks, antimonarchical
Moroccans, anti-Franco Spaniards, and anti-Salazar Portuguese participated in meetings, rallies, and seminars in France. Left-wing French
political parties and trade unions offered on-again, off-again logistical
and moral support (Miller 1982).

As for the mass of Algerian workers in France, they did not mobilize
behind the movement for independence until the mid-1950s, largely
out of fear of reprisals from French officialdom (Bourdieu and Sayad
1964). Caution receded as the National Liberation Front (Front de Libération Nationale—FLN) grew into a formidable threat to de Gaulle
and his government. During the war from 1958 to 1962, the Algerian
community in France was the stronghold of the Messalist National Algerian Movement (Mouvement National Algérien), the FLN's main organizational rival.[12] After independence, Algerians in France organized

often significant political dissidence against the regime in Algiers. The community thus became a focus of FLN concerns and mobilizational efforts (CEDETIM 1975, p. 101).

Most homeland governments, in fact, were intent on controlling their expatriate citizens and on blunting political opposition in their ranks. However disparate their motives and approaches, all established networks of consular services and other official organizations in France to shore up support and cultural cohesion among "their" emigrants. To the same ends those governments sponsored and subsidized in France ostensibly apolitical "homeland fraternal organizations" (Miller 1981).

The Algerian regime, in particular, exerted great influence abroad through the Fraternal Association of Algerians in Europe (Amicale des Algériens en Europe—AAE). It emerged in 1962, when cadres of the wartime FLN federation in France simply became officials of the new organization. Algeria's government considered the AAE to be the major instrument for the implementation of its emigration policies and the legitimate representative of France's Algerian population.

The AAE served as a guarantor of order, an instrument to secure the political and social *encadrement* of the emigrant community. Through its myriad cultural and educational projects, it strove to nurture national identity and to prevent the assimilation and acculturation of Algerians into French society. Algerian elections and governmental consultations proceeded in France under its watchful eye. In a reflection of the Algerian regime's political leanings, the AAE and its trade union branch, the General Union of Algerian Workers (Union Générale des Travailleurs Algériens), maintained close political contacts with the PCF and the General Labor Confederation (Confédération Générale du Travail—CGT) (see Miller 1981, pp. 34–38; and Wihtol de Wenden 1982). Although the governments of several other immigrant homelands—Morocco, Tunisia, and Senegal, for example—also established networks of vigilant, overbearing official organizations in France, none attained quite the same reach as the AAE, which by the 1970s claimed one-tenth of the Algerian community in France—100,000 people—as members (Miller 1982, pp. 38–39).

As for Southern European governments, Spain's Generalissimo Franco monitored emigrant political activity by means of consular offices and, after 1956, the government-financed Spanish Houses (Casas de España) that were set up in major French centers of Spanish settlement. In 1969 the regime developed the Federation of Spanish Associations in France (Federación de Asociaciones Españoles en Francia—FAEEF). The FAEEF became the sole recipient of government subsidies and was supposed to counter the influence of trade unionists and Communists among emigrant Spanish workers (Sorel 1974, pp. 33–42; Dianteill 1992). From Lisbon, meanwhile, the like-minded Salazar and Caetano regimes were working to organize France's increasingly numerous Portuguese immigrants into more than 100 local cultural associations under their influence.[13]

Postwar Italian governments, in marked contrast, maintained emigrants' identification with Italy by granting financial assistance to trade union and social welfare organizations across Europe—whether they were affiliated with the Catholic church and the Christian Democrats, the Socialists, or the Communists. The Christian Associations of Italian Workers (Associazioni Cristiane dei Lavoratori Italiani—ACLI), formed in 1944 on a base network of Christian Democratic charitable aid societies and Catholic Missions, were favored recipients, yet antigovernment forces received their share as well. Governments in Rome also reactivated and enhanced the consultative organs for Italian emigrants that had existed in several countries, attached to the consular offices, before the Fascist period. And although they did not for a long time permit emigrants to vote at consulates abroad, authorities in Rome instituted special train and ferry fare reductions and waivers for all returning emigrant voters (see Cases Méndez 1979; Schmitter Heisler 1985).

Thus the homelands remained a focal point of immigrants' political concern. But the French institutional context was gaining in importance. The French government's selective, uneven treatment of the various national communities within the immigrant population was reinforcing the collective, ethnic identity of each. Those from European Community member states began to enjoy clear privileges. Furthermore, France maintained close ties with many of its former African colonies, and special treaties specified the rights of immigrants from those new nations (Martin and Miller 1982, pp. 39–41).

The labor market, too, was becoming increasingly segmented: immigrants from Southern Europe tended to occupy a rung above the latest, non-European arrivals, who performed the most dangerous and demeaning jobs. A government report, written by M. Corentin Calvez for the Economic and Social Council in 1969, clearly differentiated European from non-European workers: the latter were regarded as an "unassimilable island" (quoted in Freeman 1979, p. 88; compare also Tapinos 1975, p. 18).

Economic forces were overriding demographic concerns, however, and changing the dynamics and nature of the entire immigration challenge. The government lost control in the face of intense industrial demand for immigrant workers. In practice, French officialdom permitted undocumented immigration. By the end of the 1960s, 70 to 80 percent of all immigrants entered France "spontaneously." Many illegals arrived on tourist visas and had their situation "legalized" once they had found employment (Thomas 1982, p. 42).

Never intending this mass of new foreign workers to become a permanent addition to French society, authorities did not effect the infrastructural adjustments needed to cope with their presence or prepare the French public for it. This institutional nonresponse helped fuel popular anti-immigrant sentiment. Through inadequate and ad hoc housing and labor policies, postwar governments unwittingly created stable immigrant concentrations and communities. France's poorest neighborhoods and municipalities—usually left-wing strongholds—bore the brunt of the costs and social tensions associated with large numbers of immigrants. Faced with these new political and economic circumstances, the French left did not even have a voice on the ONI administrative council.

The "assimilation machines" of the interwar period, the PCF and the CGT, still functioned for postwar Italian and, to some extent, Spanish and Portuguese workers. Immediately after liberation, the major left-wing Italian and Iberian labor unions and parties had established an organizational presence in France. An emigrant press had developed rapidly. In keeping with Lenin's Third International formula of "one working class and one working-class party in every state," however, the French Communist Party soon required foreign Communists to work within it and the CGT.[14] Foreign Socialists also largely melted into the French party and, by the late 1960s, the often like-minded Democratic French Labor Confederation (Confédération Française Démocratique du Travail—CFDT) (Jyotsena 1973; see Pike 1984).

But large-scale non-European immigration added a new, racial dimension to the foreign-worker phenomenon. Confronted with rising xenophobic sentiment among their membership, both the Communist and noncommunist left had difficulty fitting the new immigrants into traditional class-based analysis (Wihtol de Wenden 1988, pp. 88–130).

Political Action

In the late 1960s the French government and society got their first inklings that the nation's foreign population had acquired a certain permanence and autonomy. Many immigrants participated in the strike activity and protest marches that rocked General de Gaulle's government in 1968. In the wake of the "events," the government expelled more than 250 foreigners, most of them not students but North African workers. Politically, the actions provided a foretaste of the new forms of immigrant expression and mobilization, combining class and ethnicity, that would characterize the 1970s (Schumann 1969; Granotier 1976, p. 239).

The Grenelle Accords that signaled the end of the unrest in the late 1960s did not directly address the foreigners' concerns. Even as their living and working conditions deteriorated further, immigrants found themselves with the same few institutional channels through which to direct their demands and opinions. Racism, rising unemployment, administrative harassment, and abuse of police power would drive Portuguese, North and sub-Saharan Africans, and, eventually, Turks to action. As immigrants and as workers, they turned into explicitly political conflicts that Presidents de Gaulle and Pompidou had tried to push into the "apolitical" realm of social policy.

No policy area illustrates this evolution in the relationship between the immigrants and the French political system better than housing. France suffered from a severe shortage of residential housing after World War II, so immigrants encountered an already tight market. Their living conditions were often reprehensible. *Bidonvilles*, Third World–style shantytowns, grew up around major French cities during the 1950s. Also meeting the housing needs of immigrants were the so-called merchants of sleep—slumlords who would rent them overcrowded, overpriced rooms (Hervo and Charras 1971).

After a series of deadly fires and other tragic events had called attention to these scandalous conditions in the late 1960s and early 1970s, Prime Minister Jacques Chaban-Delmas moved to destroy the *bidonvilles*.[15] His expedient eradication program displaced thousands of foreign-worker families. When neither replacement housing nor clear demonstrations of support from the French left materialized, a wave of protests and clashes erupted between evicted immigrants and French police, particularly around Paris.

One of the most celebrated conflicts occurred in 1969 in the Parisian suburb of Ivry, where some 700 Malians housed in a former chocolate factory went on a rent strike to protest both an increase in their rents and substandard living conditions. Ivry's Communist city government opposed the strike, while bands of extreme leftists backed the protesters. The rent strike went on for almost a year before satisfactory alternative housing had been provided for the strikers. Similar confrontations occurred across France into the 1970s (see Gorz and Grani 1970).[16]

In housing—as in job training, language instruction, and other areas of special concern to immigrants—no global policy worthy of the name emerged. The French government's preferred tack was to set up an array of specialized, functionally specific organizations. For example, the National Society for the Construction of Worker Housing (Société Nationale de Construction de Logements pour les Travailleurs—SONACOTRA), created in the late 1950s with 55 percent of its shares owned by the government, managed most of the hostels for single male workers (SONACOTRA 1979).

By the early 1970s, three ad hoc institutional responses to the immigrants' housing predicament had developed: the *bidonvilles* had given way to resettlement in temporary housing *(cités de transit)*, in private dwellings or public housing projects *(habitations à loyer modéré—HLM)*, and hostels *(foyers)* (Freeman 1979, pp. 91–92). This trio of "solutions" to the housing problem corresponded neatly with the different policy aims for different immigrant groups, with "the HLM dwellings for those who are to remain, the *cités* for those who may or may not remain but are kept segregated until the choice is clear, and the *foyers* for those who are not desirable as permanent residents" (Verbunt 1985a, p. 149).

Thus institutional mechanisms led to the immigrants' concentration by nationality and socioprofessional status in certain types of housing and in certain towns, neighborhoods, and even buildings. Immigrants were far more likely than French citizens to live in collective and substandard housing, and within that category a hierarchy of housing conditions obtained, with certain national groups at the top (Italians and

Spaniards) and others in the middle (Portuguese) or at the bottom (North and sub-Saharan Africans and Turks) (Cordeiro 1985a; compare Rex and Tomlinson 1979).

This and other forms of discrimination and racism drove the immigrants to act. For more than a decade the French left had fought for passage of a law punishing racist words and deeds, one stronger than the legislation passed in 1939 and still part of the legal codes. The new law became a reality in July 1972 (Edmond-Smith 1972), but enforcement remained limited. Physical attacks against non-European immigrants in particular were increasing in number and ferocity. Throughout 1973, immigrant-led protest marches wound through the streets of Paris, Marseilles, Lyons, and other French cities.

In 1972 the government had announced more restrictive policies toward illegal aliens in informal administrative memoranda known as the Marcellin-Fontanet *circulaires*. Named for the ministers of the interior and of labor who initiated them, they attempted to link immigration more tightly to the labor needs of the French economy. In the process they also converted the lack of proper papers and permits into a threat to the public order (and thus grounds for expulsion from France). This change compelled North Africans and other particularly vulnerable immigrants to organize hunger strikes and occupy buildings throughout France (Miller 1981, pp. 100–102). Supporting the protests were the newly formed Marxist-Leninist Movement of Portuguese Workers Abroad (Mouvement des Travailleurs Portugais à l'Etranger), Spanish leftists, and like-minded militants assembled around the anti-imperialist CEDETIM center in Paris (CEDETIM 1975).

The shadowy Arab Workers' Movement (Mouvement des Travailleurs Arabes—MTA), a multiethnic Marxist-Leninist entity, surfaced during this period in Marseilles and Paris and launched both violent and nonviolent actions. The MTA criticized both the CGT's "paternalism" and the CFDT's "overemphasis on specific issues"; revolution was its goal ("MTA" 1973). It called several general strikes. These marked the first attempts to coordinate "autonomous" (in relation to French and homeland organizations and officials) immigrant-worker protests. Despite opposition from all the major French political parties and trade unions, as well as the AAE, many North African workers in the Midi and the Paris region joined in the work stoppages (CEDETIM 1975, pp. 278–280). The CGT, CFDT, and Fédération de l'Education

Nationale (FEN) cosponsored antiracist rallies in a number of cities in an attempt to steal some of the fire from the MTA (Gani 1972, pp. 227–231; Allal et al. 1977; *Le Monde,* September 16–17, 1973).

In the workplace, meanwhile, many foreign workers, especially those who at home had experienced governmental repression of labor unions or collusion between corporative unions and authoritarian regimes, were chafing at what they saw as artificial restrictions imposed by the French left. The strategies they favored drew in the beginning on solidarities rooted in the rural realities of their countries of origin: instead of individual mobilization or collective action, clans grouped behind traditional leaders (Ben Tahar, 1979, p. 178). Such workers formed the majority in several key industrial sectors. Finding their demands abandoned whenever French labor organizations no longer needed their participation in a specific job action, in retaliation they sometimes moved en masse from one trade union to another (Miller 1981, p. 150).

Eventually the newer immigrants, including some who were incorporated into indigenous organizations, grew to resent their second-class status (Reynaud 1971). Their reaction was explosive. In a series of wildcat strikes, they underscored that their interests did not intersect completely with those of the major French trade union federations and left-wing political parties. Starting with a strike by North African workers at the Peñarroya plant in Lyons in late 1971, the movement spread throughout France in 1972 and 1973 (see Mehideb 1973). Simply by the fact that they involved noncitizens, these job actions took on political significance. As Miller argues, they "signaled the emergence of foreign workers as active participants in French labor disputes" (1981, p. 91).

At first these strikes won the support only of far left *groupuscules.* Gradually, however, the mainstream French left was awakening to the foreign workers' cause and moved to incorporate their demands and to uphold even their unauthorized job actions. Fear that immigrants might join rival organizations was as strong a motive as any awakened sense of worker solidarity. The fierce rivalry between French Communists and Socialists bred competition for immigrant members, giving the foreigners leverage (Briot and Verbunt 1981).

Both parties, and especially the PCF, were increasingly successful in drawing foreign workers into their ranks. Intent on reversing the steady erosion in their social and political influence since the war,

French trade unions worked even harder than the parties to organize the immigrants, focusing on legal restrictions against foreign workers' acceding to positions of real authority and responsibility in factories. The CGT alone counted some 2 million foreign members by the early 1970s (Miller 1981, pp. 59–62). Thus the French left as a whole gradually grew more sensitive to the needs of non-native workers. Its organizations exhibited greater tolerance for the specific nature of many of their demands, and less for discrimination.

The immigrants' post-1968 militancy had an equally clear effect on their relationship with French "solidarity groups." Since World War II these voluntary associations had interceded on foreign workers' behalf with government social welfare organizations and bureaucrats and taken care of needs not met by the government. Faced daily with the immigrants' harsh lot, they gradually redirected their efforts to include demands for policy changes and for civil and political rights for immigrants (Briot and Verbunt 1981, p. 139). In 1966 a dozen left-wing Catholic solidarity groups in the Paris region united into the Federation of Support Associations for Immigrant Workers (Fédération des Associations de Soutien aux Travailleurs Immigrés—FASTI). Along with groups such as the Protestant social action committee CIMADE and the Movement against Racism and Anti-Semitism and for Peace between Peoples (Mouvement contre le Racisme et l'Anti-sémitisme et pour l'Amitié entre les Peuples—MRAP), which was close to the CGT and PCF, the FASTI declared its support for the immigrants' struggles of the 1970s. This solidarity created tensions with public authorities, who threatened to withhold their subsidies (Wihtol de Wenden 1978, p. 90).

French churches also developed a more activist attitude toward immigrant political participation. Many provided places in which immigrants could conduct their hunger strikes, and bishops in Lille, Lyons, and elsewhere spoke up in their defense. Progressive Catholic organizations such as the Catholic Committee against Hunger and for Development (Comité Catholique contre la Faim et pour le Développement), the Young Christian Workers (Jeunesse Ouvrière Chrétienne—JOC), and Catholic Workers' Action (Action Catholique Ouvrière—ACO), many of whose members were also union organizers, took the lead in pushing for such activism (Verbunt 1980, pp. 281–296).

The early 1970s, then, witnessed a decline in paternalism as the immigrants' trade-union, party, and solidarity-group allies adjusted to increasingly independent and confrontational immigrant political activity. Initially, legal restrictions on such participation and on access to public funding gave the immigrants little choice but to rely on their French allies, and most of the immigrants' own organizations welcomed such collaboration.

But the increased solidarity generated its own concerns. The mainstream French left saw immigrants' mobilization along ethnic lines as merely a preparatory form of social organization that would facilitate their insertion into the trade unions. Foreign-worker activists sometimes recoiled at seeing their struggles harnessed to what was "essentially a French structure of organizations and relationships, and channeled into a particular framework of ideology and action" (Grillo 1985, p. 254). In spite of the legal barriers, therefore, autonomous immigrant associational activity and other forms of immigrant mobilization gained in strength and confidence after 1968. Many of the associations forged an underground political presence to complement their traditional cultural and social welfare functions (Briot and Verbunt 1981, pp. 147–148).

By the mid-1970s France was startled to realize that since the war it had unwittingly imported not temporary, expendable laborers but durable immigrant communities. More and more, foreign workers were unwilling to accept the subproletarian existence to which the host society relegated them. Institutional processes in France were channeling the immigrants' political mobilization, but in ways that were sometimes not intended or expected. In return, immigrant political activity was provoking surprisingly significant institutional changes, which in turn instigated a new series of mutual reactions.

2

France, 1974–1992

In the early 1970s immigrants found existing routes of political access blocked by their divided, self-serving host-society "allies." More and more politically active and independent-minded, they sought other, less constrictive channels. Resorting increasingly to confrontational tactics, they were changing the ways in which French political parties, trade unions, and solidarity groups responded to their demands. Like them, French policymakers finally had to accept that immigration had become a full-fledged political and social issue. The government soon provided its own more thoroughgoing response: in 1974 it instituted a ban on new immigration. The effect of this move was to consecrate and hasten the stabilization of France's immigrant communities.

Whatever their long-range goals, the immigrants themselves put aside plans to return to the homeland soon and concentrated more single-mindedly on formulating demands on the host society. Their strategies were inevitably shaped by the nature of the interaction between French institutions and the foreign workers and their children. Class-based channels of participation, though growing wider, were the only ones available to immigrants before the Socialists' electoral triumphs in 1981.

In the afterglow of François Mitterrand's historic victory, he and his governments widened immigrants' access to French politics through trade union and other class-based activity, and increased to a meaningful degree their opportunities to organize politically on the basis of ethnicity, race, and even religion. The governing left's policies, combined with the effects of French citizenship law, helped give rise to an antiracist social movement and other forms of political mobilization among foreign workers' children. At the same time, the Socialists' electoral tactics propelled France toward a new politics of hate. By the early 1990s, the nation faced widespread suburban unrest and ethnic/racial tensions.

The Giscard *Septennat*, 1974–1981

THE END OF LAISSEZ-FAIRE

Until the 1970s, containing immigration issues in the *communes* (localities) had helped national political elites defuse racial and ethnic tensions. Gary P. Freeman has noted that up to that point, "[e]xcept for the periodic crises, and the more and more insistent push from the anti-immigrant forces to halt nonwhite immigration, the race relations issue was not very salient to political leaders" (1979, p. 128).

But the "social costs" of immigration were mounting, and the ramifications of the 1973 oil crisis brought the issue to a head. President Georges Pompidou had moved to slow immigration with the 1972 Marcellin-Fontanet *circulaires*. His successor, Valéry Giscard d'Estaing, completely abandoned laissez-faire immigration policy. In July 1974 Giscard issued two *circulaires*, which temporarily suspended new inflows and halted the "reunification" of foreign workers' families. The Council of State, France's supreme administrative court, overturned the latter in 1975.

Promising a more coherent approach, the Giscard administration vowed to integrate immigrants who already resided in the country into French society. The government's Seventh Plan (1975–1981) became the first to incorporate concerns that touched on aspects of immigration besides those affecting France's political economy (see Lebon 1977; Costa-Lascoux 1980). Many of those good intentions, however, failed as a result of inadequate funding.

Efforts to stop immigration also met with only limited success. From 1974 onward new labor immigration slowed, but family reunification and illegal immigration continued. Moreover, France continued to be a haven for political refugees, both legal and clandestine, from South and Southeast Asia, Central and South America, and the Middle East (Martin and Miller 1982, pp. 51–53, 81; Weil 1991b, pp. 84–86). Control of France's borders beyond established checkpoints proved impossible. Nor did monetary inducements designed to encourage legal immigrants to return to their homelands yield significant results. The famous *aide au retour*, instituted in 1977 by Secretary of State for Foreign Workers Lionel Stoléru, was specifically designed to hasten the departure of North and sub-Saharan Africans; but more Iberians took advantage of the offer than anyone else—two-thirds of the 100,000 people who accepted the money (Rocha Trindade 1981, p. 68). Less than one-third (31 percent) of those departing had been unemployed. The government realized that the scheme had backfired and in July 1980 suspended Portuguese and Spaniards from eligibility for the program, which was dropped altogether in 1981 (Lebon 1979, pp. 37–46).

A few years earlier the *aide au retour* had run afoul of the Council of State, which questioned the Ministry of Labor's competence to enact such a program through a *circulaire*. In fact from 1975 to the mid-1980s the Council nullified more than a dozen measures taken by governmental officials. Those limits to its control notwithstanding, only the executive branch, unburdened by advisory committees and other consultative requirements, was able to take quick decisions. The very multiplicity of legal texts on immigration and their obscure and contradictory aspects opened the way for bureaucratic discretion. The government consistently employed *circulaires,* instruments with little legal force, to guide French immigration procedures. Designed to facilitate the working of the administrative machinery, the *circulaire* became the immigration "Bible" and marching orders for confused bureaucrats (Briot and Verbunt 1981, p. 65).

Civil servants thus remained responsible for the day-to-day "management" of immigration—entries and departures, work and residence permits, and so on. They reacted primarily in ad hoc fashion to the economic needs of the moment, tempered by political, demographic, social, and cultural interests (Verbunt 1985a, pp. 156–157). Usually, the new policies and procedures were grafted onto existing ones, which resulted in incremental and sometimes conflicting changes. The fundamental system was left undisturbed. "Far from according immigrants the same political rights as the French," Eric-Jean Thomas has observed, the multitudinous laws and procedures "entangle[d] them in a web of regulations and confer[red] inordinate power on the administrative authorities" (1982, p. 43). They added to the immigrants' insecurity.

Bureaucratic practices also provided a framework within which to continue to make distinctions between "good" and "bad" immigrants, which only encouraged ethnic distinctions and consciousness: "the distinguishing criterion has been the likelihood of the group's integration or assimilation. Demographic interests demanded the assimilation of some immigrants, while social peace demanded the exclusion of others" (Verbunt 1985a, p. 146). The administration, police, and social services treated Europeans' requests with more openness and greater dispatch. Identity checks (or "controls") affected non-Europeans to a disproportionate degree. Discrimination, commonplace at the local level, flowed from the highest levels of government: President Giscard promised Portuguese President Eanes that his countrymen would benefit from privileged treatment in France; he did not even need to sign any bilateral agreement or pass any legislation or *décret,* relying on administrative procedures to assure such treatment (Bruschi and Bruschi 1985, pp. 291, 297).

THE WEAKENING HOLD OF THE HOMELANDS

French authorities continued to cooperate extensively with their counterparts in the immigrants' countries of origin. They tolerated immigrants' participation in politics there, even campaigns for homeland elections on French soil.[1] After all, maintenance of ties with the homeland tended to discourage immigrants' mobilization in extreme left- or right-wing organizations and their demands on French institutions even as it eased their eventual "reinsertion" into the homeland.[2]

Nevertheless, as the immigrants' political demands centered more and more on the concrete problems associated with their life in France, there was a noticeable decline in organized political activity geared toward the countries of origin. The immigrants' periods of residency in France had lengthened, and immigration had become a fairly stable, family affair. Also, the French left's insistence that foreign Communists work within its organizations reduced the salience of much homeland-oriented participation; the immigrants' demands, even when targeting their homelands, were fusing with those of the French working class.

Perhaps even more important was France's relatively well-developed and steadily more inclusive social welfare system (see Freeman 1979, pp. 168–172). In 1980 the Council of State even ruled that the immigrants' right to lead a "normal family life"—which it had cited to overturn restrictions on family reunification—gave the second wife of a polygamist from Benin the right to join him in France and to draw public assistance on an equal basis with the first spouse (Fornacciari 1986, p. 93). More than in Switzerland, as we will see, social policies in France reduced pressures on homeland regimes to intervene there (Schmitter/Heisler 1983). Institutionally, none of the homeland governments operated in exactly the same way in the various host societies.

The networks of official and homeland fraternal associations that worked among the expatriate communities remained active. Within the Italian and the Iberian immigrant communities, religious associations with close ties to consular staffs continued to preach love of the homeland. Yet these and other homeland organizations increasingly served more as social clubs for the celebration of a common cultural heritage (Verbunt 1980, pp. 251–255).

The governments and political movements of the Southern European sending countries stopped policing their nationals' political behavior, although they did work to maintain their interest and involvement in homeland politics. Traditionally broad-minded, Italian authorities organized the National Conference on Emigration in 1975, which laid the foundation for a new consultative network more responsive to emigrants' demands. Spain's democratic, post-Franco government set up special emigration committees in each consular district in France to draw up proposals regarding the distribution of government subsidies among associations (Foschi 1977; Cases Méndez 1979).

Newer to France, the Portuguese clung a bit longer to their homeland ties, even while the host society began to take on more political importance for them. A group of immigrants in 1977 occupied the offices of the Portuguese Secretary of Emigration in Paris to try to influence bilateral talks between France and newly democratic Portugal. After several failed attempts to provide the institutional means through which Portuguese in France could actively participate in the politics of their homeland, in 1980 the Soares government in Lisbon created a Council of the Portuguese Community in France (Conselho da Comunidade Portuguesa em França—CCPF) along the Spanish model to advise it on emigration policy. Such structures "compel[led] their association-type movements to organize themselves internally and *inter se* with a view to better representation within the consultative bodies. This [was] an advance, therefore, in the direction of structuring the immigrant communities" (Cases Méndez 1979, p. 221).

The Algerian government at first resisted any erosion of its political influence. The AAE retained its coercive role, continuing to track antigovernment activities abroad with the assistance of the Algerian secret police. Significant numbers of Algerians took part in elections and referenda in their homeland. More than 100,000 in the Paris area alone voted on a national charter in 1976, and in 1977 four AAE officials won Algerian National Assembly seats (Miller 1982, pp. 27–40). Eventually, however, even the AAE had to acknowledge the immigrants' changing political focus. The realities of racism, the workplace, and the suburban housing projects induced Algerian immigrants, even more than others, to direct their demands toward the host society. Bypassed in several immigrant protests in the mid-1970s, the AAE by late in the decade had shifted its efforts more toward solving problems in France (Leveau and Wihtol de Wenden 1985; see also *Libération*, Nov. 3, 1988). President Houari Boumediene died in 1979; his successor, Chadli ben Djedid, brought new flexibility and pragmatism to relations between Algiers and the Algerian immigrants in France (Kepel 1987, p. 91).

Only among the most recent immigrants and the political refugees did the homeland still exert a determining political hold. For example, Turkey's government sent teachers, fully accredited by the French Ministry of Education, to instruct the children of Turkish workers in the language and culture of the homeland. Its nationalistic associations, including consulate-run Turkish Houses (Tuerk Evi), bolstered support for the regime. Left-wing Turkish groups shunned the consulates and government offices but had close ties with opposition movements in Turkey.[3]

WIDENING POLITICAL RIGHTS

Despite the growing stake that all immigrants had in the host society, few meaningful channels for political expression were available to them before 1981. They could participate in the activities of certain public-service bodies, such as parent-teacher associations, family welfare associations, and the governing boards of secondary schools and universities. They had voting rights in chambers of agriculture and industrial conciliation boards *(conseils des Prud'hommes)*, although they could not stand for election (Lahalle 1975). They could likewise join French associations. With their membership held to a maximum of one-quarter of the total, however, they often found it difficult to have their interests taken seriously (Briot and Verbunt 1981, pp. 55–56; see also Bonvin and Thery 1977). The government deported thousands of foreign activists annually for disturbing the "public order." The Interior

Ministry dissolved several well-known, established immigrant associations.[4]

At bottom, immigrants continued to enjoy quite extensive "social" but very few "political" rights. Still in force was the ban on unauthorized foreigners' associations, as well as the requirement that they maintain political neutrality. In response, immigrants continued to target social policies with unconventional actions throughout the seven years of the Giscard presidency.

French immigration scholar Gilles Verbunt has argued that "[w]hatever positive changes have taken place in the social situation of immigrants are more a result of work done by motivated individuals, immigrant organizations, labor unions, and other organizations than of the efforts of official policy" (1985a, p. 153). The immigrants' unorthodox, confrontational protests of the early and mid-1970s "had proven [their] mettle . . . and the necessity of bringing this increasingly combative group into the mainstream of the labor movement in France" (Miller 1981, p. 95; see also CFDT 1974). The major French trade unions and left-wing political parties, which traditionally dominated and channeled social conflicts, brought pressure to bear on policymakers.

Government officials played a predominant role during this period. They enacted reforms in employee institutions in the 1970s partly to remove issues that served to unite immigrants and the political opposition. But the French left's efforts also helped to hasten the changes. Since World War II a complex system of representation has operated in French firms to give employees a voice in their management. Legal restrictions had barred most immigrant workers from voting in elections for work committees and employees' delegates; French administrations had judged such participation too similar to the exercise of political rights (Akkacha 1973, p. 501; Minet 1984).

The French left championed a 1972 law that extended the voting and eligibility rights of foreign workers. Follow-up legislation in 1975 went even further in securing their right to stand for election to work committees, although foreign candidates still had to be able to "express themselves" in French (Wihtol de Wenden 1978, pp. 120–122). The same statute removed discriminatory conditions that had prevented foreign workers from serving as trade union delegates. In addition, immigrants from outside the European Community (EC) became eligible to hold office in administrative and policymaking bodies of trade unions, provided that they could speak French and had worked in France for at least five years.[5]

Also in 1975, immigrants won the right to become shop stewards on the same basis as French workers. With their participatory opportunities in the workplace thus augmented, officials hoped, immigrants could be wrested from the CGT's mobilizational control in the factories (see Kepel 1987, chap. 3). Paul Dijoud, then secretary of state for foreign workers, hailed the new laws as the "confirmation of the government's dedication to assuring the equality of social rights between foreign and French workers" (*Journal officiel—Assemblée Nationale*, June 16, 1975, p. 4241).

Inequities persisted, however. Discrimination within the trade union organizations responsible for drawing up slates of candidates could easily operate to exclude immigrants from full participation at the factory level. The same was true of the ill-defined language requirement (Minet 1984, p. 13; Briot and Verbunt 1981, p. 36).

CONFRONTATIONAL PARTICIPATION

Compounding the common, de facto discrimination in elections to employee associations were other indications that solidarity would not materialize overnight. By the mid-1970s the mainstream left was clearly moving closer to making the immigrants' demands its own. But French workers' organizations continued to dodge several of the immigrants' specific problems: lower wages than those of native workers, cases of alleged management racism, especially dangerous working conditions, inadequate company- or government-provided housing, and employment insecurity (Miller 1981, p. 148; Cerny 1982, pp. 60–61). Accordingly, the wildcat strike remained an important tool of protest for immigrants. The spontaneous, unauthorized job action by the mainly sub-Saharan African sewer workers of Paris 1977 stands as a case in point (Minet 1978, p. 10).

At the same time, unconventional actions persisted outside the factories. Learning from their struggles earlier in the 1970s, immigrant activists were working to achieve a higher degree of coordination. They organized foreign worker "congresses" and addressed joint lists of demands to French authorities. During the run-up to the presidential election of 1974, North African militants of the multiethnic Emigrant Movement Front (Front de Mouvement des Emigrés) campaigned for left-wing candidates sympathetic to their interests and organized a symbolic presidential campaign, "nominating" one of their leaders, Djelali Kamal, for the office.[6]

There followed a period of intense protest activity. The immigrants involved presented themselves explicitly as workers who happened to be foreigners. Yet clearly competing in their protests with class interests were the ethnic-based political identities that French immigration policies had encouraged, as well as a more general immigrant consciousness fostered by a common experience of social and political marginalization (see Wihtol de Wenden 1986b).

As before 1974, terrible living conditions continued to spark foreign-worker agitation in France. The protesters widened and coordinated their actions after French authorities slowed immigration. They welcomed support from the French left but stressed the need for both their movement's autonomy and its multiethnic composition (SONACOTRA 1978, p. 3).[7]

In late 1973 and in 1974, thousands of African workers housed in quasi-public dormitories in the Paris region participated in coordinated rent strikes. Immigrants housed in the hostels constructed and managed by the government-controlled SONACOTRA agency followed their lead and launched a movement to oppose rent hikes and to demand greater tenant rights and even Islamic prayer rooms. North Africans, sub-Saharan Africans, and Portuguese together also claimed the right to assemble and to form their own autonomous renters' associations to negotiate with SONACOTRA management (Verbunt 1980, pp. 319–321; see also SONACOTRA 1979, preface).

The wave of protests started in the Communist Red-Belt suburbs of Paris in 1974. It spread from hostel to hostel to reach other regions of the country as well as housing run by other quasi-public bodies and by employers. The strikers withheld rents and stymied government efforts to suppress their movement. Rallies and demonstrations in support of the protesters drew crowds of thousands. With up to 20,000 participants at some points (over one-fifth of all hostel residents), the SONACOTRA strike "became a largely autonomous protest movement which eventually led to criticism of all aspects of French policy toward foreign workers" (Miller 1982, p. 54).

In the absence of institutionalized patterns of conflict resolution and recognized immigrant representatives, French institutions had difficulty dealing with the protests. Local PCF and CGT officials were visibly upset by the uncontrolled nature of the movement on "their" turf.

Late in 1975 they joined with their allies in the AAE to mediate an end to the SONACOTRA unrest in the Paris area. Several dormitories wherein the CGT was strongly represented did agree to the compromise settlement, but most of the strikers refused the accord, since it had been negotiated without them and failed to go beyond rent reductions (SONACOTRA 1978).

The government also encountered severe problems in attempting to negotiate a settlement. When negotiations with the strikers' Coordination Committee failed to make any headway in 1976, Minister of the Interior Michel Poniatowski deported several dozen movement leaders on Good Friday. That symbol-laden move sparked denunciations from the Catholic church, the left, and such luminaries as Jean-Paul Sartre and Simone de Beauvoir. Although the Council of State eventually overturned the deportation orders for most of those concerned, 500 were forced to leave for having disturbed the "public order" (Harbi 1977).

The harsh government reaction emboldened the protesters. Demonstrations multiplied throughout the late 1970s, as did clashes between strikers and the police. Legal assistance provided by French allies enabled the SONACOTRA strikers to continue their protest until 1980, by which time most participants had agreed to a settlement. By then, the five years of protests had cost the French government about $50 million in lost rent receipts "and much more in public embarrassment and frustration" (Miller 1981, p. 88).

Spurred by the tenacity of the SONACOTRA strikers, antiracist protests proliferated after the 1974 immigration stoppage. Foreigners organized rallies and marches to condemn anti-immigrant violence and went on hunger strikes. They were equally active in their opposition to the laws and procedures tightening controls over work and residency permits that came into effect between 1974 and 1980, as the government struggled to reassert its authority over immigration.

After 1977 the government adopted a noticeably tougher line that managed only to politicize the immigration issue even more, arousing both parliamentary debate and nonparliamentary opposition. Legislation and its enforcement targeted non-Europeans more than immigrants from within the European Community. In 1979 and 1980 immigrants of many nationalities banded together to oppose the proposed (but never enacted) "Stoléru reform" to limit renewals of work and residency permits, as well as the "Barre-Bonnet laws" (named after the prime minister and the minister of the interior and passed in January 1980), which tightened regulations against illegal aliens and made deportation procedures easier. Immigrant leaders condemned the measures for sharpening "juridical balkanization," the discrimination between Europeans and non-Europeans (Miller 1981, pp. 88–101; *Le Monde,* May 29, 1979).

INSTITUTIONAL RESPONSES AND THE DECLINE OF PROTEST

The immigrants' confrontational protests and other aggressive political actions through the late 1970s thrust debate over immigration to the center of French politics. Major newspapers devoted considerable column space to the more unorthodox protests. The wildcat strikes compelled the minister of labor to ask several North African governments to control their rebellious nationals in France. Heated parliamentary discussions sometimes took on wider political significance by intensifying confrontations between the French right and left, and between the PCF and the Socialist Party (Parti Socialiste Français—PS) (see *Journal officiel—Assemblée Nationale,* first sessions, April 29, 1976; April 27, 1977, pp. 2375–82; April 17, 1980).

The immigrants addressed themselves directly to the bureaucracy by means of novel tactics and strategies that won for them more influence than might have been expected. All the while, French authorities made it clear that they viewed the supposedly apolitical protests against social conditions as "so many transgressions of the political principle of political neutrality" (*La Croix,* Nov. 23, 1973, p. 1). Ironically, though, the immigrants' confrontational actions thereby contributed to the political co-optation of their fights: in order to give the impression to itself and to French society that it had matters under control, the government provided an institutional response intended to retrieve possession of the source of social conflict (Wihtol de Wenden 1988, pp. 220–224).

Though clearly worried about legitimating the foreign workers' protests over housing by acceding to their demands, in the second half of the 1970s President Giscard d'Estaing announced the government's commitment to programs designed to improve immigrants' housing. The SONACOTRA movement forced rent decreases and changes in the renters' legal status. As a direct result of the publicity generated by the strikes, the government came under intense pressure to allocate more money for housing for foreign workers and to widen their access to subsidized housing. The illegal immigrants' hunger strikes and protests of the mid-1970s and thereafter likewise convinced the government to regularize the status of many participants and to reconsider its policies toward illegal immigration (Costa-Lascoux and Wihtol de Wenden 1981).

Just as the government responded to the immigrants' assertiveness by modifying procedures and laws, so, too, did the institutions of the left—the PCF, PS, CGT, CFDT, and the solidarity groups close to those organizations politically—move to offer more reliable and comprehensive material and moral assistance. Thus, despite their conflictual relationship with the SONACOTRA strikers' Coordination Committee, the CGT and CFDT reaffirmed their support for the immigrants' right of association and for greater participatory opportunities in the workplace (Verbunt 1980, pp. 310–340). And by the decade's end, immigrant-worker leaders had grown more familiar with the "rules of the game" in France. They came to realize that although protests could produce important gains, complete autonomy threatened to degenerate into debilitating political isolation.

Greater numbers of immigrants were involving themselves in French politics through membership in political parties. Although few belonged to the PS in the late 1970s, the PCF had some 25,000 foreign members, more than any other host-society party in Western Europe. French trade unions still served as the most important vehicles for the immigrants' class-based participation. Even so, unionization among immigrant workers hovered at around only 10 percent during the 1970s, in contrast to 20–25 percent for French workers. In France's labor-importing neighbors, West Germany and Switzerland, two to three times as many foreign workers were unionized. The overall weakness of French trade unions relative to those elsewhere in Western Europe partly explains the discrepancy, along with the fact that many foreigners worked in weakly unionized sectors like construction. In traditional labor strongholds like metalworking and textiles, by contrast, union locals had almost as many foreign members as French (Minet 1984, p. 6; Miller 1981, pp. 184–185; compare Coeuret 1974).

As before, many Italian and Spanish immigrants participated in French politics through membership in the PCF and the CGT. The Portuguese Communist Party had an extensive organizational network in France and worked outside of the homeland government's purview and under the skirts of its French counterpart. Homeland front organizations like the Association of Portuguese Natives (Association des Originaires du Portugal—AOP) helped spread the Communist viewpoint throughout the community in France.[8]

The CGT and the PCF hesitated at first to drop their insistence that foreign workers follow the French Communist leadership on matters concerning host-society politics. These organizations stressed that even with their specific demands and needs, foreign workers remained an inseparable part of the overall French movement. In this optic, French Communists strove to increase the number of foreign unionists by means of tightly controlled local and departmental "nationality groups," special bodies alongside regular union structures.[9]

The CFDT and the Socialists also continued to see immigrants as part of their class strategy. But their Catholic and *auto-gestionnaire* (self-management) members pushed them to display greater tolerance earlier on for the "specific" nature of many of the foreign workers' demands. In the CFDT truly autonomous foreign-language groups formed. In several Renault plants (Flins, Cléon, and Choisy) in 1975, foreign-worker participation in employee delegate elections very clearly contributed to the CFDT's progress at the CGT's expense (CFDT 1978; Verbunt 1980, pp. 227–229).

In both major labor federations more immigrants were rising through the ranks to become trade union officials, delegates at national labor conferences, and employee delegates. The moral and symbolic weight of the immigrants' presence largely compensated for their lack of financial and political resources. As before, they gained added leverage from competition between rival elements within the mainstream left.

The greater sensitivity and responsiveness of the French left engendered a "growing, if still uneasy symbiosis" between it and foreign workers (Miller 1981, p. 95; PS 1979). This enhanced rapport encouraged the latter to undertake actions that were class based but also institutional. Even though not all of immigrants' demands melted easily into the common pool of grievances, by the late 1970s their struggles increasingly took place within the broader context of the mainstream labor movement. Independent workplace protests steadily declined. In the automobile industry (the Renault plants at Ile Séguin, Billancourt, and Flins) from 1975 through 1980, during the celebrated strike of the Paris Metro cleaners in June 1977, at the nuclear generator at Malvilles in 1979, in the mines of Lorraine in 1980, and elsewhere, immigrant labor militancy unfolded under the aegis of the CGT and the CFDT (Minet 1984, p. 21; Verbunt 1980, pp. 361–368).

Employers and the police did not hesitate to try to exploit ethnic differences to weaken strike activity, and government officials occasionally deported striking foreign workers.[10] Generally, however, French governments accepted their work-based participation. In fact, acceptance of a wider role for immigrants in French political life was gradually building. During the Giscard presidency the Interior Ministry grew more liberal in its handling of immigrant associations. By 1978 officials were rejecting only 7 percent of requests for authorization, and a 1979 law required the administration to provide an explanation for any refusals.[11]

There was nevertheless a clear limit to such political openness. The non-Communist French opposition, shut out of national power but in control of a number of *communes,* was drawing inspiration from the Belgian model of local-level consultative councils for immigrants (*Conseils Consultatifs Communaux des Immigrés*—CCCI). Several experiments proceeded along these lines as early as 1971; and after the 1977 municipal elections, some fifty Socialist-led Union of the Left communal councils set up some form of consultative body for immigrants.[12] They varied in their mode of operation, in their degree of institutionalization, and in the level of direct participation they provided immigrants or their associations. Most, however, dealt with the same sets of problems salient to immigrant workers and their families: housing, education, job training, relations with the French bureaucracy, and employment (Charlot 1978; Wihtol de Wenden 1978, pp. 56–65). National government officials were highly suspicious and insisted that the councils observe political neutrality. When Chambéry endeavored to establish a full-fledged Belgian-style CCCI in the late 1970s, Interior Minister Christian Bonnet twice dissolved it (PS 1977; CLAP 1981).

Thus, despite the political advances won, the workplace remained the only area wherein *de jure* equality for immigrants had been approached. The gulf between their trade union and professional rights and their rights to participate in French political life had not closed significantly. "Industrial democracy," to borrow Miller's term, remained the "primary legitimate channel of foreign worker participation in public affairs" (1981, p. 147; compare also Beylier 1978).

The Mitterrand Experiment, 1981–1991

EARLY CHANGES IN POLICY AND DISCOURSE

The trend toward sociopolitical integration accelerated sharply after the Socialists came to power in 1981. Though not making them a top political priority, François Mitterrand and the Socialist Party platform promised better treatment and greater political rights for France's immigrants—including local-level voting rights. During his campaign, the new president had repeatedly announced his intention to welcome especially non-European immigrants and their families into the "national solidarity" that would be a natural corollary to French solidarity with their Third World homelands (Costa-Lascoux 1982).[13]

After Mitterrand's victory, immigrants flocked to the Place de la Bastille to celebrate, a scene evocative of the parade of the united "people of the left" in 1936 (Leca 1985, p. 13). Catherine Wihtol de Wenden (1988) has documented the immigrants' "passage to the political" ("le passage au politique") in the period that followed: whereas once they had turned problems that French society had deemed to be social into political ones, they now progressively received and acted on new institutional possibilities to participate as nearly full-fledged actors in French politics.

Undeniably, Mitterrand and the PS reduced the insecurity of foreigners and their children residing in France. Their ability to organize on the basis of class, ethnicity, race, and religion expanded significantly. However, the governing left soon became preoccupied with forces engendered by previous regimes' policies and nonpolicies, as well as with its own internal divisions. Within a few years the limits to governmental action and the sometimes unintended effects of Socialist policies became clear.

In June 1981 François Autain, the new secretary of state for immigrants *(secrétaire d'état chargé des immigrés)*, made it clear that the two main objectives of French immigration policy were to remain intact: stopping the influx and absorbing the immigrants already settled in France. Once in power, though, Mitterrand and the PS moved quickly to implement several of their campaign pledges to the immigrants. The new government enacted more liberal policies toward family immigration, strengthened the immigrants' protection against administrative abuses and deportation without due process, and implemented a one-time "regularization" program for undocumented foreigners.[14] The "executive and administrative style" that had dominated immigration policymaking before 1981 gave way to a more inclusive and rights-oriented approach (Wihtol de Wenden 1988, p. 288).

The new government issued a qualified guarantee that immigrants would no longer face expulsion for participating in militant trade union activity. The Auroux Laws of June 1982, which augmented labor rights generally, removed the requirement that immigrants be able to express themselves in French in order to run for election to employee institutions and made foreign workers eligible to sit on the *conseils des Prud'-hommes*. In the 1982 elections for these labor-relations tribunals, the immigrant vote saved the CGT and the CFDT from disastrous slippage in several voting districts (Dias 1983).[15]

The legal changes, combined with the direct political access now enjoyed by the immigrants' allies on the left, increased opportunities for class-based action, including a new wave of immigrant worker strikes at a number of French automobile plants from the summer of 1981 to early 1983 (Benoît 1982; Wihtol de Wenden 1985). Even in those industrial plants in which immigrants constituted the overwhelming majority of members, their strikes displayed a more professional character than before. Collaboration with French unions was extensive.

THE FLOURISHING OF ETHNIC AND MULTIETHNIC ASSOCIATIONS

Other new channels of political opportunity opened to foreigners by the Socialist government were to prove even more fundamental and consequential than their expanded opportunities to participate in the workplace. For a commitment to cultural pluralism figured in the Socialist program. The ethnic "label," long denied and denounced in Jacobin France, received unprecedented official acceptance, even encouragement. National officials expanded on initiatives developed by left-wing municipalities over the preceding decade. The PS acknowledged that immigrants would remain in France and emphasized their right to live and work there without abandoning their cultural/ethnic identity. Private radio stations became legal in November 1981, offering a highly prized cultural outlet for foreign workers and their children (Verbunt 1985a, pp. 147–152).

Most significantly, the Association Law of 9 October 1981—enacted at least in part as a result of efforts by immigrants and their allies—replaced Daladier's decree-law of 1939. Foreign associations thereby became subject to the same conditions as "French" associations: that is, making a simple declaration to the Ministry of the Interior. Immigrants likewise won the right to act as administrators of their own and French associations and, like them, to receive public funding (FONDA 1983). The official Social Action Fund (Fonds d'Action Sociale—FAS) received a mandate to disperse such monies.[16] The next year the government revamped the FAS, decentralizing it and seating representatives of the *"communautés étrangères"* on the regional and local boards (Safran 1985, p. 54). Immigrants (appointed by the secretary of state for immigrants) entered the FAS administrative council in 1983 (see Planchais 1986).

The government neglected at first to inform foreigners adequately of their new rights, but the situation slowly improved. The new funding dynamics influenced many of the immigrants' voluntary-association allies on the French left. Before 1981, as we have witnessed, they had often made immigrant demands their own, serving as a "shield" for their vulnerable "charges." They had received quite generous financial support from the French state in appreciation for their provision of social services and other humanitarian assistance that would otherwise have been in its realm of responsibility and more of a political issue.

Now, however, these groups had to compete with the immigrants' own associations for government largesse and for the right to represent the immigrant communities: "the cake is the same size, but there are more pieces" (Comité d'Etudes et de Liaison "Etrangers" 1983, p. 32). The social Catholic Federation of Support Associations for Immigrant Workers (FASTI), Catholic Workers' Action (ACO), the Young Christian Workers (JCO), the Protestant social action committee CIMADE, and the pro-Communist Movement against Racism and Anti-Semitism and for Friendship between Peoples (MRAP) eventually had little choice but to respond with greater respect for the immigrants' political autonomy and a willingness to collaborate on an equal basis (Verbunt 1985b). As with French trade unions and left-wing political parties, competition between the immigrants' solidarity-group allies heightened the value of the immigrants to them (see Verbunt 1982).

Associational life among immigrants themselves received a decisive stimulus from the new law. The number of associations skyrocketed after its passage (see Table 11), exceeding 4,200 by the mid-1980s. Reflecting the diversity of the immigrant communities themselves, their associations represented virtually all possible currents, "from moral exhortation to calls to radical action" (Briot and Verbunt 1981, p. 136).

Much of the new activity proceeded along ethnic lines. Legal repression and official encouragement of immigrants' ties to their countries of origin had fed a "homeland hangover"—the continuation of patterns of participation characteristic of the societies from which the immigrants arrived. This condition clearly contributed to the early salience of ethnic and cultural organizational differences within each national community.

But over time, the government's long hierarchization of the immigrants came to matter more. Effectively ranking the immigrants by nationality, postwar French governments had linked each group some-

Table 11 Number of immigrant associations declared in the *Journal Officiel*, 1981–82

	Number of associations	
Immigrant group	May 1981	March 1982
African	9	59
Algerian	3	14
Asian	13	22
Foreign workers (grouped)	1	10
Islamic	7	42
Italian	7	19
Moroccan	6	30
North African (unspecified)	2	35
Portuguese	25	69
Spanish	12	19
Tunisian	2	7
Turkish	18	25
Others	17	51

Source: Data derived from Comité d'Etudes et de Liaison "Etrangers" (1983), p. 55.

what differently to the political process. Even though this ordering of immigrants by national background steadily lost its legal foundation in many policy areas, in practice authorities continued to discriminate on that basis.

Distinct national organizational patterns resulted. The provision of social services and religious and folkloric activities remained important for most ethnic-based associations, as it had before 1981. But many groups now broadened their actions to defend the national (or regional) ethnic group's cultural identity and worth in France; some voiced demands for greater freedom of political expression (Dias 1986).

Such an evolution was apparent among Algerian organizations. The mass-based AAE still dominated the Algerian community's associational life in France; emigrant opponents of the FLN government in Algiers grouped around the Ben Bellist Committee of Algerian Workers (Comité des Travailleurs Algériens—CTA). Since the late 1970s, both organizations had been expending more effort defending the interests of Algerians vis-à-vis French society. The CTA urged its members to join French labor organizations and to fight within them for greater sensitivity to their needs and to those of the Algerian opposition.[17]

Tellingly, in 1981 a group of Algerian militants founded the Association of Algerian Workers in France (Association des Travailleurs Algériens en France—ATAF) to serve as a more autonomous community representative. The ATAF cared more about the conditions of the immigrant workers in the host society than about its compatriots in Algeria. A movement of militant elites, it did not have a mass base, although it made recruiting forays into regions of particular Algerian concentration.[18]

Southern Europeans organized in different ways. Despite the widespread belief that it had melted without a trace into French society, the Italian community nurtured a vibrant associational movement that developed markedly in the freer post-1981 environment. Citizens of a fellow EC member state, Italians escaped the brunt of anti-immigrant sentiment, and their organizations did not try to create an independent political presence in the host society. Most organizations enjoyed friendly, mutually supportive relations with officials in Rome and at consulates in France. Under their guidance, coordination among associations grew even closer. Local cultural and regional associations, parents' groups, and sports clubs predominated (Campani 1983 and 1985).

The Spanish associational pattern resembled the Italian, although

Spaniards exhibited a weaker relationship with the homeland. By the late 1960s the Spanish "colony" in France was aging, and the foreign workers were becoming "less concerned with their savings and more with their children's future" (Taboada-Leonetti 1987, p. 158). In response the Spanish Catholic church had helped found a network of apolitical parents' organizations, the Association of Parents of Emigrated Spanish Families in France (Asociación de Padres de Familia Españoles Emigrados en Francia—APFEEF). But the social Catholicism that motivated many of the priests and parents active in the parish-level organizations had created some tension with homeland officials. The APFEEF, which would eventually count some eighty-five member associations, did not declare itself a national federation until after Franco's death in 1975. Organizationally, if not necessarily ideologically, it separated itself from the Catholic church enough to include activists from the Spanish Communist Party (Partido Comunista Español—PCE), the workers' committees (comisiones obreras—CCOO), and the CFDT-affiliated Spanish "neighborhood committees" among its ranks (Dianteill 1992).

After the generalissimo's death, a number of prominent anti-Francoists took over the management of the other major Spanish organizational network, the Federation of Spanish Associations in France (FAEEF), which Franco had supported. Many formerly excluded associations soon joined.[19] Despite the FAEEF's professions of political autonomy and nonpartisanship, the influence of members or sympathizers of the PCE and the CCOO became quite strong in this network. Between them, the FAEEF and the APFEEF accounted for 70 percent of Spanish associations in France. Neither evinced any special loyalty toward the government in Madrid. After 1981 they worked together on projects to combat racism in France and to lobby for the immigrants' right to vote in local French elections.[20]

The burgeoning Portuguese associational movement resisted more persistently the trend toward coordination, yet it, too, yielded to the structuring forces at work. France's Portuguese community, which in some areas included entire villages that had uprooted and emigrated, produced a riot of mostly local dance, music, theater, religious, and football clubs that strove to maintain Portuguese culture. The Council of the Portuguese Community in France (CCPF), instituted by the Portuguese government in 1980, worked steadily to reduce associational "atomization."[21]

In 1982 the Center for the Study and Dynamics of the Portuguese Emigration (Colectivo de Estudos e Dinamizaçao da Emigração Portuguesa—CEDEP) made its début and joined that battle. Consisting at first of a handful of Portuguese militants in Paris, the CEDEP's main objective was to create a truly independent, unified Portuguese associational movement rooted firmly in a pluricultural French society. It advocated collaborative actions with the French left and with the organizations of the other immigrant communities (CEDEP 1983).

Institutional structuring, then, produced a common experience in France for members of each ethnic/racial group. Political differences among immigrants that had their roots in the same homeland were fading steadily, albeit at different rates. Each national community's associations showed a growing tendency to share an interest in their community's treatment in the host society and sometimes even to harmonize their actions.

This trend within the Southern European and, to a lesser degree, the Algerian immigrant communities was evident by the early 1980s. It also affected the newer communities, such as the Turks. The Turkish network of organizations was polarized along ideological lines, with the full panoply of Turkish political currents reproduced on French soil (Liger 1972). Islamic centers and religiously affiliated Turkish teacher-parent associations had formed in many localities to provide instruction in language and the Koran. Particularly after the 1981 officers' putsch, the secular Turkish government countered their appeal by supporting a range of ostensibly autonomous conservative associations in France (Legrain 1985, p. 10). Turkey's ethnic fragmentation also found an echo in the host society: Kurds and Armenians had their own associations, which government officials and other Turkish immigrants alike repudiated.[22]

In addition to those associations, which have remained important and active, a collection of left-wing Turkish organizations developed in France after 1981. Their activities and goals gradually converged as their interest in the problems of Turkish workers in France grew. These mostly Paris-based associations brought many regional associations under their rubric and intensified their actions.

Even though some of these leftist associations maintained ties with political parties and movements in Turkey, they rarely received their marching orders from there. Often they allied themselves with corresponding French movements. For instance, the Union of Turkish

Workers (Union des Travailleurs Turcs—UTT) and the Cultural Union of Turkish Workers (Union Culturelle des Travailleurs Turcs—UCTT), both formed in 1981, worked closely with the French Communists; nevertheless, as the French manifestation of the Turkish Maoist movement, the UCTT's focus deviated somewhat from that of the Communist mainstream.[23] Other Turkish organizations were more autonomous and concentrated on the day-to-day problems faced by Turkish workers in the host society.[24]

Although the left-wing Turkish associations at first shunned one another, Turks could not long ignore the commonalities of their experience in the host society. The organizations started to join in a common effort whenever a problem arose affecting the Turkish community as a whole. Several of the Paris-based associations put aside their differences and united to denounce racism and anti-immigrant violence, "just as the blacks did in the United States," and to participate in marches and rallies.[25]

Thus changes in French government policies and administrative procedures after 1981 caused a burst of associational activity and stimulated the consolidation of immigrant associations along ethnic lines. Socialist officials further instigated the development of ethnic political identities by pressuring amenable municipalities to establish consultative bodies for immigrants. In most cases the foreign delegates spoke for immigrants of a single nationality or ethnic background. Authorities usually dealt with certain leaders of a given national group and passed over others. In so doing, French officials contributed yet again to the political structuring of the immigrant communities.

Only rarely did immigrants have much influence on the selection of their representatives. Accordingly, when the Socialist government itself instituted a national-level consultative body, the National Commission for Immigrant Participation, in 1983, the Ministry of Solidarity appointed the immigrants sitting on it.[26] Representatives elected by the *communautés étrangères* did sit on national- and department-level advisory bodies responsible for social assistance to the immigrant population. Those foreigners, however, participated only in their capacity as trade union or social service representatives, not as immigrants per se (Safran 1985).

Whatever the shortcomings of the consultative bodies at any level, they did create opportunities for contacts not only between French citizens and immigrant communities but also among the various national communities themselves. More generally, the associations of immigrants from the various national groups were learning from one another how to articulate demands and how best to influence French politics. Simultaneously, the French government was working to reduce discrepancies in the different national groups' political and legal status.

All these factors produced a gradual convergence in the strategies, goals, and tactics of many immigrant associations. Some truly multiethnic associations of women, many of them neighborhood-based, quickly formed in the more tolerant political climate. Yet cooperation among ethnic-based associations remained more common. The most prominent case of such collaboration occurred on the eve of the immigration stoppage late in 1973, when seven autonomous, ethnic-based immigrant associations—all left-wing, national-level organizations based in Paris—founded the Immigrant Workers' House (Maison des Travailleurs Immigrés—MTI). The MTI worked to transcend ethnic divisions and coordinated member associations' activities with the aim of improving the lot of all immigrant workers, as workers, in France.[27]

The legal changes of 1981 provided the occasion for the interethnic movement to widen its scope and develop a truly political mission. In 1984 the Council of Immigrant Associations in France (Conseil des Associations Immigrées en France—CAIF) superseded the MTI. The leaders of fourteen national-level, ethnic-based umbrella associations sit on the CAIF, with one or more ethnic-based organizations representing the Algerian, Tunisian, Moroccan, sub-Saharan African, Spanish, Portuguese, and Turkish immigrant communities.

From the outset, CAIF leaders spoke of a single "Immigrant Worker Associational Movement." Through its technical and financial assistance and coordinating capabilities, the CAIF defined itself as this movement's nerve center. Its leaders dedicated themselves to bringing together the very diverse immigrant associational components of all nationalities in order to defuse lingering political rivalries rooted in the politics of the homelands (Mellouk 1985).

Although the CAIF insists that it is autonomous and espouses no particular ideology, in reality it has had a very close relationship with the French Communist Party and its allied CGT trade union (as well as with the left wing of the CFDT). Consequently, for the CAIF the Communist vision of class struggle has taken precedence over issues of ethnic identity, although these bases of mobilization have been seen as complementary. The CAIF's ultimate objective has been to get the immigrants to agree on a set of major demands to advance in common with the French labor movement, while the national communities and associations freely work to fulfill their own individual agendas (CAIF 1986).

THE POLITICS OF ISLAM AND THE LIMITS OF REFORM

Even as the immigrants' associational movements were prospering under the left, Islam was emerging as a form of multiethnic political mobilization that tested the limits of the new tolerance. The CAIF and other immigrant associations were enjoying some influence on the immigration debate at the national and local levels: the French media and public officials occasionally took notice; publicity over such institutional activities was generally favorable. Islam, on the other hand, caused upset in the host society.

Muslim associations and brotherhoods had existed for decades in France. Many received support from or were directly controlled by movements or regimes in the Muslim world. Money—"petrodollars"—flowed particularly profusely into France after the oil shocks of the 1970s (Kepel 1987, chap. 2).

France's Muslims, however, largely resisted both homeland and French efforts at coordination and effective control. The vast majority belong to the Sunnite branch of Islam, which has no hierarchical structure or magistracy. Some movements, like Faith and Practice (Foi et Pratique)—a branch of the pietist Sunnite Society for the Propagation of Islam (Jama 'at al Tabligh) that established a congregation in Paris in 1972—required the faithful to isolate themselves from French society (Legrain 1985). Others mediated with French authorities on their followers' behalf. The Paris mosque, which dated from 1926, liked to present itself as the official representative of Islam in France. But in reality there was no unifying structure to speak for the community or to serve as its official negotiator with French authorities.

The Socialist-led government tried to change that situation after 1981. In the 1950s Prime Minister Guy Mollet had named Si Hamza Boubakeur, an Algerian deputy to the French parliament who maintained close ties to expatriate *harkis*,[28] rector of the Paris mosque. Both before and after independence, Algerian nationalists denounced him as a traitor, and Moroccan and Tunisian officials resented Algerian "domination" (see Legrain 1985). Si Hamza's political support in the

French government evaporated with Mitterrand's victory, and he re-signed in 1982. Cheikh Abbas, an Algerian functionary with ties to the AAE, was selected to replace him (Kepel 1987, chap. 7).

Muting the impact of that change in leadership of the Paris mosque was the proliferation of Muslim associations of all types in the freer post-1981 legal environment. One segment limited itself to religious practice and instruction. The construction of mosques in France had accelerated during the mid-1970s: from 131 in 1976 to more than 300 in 1979.[29] After 1981, religious demands from an increasingly familial population combined with the new associational possibilities to stimulate such development further. By December 1984 there were more than 600 Islamic places of worship in France. Alongside them Muslim cultural associations began to intervene more often on their coreligionists' behalf at social welfare offices, schools, police stations, and city hall (Etienne 1989). Islam's increasing "visibility" often provoked a local political firestorm (Legrain 1985, pp. 23–24). Government officials and religious groups in Saudi Arabia, Libya, Morocco, Iran, Tunisia, and elsewhere financed many of the mosques. They were intent on removing the mantle of Muslim leadership that French authorities had effectively conferred on Algeria (see Kepel 1987, chaps. 5 and 6). This foreign connection contributed to misgivings in the indigenous population.

Islam was emerging in the workplace as well. Foreigners confronted both a reduced threat of deportation for participation in job actions and an increased threat of unemployment from automatization in French factories. The combination gave an impetus to class-based participation. Moroccans, normally not as militant as their Algerian and Portuguese colleagues, spearheaded the wave of immigrant-led strikes against Renault, Citroën, and Talbot automobile plants in several areas of France from the summer of 1981 to early 1983. Yet it was as unskilled workers *(ouvriers spécialisés)* and not as immigrant workers that most participated.

But for the immigrants those conflicts were not simply class struggles. Besides advancing work-related issues and demands for improvements in employer-provided housing and job training, the strikers demanded Islamic prayer rooms in the factories. Islam was hardly a newcomer there; an imam had been present at Renault-Billancourt as early as 1933 (Garache 1984), and several other Renault plants had installed prayer rooms in response to foreign-worker petitions in the late 1970s (Kepel 1987, pp. 145–153). What was new in the 1980s was that Islam, and not the trade unions or the immigrants' own ethnic-based associations, functioned as a factor of mobilization and unification in the automobile plants. The strikers brought in religious leaders to facilitate cooperation among the various national groups present (Wihtol de Wenden 1985; see also Benoît 1982).

As before, competition within the pluralistic French labor movement worked to the immigrants' advantage. The independent Confederation of Free Unions (Confédération des Syndicats Libres—CSL), which dominated the Talbot and Citroën factories, underestimated the importance of the immigrants' demands and lost their support as a result. The CFDT enjoyed some success in organizing the less religious. The CGT, on the other hand, used the "language of Islam" to "launch an offensive against the CSL" (Kepel 1987, p. 155). It backed calls for factory prayer rooms and created a "collective" of sympathetic imams at Renault's Billancourt plant to "protect the mosque from any deviation." Employers relented and found to their relief that practicing Muslims participated less often in trade union and strike activities. Soon, management adapted the rhythm of work on the lines to the cadences of Islam (Subhi 1985; see also Gaudemar 1982).

The strike movement had grown into a fight for the improved status of immigrant workers in heavy industry, beginning a new generation of labor struggles. The immigrants' militancy, albeit along institutional channels, rattled French authorities. Fear of Islamic fundamentalism and foreign influence provoked official overreaction to events. Labor Minister Jean Auroux asserted that "we are in a secular state, and we damned well intend to keep things that way." The striking immigrant workers were, Prime Minister Mauroy declared, "agitated by religious and political groups acting on agendas that have little to do with French social realities."[30] Not in a militant fashion, but along utterly institutional participatory channels and despite its potential for maintaining social peace, Islam was troubling France's secular republican political system (see Barou 1985; Leveau 1992).

In other important respects, as well, the immigrants could sense that the bloom was off the rose. The promised extension of limited suffrage, for instance, never materialized. The PS had joined the far left and the churches in supporting local-level voting rights for immigrants by the late 1970s. But the Socialists' Communist allies repeatedly opposed granting immigrants voting rights. Instead, placing an accent on internationalism, they advocated their full social and trade union rights in

France and the fight for democratic rights in their homelands (CGT 1981).

When the PS undertook to incorporate the immigrant population into French society outside the factory, it thus risked the ire of its Communist partners. From the other flank the opposition right harshly attacked all liberal measures toward the immigrants. Further constricting the Socialists were the consequences of their own reforms, many of which were incomplete. Practical decisionmaking on immigration regulation was still the responsibility of a wide range of ministries and agencies whose agendas often conflicted. "Administrative inertia" continued to "blunt the force of progressive policies and programs," even if some of the more flagrant bureaucratic abuses had been removed (Bruschi and Bruschi 1985, p. 296).

The country's "state of values" (l'état des moeurs), President Mitterrand eventually decided, was not yet ready for immigrants to vote in French elections at any level.[31] And though limited by juridical safeguards, the state retained the authority to expel immigrants for disturbing the still-undefined public order.

Discrimination between nationalities also persisted. The Badinter Law of June 1983 (named after the minister of justice) allowed police to consider, among other things, hair and skin color when deciding whom to stop for identification checks or to question about crimes. Not being white remained grounds for suspicion—what immigrants of color refer to as the "dirty mug crime" (le délit de sale gueule). The visa system was extended to apply to Turkish visitors, while the nationals of former French colonies, refugees, and citizens of EC member nations continued to enjoy privileged treatment. Only a few years after the left's historic initial victory, domestic and international constraints had forced the Mitterrand/Mauroy government to abandon its experiment in redistributive Keynesianism and had torn apart the Socialist-Communist alliance (see Hall 1986, chap. 8). By then, the movement to open institutions to the immigrants had run its course.

The Second Generation and the Social Explosion over Immigration

A NEW SOCIAL MOVEMENT

The limits of the reforms of 1981–82 notwithstanding, it remains true that by having opened new participatory channels to the foreign workers, the left dissuaded them from employing confrontational political tactics. The institutional system had defended itself with remarkable flexibility. When officials had realized that the immigrants were not going to go home and were not going to remain politically passive, they had granted them greater political rights. As the immigrants made use of those opportunities, and partly in line with them, the nature of their participation changed. Although the first immigrant generation guarded its hard-fought political autonomy and the specific nature of its demands, by the early 1980s foreign workers were clearly shifting from "out-of-channel" to more assimilative forms of participation, despite the hostile French reaction to even a nonmilitant Islam.

Less institutional forms of political protest did not simply disappear after 1981: the more vulnerable immigrant groups took up the confrontational tactics that the more established ones were abandoning. During the 1980s, most notably, illegal Turkish, Moroccan, Yugoslav, and other immigrants organized hunger strikes, occupied factories and public buildings, and mounted public demonstrations to secure legal status (Wihtol de Wenden 1984).

It was at this point that an additional, even more noteworthy factor became important: the appearance of a "second generation" of immigrants that had developed new forms of political activity. For the full century of large-scale immigration to France, a second, third, and more generations of immigrants had lived in the country. Yet it was not until after World War II, when the apparently "unmeltable" sons and daughters of non-European workers cast doubts on the assimilative powers of French society, that the second generation acquired collective visibility.

The governing left did much to spur the formation of a politically active second-generation subculture, but it was the heavy family immigration into France from 1965 to 1972 that had made for the rapid growth of this age cohort and the challenges associated with it. Its incredible ethnic diversity reflected the successive waves of immigration into the country. Already almost a million in number by the mid-1970s, second-generation immigrants typically occupied the same undesirable occupational substratum as their parents. In 1976 one-quarter of skilled workers' children, one-third of semiskilled workers', and almost half of unskilled workers performed the same job as their fathers. A much higher percentage of immigrants' children (30.3 percent of those without French citizenship in 1982) were unemployed than those of French stock (25.2 percent). They suffered from both a lack of adequate training and employer racism (Clévy 1976, cited in

Wihtol de Wenden 1988, p. 203). Many of those in the second generation with jobs held temporary positions offering no sense of security or permanency.[32]

In spite of the parallels between their socioeconomic situation and that of the first generation, these youths created their own subculture. Caught between the host society and their parents' homelands, most saw themselves as being "from France," the place of their birth and/or upbringing. Their collective behavior and sense of identity came to have less to do with the particularities of their ethnic origin, nationality, or social-class status than with the web of political, cultural, and economic relations in which they moved (Leclerq 1985; Leveau and Wihtol de Wenden 1988). They had very different political expectations and demands and adopted different participatory forms, largely because of the nature of the institutional factors acting on them.

Abdelmalek Sayad (1981); Claudio Bolzman, Rosita Fibbi, and Carlos Garcia (1987); Jacqueline Costa-Lascoux (1987); W. Rogers Brubaker (1992); and other scholars have drawn special attention to one such causal factor: in contrast to nations like Germany and Switzerland, whose citizenship laws are based on blood ties or descent (*jus sanguinis*), France has long had a much more inclusive definition of citizenship that incorporates notions of territoriality as well (*jus soli*). Thus a child born in France of foreign parents who has spent the preceding five years there and has not been convicted of certain crimes can acquire citizenship automatically at age eighteen (Article 44 of the Nationality Code of 1945). Anyone born in France who has at least one French-born parent is a citizen at birth (Article 23). This latter provision includes not only all third-generation immigrants but also the French-born progeny of Algerians born before their homeland gained its independence in 1962.[33] French naturalization procedures are also quite liberal. As a result, most of the estimated 400,000 second-generation Algerians born in France since 1963 and two-thirds of the 1.2 million noncitizens under eighteen will become French (Jean 1981; Brubaker 1992, chap. 1). This mechanism virtually ensures the eventual "civic incorporation" of France's immigrant communities (Brubaker 1992, chaps. 4 and 8).

What it does not do is determine the nature of that process of incorporation. Limited opportunities for individual socioeconomic mobility, together with relatively easy access to French citizenship and full political rights, encouraged second-generation immigrants to undertake group-based organization (see Huntington and Nelson 1976, chap. 4). In fact, the centralization of the French political system—the distance separating society and state and the absence of bridges across it—has long encouraged outsider groups there to develop social movements and to engage in direct-action tactics (see S. Berger 1972; Grémion 1976; Cerny 1982). These and other institutional features were important in channeling second-generation immigrants' participatory energies. To understand why they have chosen the particular collective strategies that they have, we need to look more closely at other aspects of the institutional context in which they have acted.

Unlike their parents, first and foremost, they typically refused to identify with the working class, rejecting a future as the "second generation of street sweepers" (quoted in Clément 1985, p. 111). This rebuff angered French Communists and trade unions, already hard pressed by the ongoing transformations of the French economy and workforce. Yet changes in the French and the world economies were weakening the French Communist Party and the trade unions, and the split between their indigenous and noncitizen components exacerbated their plight. This important transmission belt, which had connected earlier foreign workers to French society, was breaking down.

The same could be said of the Catholic church and the army. All these old "integration machines" were less and less able to assimilate and socialize the newer, non-European immigrants (Leca 1985). For their children, the task came to fall almost entirely on the schools, which held to their traditionally assimilative ideology. Educational "tracking" served to exclude immigrant children from remunerative careers. In fact the schools tended to marginalize all those whose cultural backgrounds rendered them unable or unwilling to adapt (Boulot and Fradet 1982; Pierrot 1985).

As a result of postwar policy choices, such people populated the *cités de transit* and the prisonlike low-income public housing complexes (HLM) of France's industrial suburbs. They took in immigrants, young workers from declining rural areas, and older workers displaced from the central cities by urban renewal. There French and immigrant children coexisted. They developed their own ways to cope with the *"rage"* bred by their marginal status and the discrimination under which they suffered. Instead of the old "universalist national institutions," the agents of socialization for them were the social workers, policemen, and local housing officials with whom they came into contact on a daily—and often conflictual—basis (Schnapper 1987–88).

The neighborhood and the housing project have become the loci of social and political mobilization. It is there that "victims of social exclusion, French and immigrants," have developed their "parallel socialization structures": "Territorialization permits the development of intermediary structures, veritable local communities that complement the state in integrating their members. In this optic, a sense of belonging to the Nation, which remains a very abstract ideal, is transmitted by belonging to the neighborhood, the place where social relations become real" (Simon 1992, p. 66).

Not surprisingly, then, the first collective actions by second-generation immigrants occurred in the suburban housing projects. Some children of Southern European and Algerian foreign workers participated in the "events" of 1968, but it was especially in the mid-1970s that members of the second generation began to react against their social exclusion. Some of them joined existing organizations, such as the Catholic JOC or the AAE's youth association. For others, juvenile delinquency provided the needed outlet (Sayad 1985; Boumaza 1985).

For others cultural activities were a way to vent frustration with their place in French society. Second-generation North Africans (nicknamed *Beurs*) got involved first, since they faced the most severe repression and discrimination. Militant theater groups presented often farcical interpretations of daily immigrant life and its problems, addressing themselves as much to French society and authorities as to the immigrant population.

Rock music filled the same expressive needs. *Beur* rock groups such as "Carte de Séjour" and the "Rockin' Babouches" sang of the second generation's trials and tribulations in French, Arabic, and the *Beur* dialect and published newsletters in which they developed their themes in greater detail. Inspired by the concerts of the same name in Great Britain, a loose collection of groups based in Nanterre formed "Rock against Police" in 1980 and 1981. It organized free rock concerts across the Paris area that often degenerated into violent confrontations between police and young immigrants and their French comrades (ANGI 1984).

The government moved to deport participants, prompting hunger strikes in Lyons and Paris to protest that action and racism in general. These ended in the spring of 1981, when the new Socialist government suspended the deportations pending a legislative study. President Mitterrand's decision was welcome, but it did not end assaults against immigrants and their children, particularly North Africans (Delorme 1984b; Battegay 1985).

The "hot summer" of 1981 in the suburbs of Lyons followed. Youngsters looted stores and stole automobiles, drove them wildly through the city, and then burned them on street corners. These so-called *rodéos* terrified the French public (Jazouli 1986, p. 81). Responding quickly to these violent outbreaks, the Mauroy government launched "Operation Anti-Hot Summer," which included summer camps by the sea and training for associational leaders. Interministerial commissions began to look in earnest for ways to get at the root causes of the disturbances. Officials also designated priority educational zones *(zones prioritaires d'éducation)* in areas of high immigrant concentration and introduced special remedial classes and instruction in the "mother" languages. French courts were handing out harsher sentences against the murderers and harassers of immigrants and their children. The new law on immigrant associations in October 1981 was at least in part a response to the preceding summer's violence (Safran 1985).

The effects were undeniable: the measures "defused the revolt that was simmering in numerous French cities, and they led hundreds of young North Africans to work within the institutions" of the host society (Delorme 1984b, p. 31). The legal changes and new programs led to intensified "in-channel" second-generation associational activity. Culture was still a potent form of political expression. It was now government funded; the *Beurs'* associations owed many of their organizational opportunities to the government, either the Ministry of Culture or the Social Action Fund (Wihtol de Wenden 1988, p. 370). Second-generation Iberians and Africans followed the *Beurs'* lead and founded political theater and rock groups and private radio stations (Delorme 1984b).

Anti-immigrant sentiment was already building as France's economic crisis deepened and as its immigrant-origin population grew more visible. The second generation's mobilization intensified this hostility. The results of the 1982 census revealed that the foreign population was growing ever more familial, with fewer economically active people than among the indigenous population, and less European (accounting for only 48 percent of all foreigners).

LE PEN AND THE ANTI-IMMIGRANT REACTION

In the municipal election and by-election campaigns of 1983, local politicians of all stripes portrayed the immigrants as a problem population. Jean-Marie Le Pen and his National Front (Front National—FN) harped on crime and "insecurity," linking their rise to the presence of non-European immigrants. The right-wing press—*Le Figaro*, as well as *Aurore* and *Minute*—depicted the second generation's political actions as dangerous infringements on French sovereignty (Plenel and Rollat 1984; Schlegel 1985b). The FN scored impressive electoral gains—around 10 percent of the vote—in several *arrondissements* of Paris and in cities such as Dreux, Roubaix, and Marseilles, which had a high proportion of immigrants, especially North Africans and *Beurs* (Schain 1987).

The far right's electoral breakthrough rocked the political establishment. The immigration issue crossed traditional party lines and defied a simple left/right dichotomy. The mainstream political parties feared a proliferation and widening of internal divisions from opening this potentially explosive dossier. The PS found itself torn between proponents of the new ethnic pluralism and defenders of the traditional Jacobin model requiring immigrants' complete, individual assimilation.[34] Nor did a coherent position emerge from the center-right, the Union for French Democracy (Union pour la Démocratie Française—UDF) and the neo-Gaullist Rally for the Republic (Rassemblement pour la République—RPR). As for the French Communist Party, its strength steadily eroded as it reaped what it had sown: "Virtually the same rhetoric that was used so effectively by the National Front in 1983 was first used by the Communist Party and some of its representatives in 1980–81" (Schain 1987, p. 239). With its "antipolitical" political discourse, the FN filled the ideological void (*Le Point*, no. 763, May 4, 1987, pp. 24–27). From March 1983 to March 1985, it received close to or more than 10 percent of the votes nationally in six elections.

Meanwhile, darker-skinned immigrants of many national backgrounds were becoming more frequent targets of attacks. Upset with the continuing racial violence and with Le Pen's electoral successes, immigrant-origin youths continued to clash with police. However, more contacts and greater mutual respect had resulted from earlier confrontations and the government's response to them. Whereas the summer of 1981 had been "hot," that of 1983—"warm" though it was—produced a less destructive reaction from the second immigrant generation (ANGI 1984, p. 39).

The spark flared in June 1983, when a policeman shot a teenaged immigrant leader in the "Minguettes" housing project in Lyons. The incident gave rise to the "March against Racism and for Equality" from Marseilles to Paris that autumn. Although *Beurs* and other non-Europeans predominated, marchers of Southern European origin also participated. French churches and solidarity groups offered active support. Nervous, the Socialist government and the trade unions only tacitly backed the peaceful protest at first. But by the time the marchers arrived at the Place de la Concorde on December 3, they numbered over 100,000 and had become a media sensation. President Mitterrand joined Coretta Scott King and Joan Baez, among other celebrities, in welcoming them ("Manifeste de soutien" 1983; *Le Monde,* Nov. 16–17 and Dec. 4, 1983; Bouzid 1984; Jazouli 1986, pp. 113–142, 175–179).

Although the disadvantaged youth of France's suburbs had many experiences in common, regardless of their ethnic or religious background, the French institutional system did not weigh the same on all second-generation immigrants, and their participatory responses varied. Accordingly, some *Beurs* organized to fight the racism that defined them as a special, especially vulnerable group. Electrified by the 1983 march, the *Beurs* began to struggle for the right to participate in the management of housing, job training, and social services (Zehraoui 1985; Jazouli 1986, pp. 113–148). In addition, the *"Beur* label" quickly became a trendy fashion statement, and *Beur* entertainers, models, and sports heroes enjoyed great popularity. As French teenagers copied the distinctive dress and mannerisms of the second-generation North Africans, Paris experienced a *Beur* cultural flowering that reminded many social commentators of New York's Harlem in the 1920s. Even *Marie-Claire,* the magazine of popular fashion, published a four-page spread on the *"Beur* look" in April 1984. Its conclusion: *"Beur* is beautiful!"[35]

In 1984 several *Beur* activists devised a powerful, symbolic action designed to reflect a more broadly multiethnic perspective: "Convergence." "France is like a motorscooter," they argued; "to move ahead it needs a mixture [of gasoline and oil]." Five squadrons of motorscooters, each representing one of the major ethnic components of France—North Africans and Turks, Iberians, Asians, sub-Saharan Africans, and the French—left from one of five French cities. They converged in Paris for a multicultural celebration. Although young Italians had no organizational representation in Convergence '84, many participated on an individual basis (Cordeiro 1985a, p. 41; Rodrigues 1985).

Buoyed by positive reaction to the 1983 march, the Socialist government had originally announced its support of the action. It withdrew the imprimatur when Convergence '84 leaders started to criticize the government for its failure to take on the National Front and racism more forcefully. The organizers had not spared their criticisms of the French Communists or the trade unions either. Along with the far left, those organizations supported the event anyway. By this time the Communists had broken with the Socialist government and took particular pleasure in associating themselves with an action that antagonized it (Rodrigues 1985, pp. 21, 43–45, 94).

Convergence was to be the harbinger of a new cultural identity, anchored both in the immigrants' respective ethnic backgrounds and in the contemporary French society of which they were the product. Yet despite its motto, "Living together with our differences," Convergence ran aground on internal divisions. A faction emerged from within its ranks to call for a broader, class-based, multiethnic movement uniting all the politically disfranchised. Such an initiative would shift the focus away from racism and "immigrant" issues to what was deemed the more fundamental problem of inequality in France.[36] The second-generation social movement, in sum, was dividing in ways that reflected the institutional forces acting on it: class-, ethnic-, and generationally based organizing all received an impetus in the French context.

With the second-generation leadership in disarray, the Socialists moved to harness the antiracist organizational potential. A handful of veterans of the 1983 march, close to the French Socialists and militant Jewish student groups, founded SOS-Racisme in 1984. Its charismatic leader, Harlem Désir, was the son of a politically active father from Martinique and a mother from Alsace. He insisted that SOS-Racisme not be considered a working-class, immigrant, or exclusively French organization: rather, it was a multiethnic movement of the "buddy" *(pote)* generation, the French and immigrant youths of the suburban housing projects.[37]

From the start, SOS-Racisme benefited from the logistical, financial, and moral support of the government, the PS, and the left-leaning press. The movement exhibited an impressive mastery of public relations techniques (Battegay 1985). Soon appearing on lapels of students, politicians, intellectuals, and movie stars alike was its main organizing tool, a plastic pin shaped like an open palm and inscribed with a pacifist message: "Hands off my buddy" ("Touche pas à mon pote"). Thousands of immigrants and French citizens joined local branches across the country. Through cultural events, vocal defense of young people's (immigrants' and nonimmigrants') rights, and media campaigns, SOS-Racisme advanced its eclectic, vaguely defined agenda. Désir, a card-carrying PS member, conferred on several occasions with President Mitterrand at the Elysée Palace (Fiévet 1984; Malik 1984).

Critics reproached SOS-Racisme for "going Hollywood" and for allowing itself to be "co-opted" by the PS. The harshest attacks came from the National Front and the Communists, the latter angry at the movement's refusal to identify with the struggles of the working class. Désir condemned the discriminatory policies of some local PCF governments, a move that further rankled the national party leadership.[38] Allied with the PCF and the trade unions, the multiethnic CAIF also fumed against the "vexing *potes.*"[39]

More than a few second-generation immigrants, too, resented what they perceived as an effort by the PS to use them to its own political ends. Some immigrant-origin youths agreed with SOS-Racisme's basic message, if not with its tactics, and took part in its demonstrations and other activities for lack of a truly viable alternative.[40] One group of *Beurs*, however, resented SOS-Racisme for ignoring North Africans' particular plight and marched in 1985 from the Barbès neighborhood in Paris to Bordeaux.

Still other second-generation immigrants opted for an expressly political effort to affirm a collective second-generation identity. In 1985 a new group, France-Plus, and a spate of local Collectives for Civil Rights organized drives throughout the country to register eligible second-generation immigrants to vote and to encourage those eligible to run for office. They criticized SOS-Racisme for "ghettoizing" young immigrants through its campaign for the "right to be different" (*Le Monde*, June 6, 1985). A March for Civil Rights in November 1985 kicked off the nationwide campaign, which transformed a seemingly individual act such as voter registration into an affirmation of a new collective identity in France.

France-Plus concentrated on the *Beurs*, but many local groups targeted second-generation Europeans and sub-Saharan Africans as well. Researchers estimated the potential electorate of North African origin (including the children of the *harkis*) alone at over one million in the mid-1980s. In the cantonal elections of 1984 more than thirty *Beur* candidates—as well as several of Southern European origin—had run for office. During this period a number of second-generation immigrants won seats on municipal councils or were appointed to municipal commissions (Khammar 1985; Wihtol de Wenden and Marie 1989).

The second generation's political awakening energized previously somnolent groups, provoking a "re-ethnicization" of earlier immigrants who "had been in the process of assimilation (such as Armenians and Jews)" (Safran 1985, pp. 61–62). Likewise, phenomena such as the 1983 march, Convergence '84, SOS-Racisme, France-Plus, and the Collectives for Civil Rights gave the activists new confidence in the validity of their claims on the French political system. Each action and movement operated on a different premise, but all started from the basis of the newly achieved rights to form associations and to receive government subsidies.[41] Furthermore, French citizenship laws and naturalization policies were such that second-generation immigrants were already or potentially full-fledged members of the national political community. The result was a multifaceted second-generation social movement fighting against socioeconomic marginalization and racism.

THE DIFFICULT COHABITATION, 1986–1988

Through struggles that were qualitatively different from those of its foreign-worker parents, with whom relations were increasingly tense in many respects, the second generation built on the gains of the first. Both generations' entry into French politics was the logical consequence of a long process of settlement in French society and French officials' response to it. The left had facilitated that entry after 1981, yet it had also opened the door wider to the National Front. By the middle of the decade the Socialists were dealing with the new politics of hate and violence that they inherited and exacerbated.

The PS continued to back SOS-Racisme, but both the divisiveness of second-generation politics and the rise of Le Pen and his movement shook it. It dropped its call for the "right to difference" *(droit à la différence),* replacing it with a campaign of "living together" *(vivre ensemble)*—emphasizing common ground instead of cultural differences. But, suffering in the public opinion polls, it backed off from immigration issues. In fact by 1986 the positions of the mainstream political parties, left and right, were converging: all agreed on the need to bolster France's borders against new immigration, tighten policy toward illegal immigrants, integrate those foreigners wishing to remain in the country, and encourage voluntary returns to the homeland. This artificial, defensive political consensus, as well as the unrealistic policy debate that resulted, made it possible for the far right to diffuse its simplistic message more widely (Hochet 1988).

The approach of legislative elections in 1986 threw fear into Socialist hearts. President Mitterrand, for ideological reasons and in hopes of dividing the right, had changed the electoral system to one of proportional representation. The strategy worked to a degree during the election, but in the process it let the *lepéniste* genie out of the bottle: the FN garnered 9.8 percent of the vote—38,000 more votes than the PCF—and elected thirty-five deputies, enough to constitute a parliamentary group. Jean-Marie Le Pen adapted his message to the changing times, linking the immigrant—specifically, the North African—presence not only with crime but even with the rising incidence of AIDS in the country. The FN was gaining working-class support and seemed to be replacing the PCF as the mouthpiece for the disaffected (Todd 1988). Certainly, it had become fully installed in French political life (P. Milza 1987, pp. 414–419; see also Jaffré 1986; and Schain 1988). Such developments overshadowed more positive ones for the immigrants as the list of municipal and departmental consultative bodies lengthened steadily.

The period of cohabitation that followed the mainstream right's narrow victory brought more-repressive immigration policies. For years, its top leaders had shamelessly bent to the political winds of the moment on these issues (see Wihtol de Wenden 1988, p. 206). The new prime minister, Jacques Chirac, made an explicit connection between delinquency, terrorism, and immigration. Identification checks and expulsions of illegal immigrants and refugees multiplied, with non-Europeans incurring much of the wrath of the new hard-line interior minister, Charles Pasqua. His policies, codified later that year, made it clear that the new government rejected the notion of a multicultural France (*Le Figaro,* June 4, 1985). The left remained silent, apparently terrified by the amount of public support for such measures (Rakotoson 1986).

The Le Pen juggernaut upset and frightened the immigrants. Yet it also had a galvanizing effect on many activists. Just as important in shaping a social movement as its network of allies is its "conflict system, consisting of representatives and supporters of the challenged political system, including counter-movement organizations" (Klandermans

1990, p. 123). Small bands of leftists, the churches, and humanitarian groups spoke out strongly. They stood with immigrants of various ethnic backgrounds and of both generations who mounted demonstrations against the government, the National Front, and the mainstream left's reluctance to attack either of them.

A turning point was reached with the student demonstrations in late 1986 and early 1987, which forced the government to withdraw planned educational reforms (the Devaquet Plan). Many in the movement of high school and college students had cut their activist teeth in the marches and rallies of SOS-Racisme. Their reluctance to forge an alliance with striking railroad workers bespoke the absence of working-class consciousness that typified much of the second generation.[42] The death of an innocent *Beur* bystander, Malik Oussekine, at the hands of the security forces underscored the stake that young people of foreign extraction had in the social struggles of their generation in contemporary France (Body-Gendrot 1989, p. 11; *Le Monde*, Jan. 13, 1987).

A few months later the government proposed a reform of the Nationality Code (the Chalandon Reform). Many leaders and intellectuals of the French right had decided that Islam, seen as blending the private and public spheres of authority irretrievably, made the assimilation of Muslims into secular, republican France far more unlikely than that of the earlier Catholic and Jewish immigrants (see Schlegel 1985a). The commission that Chirac appointed to devise a plan proposed eliminating the automatic nature of second-generation immigrants' accession to French citizenship, in order to stem the "mass" naturalization of second-generation immigrants and to revalorize the acquisition of French citizenship. The list of offenses that precluded it was to grow significantly longer. The government eventually backed off on requiring evidence of assimilation and an oath of allegiance. Yet a conscious, expressed desire to be French would become the *sine qua non* of citizenship acquisition (*Le Monde*, Nov. 5, 1986).

The government found itself confronted not only with "symbolically resonant opposition" based on defense of France's tradition of inclusiveness and equality (Brubaker 1992, p. 155) but also, quite simply, with a muscular, proven political threat. The immigrant-origin communities made it apparent that they did not want to assimilate. The same student groups that had doomed the proposed Devaquet reform began to take to the streets again, and Prime Minister Chirac quickly put the reform on ice. Jean-Marie Le Pen taunted the government for "demeaning the Republic by capitulating before the ukases of Harlem Désir and SOS-Racisme" (quoted in Birenbaum 1987, pp. 13–14).

An emotional, fragile movement, organized antiracism fluctuated and evolved, partially in response to events created by its adversaries and allies. SOS-Racisme had appointed itself the mouthpiece of the antiracist youth movement. Increasingly, however, its momentum was flagging: the Palestinian issue divided its Jewish and Muslim members, and its cozy relationship with the Socialists limited its reach and effectiveness. France-Plus, on the other hand, persisted in its voter registration and education efforts. New groups such as the Arab Youth of Lyons and Its Suburbs (Jeunes Arabes de Lyon et Sa Banlieue) and several other *Beur* groups sprang up in opposition to both the "feel-good" antiracism of Harlem Désir and the Chirac/Pasqua regime (*Libération*, Nov. 30, 1985; Kepel 1987, pp. 347–348).

The multiethnic CAIF, too, struggled from its Parisian headquarters to widen its reach in the immigrant communities. In late 1987 the CAIF leadership persuaded some twenty youth, women's, and first-generation immigrant associations in France to form Mémoire Fertile (Fertile Memory). This short-lived effort advanced a "unitary approach" that involved both the first and second generation of immigrants and stressed the importance of common action between immigrant and minority communities and the French working class (Perotti 1988).

THE RETURN OF THE SOCIALISTS

With the right stumbling, the left gradually rediscovered solidarity with the foreign-origin population. Painfully, the Communists were realizing just how deeply the restructuring of industry and urban areas had affected the French working class: changes in its position in society, composition, and aspirations had transformed its relationship with the PCF and CGT (Boumaza 1988).

With the upcoming presidential campaign in his sights, moreover, François Mitterrand retook the high ground in the immigration debate in 1987 and 1988. Once again he spoke of granting municipal voting rights to noncitizens, rejected any tightening of naturalization laws, and vowed to overturn the draconian Pasqua Law if the left regained its governing majority in parliament. Political strategy played a role here: thanks in part to efforts by France-Plus, second-generation immigrants accounted for 3 percent of the electorate nationwide and more in some localities (*Libération,* April 22, 1988).

Arezki Dahmani, president of France-Plus, warned that "there are racists on the left as well as on the right" (quoted in *Libération,* Feb. 25–26, 1989). Even so, most of the new voters leaned toward the Socialists. In first-round balloting in the 1988 election, Mitterrand won the backing of nearly half of second-generation North Africans. Railing against the "arrogant *Beurs*" (*Le Monde,* April 4, 1987), Le Pen had again mounted an effective campaign. Stunned by his 14.5 percent showing nationally—which translated into 4.5 million votes—between 80 and 84 percent of the *Beurs* chose Mitterrand over Chirac in the second round (*Libération,* May 18 and 28–29, 1988). The president's reelection brought thousands of relieved immigrants into the streets of many French cities and towns.

Soon the Socialist mayors of large cities like Bordeaux, Toulouse, Lille, and Grenoble began opening their ranks and their candidate lists to *Beurs,* Portuguese, and Asians. In the 1986 legislative contests, *Beur* slates had appeared in the Hauts-de-Seine, the Bouches-du-Rhône, and other immigration "hot spots." By 1988 more than 600 *Beurs* and young people of *harki* stock figured on the slates of the PS, the PCF, Chirac's RPR, the Christian Democratic Party, and the Republican Party (*Libération,* April 11, 1989).

The minority Socialist government that emerged from the legislative elections that June kept most of its campaign promises. A few months after his victory, President Mitterrand reportedly offered a state secretariat to Harlem Désir. (Désir loyalist Deputy Julien Dray filled the post.) The Socialists again judged local suffrage too inflammatory an issue but agreed to study the matter further. Jean-Marie Le Pen fumed; but under the reinstituted two-round, majority electoral system, his party had captured only a single seat in the Assembly. The mainstream political parties, especially the PS, breathed a sigh of relief (C. de Rudder 1989).

ISLAM AND THE SUBURBAN CRISIS

The Socialists' complacency proved premature. Le Pen had shifted political discourse about immigration in France decisively toward an insular, right-wing populism. At the same time, after Mitterrand's reelection the immigration challenge merged inexorably with much broader urban and social crises that defied simplistic answers.

The result proved to be political dynamite. And although the explosive potential had been building long before the left came to power, its policy responses to immigration since 1981 had helped light the fuse.

Of course, 1981 had not been 1936. The left had also increased the foreign-origin communities' ability to protect themselves and integrate into French society. They had been undergoing a centralizing, moderating process that a number of observers started to take as a sign of true political integration (Wihtol de Wenden 1990). In 1991 immigrant associations celebrated the tenth anniversary of their new legal status. As the foreign-worker generation neared retirement age, with some retreating into folkloric activities, a new, French-born associational leadership was emerging. It pushed the culturally geared ethnic associations to see themselves as part of a complex process of integration implicating more than just a single national group. A further strengthening of immigrant associational networks, localized around new businesses and entrepreneurial efforts, was evident in several regions (Toulat 1992). Private radio stations continued to serve an important role in unifying and coordinating communities—not only the *Beurs* but others as well, including blacks (Radio Nova), Italians (Radio Vesuvio), and Portuguese and Spaniards (Perotti 1991, p. 51).

Homeland governments struggled to find an accommodation with the ethnic-based associations, now firmly rooted in the French institutional context. Several governments beefed up their consultative networks and cultural activities and launched new initiatives to retain influence over what were in actuality no longer entirely "their" communities.[43] In fact, forms of reverse participation were emerging: several Portuguese, Polish, and North and sub-Saharan African associations "adopted" villages in their homelands. They soon began to serve as a liaison between the homeland and the French voluntary sector interested in Third World development (Toulat 1992).

Immigrant workers, in the meantime, moved more securely into the institutions that French workers were abandoning. A new wave of strikes hit France in the fall of 1989, most notably at the Peugeot plants in Sochaux and Mulhouse. Like the 1982 strikes of the immigrant *ouvriers spécialisés*, these involved a reaction to the redefinition of factory work and the future of unskilled labor in the face of technological change. Immigrant workers—North Africans, Turks, and Portuguese were most numerous—participated in the protests as workers like any others, even as they invested strike activity with their own specific demands. The lessons of the long process of restructuring French industry had changed the indigenous labor movement's attitudes toward the immigrants definitively, and strikers repelled employers' attempts to divide them along the lines of ethnicity or professional category (*L'Europe multicommunautaire* 1989–90, pp. 115–119).

The second generation still largely ignored the class struggle, directing its energies into electoral efforts instead. By 1988 more than 600 young people of North African, Southern European, and other foreign origins figured on the candidate slates of all the mainstream parties. The next year two *Beurs*—one a Green and the other a Socialist SOS-Racisme activist—won election to the European Parliament. In the municipal elections later in 1989, more than 300 second-generation immigrants won local-level office. In addition to the candidates put forward by French parties, grass-roots, "independent" lists appeared on the municipal ballot in Lille, Saint-Étienne, and Bron—where they obtained from 1 to 3 percent of the first-round vote (Bouamama 1989; *New Statesman*, Oct. 19, 1990).

Second-generation associations flourished. More and more youth of other ethnic backgrounds followed the *Beurs'* lead, in particular sub-Saharan Africans and Portuguese intent on breaking out of the "communal trap" represented by the first generation's ethnic-based associations. French society's apparent indifference toward second-generation Europeans' limited socioeconomic mobility thus encouraged even them to organize collectively (see Cunha 1988).

The second immigrant generation has not, generally speaking, rejected the French political system or republican values. The vast majority of these young people have either remained apolitical or chosen legal and institutional means of participating in that system: they have not contested France's democratic, lay values or its defense of individual liberty.

Second-generation non-Europeans have nevertheless deeply shaken French society. Islam, yet again, has been the major reason. Many first-generation immigrants have been active in Islamic associations and mosques with ties to the homelands, although much of this involvement has represented a purely religious interest and a virtual withdrawal from French political life. And the main mosque in Paris, once such a source of conflict in the North African Muslim community, has benefited from more cordial relations among Algeria, Tunisia, and Morocco (Reverier 1989).[44] But regardless of some social commentators' fears, Muslim fundamentalism has never won many converts in France, least of all among the younger generation of North and sub-Saharan Africans and Turks. Moreover, second-generation Muslims have shown very little nostalgia for the "homeland," as disappointed official homeland associations and governments have discovered when attempting to win them over (Malaurie 1990).

As their economic and social integration in France has stalled, however, many of these youngsters have mythologized the Arab world. "Globally accepting [French] society's values," they nonetheless hope "to maintain a group identity." Islam has become for them both a mouthpiece and a negotiating tool in a painful process of integration—just as the Communist Party was for French and immigrant workers from the 1920s to the late 1960s (Leveau 1989, p. 23).

This transformation, as well as its wrenching effect on the French polity, was apparent during the "scarf affair" in the autumn of 1989. Citing a 1937 decree-law against promoting religion in public schools, officials at a *collège* in Creil refused admission to three Muslim girls who insisted on wearing the *hijab*—the traditional scarf covering the hair, ears, and neck—to class. What should have been merely a minor local news story set off a fierce two-month furor that opened divisions within French political families and the antiracism movement. As Muslim women marched in Paris for the right to wear the *hijab*, members of the government opposed each other publicly. Trade union officials and many intellectuals insisted that religious symbols be banned in public schools. France-Plus agreed, but SOS-Racisme demanded that the minister of education readmit the three students, for "under no circumstances should a punishment be levied on students on account of their faith" (*Le Figaro*, Oct. 6, 1989).

The controversy forced the nation to debate the role of the immigrants and Islam in France's secular society.[45] Opinion polls indicated growing intolerance toward Muslims and, subsequently, Jews. Mosques and synagogues were desecrated and destroyed, and physical assaults on non-European immigrants were increasing. Provisions of a new immigration law in August 1989 (the "Loi Joxe") and a Communist-sponsored antiracism law that passed in July 1990 strengthened France's legal weapons against racism (*New York Times*, Dec. 7, 1989; Costa-Lascoux 1990).

The absence of an effective spokesperson for France's Muslims had long frustrated French officials and contributed to Islam's image as a threatening, inscrutable force. Concern over the spread of both anti-Muslim sentiment and Islamic fundamentalism spurred Interior Minister Pierre Joxe to double his efforts to encourage the selection of moderate imams and the development of a national "consistory"—such as already existed for France's Jews and Protestants—to provide structure to France's Muslims and a reliable interlocutor to the French government. Joxe appointed ten respected members of the Muslim establishment to the new Council for Reflection on Islam in France (*L'Express,* March 16, 1990, p. 12). But these attempts to develop a "Gallic Islam" met with limited success. Instead they often heightened tensions within the far-from-monolithic Muslim population (Lochon 1990).

In response to the mounting violence, the government of Prime Minister Michel Rocard tightened controls against illegal immigration and unveiled an expensive program to speed up resident immigrants' integration. Unfortunately, his policies, implemented by means of some 400 individual contracts between the state and local officials, largely repeated measures in effect since the mid-1970s: teaching secular values in schools, sprucing up the HLM, and developing neighborhood parks and youth centers. Left to fester were the deeper problems of the suburbs, where chronic unemployment, drugs, crime, and despair were rampant (*Le Monde,* Sept. 21, Oct. 11 and 16, 1990).

The inadequacy of the governmental response became apparent in the fall of 1990. Almost a decade after the "hot summer" of 1981, riots once again spread across France from the tinderbox of Lyons's suburbs. They started in Vaulx-en-Velin, a suburb of Lyons that national and local officials had celebrated as a showpiece of suburban renewal. Soon, in dozens of cities, poor youth of immigrant and native French stock were looting stores and setting fires in commercial districts. The disturbances often began with a clash between young people and the French police, whom many residents accused of racism and heavy-handedness.

In the early 1980s the French government had answered the angry protests of the second generation first with police repression and then with the institution of locally based structures and subsidies that facilitated its cultural and political expression. These measures created points of contact and discussion between French officials and society and the young people. This reactive institutional tinkering largely explains why the French suburbs faced only petty delinquency and cultural militance instead of the full-scale riots that occurred in Britain during the same period (Jazouli 1986; see also Maffesoli 1978; Freeman 1979).

The French political system had thereby integrated the second-generation leadership, who became the organizers of the antiracism movement. Examples of successful integration through traditional professional and individual channels multiplied among second-generation immigrants, and not just among those of European origin. What Wihtol de Wenden has termed a *"beurgeoisie"* emerged: *Beur* activists running the local associations in the housing projects, young suburban professionals forming self-help groups, and entrepreneurs entering into multiethnic business ventures such as the "California Burger" fast-food stand in Nanterre. These new elites, many of them women, acted as brokers between their generation and French society (Wihtol de Wenden 1990).

But socioprofessional mobility has remained beyond the reach of most, the *Beurs* in particular. The industries that needed foreign workers after World War II have undergone a drawn-out, painful period of restructuring and today provide fewer and worse jobs for their children. In France widespread unemployment has largely precluded even a reasonable possibility of individual socioeconomic advance, which, as we will see, has kept many of Switzerland's second-generation immigrants from opting for collective "voice" over individual economic "exit."

Those who took part in France's *"intifada* of the suburbs" in 1990 were the youngest and most marginalized immigrant-origin and French youths. They had no connection to or memory of earlier struggles. With few opportunities for professional mobility, disaffected suburban youth have developed "parallel survival networks": a shadowy, underground economy of petty delinquency and drugs organized around loose youth bands, some multiethnic and others reinforcing ethnic and social differences. They have had frequent run-ins with local police officials, who have dubbed them the *zoulous* (Jazouli 1991).

Their alienation was manifest yet again in the "suburban fever" of autumn 1991, as angry incidents between groups of youngsters and the police and commercial security forces escalated into riots. The epicenter of this wave of violence was Mantes-la-Jolie, outside Paris (Yvelines). In the city's Val-Fourré housing project (50 percent immigrants), some 150 youths of primarily North African origin looted businesses, burned cars, and attacked firemen. The troubles soon spread, mushrooming into a national obsession.[46]

These acts, like the *rodéos* of the early 1980s, were illegal and violent, to be sure. But all other means available to these youths of making their demands known to local politicians and law enforcement officials had proved sorely inadequate. Since collective violence had earlier provoked policy responses from French officials, some young people reasoned that the time had come to give the government a "booster shot" (Commission Nationale Consultative des Droits de l'Homme 1992, pp. 211–218). Illegitimate in itself, collective violence thereby came to be seen as the sole effective means of obtaining legitimate goals.

Ease of access to citizenship was a critical factor. It accounted in large measure for the near stabilization in the total number of foreigners registered in the 1990 census (Lebon 1991). It gave the second generation a claim on French society that was far clearer and less open to challenge than their parents'. But it did not guarantee sociopolitical integration. Non-Europeans represented almost two-thirds of the foreign population residing in France in 1990, up from 57 percent in 1982. The racist reaction to their presence metastasized. Second-generation immigrants with French citizenship and darker pigmentation thus found themselves treated as unwelcome foreigners. Marginalization affected Antilleans and Guyanans (from France's overseas *départements*) as well as noncitizens.

And the *harkis*, finally, discovered that French citizenship did not automatically bring many benefits in terms of living conditions and employment opportunities. In June 1991 second-generation *harkis* occupied public buildings and clashed with French police across the south of France. Unlike their parents, who had cried "We are French!" these protesters stressed their collective identity as children of the *harkis*. Just as with the *Beurs*, this change of "label" reflected a widening generation gap. The young *harkis* have undergone an evolution similar in several respects to that affecting second-generation immigrants, even though their sociopolitical demands have often diverged (*Le Monde,* June 25 and June 30–July 1, 1991; Roux 1992).

By the early 1990s it had become difficult for any government in France to undertake large-scale projects in favor of immigrants, especially "Arabs." The political climate in the suburbs continued to deteriorate, with extremists of all ilks profiting from the social unrest. As it merged with the deep-rooted social problems in which it had in fact always been embedded, the immigration issue was proving too divisive and explosive for bipartisanship and incremental legal changes. Thus trapped, the government again tried to depoliticize the issue.

In March 1990 Michel Rocard had instituted the High Council for Integration of Immigrants (Haut Conseil à l'Intégration—HCI), comprised of nine members from the major French political families, to develop politically balanced and palatable solutions. While the HCI was deliberating, the government had centered its attention on the rehabilitation of France's 400 "most disadvantaged" neighborhoods and suburbs. At SOS-Racisme's behest, in the wake of the 1990 riots President Mitterrand had convened representatives from a cross-section of France's hardest-hit areas at the First Estates-General of the Neighborhoods. That December, he had presented a five-year plan for the suburbs, speaking of the need to beef up police patrols, reduce financial disparities between rich and poor cities, and end residential segregation (*Libération*, Dec. 4, 1990). Later that winter, during the Persian Gulf War, which had seriously divided the immigrants and their organizations, France's already shaken immigrant neighborhoods had faced an upsurge in police harassment and racist incidents (see *New York Times*, Feb. 8, 1991; *Le Monde*, March 14, 1991).

French authorities responded by clinging even more desperately to the inadequate policies of the past. The HCI presented its first report to the government in February 1991. It underscored the need for greater administrative coherence and "patient, vigorous, and inventive" measures to integrate non-Europeans. The report made clear that all immigrants "should 'accept the rules' of French society and adhere to a 'minimum of common values' so that their 'fusion with the national collectivity' continues to enrich it and to contribute to its development.''[47] The Council, in effect, reaffirmed the traditional model of individual integration, that is, assimilation. As if to drive home the point, the new government under Edith Cresson in May 1991 included a secretary of state for integration (*sécrétaire d'état à l'intégration*), Kofi Yamgnane, a man of Togolese origin who is the perfect embodiment of this Jacobin tradition (*Le Monde*, April 30 and May 19–20, 1991; *Libération*, May 25–26, 1991).

The months that followed saw not only renewed suburban rioting in Mantes and elsewhere but also a noticeably harsher discourse on immigration. Dedication to the hard work of tackling the suburban crisis had given way only to crass political posturing (see, for example, *La Croix* and *Le Figaro*, June 21, 1991). Even mainstream politicians unabashedly espoused Le Pen–esque "populism." The new harshness put the government on the defensive. Prime Minister Cresson announced that France would not tolerate illegal immigrants and talked about sending them back in chartered planes (*Le Figaro*, June 21, 1991; *Le Monde*, July 11 and 16, 1991). Writing in *Le Monde* (July 13, 1991), Robert Solé captured well the discomfiture of the French political class: "An electoral issue par excellence, immigration/integration risks losing its seasonal character, becoming the object of a permanent debate played out in incidents in the suburbs and in more or less controlled rhetorical outbursts. It is only wishful thinking to try to depoliticize it and keep it out of fights between parties."

The riots that fall would prove him right, as would the continuing shameless exploitation of the immigration issue for political purposes. In an interview with *Figaro Magazine* (Sept. 21, 1991) former president Valéry Giscard d'Estaing referred to immigration as an "invasion" and called for naturalization based on blood ties to prevent the "abuse" of French citizenship laws. Jacques Chirac, who only a few months before had expressed sympathy with French workers reacting against the "noise" and "smell" of foreigners (*Le Figaro*, June 21, 1991), applauded Giscard's position. Prime Minister Cresson condemned him in abusive terms.[48]

What French officialdom was failing to provide, meanwhile, was a positive, innovative response to the country's very serious social problems. Just after the 1991 riots the National Assembly took up "anti-ghetto" legislation proposed by Michel Delebarre, minister of cities and land management. Parliamentary debate was animated primarily by fear that the suburban housing projects were degenerating into full-blown, "American-style" ghettos (*Libération*, May 28, 1991).

Similar concerns obsessed the High Council for Immigration. Its third report, presented to Prime Minister Pierre Bérégovoy in February 1992, further developed a model of integration firmly in the Jacobin tradition: equal rights and obligations for all were to generate solidarity between the different ethnic and cultural components of French society. Appearing in the highly charged period following the electoral success of the fundamentalist Islamic Salvation Front in Algeria, the report defined and defended "French values." It strove to remove weapons from the National Front's anti-immigrant arsenal by sharply rejecting

"Anglo-Saxon ethnic pluralism" (*La Croix,* Feb. 7, 1992; *Journal du dimanche,* Jan. 5, 1992). As Pierre-Yves Le Priol remarked in *La Croix* (Feb. 7, 1992), "It is perhaps twenty years' promotion of the *droit à la différence* that has given up the ghost with the new report of the Nine Wise Men and Women of the High Council for Integration."

Thus the official response to Le Pen and the immigration challenge remained limited to harping on the simplistic opposition between the "good" French model of individual assimilation and the "bad," "tribal" American and British "communitarian" model—wherein group-based organizations mediate the process and allegedly lead to the formation of ghettos (see Weil 1991a). Such reasoning led Jérôme Dumoulin to argue in *L'Express* (Feb. 13, 1992) that "France is the best-armed country in Europe, intellectually and historically, to control immigration."

But the HCI added a new twist to integration *à la française:* it expressed regret at the absence of representative interlocutors for Muslims at the national and local levels. Contrary to traditional Jacobin ideals, in fact, the Council celebrated voluntary associational life, especially at the local level, as the ideal means for expressing cultural and ethnic diversity, dealing with the problems of daily life, and stitching together the "social fabric" (P. Farine 1991; *La Croix,* Feb. 7, 1992).

What that argument ignores is the very real selections that French authorities have always made on the basis of ethnicity and nationality. It was contradictory for the HCI to deplore the absence of a structured associational movement and of reliable Muslim interlocutors on the one hand and to condemn the "communitarian drift" *(dérive)* on the other (see *Migrations-société* 4, March–April 1992, pp. 54–68). One can argue that Islam offers a dangerous channel by which outside money and influence may flow into France and that it was a mistake to allow the introduction of mosques in the workplace and native-language instruction by foreign teachers paid by homeland governments (see Griotteray 1984, pp. 114–115; Weil 1991a, p. 246). These supposedly wrongheaded moves, however, have resulted more from decisions by French authorities than anything else. Although certain republican values emphasizing equal treatment and inclusion may indeed have survived in France (see Weil 1991a; Brubaker 1992), officials have not always respected the letter or the spirit of the law.[49]

It is also unwise to ignore the institutional forces that have fed second-generation immigrants' collective identity and have in some cases driven a wedge both between the immigrant generations and between the *Beurs* and other European and non-European immigrant-origin communities. The government's tactics have alienated second-generation movements. Even the privileged SOS-Racisme has found itself dealing with a political system that on the one hand tries to co-opt it, and on the other offers it a certain degree of access to political and public life. SOS-Racisme had squabbled with the government during the "scarf affair," later initiating talks with the Greens. Harlem Désir had embarrassed the Rocard government early in 1991 by helping organize a demonstration against the Persian Gulf War. And virtually all the antiracist and immigrant groups denounced President Mitterrand's defense of the concept of a "European citizenship" in the Maastricht Treaty, to which the heads of European Community member states agreed in December 1991.[50]

Angered at the Socialists, Harlem Désir resigned as head of SOS-Racisme in September 1992. He quickly formed a political party, "The Movement"—something of a French "rainbow coalition." Left-wing Socialists, Communists, and ecologists joined it in calling for a popular force for "a France and a Europe" that would be "more social, more ecological, closer to the people, and more open to the world" (*Die Tageszeitung/Bremer Ausgabe*, Oct. 5, 1992; see also *Frankfurter Allgemeine Zeitung*, May 2, 1990; and *Le Monde*, March 14, Dec. 12 and 17, 1991).[51] Meanwhile, SOS-Racisme (under new leadership), France-Plus, and the other second-generation organizations struggled to regain their momentum as fear of a wave of Islamic fundamentalism spread throughout the French political establishment (*Libération*, Sept. 7, 1992).

The second-generation movement thus bore witness as before to the complex, often contradictory institutional context within which it evolved. What Rémy Leveau has written of the *Beurs* could be applied to the entire second generation: "They are not immigrants, not quite citizens, but the members of a minority community that aspires to a common collective existence and looks to preserve their collective identity in order to integrate better" (quoted in Wihtol de Wenden 1988, p. 370). They show no signs of accepting assimilation. In their desire to participate as collective actors—as (multi)ethnic or genera-tional communities—they continue to be a new and disruptive force in French social and political life.

A Policy Impasse?

The immigration challenge of the 1990s hardly resembles that of two decades ago. Through their struggles, earlier foreign workers—the first immigrant generation—contributed to the progress of social democracy in France; their children have contributed to the extension and enrichment of political democracy. Once the most marginal and least autonomous of social actors, immigrants of both generations have become bona fide political actors. They have introduced novel, effective forms of political participation to French politics.

Institutional factors, not the immigrants' ethnic background or their working-class status, have produced their distinctive, evolving participatory pattern. After their initially confrontational tactics produced an institutional response, first-generation immigrants of all nationalities and national origins settled into "in-channel" modes of ethnic associational and labor activity. Their children mobilized in the name of a different, shared institutional experience and devised their own array of strategies to express themselves. Supporting a vibrant political life and sometimes affirming new collective identities, they and their parents have influenced French politics, policies, political discourse, and culture (see Wihtol de Wenden and Marie 1989).

Of course, as Gary P. Freeman has argued, "Either the development of a political consciousness among migrants or their integration into national working-class organizations spells the end of many of the benefits of alien labor" (1979, p. 5). French officialdom confronts a serious dilemma. On one side the presence and political participation of the immigrants have fed a potent racist reaction. Jean-Marie Le Pen and mainstream politicians on the right have exploited the public uproar over riots and immigration in general for political advantage. Growing numbers of illegal immigrants and refugees have provided additional points of confrontation and more grist for the National Front's mill (*Le Figaro*, May 14 and 15, 1991; *La Croix*, May 28, 1991).

On the other side there is the politically active and substantial immigrant population. Its social and political integration has clearly become one of the most urgent and formidable tasks facing France. Fueled by unemployment and racism, new outbursts of rioting continue to break out in French cities. As Michel Noir, the centrist mayor of Lyons, has observed, "Slowly but ineluctably, the malfunctionings of our society are felt in our cities, which are the dumping place for our increasingly two-speed society" (*New York Times,* June 15, 1991).

Hobbled by the intense anti-immigrant feeling in France national authorities have had precious little room in which to maneuver. They have been unable or unwilling to make the institutional innovations needed to defuse the political crisis of social control in the suburbs and decaying inner cities. The relatively high rate of civic incorporation of immigrants there—compared with nations like Switzerland and Germany (Brubaker 1992, chap. 4)—has made a continuing dialectic unavoidable. But does the policy impasse of the early 1990s signal a definitive, dismaying dénouement of the complex interplay between French institutions and the immigrants? Does such institutional blockage and buildup of social tensions develop also at the local level, where the problems associated with the immigrants have accumulated? To make that determination, we must turn to the country's troubled urban areas.

3

The Local French Cases: La Courneuve and Roubaix

In the preceding chapter I have argued that at the national level in France institutional factors have overwhelmed ethnic and class factors in determining the evolution of immigrant political activity—that is, institutional channeling has determined whether class or ethnicity or a mix of each has served as the basis for such mobilization. The nature of institutional opportunities, constraints, and support vis-à-vis immigrants has accounted for their adopting homeland-oriented, confrontational, or assimilative political tactics. According to this interpretation, the positions of host-society institutions, in return, have developed along and in interaction with immigrants' participation.

For this analysis to be anything more than suggestive, however, I must move beyond description and try to isolate and assess causal variables across cases. Each successive layer of case-study evidence—first from the national and local levels in France, then from the national and local levels in Switzerland—contributes a critical piece to my argument. Careful comparison will reveal that institutional factors have indeed played the determining role in producing the patterns of ethnic relations observed.

Here local-level comparison looms critical. Urban centers have absorbed most of the immigration wave in Western host societies. There the immigrants' "adaptation" problems have become linked with those associated with urban life and interethnic cohabitation (Simon 1992, p. 45). In France, as we have seen, the labor market and the government's immigration policies and nonpolicies pushed foreign workers and their families into the poorest neighborhoods and municipalities.

It was by containing immigration issues in the *communes* that French political elites managed to defuse racial and ethnic tensions up through the 1970s (Freeman 1979, p. 100).

France's centralized form of government has left local governments with little autonomy or power. They have been legally required to submit balanced budgets and to pay in full all incurred debts. Local authorities have had to operate in a blizzard of administrative decrees and circulars establishing national standards for a wide variety of services, procedures, and activities. Before 1981, furthermore, the prefects—as representatives of the national government—could annul most policies of any municipality (Schain 1985, p. 3).

Despite those legal limitations, however, French *communes* could exercise important discretionary powers. Local officials guarded the "public order" whose violation constituted grounds for the deportation of foreigners. In addition, local authorities enjoyed considerable control over the initiation and implementation of housing, educational, and cultural policies and thus played a significant role in the integration of immigrants (Freeman 1979, p. 97; compare Grémion 1976; and Tarrow 1977).

As a result, localities often developed highly divergent approaches to dealing with such issues. These had a clear impact on the nature of immigrant political mobilization. National-level institutional factors did retain their important channeling effect at the local level: residential segregation, the narrow opening to class-based immigrant participation, de facto discrimination on ethnic and religious lines, the laws governing associational and other political life, and the relative inclusiveness of French citizenship laws and naturalization policies. Yet the attitudes and policies of authorities and the responses of trade-union, political-party, and solidarity-group activists at the local level also structured the immigrants' participation in significant and often unexpected ways.

The pair of French *communes* examined here, La Courneuve and Roubaix, contain comparably large foreign populations of similar socioeconomic status, and they allow for the comparison of several communities of the same ethnic/national background. In each city officials and institutions linked immigrants to local politics in very different ways. The result was distinct participatory patterns that, while fitting into the general contours of the national-level pattern, revealed the powerful effects of local-level institutional structuring. Immigrants of the same ethnic and class background adopted noticeably different participatory forms in the two cities.

It is easier at the local than at the national level to isolate and assess the differing, interacting impact of class, ethnicity, and institutional channeling on immigrant political activity. It also becomes possible to determine how much freedom of maneuver municipal officials actually enjoy in centralized France and how much influence local marginalized groups can hope to exert. Given the centralization of French politics and the suspicion with which French governments have viewed associational participation, the wide gap between the political system and the immigrants encouraged them, when they found their individual mobility blocked, to resort to organized, confrontational tactics that proved quite effective in provoking a response from French institutions.

After their triumphs in 1981, the Socialists legitimized and subsidized the immigrants' associations and effected the political decentralization for which many in the PS had long called. In March 1982 the Mitterrand-Mauroy government abolished the central government's "tutelage" *(tutelle)* over local authorities, replaced the prefects with elected executives, and recognized the regions as bona fide local authorities. Paris offered financial assistance to municipalities *(contrats d'agglomération)* to encourage immigrants' integration into the neighborhoods (Moreau 1986; see Ginioux and Minces 1983, annexe 1).

But even as decentralization increased the immigrants' organizational opportunities and brought the political system closer to them, it gave free rein to local mechanisms of segregation, which maintained and strengthened the forces that led to their marginalization (Wihtol de Wenden 1986a). Their struggles multiplied with local politicians, who, intent on consolidating their bases of power, still prized electoral over associational participation. Highly touted programs failed to translate into discernible changes in many neighborhoods, since it was now easier for local political clientelism to gum up the best-intentioned national policies (see *Migrations-société* 12, Nov.–Dec. 1990, pp. 91–109).

Moreover, the new points of political access served as openings not only for immigrants but also for grass-roots racism and the National Front. In the early 1980s the FN did best in cities that, like La Courneuve and Roubaix, had a high proportion of immigrants ($r = +.50$

Pearson product correlation at the 99 percent level), especially North Africans ($r = +.50$ at the 99 percent level) (Schain 1987). The experiences of those two cities, in sum, can reveal much about the evolving relationship between immigrants and politics in France.

La Courneuve

The "typical" Parisian Red-Belt suburb—if ever there was such a thing—La Courneuve, a small city of 40,000 in the 1970s, lies in the department of Seine-Saint-Denis northeast of the capital. It affords an example of how strongly local Communist political domination was able to influence the immigrants' sociopolitical integration. The participatory pattern developed there diverged in several key respects from those found in other institutional contexts.

La Courneuve has been one of the most industrialized communities in one of France's most industrialized departments since the railroad line linking Paris with the manufacturing basin of the north passed through in the late nineteenth century. Some of France's and the world's major manufacturing concerns established factories in La Courneuve in ensuing years (Breton 1983, pp. 16–17). The labor movement accompanied the arrival of heavy industry, and the city had high rates of unionization. Not coincidentally, it became a Communist stronghold in the years just after World War II. Once the Communist Alphonse Rollin had won the mayor's office in 1953, support for the PCF in La Courneuve held fairly firm (see Table 12).[1]

Immigrants contributed heavily to the city's postwar economic development. Seine-Saint-Denis's industrial base, as well as the bedroom-community function that it played for Paris, made it a magnet for immigrant workers and their families up through the 1960s. That influx stabilized after 1968: La Courneuve's blue-collar employment base was precisely the type most affected by the deindustrialization process that began in France in the 1960s. As industry shifted outward to more distant suburbs or to the Third World, the working class fell from 55.8 percent of the city's employed population in 1954 to only 47 percent in 1975. At that time foreigners made up around one-fifth of the city's residents and an even greater share of its workers (Guillon, de Rudder-Paurd, and Simon 1977, pp. 3–19).

Table 12 Percentage of votes for the PCF in La Courneuve, 1947–1989

Year	Municipal elections	Legislative elections
1947	49.5	—
1953	46.1[a]	—
1958	—	43.4
1959	56.1	—
1962	—	59.2
1965	67.3	—
1967	—	52.2
1968	—	47.1
1971	70.2[b]	—
1973	—	47.3
1977	74.6	—
1978	—	48.9
1981	—	53.8
1983	68.6[b]	—
1988		
First round	—	38.3
Second round	—	52.5
1989	65.3[b]	—

Sources: Breton (1983), pp. 243–269; Election Commission, La Courneuve; and *Le Monde,* May 10 and June 13, 1988; March 14, 1989.

a. PCF + PSU.

b. PCF + PS.

The ethnic composition of La Courneuve's immigrant population resembled that of the Ile-de-France region. The Italians had been there from early in the century; most Spaniards arrived from 1956 through 1965. The wave of Portuguese immigration crested in the department in the years 1966–1970. In the period before the immigration stoppage of the mid-1970s, La Courneuve experienced a decline in the European-origin immigrant population and a pronounced increase in the North and sub-Saharan African and Turkish communities. All national groups registered fewer entries after 1975, but the share of women and families was growing (*BM*, May–June 1975).

A LOCAL MOBILIZATION SYSTEM

La Courneuve's Communist governments slavishly followed the policy shifts of the national PCF leadership with regard to immigration. More than any other factor, its edicts regulated the relationship between the immigrants and city officials in La Courneuve. They worked to mobilize and control the immigrants' political participation, forcing it into class-based and homeland-oriented forms that jibed with the Communist political program of the moment.

La Courneuve had gained national notoriety for its many immigrants, largely because of their living conditions. From the mid-1950s a horrible shantytown with no electricity or running water, "La Campa," had "housed" thousands of Spanish, then Portuguese and Algerian immigrant workers on the city's border with Aubervilliers. The squalor there was so shocking next to the prosperity of Paris that some tourist buses included it in their tours. To the Communist municipality, that "open wound" was a source of embarrassment, rage, and increased party membership—"La Campa" supported several PCF cells (Breton 1983, pp. 37–43, 53–56).

Media coverage, the pressures of rising land costs in the capital, and Communist complaints eventually compelled the national government and the city of Paris to replace the *bidonville* with a massive housing project in the mid-1960s. With the starkly unromantic, if apt, name of "The 4,000"—the number of apartment "cubes" it contained—the collection of concrete towers nearly doubled the previous population of the entire city, accounting for 43 percent of its residents and one-third of its housing stock. "The 4,000" became the place where city and national officials in Paris shunted immigrant workers, *harkis*, and migrants from the overseas departments and territories.

"The 4,000," outside the jurisdiction of La Courneuve's officials, deteriorated rapidly. The Paris Public Housing Office had provided for no schools, recreational, religious, financial, or health facilities in the "city within a city." With "The 4,000" reserved almost exclusively for families, single (male) immigrant workers lived in several employer-owned hostels in La Courneuve. La Courneuve's Public Housing Office, headed by the mayor, also built several hostels and low-income housing complexes (HLM) controlled entirely by the city. Determined to eradicate the final vestiges of the shantytown on the city's edge, the city council also permitted the quasi-public SONACOTRA to construct a hostel in La Courneuve in 1968.

This low-income housing came to define the city as a whole. The racist violence and the despair associated with the projects exercised a grim fascination on the French media. By the mid-1970s "La Courneuve" had become synonymous with "Harlem" or "the Bronx." City officials and residents resisted such negative categorizations, yet even Mayor Marson made only modest claims for La Courneuve: "It's not Paris, not even Saint-Denis or Montreuil . . . a city a little 'uncouth' but also endearing, full of human richness" (Breton 1983, pp. 9–11).

In typical Communist fashion, the city government worked to mine that richness electorally by providing key constituencies with a wide range of services. Municipal officials embarked on a massive program of renovation and construction designed to provide a viable downtown commercial district and new cultural and educational facilities. With names like the Youri Gagarine Children's Home (1970), the Salvador Allende Medical Center (1974), and the Julius and Ethel Rosenberg Nursery School (1976), there could be little doubt about the political complexion and priorities of the municipality (*BM*, Sept. 1978).

Communist officials strove to balance those local efforts with a reluctance to tax further their already "overburdened" populations. Municipal dependence on the state for loans and grants grew irresistibly. The local government often proceeded with projects before receiving authorization from Paris and sometimes even when it failed to win authorization. It would then move to mobilize the affected populations in La Courneuve and employ the ensuing hue and cry to pry concessions from the prefect and government ministries (Montaldo 1978, pp. 140–141).

Communist mayors, in fact, took pride in their ability to use popular mobilization as a means of confronting the state and gaining benefits they would not otherwise obtain. They worked to control all political activity in La Courneuve. The municipality endeavored to integrate local associations into policymaking, mobilizing every possible constituency, including immigrants. Officials rented automobiles and meeting places and sold office supplies to associations for token, heavily subsidized sums. They awarded grants and loans, favoring groups close to the PCF and political, social, and cultural events initiated by the municipality. Those "clearly identified with the political opposition" or advocating "objectives not compatible with important aspects of local policy" faced tremendous obstacles and were "isolated from the decision-making process" (Schain 1985, p. 130).

Immigrants received no special political treatment. Whether members of an association with municipal contacts or not, "any Courneuvians, regardless of their citizenship status or national origin, could deal directly with the city government."[2] Mayors did traditionally appoint a city councillor to be in charge of "immigrant worker affairs," just as such adjuncts existed for other pet constituencies (the handicapped, the elderly, young people, women). They amounted to mere go-betweens between those groups and city hall and local Communist Party headquarters.

The immigrants were expected to join the traditional organizations of the French working class. They were "visible victims of world capitalist exploitation." Through their participation in the French labor movement, they would both assist it in its mission to transform French society and gain the skills they would need to effect similar changes upon their return to their homelands (*JA*, March 2, 1978).

With the connivance of the municipality, labor militancy broke out frequently in the years following World War II. It increased in the 1960s as La Courneuve lost industrial jobs at an ever faster rate. The wave of strike activity in 1968 affected the city deeply, and it involved foreign workers as well as French natives. Strikers idled over seventy factories, occupying forty of them. The municipality offered its full backing and sent food to sustain the protesters (*JA*, May 11, 1978).

This unified strike activity, along with the immigrants' own confrontational protests across France in the years following, convinced French Communists of the value of harnessing such activist potential. To them it seemed entirely appropriate that foreign workers' only legitimate access to French politics should be through participation in the French labor movement. Throughout the 1970s immigrant workers participated in the job actions that took place in the factories of La Courneuve. Local French trade unions—the CGT and often also the CFDT—and the PCF would normally make an express appeal to immigrant workers for their participation in marches, demonstrations, or strikes against a company or the government.

Immigrants constituted the majority of workers in several local plants, and they themselves initiated many of the more aggressive strikes and factory occupations. The municipality and the local Communist organizations rallied around these actions. The PCF and CGT harshly rebuked attempts by employers to divide striking French and immigrant workers: "Isn't the exploitation of the immigrants just another of the bosses' means to pressure workers and to maintain miserable working conditions?" (*JA*, May 8, 1975).

Testing the Communists' solidarity with the immigrants were the severe economic difficulties that threatened La Courneuve's employment base throughout the period. Almost 100 companies there folded between 1960 and 1974. More closings and layoffs followed through the rest of the decade. Sometimes the efforts of French and foreign workers, public officials, and trade unionists would result in a victory for workers that spared their jobs or wage levels. But in the end, all the major industries in the city laid off workers. In 1977 one worker out of five in the department was on the dole (*JA*, May 5, 1977).[3]

One closing hurt particularly badly: the Mécano electrical turbine factory, standing between "The 4,000" and city hall, was the industrial heart of La Courneuve. Owned by a Paris-based multinational, Marine de Wendel, it had dominated the city both physically and in employment terms since 1912. The announcement that it was slated to close in 1976 touched off several years of bitter, often violent struggles that involved the entire town.[4]

"All Courneuvian workers," then, had "the same enemies" (*JA*, June 30, 1977). Communist-sponsored festivals and social gatherings, where North African *cous-cous* held the culinary place of honor alongside Alsatian *choucroûte*, facilitated contacts between immigrant workers and Communist organizations. The local press reported triumphantly the number of new PCF and CGT members that never failed to result. Immigrants active in those movements attended "debates" at election time to pose appropriate questions to PCF candidates about the immigrants' role in French social and economic life. Whenever the government introduced immigration procedures that the PCF and CGT opposed, meetings were called at which carefully selected immigrant workers would explain their problems and difficulties. It was there that the immigrants made the most of their truly political contacts with city officials (see *JA*, March 13, 1975; June 17, 1976; Nov. 10, 1977).

French-led solidarity groups could be highly effective in encouraging and manipulating immigrant political participation in La Courneuve— provided those groups were sufficiently friendly with the PCF, the CGT, or at least the CFDT. Communist-backed renters' associations, for example, actively enlisted immigrant involvement in their fight for improvements in living conditions and the legal transfer of "The 4,000" to the city of La Courneuve.[5] Churches and religious associations, on the other hand, lacked real influence with the Communist municipality.

The small, heterogeneous, left-wing Unified Socialist Party (Parti Socialiste Unifié—PSU), a staunch defender of immigrants and their right to participate in French politics, had only a minor presence in the city. Ecologists, who formed one important wing of the PSU, dominated the local branch. Although it sometimes ran its own slate in local elections, the PSU proved far more loyal to the PCF locally than at the national level.[6]

In such a local mobilization system, the immigrants' political participation reflected first and foremost its perceived value to the Communist municipality. The more likely immigrants seemed to be able to help it fulfill its program, the more substantive policy gains they made and the more local militants took an interest in their causes. The same applied to the immigrants' homeland-oriented participation: Courneuvian authorities stifled opposition to governments friendly to the PCF, and those governments' official homeland organizations profited from municipal recognition and aid (see, for example, *JA*, April 29, 1976).

Local Communists, echoing the national party hierarchy, emphasized internationalism and worldwide working-class unity. The municipality held seminars and festivals that gave ideologically correct foreign workers and their families the chance to become acquainted with "their" countries. The local PCF called for the immigrants' full social and, especially, trade union rights; yet it did not advocate granting them voting rights: "To respect the immigrants' right to be different and to struggle so that they can exercise their civic rights in their homelands is the best evidence of attachment to democratic liberties and of respect for the national personality of each immigration" (*JA*, Oct. 3, 1975).

The municipality's approach to immigrants and their needs, in other words, reflected a close connection with the international struggles at which the Communists were targeting their efforts. The immigrants' class-based participation in La Courneuve, accordingly, often intertwined with that directed toward their homelands. Rank-and-file French Communists would demonstrate along with the immigrants for or against significant political developments in "their" countries. By joining the PCF and the CGT, it followed, the immigrants would simultaneously be fighting for positive change there (see, for example, *JA*, April 28, 1977).

The local party, for example, praised the Algerian government in particular for the "exemplary concern" it showed for its nationals in France. City officials viewed the FLN-backed AAE as the representative of all Algerians there. Efforts by opponents of the ruling regime to organize in the city met with stiff resistance from local authorities (*JA*, March 27, 1975; March 6, 1980; Jan. 21, 1983). Municipal officials consulted with both the local and Parisian AAE branches and included AAE officers and members in all the cultural expositions, marches, delegations to the prefect's office, and other protests organized on behalf of La Courneuve's working class. The AAE returned the favor by encouraging its constituents to join the PCF and the CGT.[7]

Local Communists, who had organized opposition to the authoritarian regimes in Iberia, celebrated the arrival of democracy there in the mid-1970s. The focus shifted from marches on the Spanish and Portuguese embassies in Paris to celebrations of Iberian cultures and expressions of support for Iberian Communists. Like their Italian counterparts, Spanish Communists had worked through the PCF and the CGT and were fairly well integrated into the local French Communist movement. Connections were close with "brother" parties in Spain and Italy (*JA*, Sept. 25, 1975).

The same was largely true of their Portuguese comrades, although that community had its own organization, the AOP. With close ties to the Portuguese Communist Party, the AOP had its regional headquarters in Bobigny and drew many members from adjacent La Courneuve. It received the same special treatment accorded the AAE and likewise urged its militants to join French Communist organizations. Neither it nor the PCF hesitated to endorse Communist candidates in Portuguese elections.[8]

Taking the place of the defunct Iberian dictatorships at the top of the PCF's list of foreign policy interests were the struggles of left-wing rebel groups in Angola, Mozambique, Djibouti, and elsewhere. The military junta in power in Turkey during the early 1980s was another prime concern. Communists in La Courneuve denounced the regime and joined marches on the Turkish embassy in Paris. The Communist Turkish opposition received considerable support and protection from the PCF and its militants. Like the Algerian opposition, non-Communist opponents of the Turkish status quo received the very coldest of shoulders.[9]

Under the force of the local Communist drive to co-opt political activity of any kind in the city, the boundary often blurred between the immigrants' political participation based on their working-class status and that directed toward their homeland. Actions whose aims did not coincide with those of the local—and by extension, the national—Communist leadership found themselves ignored or actively suppressed. When faced with unorthodox and aggressive forms of protest by immigrants, the Communists moved quickly to channel them into—or at least to package them as—an aspect of the class struggle.

In La Courneuve, then, what constituted institutional participation and expected and "proper" immigrant behavior differed from that in the nation at large. City officials sprang to the defense of protests such as the SONACOTRA strikes. In the mid-1970s, the mostly Algerian and Portuguese residents of the SONACOTRA-managed hostel in La Courneuve were among the first to join the renters' strike movement that broke out in nearby Saint-Denis. The municipality voiced support for the strikers even while it worked with the CGT and the AAE to negotiate a separate settlement for the hostel in La Courneuve, which became the first one to settle in such a manner. In addition to granting concessions on rent increases, the housing authority dropped legal actions against the protesters and promised to widen resident participation in management. City officials participated in the celebratory slaughtering of a kid to mark the victory (*JA*, Dec. 11, 1975). They argued that the immigrant workers' growing militancy and their mobilization alongside the organizations of French labor would help all workers: "The important successes registered in La Courneuve to keep factories open (Rateau, Satam, etc.) and to improve working and living conditions (SONACOTRA, Béguin, Babcock, etc.) are the fruits of this union. That is what the bosses want to crush" (*JA*, April 29, 1976).

The immigrants who worked in factories in La Courneuve engaged in several wildcat factory strikes and, like their counterparts across France, also resorted to confrontational tactics in their fight against racism and the national government's immigration policies and procedures. All such activism found favor with the municipality and other Communist officials and trade unionists. They offered every kind of assistance to the protesters, sometimes to the point of dragging the immigrant strike leaders to the prefecture in Bobigny to complain. The local and national Communist press publicized the activity and interpreted it to fit the party line. Heatedly denying charges of co-optation, the Communists counted as their own the gains produced.[10]

The more combative the immigrant workers were, the greater was their utility to a French labor movement in need of energetic new recruits. But in the Communist perspective, ethnicity did not constitute an acceptable basis for political organization except when it advanced working-class integration. Autonomous ethnic associations met with resistance from city hall. La Courneuve's imposing municipal cultural center, a common feature in Communist *communes,* stood guard against any instances of "spontaneous," unauthorized immigrant (or French) political mobilization (see *BM,* Sept.–Oct. 1983).

A "subterranean" network of informal ethnic groupings had existed in La Courneuve for decades. Stable organizations were a rarity, yet their number did grow after the modification of the national associational law in 1981. The municipality recognized and maintained regular contacts only with associations that toed the PCF's line. Thus Mayor Marson could argue that the AAE and groups related to it (such as the Franco-Algerian Sporting Club) were "the only Algerian associations in town," denying the presence of groups opposed to the FLN. After their legalization in 1981, "acceptable" existing associations of sub-Saharan Africans and Italians also received official recognition (*JA,* Oct. 23, 1981).

The Mitterrand-Mauroy government also legalized local private radio stations, and the "pirate" Radio 4000 that had been broadcasting out of that complex left the underground. It quickly announced its intention to act as the sounding board and soapbox "for those who have never had one, immigrants included." In typical fashion, the city council set up an association to coordinate and oversee Radio 4000 and other local stations (*JA,* Oct. 2, 1981).

At bottom, local officials preferred direct immigrant-municipality contacts to any autonomous associational presence. City hall tried to weaken any association, cultural or otherwise, that was hostile to PCF strategy. The less-than-hospitable environment led some national groups to forgo organizing in La Courneuve altogether: no autonomous local Spanish or Portuguese organizational presence developed, since the PCF was to be the forum for Iberians' activity in France.[11]

For the most part, the Communists' strategy worked with the first generation of foreign workers. By participating under the aegis of the

PCF and the CGT, they won some influence within local political circles. Grateful trade union leaders freely acknowledged, for example, that in the elections to the *conseils des Prud'hommes* in 1982, the immigrant workers played a crucial role in the CGT's retaining its supremacy in area factories.[12] Mobilized or not, however, the immigrants' class-based participation was slackening by the early 1980s. This decrease in militancy paralleled that of the French workforce in general.

The 1980s brought other distressing developments for the PCF. Racism intensified in La Courneuve and created a new basis for political mobilization that crossed traditional social-class divisions. The flight of many indigenous families from the deindustrializing Red-Belt suburbs actually caused the share of immigrants in the total population of cities like La Courneuve to rise after 1974. As the economic crisis deepened, foreigners became ever more frequent targets of hostility, with children figuring among the victims. The city's long-standing nationwide reputation for violence gained new currency (*BM*, April 1982).

PCF officials in La Courneuve, as nationally, initially spoke of the strong solidarity that bound together all workers in the city. Racist and anti-immigrant acts brought a swift, fierce reaction from local authorities. At the same time, municipal officials blamed the national government for reneging on its reponsibility to address the housing, education, and training needs of the immigrants—described as "victims of social discrimination." Such burdens, they contended, were falling unfairly on France's working-class *communes*. As early as 1969 the Communist mayors of the Paris region had protested against the "inequitable distribution" of immigrant workers and their families. By the mid-1970s this idea was figuring prominently in the statements of local PCF officials, always accompanied by assertions of solidarity with immigrant workers (see, for example, *JA*, Jan. 30, 1975).

And they did not always limit themselves to rhetoric. By the late 1970s formal protests had degenerated into "crude actions directed against both immigrants and French workers from overseas territories." During the presidential campaign of 1981, "these actions emerged as a coordinated campaign led by the national leaders of the Communist Party" (Schain 1985, p. 81). The most infamous incident along these lines took place in 1980 in the southern Paris suburb of Vitry, where the Communist mayor led a group of city councillors and "irate citizens" in razing with a bulldozer a newly installed foreign workers' dormitory. Backed by the PCF candidate for president,

Georges Marchais, the Communist mayors of Seine-Saint-Denis—including La Courneuve's James Marson—issued a declaration of support for the mayor of Vitry.[13]

THE SECOND GENERATION

The hardening of the Communist position on immigration also owed much to the growing restlessness of the second immigrant generation. Unlike their parents, these youngsters resisted the PCF's attempts to mobilize them politically. The partially successful effort to bring this generation into the working-class fold occupied local officials for the next decade.

Second-generation immigrants were not a negligible quantity in La Courneuve, where over 42 percent of foreigners were children under age sixteen. They occupied between 20 and 30 percent of the places in the city's schools from the mid-1970s through the 1980s. High rates of scholastic failure—and, when they got older, unemployment—plagued most of La Courneuve's young people. The children of foreign workers accounted for a disproportionate share of those affected (Guillon, de Rudder-Paurd, and Simon 1977, pp. 100–105).

The local government responded to the problems of the city's younger residents in ways that fitted with its own political agenda. Youth festivals brought together those in the working class, regardless of citizenship status, under the Communist banner. The youth section of the CGT and the activist Catholic JOC received municipal assistance as they worked to organize the immigrant workers' children. The city also organized events for them at the municipal cultural center (*JA*, March 25, 1976).

Such events failed to attract large numbers of second-generation immigrants or French teenagers. Some of them complained to researchers that "there was always some guy there giving a speech like at city hall." Others said that they "gagged on the perfume of social assistance that hung over the place" (Fagnen 1981).

The more radical second-generation immigrants soon bypassed the municipality-approved forms of participation and developed their own. In the wake of Vitry's Communist bulldozer in 1980, a spate of local "Rock against Police" (RAP) movements appeared. RAP considered delinquency to be "a legitimate response to the repressive actions of the State, as relayed by local authorities and especially by Communist mayors." In "The 4,000," instances of the petty crime, drug culture, squatting, and occasional violence of which RAP approved multiplied (*Libération*, Jan. 12, 1981).[14]

La Courneuve still lacked an organized second-generation presence. But it did have Jimmy Kiavué, one of the charismatic associational gadflies who did more than anyone or anything else to fill the cultural and social needs of the second generation of France's industrial suburbs. Like Harlem Désir, Kiavué had an Antillean father and a French mother. He had knocked about the northern suburbs of Paris for years, organizing militant cultural and recreational groups wherever he went. In 1981 he arrived in La Courneuve, where he founded the Movement for Alternative Artistic Actions (Mouvement pour d'Autres Actions Artistiques—MAAA). The MAAA took over a cinema in the city that a Spanish immigrant close to the local PCF had unsuccessfully attempted to turn into a concert hall. The Yuro Théâtro—named after the Bolivian village in which Che Guevara was killed—became for eight months a fulcrum of avant-garde and *Beur* culture. French music publications and the cultural pages of the major Parisian dailies began to contain glowing reviews of events at the Yuro, the new "Broadway in La Courneuve" (MAAA–Yuro Théâtro 1982; *Libération*, Oct. 3, 1981; see also *Le Monde*, June 12, 1982; *La Vie*, July 22, 1982).

Given the great need for such a cultural outlet in the city and the positive effect on La Courneuve's image as a result of all the press coverage, municipal authorities at first applauded the Yuro Théâtro (see Battegay 1985, p. 116). It became the object of praise, financial beneficence, and technical assistance. Officials talked about incorporating it into their fight against "false solidarities, unemployment, and delinquency" (*JA*, Dec. 11, 1981). Yet the municipality was also suspicious and fearful of the MAAA's spontaneity, "just as it feared everything that took place outside it" (*Libération*, Nov. 28, 1981). Tensions between city hall and the second generation erupted into open conflict in March 1983, when RAP organized a massive concert that degenerated into a free-for-all between youths and police. The shocked municipality asked rhetorically: "Wasn't the rock concert merely a cover, a cynical provocation from the outside, designed to spread disorder in a working-class suburb?" (*JA*, March 18, 1983).

Suspicion subsequently fell on all activity by young people outside municipal and PCF purview. The city beefed up its program of cultural events aimed particularly at North African and Iberian immigrants and their families. With the national government's financial backing, it quickly opened a meeting place *(bourse des associations)* for all officially sanctioned associations in "The 4,000," where they would be under its watchful eye. Not coincidentally, around the same time a local youth employment service opened to assist young Courneuvians of all ethnic backgrounds and nationalities (*JA*, April 1, 1983; *BM*, March 1983).

THE EXTREMIST REACTION AND THE REBIRTH OF SOLIDARITY

The issues of crime and drug use soon obsessed the municipal government. City officials talked up their role in convincing the police to introduce several roving bands of "beat cops" *(îlotiers)*. Early in 1983 Mayor Marson's administration established a special commission on security issues and produced figures to demonstrate that its efforts had helped lower the crime rate (*JA*, Jan. 21 and March 11, 1983).

The mayor and his administration hoped that the tough new approach would defuse support for the National Front. "Crime, security, and Arabs" had become the FN's "electoral mantra," and more and more Courneuvians were taking up the chant.[15] Local and regional FN organizations responded hysterically to the militancy of the *Beurs* and others of the second immigrant generation. Their citizenship status did not matter as much as their refusal to become "good Frenchmen" and assimilate as individuals into the host society.[16]

The PCF held its own in the 1983 municipal elections, but the gains registered soon thereafter by the National Front shook the city's political establishment. Table 13 shows the amazing rapidity with which the Front's influence grew in La Courneuve: from less than 1 percent in the 1979 European election to almost 15 percent in the 1984 reprise. Disaffected working-class voters appeared to account for a share of the FN's impressive totals. The PCF's need to reinforce working-class unity had caused it to deny the tensions that often existed between French and immigrant workers.

One result of the *lepéniste* successes in La Courneuve and in other PCF bulwarks was the gradual rediscovery of historically left-wing concerns about French society's outcasts. As the industrial suburbs of Paris hemorrhaged more jobs and companies, and as the National Front surged in popularity, the PCF panicked. Even though the immigrants could not vote, their presence in the ranks of the working class was swelling in importance. The party's only true hope appeared to lie in a return to solidarity with them and the other poor and disfranchised.

Table 13 Percentage of votes for the FN in La Courneuve, 1974–1989

Year	Election	FN
1974	Presidential election (first round)	0.6
1979	European election	0.9
1983	Municipal election	—
1984	European election	14.9
1985	Cantonal election	17.0
1986	Legislative election	14.6
1988	Presidential election (first round)	14.4
1988	Legislative election	14.6
1989	Municipal election	—[a]
1989	European election	16.0

Sources: Election Commission, La Courneuve; *Le Monde,* May 10 and June 13, 1988; March 14 and June 20, 1989.

Note: Percentages for presidential elections are of total number of properly marked ballots. Percentages for other elections are of total votes cast.

a. There was no separate National Front slate, but two FN municipal councillors were elected from the Union de la Droite slate.

A tragedy gave a fillip to that transformation in outlook. In July 1983, a drunk Algerian War veteran shot out into a courtyard in "The 4,000" where a group of Muslims were celebrating the end of the holy month of Ramadan. He killed nine-year-old Toufik Ouannes, a *Beur.* The municipality employed the harshest terms to condemn the tragedy, mourning the loss of "one of ours" and linking racism to anti-Communism. It vented its spleen equally against the violent reaction that the murder elicited among immigrants in "The 4,000" (*JA,* July 21, 1983).

A few months later, the organizers of the 1983 March for Equality and against Racism pointed to the murder of Toufik Ouannes in La Courneuve as one key trigger of their movement. Posters carried by several participants bore Toufik's likeness, along with slogans denouncing the racism that led to his death. The marchers entered La Courneuve on December 3 and were greeted by a support group comprised of the mothers of Toufik's friends, as well as leaders of the local PCF,

CGT, CFDT, and PSU. Since the murder had occurred in their city, elected officials displayed far greater sympathy and solidarity with the marchers of 1983 than did the national PCF. The entire procession headed to the cemetery where Toufik lay buried, and a wreath was laid on his grave. The symbolic force of the act drew intense media attention to the city (*Huma-dimanche*, Dec. 4, 1983; *Sans frontière*, Jan. 1984).

Quickly taking the offensive, the municipal government reasserted its authority over the volatile situation in La Courneuve. In 1981 the city's newly reelected deputy, Jack Ralite (PCF), had become the minister of health in Prime Minister Pierre Mauroy's cabinet and had led an official government delegation on a tour of La Courneuve and "The 4,000." After years of intense wrangling and a surprise visit from President Mitterrand himself in the summer of 1983, La Courneuve finally attained control over "The 4,000" in March 1984.[17]

Then, in July 1984, under the specious pretence of health and safety violations and noise pollution, local authorities closed the Yuro Théâtro. They had determined they could not control or even direct it.[18] The city organized a memorial service for Toufik Ouannes on the anniversary of his death, the same day that the closing was announced, hoping to blunt charges of anti-immigrant racism (*JA*, July 6, 1984).

In a move to fill organizational space in the city with friends, the city government next instigated the creation of ideologically acceptable immigrant associations. A naturalized Turkish municipal employee headed the local branch of the pro-Communist, Paris-based Turkish Workers' Union, which received start-up funds and a meeting place in the municipal cultural center in 1984.[19] The small Malagasy, Comorian, Moroccan, and Antillean communities received a similar push to form ethnic associations, as did immigrant women. These associations were to direct all political activity into channels favored by the local PCF and to discourage the formation of groups inimical to the party's interests.

Similar reasoning led La Courneuve's Communist leaders to court local Muslims. In April 1983 an Algerian imam established an Islamic association whose purpose was to construct a prayer room and Koranic school on the ground floor of one of the buildings making up "The 4,000." The municipality monitored the development carefully, but the Muslims acted independently of any movement or government. The dues of believers, who were of a number of nationalities, provided its sole source of financing. The mosque association aspired to no explicit political role, since "when there is politics, that means there can be no religion."[20] Despite such indifference, as well as the possible electoral costs, elected city officials attended Muslim holiday celebrations (*JA*, Oct. 16, 1981).

Grudgingly, the local government even tried to accommodate those elements within the second immigrant generation that, albeit more autonomous than the PCF would have liked, did not openly deride the party. Convergence '84 received the unsolicited support of the national PCF hierarchy, making the choice to support it easier for Communists in La Courneuve. A squad of motorscooters from Roubaix passed through the city on their way to Paris. Mayor Marson ushered them into a factory, where they met with workers but declined to embrace the class struggle. Ignoring that slight, the mayor condemned both racism and "the effort by some political groups to push a profoundly just movement onto the slippery slope of anti-Communism" (*JA*, Dec. 7, 1984).

That was a clear reference to the ties of some in the *Beur* movement to the Socialists. In 1984 a branch of SOS-Racisme formed in "The 4,000." It found few friends in city hall, and municipal pressures helped hasten its demise (*Le Matin*, Dec. 19, 1986). Winning official favor, by contrast, were the "anti-*potes*" *Beurs* who marched in 1985 from Barbès to Bordeaux, Iberian and Italian youth groups sympathetic to the PCF, and especially the voter registration drives of France-Plus, which the municipality hoped would add to the Communist electorate. In fact, Communist activists worked independently to register eligible second-generation immigrants, *harkis*, and Antilleans in La Courneuve (*JA*, Dec. 6, 1985; Servet 1985).

Thus by the mid-1980s local Communists had joined the national party in reaching out to second-generation immigrants, and in La Courneuve they were notably more effective than at the national level. Anyone who bypassed the encapsulating network of local Communist institutions still encountered intense hostility: as the CGT saw it, for instance, "the fight against racism is not simply a subject of humanitarian concern, it is a class struggle" (Thépaut 1985, p. 1).

The National Front hoped to exploit the PCF's new tactics. Its press made frequent reference to La Courneuve, the archetypical "immigrant-plagued" industrial Red-Belt suburb. Far-right newspapers and leaders blasted it as an "overly lenient *commune* in which thieves and aggressors can escape punishment" (*Minute*, March 31, 1984; see also *National*

Hebdo, Oct. 9, 1986). Le Pen's forces received an impressive 17 percent of the vote in the 1985 cantonal elections and 14.6 percent in the 1986 legislative elections. Over the same period, the Communists' vote total fell from 38.3 percent to 23.2 percent.

In such a politically polarized environment, it was easy for racist violence to spread. In 1986 another foreign worker's teenaged child was murdered, this time in a local bar—ironically, named the "Tout Est Bien" (All Is Well). Crying, the victim's brother first announced his intention "to return home to Algeria." Then one of his friends pointed out that he had been born and always lived in France and had not felt comfortable in Algeria during a visit with relatives there over the summer holiday.[21] So instead he and his friends formed the Abdel Benyahia Justice Committee to protest police and court handling of the affair. It received permission to set up shop in the municipality-provided *bourse des associations,* as well as the local administration's moral and financial support (*Libération,* Dec. 8, 1986; Laigre 1987).

The Abdel Benyahia Justice Committee participated enthusiastically alongside college and high-school students in La Courneuve in protests later that year against the proposed Devaquet educational reform and Chalandon reform of the Nationality Code. Their chants and banners made no mention of the working class, but the Communist municipality and allied organizations jumped on the bandwagon: they touted the events as an indication of young people's awakening class consciousness and offered financial support. The young immigrant and French students remembered the PCF's past "indiscretions" and remained wary of efforts to co-opt what they described as *notre truc à nous* (our own thing). They nevertheless willingly accepted the Communists' largesse and seemed positively disposed toward the municipal government.[22]

Sadly, La Courneuve's history repeated itself once more in the summer of 1988. The death of an apparently innocent *Beur* in a confrontation with traffic police sparked riots throughout the city. The violence witnessed the first important intervention by the resuscitated local branch of SOS-Racisme, which transmitted the demands of the victim's family and friends for justice. City hall condemned the actions of the police but, ever loyal to the PCF, accused the Socialist government of using SOS-Racisme to whitewash the whole affair (*Libération,* July 15, 1988; *Le Monde,* July 19, 1988).

The National Front, from a very different political angle, held the ground that it had won in La Courneuve: Le Pen received 14.4 percent of the local 1988 first-round presidential vote (see Table 13). The Communists withstood further losses, however, holding steady at 24.6 percent. They bounced back to 38.3 percent in the first round of the ensuing legislative elections. In 1989, as before, the mainstream left and right ran unified slates in the municipal elections. Mayor Marson's Union of the Left nearly matched its showing of 1983, with 65.3 percent; still, the municipal council would now contain two members of the National Front, whose candidates figured on the Union of the Right list (*Le Monde*, May 10, 1988, and March 14, 1989; *Libération*, June 13, 1988). The FN did well in the European elections later that spring. Yet its 16 percent of the vote, while placing it a close second in the balloting, was well below its party's departmental average for Seine-Saint-Denis (at 17.5 percent); the Communists' 35.5 percent, well above (at 19.7 percent).[23] As then–Prime Minister Michel Rocard argued, the PCF might indeed have become a "regional party"; but cities like La Courneuve did remain their strongest region (*Le Monde*, March 21, 1989).

The PCF was in the painful process of realizing just how deeply the restructuring of industry and urban areas had affected the French working class: changes in its position in society, composition, and aspirations had transformed the traditional context of municipal policy. As the high cost of living in Paris pushed out its middle class, the populations of traditional working-class fiefs like La Courneuve were home to proportionately more salaried employees and managers, as well as immigrants. As a result, "municipal leaders found themselves disoriented in the face of a population that they no longer recognized" (Robatel 1988, p. 438).

By the late 1980s the local government did not enjoy wide latitude. La Courneuve faced a myriad of interconnected problems: rising unemployment, rampant racism, fear of insecurity and crime, and a potent National Front. The city had become a national symbol of French urban decay, and local authorities could do little on their own to reverse it. Gamely, though, La Courneuve's Communist officials were laboring to maintain their control while adapting to the new challenges. Their mobilizational approach to immigrant political participation did not change fundamentally. At the very least, the local PCF managed to reach an accommodation with the immigrant communities and even most elements of the second-generation social movement. They all exhibited greater class consciousness than their counterparts in cities where the Communists had not enjoyed such political strength. Those in the immigrant-origin population who did not at a minimum tolerate their interference either organized elsewhere or not at all. Generational and ethnic-based organizing remained tributary to the working-class movement. As a result, the participation of both immigrant generations in La Courneuve continued to differ in form and basis from the overall national pattern.

Roubaix

In centralized France national-level institutional channeling has set the general parameters for immigrants' political activity. Within those constraints, however, their relationship with municipal governments and other local institutions has varied greatly, producing distinctive participatory patterns. La Courneuve offers an instance of mobilized immigrant political participation, with the French Communist Party attempting to control and co-opt it in all its forms. Roubaix, on the other hand, demonstrates that a strong local network of sympathetic French activists and solidarity groups can help a disadvantaged population like the immigrants take fuller and freer advantage of existing routes of political access, at least up to a point.

Roubaix presented immigrants with a more open political opportunity structure. In large measure, it was the historical legacy of municipal socialism and Catholic social activism. One of the nation's first and foremost industrial centers, Roubaix was the "French Manchester," with its destiny tied to textiles. It was also "the holy city for the proletariat everywhere," in Jules Guesde's phrase (quoted in Piat 1981, p. 43). The French Workers' Party (Parti Ouvrier Français—POF) found fertile ground there for its reformist message of social change and local autonomy in the late nineteenth century. In 1892 Guesdist leader Henri Carette won Roubaix's mayoral race, one of the first such victories for French socialism. The next year Guesde himself became the city's deputy in the National Assembly. In a choice of words that would later seem ironic indeed, Alfred Merrheim, one of the leading theorists of revolutionary socialism, at a 1906 CGT congress referred to Roubaix as the "Guesdist mecca."[24]

Harsh anticlericalism marked the rhetoric of the POF. But Roubaix had a strong Christian socialist tradition as well, and it influenced the policies and programs of local governments. Marc Sangier's Sillon and the Chrétien Social movement took their first steps in the region. The "worker priests" of the Nord often sided with factory workers in their struggles against the textile bosses in the late nineteenth and early twentieth centuries (see Vinatier 1984). Some of France's earliest strikes and protests, many of them extremely bitter and violent, peppered the industrial history of the city.

The effects of the Catholic social action perspective were apparent in the mildly Marxist ideology and the system of "municipal socialism" that Roubaix's mayors introduced. At a time when the central state provided for few of French cities' services and infrastructural needs, the municipal government in Roubaix set up a highly developed and diversified network of social welfare assistance and organized educational, recreational, producer, and employer associations (Vaulont 1977).

Pious Belgian Catholic immigrants contributed significantly to the blending of Christian social activism and reformist Socialism that would become hallmarks of Roubaix. The city became a major immigration center long before 1945, in contrast to La Courneuve. With legal restrictions and demographics limiting the employment of women and children, Roubaix's textile industrialists looked across the nearby frontier to Belgium for unskilled workers for their factories. Incredibly, by 1891 over half of Roubaisians held Belgian citizenship. Many other Flemish workers commuted weekly, *frontaliers* who returned to their families each weekend.[25] The Belgians brought with them Socialist ideas from the north, where the new ideology had advanced further than in France. They also had a greater predilection for associational activity than the French, and they quickly developed numerous political, social, and cultural groups (Marty 1982, p. 76).

Even very large immigrant communities managed to integrate into the ranks of the *Roubaignos* (native Roubaisians) through their membership in the working class. The Belgians and, later, a smaller community of Poles faced xenophobic hostility before they slowly melted into the French labor movement and French society. At the close of the nineteenth century, immigrants from Germany, England, the Austro-Hungarian Empire, and Italy underwent a similar process of assimilation (Marty 1982, p. 8).[26]

As those immigrants became French workers and citizens, and as growth in the textile industry slowed, the share of foreigners in the total population of the city declined steadily after the turn of the century, until a new influx into the city began after World War II. Workers from Italy took the place of the Belgians and Poles in the 1950s. Algerians (including many *harkis*), Moroccans, Spaniards, Portuguese, and sub-Saharan Africans followed them in successive waves, with 1962 marking the real beginning of the flood. By 1975 nearly 20 percent of Roubaix's residents were foreign-born. At the end of the decade 84.5 percent of the immigrants there were still manual, unskilled, or skilled workers (Abou-Sada et al. 1981, p. 73).

Observers have described Roubaix as an "American" city: ringed by wealthy neighborhoods and suburbs, its central section housed poor French and foreign workers. Entire city blocks of decrepit employer-constructed housing units lined the streets of the inner city, stark reminders of the meteoric development of textiles in the nineteenth century. Many took the form of the *courée:* ten to thirty buildings with communal sanitary facilities surrounding a narrow, sunless courtyard. Because they were cheap to buy and rent and relatively amenable to the needs of the extended families that typified the North African and Southern European immigrations, those "minighettos" came to shelter much of Roubaix's foreign population—75 percent in 1975. Members of the various national groups clustered by *courées* and by neighborhoods, a situation that incubated ethnic-based political consciousness. The city also contained its share of HLM, a SONACOTRA-run worker hostel, and half a dozen *foyers* (Marrucho 1982b, pp. 39, 49–54).

AN ACCOMMODATING POLITICAL OPPORTUNITY STRUCTURE

From 1942 to 1977 Roubaix Socialists led a coalition of non-Communist leftist and centrist elements in a happy governing consensus. As opposed to the Red-Belt PCF municipalities, the less monolithic left-wing governments in Roubaix downplayed class struggle and a rigid, universalistic party ideology. They emphasized inclusiveness and local control and initiative. In contrast to the one-sided support for pro-Communist homeland movements in La Courneuve, consequently, elected officials in Roubaix allowed homeland organizations of all political leanings to operate in their city. The municipality expected them to provide material and emotional support to their expatriates, even while accepting Roubaix's share of the burden. Even conservative groups met with acceptance. Thus political divisions rooted in the countries of origin persisted longer than in La Courneuve. Absent the backing of interested local French officials and activists, however, homeland-oriented immigrant participation rarely took the form of vocal protests, street demonstrations, or other confrontational actions.

The AAE had a strong hold on the Algerians of Roubaix, where it maintained a major regional center that provided Arabic courses, cultural activities, and various forms of social services and counseling. But the Algerian opposition was also active, most notably the Union of Algerian Workers' Syndicates (Union des Syndicats des Travailleurs Algériens).[27] City officials treated the AAE as the primary representative of Roubaix's Algerian community. They knew that the AAE bristled at the mere mention of the FLN regime's enemies, of course, and did not hesitate to sow the seeds of discord for tactical advantage: they claimed that their concern for the community applied "without distinction to both the partisans and the adversaries of the political regime in power in Algeria" (*VN*, Jan. 8, 1974).

Official Portuguese associations, similarly, reflected homeland political divisions that were just receding within what was a relatively new immigrant community. Portuguese consular officials and religious organizations devoted more resources to Roubaix and the Nord in general than to almost any other region outside the Ile-de-France. Remaining aloof from them were militants of the Portuguese Communist Party and its affiliated AOP, acting under the umbrella of the PCF. Unlike their counterparts in La Courneuve, authorities in Roubaix stayed clear of all internal Portuguese disputes. Yet they clearly favored official diplomatic representatives after the fall of the Caetano regime and deferred to them when a problem arose in the Portuguese community (Marrucho 1982b, pp. 73–113).

The Italian and Spanish communities were more tightly knit than the Algerian and Portuguese. Fraternal organizations of Italian Catholics and Communists both worked closely with consular officials in Lille and served as social-service providers and cultural clearinghouses for the community. The same was true of the official "Spanish House," which had its headquarters for northern France in Roubaix. The municipality's relations with the official Italian and—after Franco's demise—Spanish associations were cordial (*VN*, Dec. 22, 1978). The diversity of the governing local coalition thus encouraged a general openness toward immigrant groups of all political and ideological persuasions, in sharp contrast to the heavy-handed Communist mobilization that characterized La Courneuve.

After their own fashion, however, Roubaix officials did take clear steps to link immigrants to local politics. By the early 1970s public workshops and round tables were examining the health, employment, and educational difficulties of postwar immigrants and their children. In 1973 Mayor Victor Provo appointed an adjunct to the municipal council to "take care of the foreigners" (quoted in *BC*, Nov. 25, 1974). The emphasis was on social assistance to solve the problems that, from city hall's perspective, capitalist exploitation had created (Ville de Roubaix 1985, p. 39).

Those problems quickly worsened. By the mid-1970s it was clear that Roubaix's textile industry was undergoing a secular decline. Employment in that sector in Roubaix-Tourcoing had fallen from 68,400 jobs in 1962 to 40,800 in 1978, and with the "factory undergoing mutation, the entire social fabric of Roubaix grew stressed" (Hilaire 1984, pp. 322–323). Heated debates over Roubaix's economic future and the place of immigrant workers in it animated Municipal Council meetings and filled newspaper columns. The municipality, echoing the Communists of La Courneuve, first called on the government to ensure a "more harmonious distribution of immigrants in the metropolitan area" (Ville de Roubaix 1985, pp. 24–26).

A major political change, however, shortly brought a fresh approach toward the participation of the immigrants in city affairs. In 1977 the era of cozy postwar political consensus ended when a Socialist-led Union of the Left slate won the municipal election. That victory and the 1978 legislative elections heralded a return to partisanship in the city. A new generation of militants in the Socialist Party determined that the time had come for Roubaix's officials to encourage the immigrants to "find their own voice" and move into the mainstream of the city's political life.[28]

Given the new local government's stance, it is not surprising that institutional participatory channels took on greater significance for the immigrants. Class, especially, was a preferred basis for organizing in the longtime leftist and industrial stronghold. The already long-standing rivalry between local Communists and Socialists and between the CGT and the CFDT union movements intensified in the late 1970s. Competition for members within this pluralistic left gave immigrants more leverage, and the political parties and trade union locals in Roubaix accepted the foreign workers' specific demands as their own earlier and more completely than in Communist-dominated La Courneuve. The

Catholic union (Confédération Française des Travailleurs Chrétiens) was also active in the city and moved to organize Southern European workers (*VN*, Jan. 15–16, 1978).

Immigrant workers participated in all the major class-based actions that punctuated Roubaix's economic decline through the 1970s and early 1980s. Their activism received much attention and praise from the municipality, French workers, and the competing organizational components of the French labor movement. Very few spontaneous strikes were initiated by immigrant workers; one or another French trade union, and often the municipality itself, tried to co-opt those that did break out.[29]

The leftist PSU did no better at the polls in Roubaix than in La Courneuve. Yet whereas the party's ecology-minded current predominated in that Parisian suburb, in Roubaix it was PSU activists concerned chiefly with France's immigrant communities who controlled the party organization. That difference had a clear effect: elected PSU officials regularly brought up the immigrants' problems and demands at municipal council meetings.[30]

In addition to explicitly working-class and leftist political organizations, Roubaix was home to a dense web of mostly left-leaning solidarity groups that were supportive of the immigrants and their causes. The city had traditionally enjoyed a deep-rooted, autonomous associational life, and officials looked favorably on and worked closely with a wide range of local organizations and clubs. The municipality provided them with meeting places and generous operating subsidies.[31]

Local chapters of important national associations like the pro-Communist MRAP and the Human Rights League (Ligue des Droits de l'Homme) had a conspicuous presence in the city. Alongside them religious organizations were heavily involved with Roubaix's immigrants. As one might expect, given the Catholic socialist tradition of the Nord, Catholic Workers' Action (ACO) and the Young Catholic Workers (JOC) were far more active there than in La Courneuve (*VN*, Jan. 8 and May 16, 1974).

Roubaix's numerous neighborhood and renters' associations, moreover, actively recruited immigrant members, whose specific demands they advanced. Large-scale urban renewal had begun in the most run-down sections of Roubaix as early as 1958. One of the neighborhoods slated for "bulldozer renovation" in the 1970s was the Alma-Gare, an old working-class, *courée*-filled maze with a large immigrant population. Local groups, including immigrant associations, banded together to form the Popular Urban Workshop (Atelier Populaire Urbain—APU) in 1974. From then until 1983 the APU initiated court proceedings, organized protests and civil disobedience, and did anything else it could think of to stop the renewal process. Eventually successful, this fight was only the most prominent instance of joint action between French and immigrant residents (Atelier d'Art Urbain 1982).

By means of the tight network of solidarity groups and the level of access they enjoyed, the immigrants had a direct pipeline to the municipality. Their allies welcomed—even competed for—immigrant members and championed their interests, instead of trying to mobilize their participation in ways amenable to one party's strategy as in La Courneuve. The immigrants' influence on the debate over immigration in Roubaix was real (see, for example, *BC,* April 9, 1979; *NE,* Feb. 28, 1981).

ETHNIC ASSOCIATIONAL ACTIVITY

Thanks to pressure from their well-connected leftist allies, the immigrants gained an official consultative voice in local politics under the new administration. In 1978 Roubaix joined a handful of French cities in establishing a full-blown Extra-Municipal Commission for Foreigners (Commission Extra-Municipale aux Etrangers—CEM). Such commissions existed for a number of specific populations besides the immigrants (for instance, youth, the elderly, and the handicapped). The municipality saw them as integral to developing full participatory democracy: "It is through this channel that, progressively, the democratic exercise of urban power will be practiced and the relationship between elected officials and the people will become effective" (Mayor Pierre Prouvost, quoted in *BC,* Oct. 3, 1977).

Inspired by Belgium's well-developed network of Consultative Communal Commissions for Immigrants, Roubaix's CEM for immigrants was meant to fill a transitional, facilitating role in their integration into all aspects of community life. The body devoted its energies to improving race and ethnic relations in the city and responding to the pragmatic, day-to-day concerns of its immigrant communities (Ville de Roubaix 1985; compare also "Le Point en Belgique" 1979).

The accent was clearly on the immigrants' national and ethnic backgrounds. Since the nineteenth century, Roubaix authorities and solidarity-group militants had seen immigrants as members of different national communities. In keeping with its *auto-gestionnaire* project, the municipality encouraged self-help, ethnic associational activity within the new foreign populations after 1945. To a far greater extent than their counterparts in La Courneuve, Roubaix's governments provided subsidies and tactical support to the immigrant associations active in the city. Accounts of the sums allocated to autonomous Italian, Portuguese, Spanish, Turkish, Algerian, and other organizations filled municipal bulletins throughout the 1970s and 1980s. Thus even before 1981 such associations in Roubaix were far more active than elsewhere in France.[32]

Reflecting the emphasis on ethnic identity was the makeup of the consultative CEM, which the municipality viewed as its primary link with the immigrant population. Officials organized it along national lines. They acknowledged that other bases of organization—such as religion, class, and political orientation—existed. But they preferred to appoint one or two representatives of each national group to the body: it was not to be dominated by the larger communities or divided by political conflicts rooted in the homelands. The CEM thus encouraged first conflict and then consolidation within the immigrant communities, which scrambled to enhance their strategic position on the Commission.[33]

Associations with close ties to the immigrants' homelands usually refused to sit on the body with representatives of their rivals. The AAE, for example, participated in the CEM but threatened to leave if the Union of Algerian Workers' Syndicates, the only other Algerian association with a palpable presence in Roubaix, also did so. The municipal government did not want to alienate an influential organization like the AAE and respected its wishes, opting for private contacts with other Algerians.[34]

The Portuguese presented even greater difficulty. Roubaix was home to proportionately more Portuguese associations of all sizes and interests than any other city in France, fourteen alone with their own meeting places. Political, regional, and religious cleavages divided the community. Providing some cohesion was France's largest single Portuguese association, the 1,000-member Luso-French Parents' Amicale, founded in September 1976. It and a cultural organization, the Filhos da Alegria (Sons of Mirth), each sent a delegate to the CEM. Their appointment irked several other Portuguese associations—especially Communist ones—because both the groups were close to the consulate. One Portuguese cultural group even mounted a counter-festival to protest its exclusion from the CEM, until the municipality appeased it with assistance in obtaining a new headquarters. Dissension gradually subsided (*VN*, Sept. 9, 1976; Marrucho 1982b).

From the start, the Italians caused fewer problems. Leaders of Roubaix's dizzying array of political, cultural, recreational, and folkloric Italian organizations met in the mid-1970s to coordinate their actions and to facilitate their integration into local society. Holding out the promise of financial assistance, consular officials initiated the efforts, which met with considerable success. All segments of the community accepted the Italian cultural clearinghouse that resulted—known by its acronym, COFIT—as their CEM delegate (*VN*, March 27, 1974).

Spanish immigrants, too, seemed generally content to have the "Spanish House" present their views on the Commission. From Catholic groups to the Socialist Workers' Party, Spaniards seemed to accept it as a fair, trustworthy agent of their interests. There was some rivalry among the Spanish associations, but disagreements evaporated as the years passed.[35]

Besides encouraging such associational streamlining within each national group, the CEM gave a fillip to all forms of immigrant associational and other institutional activity. City councillors began to receive letters from immigrants, a form of political contacting in which noncitizens rarely engaged elsewhere in France.[36] The change in the law governing foreigners' associations that followed François Mitterrand's electoral triumphs in 1981 also had a stimulating effect. The reform legitimated the organizing that sympathetic Roubaix authorities had long tolerated, and the municipality organized a training workshop for immigrant associational leaders. Roubaix came to rank near the top among French cities in its number of immigrant associations (Hilaire 1984, p. 336).

Authorities there gently but insistently prodded previously unorganized immigrants—for example, those from the Cameroons, the Ivory Coast, and Laos—to form their own ethnic-based groups, whose representatives then sat on the CEM.[37] Much to officials' disappointment, however, the city's small and rather dispersed Turkish community produced only one conservative, contrary religious association: the Islamic Cultural Association of Turks, founded in 1982, ran the only Turkish mosque in the north of France. It took part in the CEM's proceedings for a while. When it failed to receive more than a few students' desks from the municipality, its leader refused to attend CEM meetings—although the association continued to have a booth at city-sponsored international festivals. Despite repeated attempts, the municipal government was unable to entice secular, working-class Turks to form an alternative, more amenable association to serve as an intermediary.[38]

That setback did not prevent the CEM from serving as a valuable forum in which minor disagreements and misunderstandings between the municipality and the immigrant communities could be dealt with before they escalated. It remained a purely consultative institution. Yet its work helped familiarize the immigrant members with the intricacies of Roubaix politics. In the process it furthered interethnic contacts and released interethnic tensions. The Festival of Friendship across Frontiers, a yearly multicultural event that was the highlight of each year's activities, provided an opportunity for cultural expression and for the advancement of mutual understanding (Ville de Roubaix 1985, pp. 71–72).

This effervescence occurred as other forms of immigrant political participation were losing intensity. Many of Roubaix's Italians and Iberians cast absentee ballots in direct European elections beginning in 1979, with several candidates even traveling from Italy to campaign (*VN*, June 11, 1979). But although cultural ties remained important, the homeland governments' political hold on the immigrants was loosening. And whereas immigrant workers played a key role in the strikes that occasionally hit local factories and in elections to the *conseils de Prud'hommes*, overall their class militancy had dropped as much as that of their French colleagues (*VN*, March 21, 1981, and Dec. 14, 1982; Hilaire 1984, pp. 322–323).

As for confrontational forms of participation, first-generation immigrants in Roubaix had never shown much of a propensity for them. They enjoyed more freedom of political maneuver than their mobilized counterparts in La Courneuve and received greater support from local institutional actors. Conflicts were rare. The SONACOTRA hostel in Roubaix, for instance, did not join in the strike movement that affected others across France from 1975 until the early 1980s.[39]

Even so, racism and discrimination were issues that preoccupied the immigrant communities well before they made it onto the CEM agenda. In a series of antiracism demonstrations in the late 1970s, immigrants marched through the streets and delivered petitions to city hall. The CEM quickly incorporated their complaints into its mandate, and the "out-of-channel" protests faded.[40]

Certain elements of the foreign population nevertheless remained outside the ambit of the CEM and local solidarity groups. Most notable among the "outsiders" were fundamentalist Muslims. Because the CEM was organized along ethnic lines, multiethnic Islamic associations encountered difficulties in presenting their demands and convincing the municipality to act on them. The international pietist movement Faith and Practice had established a mosque in Roubaix in the mid-1970s. After almost a decade of working with the blessing and aid of the bishop of Lille, Algerian consular authorities inaugurated a mosque next door in Lille in 1980 for the "Muslim community of the Nord." Neither religious project caused undue concern to Roubaix officials (*Le Monde*, June 22–23, 1980; Kepel 1987, pp. 118, 296–297).

But in May 1980 an Islamic and Arabic Language Association, comprised largely of former *harkis* highly critical of the Algiers regime, tried to purchase an abandoned textile factory building to convert into a mosque. The municipality rebuffed the attempt, even though it had itself refused to buy the structure. Its good relations with Algerian officials and the AAE seemed to motivate the action. The Islamic association's leaders, three imams, accused the municipality of racism. They initiated court proceedings under the 1972 antiracism law against the municipality and CEM president Marc Vandewynckèle. Meanwhile, 200 of the association's supporters occupied the building in question, refusing to leave until ownership had been transferred to their organization. Authorities refused to make any concessions, charging that no religious sect merited special treatment in France (*NE*, May 18–19 and 20, 1980).

Local officials bore little blame for igniting the protest. Divisions within the region's Muslim community were at the root of the dispute. The occupation continued until the risk of a prolonged conflict, negative local reaction, and bad publicity nationwide apparently forced the municipality's hand. It finally agreed to help the rebel organization find a "suitable" location for a Koranic school and mosque (*NE*, Jan. 6, 1981).

The hot issue cooled over time. The CEM quickly took up Muslim concerns and offered the *harkis* (or "French Muslims," as some in this proud community preferred to be called) a seat on the body (which they refused).[41] In 1982 they formed their own sectarian political party, the Algerian People's Party, but it failed to win a large following. Over the next few years the rapprochement between the *harkis* and the mosque of Paris, firmly in the Algerian government's control by the early 1980s, could be felt in Roubaix. In the face of a common, often harsh experience as Muslims in France, the two camps were slowly putting the old divisions behind them (*VN,* April 19–20, 1980, and Nov. 6–7, 1983; Kepel 1987, pp. 311, 327–328).

THE RACIST REACTION

In Roubaix the 1980 mosque incident had marked Islam's painful entrance onto the local political scene. Public opinion polls indicated that it evoked fears of foreign intervention and terrorism among the populace. When economic and social troubles failed to abate in the early 1980s, an anti-immigrant reaction shook local political life to its foundations (*NE,* June 7 and 15–16, 1980).

Drug use and crime rates escalated in tandem with the city's economic troubles. Socialist Mayor Pierre Prouvost hardly exaggerated when he observed that Roubaix suffered from a "fever of fear" and was "sick with crime and delinquency" (*NE,* June 15, 1982). As elsewhere in France, the immigrants came to be seen as the carriers of that malady; local political commentators began to speak of "Roubaix-Medina." Despite real improvements in the immigrant condition after 1981, racist incidents proliferated.

The municipality roundly condemned anti-immigrant violence and organized antiracist exhibits to educate residents. At the same time it limited family reunification to foreign workers who could prove that they had employment in the city proper. It refused to construct hostels for immigrant workers in newly renovated neighborhoods. Only when Roubaisians felt that "a quantitative equilibirum had been attained," Mayor Prouvost argued, could efforts at integration go forward (quoted in *NE,* June 8–9, 1980).

Roubaix's web of solidarity-group activists held firm. By the end of 1980 an Anti-Racism Collective was in place. It oversaw all aspects of the fight against both national legislation perceived as anti-immigrant and racist incidents at the local level. The PS, the PSU, the PCF, trade unions, and religious groups joined together under its auspices in several well-publicized campaigns against racism (*VN,* March 14, 1981).

Anti-immigrant activity had a long history in Roubaix, as the violence and discrimination suffered by earlier immigrants from Belgium, Poland, and Italy testified. Yet there had never been an organized xenophobic movement until 1982, when a local businessman, Marcel Lecluse, formed Roubaix for the Roubaisians (Roubaix aux Roubaisiens—RAR). It claimed to be apolitical, but its positions dovetailed with those of the National Front. The RAR harped on the twin issues that were dear and closely linked to the extreme right across France: insecurity/crime and fear of "Arabs" (all North African and Turkish immigrants). Any and all instances of immigrant involvement in French politics—even in a consultative body like the CEM—aroused its wrath.

The RAR's first test came in the 1983 municipal elections. Its candidates pledged "to resolve the problem of insecurity in two weeks through the massive intervention of the forces of law and order" and to abolish the CEM and all other "threats to French sovereignty" (Marcel Lecluse in *NE*, Feb. 15, 1983; see also *VN*, Dec. 4, 1982). Jean-Marie Le Pen tendered his support, but the RAR declined his offer to campaign in Roubaix.

Political observers had predicted a tally for the Lecluse slate of no more than 3 percent. It received 9.6 percent of the vote and two seats on the Municipal Council. Of Roubaix's forty-five voting precincts, those in the northern and eastern sections, which traditionally supported Socialist and Communist candidates, went heavily for Lecluse. In other sections of the city, a "halo" effect was evident: Lecluse did poorly in precincts with many North Africans and Southern Europeans but well in adjoining precincts. Somewhat lower tallies came in the wealthier residential areas of south- and west-central Roubaix, where relatively few immigrants lived (*VN*, March 7, 1983; Etchebarne 1983).[42]

It was in the affluent neighborhoods that the center-right coalition headed by André Diligent, a national leader of the Christian Democrats (Centre des Démocrates Chrétiens), was strongest (see Table 14). The victory secured by his slate ended seventy-one years of uninterrrupted left-wing dominance. The new mayor had profited electorally from the RAR vote. He had a history of Catholic social activism, however, and his administration represented an amalgam of centrist politics and Catholic charity. Politicians from the classic right and the Catholic center sat on his cabinet (*NE*, Sept. 21, 1984).

Diligent's position on immigration mirrored his political philosophy:

Table 14 Distribution of votes in municipal elections in Roubaix, 1983 and 1989 (%)

Year and district/round	Participation	Candidates and parties		
1983		Diligent (Christian Democrats)	Prouvost (PS)	Lecluse (RAR)
Center	73.3	50.9	33.9	8.4
East	73.5	41.7	40.4	9.6
North	69.0	45.9	35.1	10.3
West	70.7	48.1	34.9	9.2
Total[a]	72.1	50.0	36.4	9.6[b]
1989		Diligent (UDF/RPR)	Carton (Union de la Gauche)	Gendron (FN)
First round	65.1	41.8	33.8	17.6[c]
Second round	—	46.0	36.1	17.9[d]

Sources: VN, March 7, 1983; *Le Monde,* March 14 and 21, 1989.

a. Plus 3.8 percent for far left parties.

b. One councillor elected.

c. RAR (Phelippeau): 4.4 percent.

d. Five councillors elected.

"I believe that all men are my brothers. Now, when my brothers come to visit, I try to make them feel at home. But I don't let them run my household" (quoted in "Qu'attendez-vous de l'Eglise?" 1986, p. 118). With the center-right in power, many of the most activist voluntary associations lost their entrée at city hall and thus much of their usefulness to the immigrants. Subsidies and quite generous technical assistance still flowed, however, to associations that did not violate Roubaix's political norms and traditions (see *NE,* March 16, 1983).

The foreigners' interests still received a public hearing, most often through the CEM. The mayor did not dissolve it, despite pressures from some quarters. He appointed a like-minded local consumer advocate to head the CEM: "To the immigrants the mayor is like a father," she argued; then, mixing her metaphors: "They have yet to cut the umbilical cord and take their own initiatives, political or otherwise."[43]

The CEM came to look more like a "racial buffer": an institution that, like riot commissions in the United States and the Community

Relations Councils in Britain, some have seen as existing merely to neutralize immigration as a contentious political issue and to contain or deflect the immigrants' demands (Katznelson 1973). The CEM's functions were reduced to relaying municipal directives to the immigrant communities and, especially, to organizing the yearly intercultural Friendship Festival. Hoping to attract French and foreign business investments, Roubaix's new mayor promoted the city as a "crossroads of nationalities."[44]

Even cultural celebrations elicited criticism from the extreme right. The administration also had to contend with many Roubaix Socialists, who, now in the opposition, adopted an anticrime, anti-immigrant line of their own. When a Diligent ally on the Municipal Council, Michel Baudry, argued for increasing subsidies to various local immigrant programs and associations, ex-mayor Prouvost quipped: "I fear that someone might well rename you Ben Baudry and loan you a North African mistress" (*VN*, Dec. 21, 1983). Mayor Diligent had earlier upbraided Prouvost for acting like an "ayatollah in exile" (*NE*, March 23, 1983).

The beleaguered mayor responded to fears about immigrants and crime by instituting a Municipal Council for the Prevention of Delinquency in April 1983. Two months later, city hall remained silent when a group of private citizens set up their own municipal security corps. They planned to work in conjunction with local and state police to reduce delinquency and to fight for the rights of crime victims. Although the Knights of Roubaix (Chevaliers de Roubaix) refused to allow North Africans to join, the mayor denied that the partially publicly financed corps constituted a "sort of Roubaisian KKK" (*VN*, June 2, 1983).

THE SECOND GENERATION

Much of this mobilization against crime came in direct response to widespread anxiety over the second generation of immigrants. They faced rates of scholastic and employment failure that seemed high even in a city in which the population at large did not fare well according to those criteria. Together with the indigenous French youngsters with whom they shared many elements of life experience, the second generation embodied all the most troubling developments that the 1980s brought to Roubaix. Some engaged in petty crime and gang activity.

As early as 1973, a full third of public-school students in Roubaix were foreign born; the share was almost half in some neighborhoods. The city offered them employment counseling and, in the early 1980s, held North African, Turkish, and Iberian "cultural weeks" to combat anti-immigrant sentiment in the schools. Although churches and other solidarity groups also worked to improve the educational and employment situation, few young people were active in their youth groups. Organizationally, the multiethnic second generation did not fit either solidarity-group activists' or the municipality's conceptualization of the immigrants as belonging to individual national communities or, consequently, the prevailing CEM format (NE, Feb. 17, 1981; VN, June 15, 1983).

Brought into the political mainstream in certain respects but excluded in others, members of the second generation in Roubaix blended assimilative and confrontational tactics far more extensively than in La Courneuve. They were just as trapped between the cultures of the host society and their parents' homelands. But because they benefited from the tolerance—if not always the total understanding—of local officials and local militants, most of Roubaix's second generation never participated in such violent events as the "Rock against Police" concerts of La Courneuve or the car-stealing rodéos of Lyons (Mulette 1981, p. 814).

Peaceful, heavily symbolic actions, on the other hand, were commonplace. The city was a major stop on the 1983 March for Equality and against Racism, for example. Left-wing solidarity groups, trade unions, and political parties came together in a broadly based coalition to prepare for its arrival. The by-then center-right municipality looked with some trepidation on the march. The publicity that the event had won by the time it reached the Nord compelled Mayor Diligent, in the end, to meet a delegation of marchers in a closed-door session. They took pains to emphasize that they "transcended traditional political cleavages" (Coordination: Immigrés 1983, p. 6).

In the wake of the march, cultural groups thrived, and Beurs and youth of other national backgrounds produced shows on local private radio stations such as Radio Boomerang and Radio Bas Canal. The neighborhoods became loci of associational activity. Each had groups working on job training, cultural expression, and antidiscrimination projects. Some of the youth associations were rooted in a single ethnic or racial background; others were multicultural in the full sense of the word. Generally, a cooperative attitude prevailed in the city, which made unified action possible on issues of major concern (*NE,* June 23, 1981, and March 17, 1982; *VN,* Nov. 22 and 26, 1983; and Dec. 14, 1983).

The exuberance and good humor of so many of the second-generation immigrants' undertakings reassured many Roubaisians who may have seen them before solely as hoodlums.[45] The local press played up the 1983 march and *Beur* culture. Out of admiration for what their children accomplished and out of fear of losing their influence on them, both the official homeland and autonomous immigrant associations began to speak to the new generation's interests and to support their activities ("Radioscopie" 1986).

Convergence '84 almost jeopardized that harmony. One of the five squadrons of the "rollers for equality" that made up Convergence began in Roubaix. Organizers selected it as the northern departure city because of its status as an immigration nerve center: "In Roubaix, coexistence already has a long history and has given rise to an intense cultural and social life. Yet it has also increasingly generated tensions that divide communities and serve as a pretext to justify unequal rights" (*NE,* Oct. 23, 1984).

The "rollers" and their coterie made a lot of noise, but they were small in number. No municipal representatives and only a handful of solidarity-group allies showed up. The event sparked controversy and division within the second-generation movement in Roubaix, as it did nationwide. With the exception of local Communists, French militants considered it politically chancy to take sides (*VN,* Nov. 4–5, 1984).

Another, very different event in 1984 sowed far greater discord. Together with the RAR, the Knights of Roubaix organized a "march against insecurity," a move that put the Diligent administration in a difficult position. The mayor had tried to make the fight against security his own and did not want to look like a "hostage to the sorcerer's apprentices" (*NE,* Sept. 20, 1984).

Less impressed was the National Front. Upset with the apolitical approach of the RAR, which it deemed too mild, the FN soon forged its own presence in Roubaix. It opposed, among other things, the municipality's "anti-French racism" in permitting the construction of mosques and demonstrations by second-generation immigrants.[46] Fear of crime was reaching epidemic proportions, fueling the far right's popularity. In the 1984 elections to the European Parliament, the Le Pen slate won 18.3 percent of all votes cast in Roubaix. A comparable slate had achieved a minuscule 1.4 percent in 1979 (see Table 15). The areas of the city that had strongly supported the RAR in 1983 contributed Le Pen's highest totals (*VN*, March 11, 1985). The left continued to hemorrhage votes, which the extreme right absorbed. The classic right and the center had slipped since the year before, too, and it was clear that some of their supporters had defected to the FN, which increased its share of the vote to just under 20 percent in the 1985 cantonal elections.

VACILLATIONS IN POLICY

Although he was ideologically closer to the national PS than to the mainstream right on the immigration issue, Mayor Diligent could not ignore the rise of the National Front. He gave the green light to the Knights of Roubaix and their surveillance and vigilante law enforcement practices. At one Municipal Council meeting he acknowl-

Table 15 Percentage of votes for Le Pen (FN) in Roubaix, 1974–1989

Year	Election	Le Pen (FN)
1974	Presidential election (first round)	0.8
1979	European election	1.4
1983	Municipal election	9.6[a]
1984	European election	18.3
1985	Cantonal election	19.9
1988	Presidential election (first round)	24.3
1988	Legislative election	19.0
1989	Municipal election (first round)	17.6
1989	Municipal election (second round)	17.9[b]
1989	European election	19.3

Sources: NE, May 7, 1974; June 15 and 22, 1981; June 19, 1984; *VN*, May 20, 1974; April 27 and May 11, 1981; March 7, 1983; June 12, 1984; March 11, 1985; *Le Monde*, May 10, 1988; March 14 and June 20, 1989; and *Libération*, June 13, 1988.

Note: All percentages are based on total votes cast. Votes unaccounted for represent invalid or blank ballots.

a. Liste Lecluse (RAR): two councillors elected.

b. Five FN councillors elected.

edged the obvious: "Immigration is our biggest problem for the rest of the century" (*VN*, Nov. 17, 1984).

The combination of a surging far right and a cowed local administration constricted the immigrants' political options and robbed them of effectiveness. But the churches, the PSU, and progressive elements in the PS proved to be resilient allies. They met with the governing coalition on several occasions to attempt to revitalize the CEM. That body, however, retreated further into quiet, folkloric activity. The city government gained national attention when it appointed an ombudswoman to help residents of the Alma-Gare neighborhood—both immigrants and natives—resolve difficulties with the municipal bureaucracy, housing and school authorities, and the police. Few new projects emerged to enhance the immigrants' political voice ("L'écrivain public" 1989).

Sometimes they needed no official encouragement. In an independent initiative unique in France, the representatives of the communities then active on the CEM—Algerians, Belgians, Italians, Laotians, Poles, Portuguese, Senegalese, Mauritanians, Moroccans, Spaniards, and *Camerounais*—issued a statement decrying the rise in delinquency and other crime in the city: "We abhor the confusion made between honest people—the majority of the immigrants—and a few easily identifiable troublemakers. We affirm our hope to continue fruitful dialogue so as to build together a better future" (*NE*, Oct. 7–8, 1984). The immigrant associations' joint declaration generated intense interest. Institutional political actions normally drew little attention except from the far right. But they gained moral force when they were couched in terms that recalled the ideals of the French Revolution and the Declaration of the Rights of Man.

Second-generation political mobilization, in the interim, had flourished, spurred by the far right's electoral gains. A significant segment of Roubaix's second-generation immigrants were participating in a new social movement that invested in a "double-barreled" strategy: symbolic, often noninstitutional forms of participation mixed with more assimilative ones. The CEM had narrowed as a channel of political access, and the majority of the newly anti-immigrant local Socialist Party had been lost as an ally. These two developments produced a broad-gauged, creative response from the second generation. A branch of SOS-Racisme formed in Roubaix in late 1984, but the unreceptivity of the local PS hurt it.[47] France-Plus had far more success, developing a

Collective for Civic Rights to launch voter-registration drives, hold debates, and put together educational projects. In collaboration with several youth associations and the PSU, the Collective added more than 400 names to the voting lists from 1984 through 1988.[48] Multiethnic cultural groups like Action-Research-Culture aroused interest as well (*NE*, Dec. 13, 1985; "Les 'Craignos' " 1990).

More-partisan political groupings existed as well. The Mirror Association (Association Miroir) engaged in cultural and political expression. In 1986 it formed France's first regional alliance of youth associations with the very similar Association Texture in Lille. They published their own newsletter and distributed symbolic French "Citizen's Cards" to first- and second-generation immigrants to protest the proposed Chalandon nationality reform. In 1987 Texture/Miroir organized a March for a Multicolor Region in Roubaix that attracted 5,000 people and its fair share of media and governmental attention (*CAIF Infos*, May 1987, p. 3).

Texture and Miroir were the first youth associations to join the multiethnic, left-leaning Council of Immigrant Associations in France (CAIF). When the Parisian CAIF created Mémoire Fertile in 1987, Miroir and Texture—along with the Femmes Maghrébines de Roubaix—ensured that the Roubaix area would be well represented among the twenty founding associations. This involvement did not prevent them from hesitating to share the CAIF's close identification with French working-class and Communist interests (Perotti 1988, p. 1).

Normally, each of the second-generation associations active in Roubaix pursued its own program. Nevertheless, they united to insist that the city government disband the Knights of Roubaix. They also reacted with one voice to outbreaks of racist graffiti and violence and to especially outrageous pronouncements from the National Front. Educational issues concerned the second generation directly, and the 1986 student protests witnessed a coordinated, enthusiastic movement in Roubaix.[49]

The diversity and complementarity of second-generation organizations and strategies found an echo in the ways in which the children of Roubaix's numerous *harkis* mobilized politically. Sharing their parents' initial refusal to identify with "true" immigrants were activists in the Association of Young Muslims (Association de Jeunes Musulmans). In contrast, the French Muslim Party (Parti des Français-Musulmans), formed in 1983, worked to unite all young French citizens of North

African descent into a potent political force. Its sympathizers rejected the *Beur* label and took to calling themselves *"calos"* (*VN*, Nov. 10 and 11, 1983; *Le Monde*, Nov. 13, 1986). Finally, in parallel to those two groups, other young *harkis* joined enthusiastically in the marches, voter-registration drives, and cultural events that defended the rights of the entire second immigrant generation.

Relations between the various *harki* currents were initially rather tense. Their parents were moving closer to the Algerian community, however, and the far right was taking aim at all Muslims. Second-generation *harkis* of all political persuasions learned to cooperate with one another and with the immigrant communities. Once again, the local political opportunity structure had helped produce a particular array of participatory forms and actors. Then, the ferocity of the anti-immigrant reaction, combined with the effects of national and munici-pal policies in response, induced their consolidation.

Electorally, the second generation was developing into a potent force in Roubaix. *Beurs* and *calos* who voted there gave overwhelming sup-port to François Mitterrand during his campaign for reelection in 1988. Their participation provided a much-needed albeit outmatched coun-terweight to the National Front (*Libération*, June 13, 1988). By 1988 it was enjoying support from between one-fifth and one-quarter of Rou-baix voters (24.3 percent in the presidential contest, 19 percent in the legislative elections). The next year the Front received 17.6 percent in the first round of the municipal elections; its 17.9 percent share in the second round won it five of the fifty-five seats on the Municipal Coun-cil. That June its percentage climbed to 19.3 in the European elections (*Le Monde*, May 10, 1988; March 14 and 21, and June 20, 1989).

In the meantime Mayor Diligent was gaining a national reputation as a public official not afraid to tackle the difficult issues of immigration, crime, and urban decay. Pressed from the left and the right by anti-immigrant rhetoric, he had decided that only one option remained open to him: to integrate successfully the city's immigrant communi-ties. He dedicated his administration to that task and appointed a special advisor on integration to his cabinet. Encouraging dialogue with all local (multi)ethnic communities was a central focus of his efforts. His dealings with Muslims eventually won him unheard-of public praise from the rector of the Paris mosque, Cheikh Abbas. A mainstream French right hungry for a way to fight off the National Front also took notice. In 1987 Diligent became the president of the National

Commission for the Social Development of the Neighborhoods, the government-appointed body in charge of suburban rehabilitation (*Le Monde*, Oct. 16, 1990; Kepel 1987, pp. 327–352).

Irrespective of the National Front's gains, Diligent's Union of the Right slate did well in the 1989 municipal elections, capturing 41.8 percent of the first-round vote and 46 percent of the second. It was even more noteworthy in that the mayor had included Salem Kacet, a *Beur* cardiologist, high enough on his slate to win a seat on the municipal council. After the election Kacet became the mayor's adjunct on health matters (*Le Monde*, March 14, 21, and 25, 1989). Not long afterward Mayor Diligent himself became one of the nine "Wise Men" whom Prime Minister Rocard named to the High Council for the Integration of Immigrants in December 1989. As co-president of the National Council of Cities, he played an instrumental role in developing the national policy response to the brewing crisis in France's industrial suburbs (Farine 1991).

Important as they were, the mayor's achievements did not noticeably alleviate the country's or the city's troubles. Many Roubaix neighborhoods festered. The Knights of Roubaix were still active. The widespread hostility directed toward local Muslims during the Persian Gulf War in early 1991 attested to the acute social tensions in the city (*Le Monde*, March 14, 1991; *Le Figaro*, Jan. 25, 1991).

Summary: The Force of Institutional Channeling

By the 1990s both Roubaix and La Courneuve embodied the worst of the ills that plagued urban France in general. Three neighborhoods in Roubaix and "The 4,000" in La Courneuve figured on the list of sixty "neighborhoods in greatest difficulty" that the government targeted in September 1990 for special financial credits and thoroughgoing assistance in integrating immigrants and "disadvantaged people" (*Le Monde*, Sept. 21, 1990; *Libération*, Oct. 10, 1990).

Both La Courneuve and Roubaix thus faced a similar policy standoff in the early 1990s. As they settled more or less permanently, the immigrant-origin populace in each city produced dynamic political actors. The second generation in both fitted into the multifaceted social movement developing across France, as the continuing civic incorporation of immigrant-origin youth combined with dismal socioeconomic opportunities. The presence and political mobilization of both immigrant generations aroused a right-wing reaction that stymied local governmental efforts to manage social conflict in blighted neighborhoods.

Within the general limits imposed by the French political system, however, institutions in La Courneuve and Roubaix linked immigrants to the local political system differently. Local officials, political parties, trade unions, and solidarity groups did not respond in the same manner to their political participation. As a result the immigrants organized distinctly in each city although they belonged to the same lower levels of the working class. Even the local branches of national-level immigrant associations based on a common ethnic identity did not behave politically in the same ways in the two cities.

Communist political domination in La Courneuve translated into a distinct advantage for immigrant political mobilization that tallied with the PCF's agenda or at least lent itself to co-optation by the party. In Roubaix a wider range of ethnic-based, class-based, and homeland-oriented immigrant groups found acceptance and support from a more diverse and tolerant governing coalition and a tight nexus of local solidarity groups and labor organizations. When the center-right overthrew the leftist stronghold in 1983, that network of leftist militants compensated to a degree for the constriction of participatory channels that the new municipal government induced. These institutional factors, more than common class or ethnic ones, continued to determine the forms and levels of immigrant participation and how elites and other political actors responded to it.

4

Switzerland
before 1974

Given the centralized nature of the French state, it is surprising to what extent local-level institutional variation has influenced the participatory channeling processes and thus the evolution of immigrant politics in La Courneuve and Roubaix. In Switzerland, by contrast, local particularities are a matter of course. Few countries in Europe, in fact, are as different from France as Switzerland. It has been an exercise in extreme federalism since a group of Germanic peasant forest communities entered into a defensive alliance in 1291. Subfederal units of government preceded the federal structure, and the cantons have been at least as diverse and strong-willed as American states. Localism, called *Kantönligeist* (cantonal spirit), has dominated political life from the start. Swiss cantons have had their own constitutions and have enjoyed considerable legal autonomy.

The federal Swiss state emerged in its present form in 1848, with the victory of the modernizing Protestant cantons over the traditionalist Catholic ones in the relatively bloodless *Sonderbund* (Separatist Confederation) civil war. Twenty-six cantons and half-cantons have since stood bound together in a confederal arrangement that balances overlapping and crosscutting ethnic, religious, and geographic cleavages. Whether predominantly French-, German-, Italian-, or Romansh-speaking, most cantons are officially monolingual, and one religion usually predominates in each: "Swiss culture functions as an accumulation of monologues," Blaise Lempen has argued. "Diverse European cultures have not so much come together in Switzerland as they have coexisted by turning their backs to each other" (1985, p. 154). The institutional linkages between cantonal and federal levels of power, normally found in federal systems to secure national political integration, have been noticeably lacking.[1]

Holding this hodgepodge together as a federation has been a set of complicated institutional arrangements. The legislature, the Federal Assembly, consists of two bodies: the National Council, which is elected by universal suffrage on the basis of proportional representation and distributes its 200 seats in accordance with the population of each canton; and the Council of States, which is elected on a majoritarian system and grants each canton 2 seats (1 for each half-canton). Executive power rests with seven federal councillors, each of whom directs a government ministry. The Federal Assembly elects them (usually from among their number) for a renewable four-year term. Balanced politically, religiously, and linguistically, the Federal Council acts on a consensual basis; each member subordinates his or her opinion to the collective will of the government. Personal rule is so disliked that federal councillors have rotated annually in the roles of president and vice-president—two strictly ceremonial offices, in any event (Lijphart 1984, pp. 23–24).

Immigration before World War II

Predictably, Swiss political institutions have coped differently from French ones with the new ethnic diversity created by the immigrants, and they have directed immigrant political mobilization in different directions. Since World War II Swiss governments and institutions have worked even more earnestly than their French counterparts to keep foreigners out of host-society politics and divided along ethnic lines.

Until the 1930s, however, immigrant politics in Switzerland largely resembled that in France. By the second half of the nineteenth century, Switzerland had changed from a country of emigration to one of large-scale immigration.[2] The liberal constitution of 1848 won the nation a reputation as a haven for refugees from repression and violence elsewhere on the continent.[3] Determining the inflow and length of stay of foreign workers fell to the federation, which by 1914 had entered into twenty bilateral international treaties. Conditions for entry were extremely lenient for both categories of foreigners, and their numbers grew rapidly: on the eve of World War I they accounted for 15.5 percent of the total resident population (17.3 percent if seasonal workers are included). Some refugees settled in Switzerland, but the majority of foreign workers spent only a few years in the country before returning to their usually nearby homelands (Schlaepfer 1969; Holmes 1988).

Thus Switzerland's foreign workers initially concerned themselves almost exclusively with the governments of their native countries. Even as they retained that homeland focus, however, they eventually developed forms of participation that targeted Swiss society and policies. Immigrant laborers, mostly Germans and Italians, played a crucial role in founding the major trade union federation, the Swiss Syndicalist Union (Union Syndicale Suisse/Schweizerischer Gewerkschaftsbund—USS/SGB), in 1881 and the autonomous Swiss Socialist Party (Parti Socialiste Suisse/Sozialistische Partei der Schweiz—PSS/SPS) seven years later (Castelnuovo-Frigessi 1978, pp. 10, 69–70).

The Swiss federal constitution does not explicitly recognize political parties, and religious and cultural divisions have made them loose federations of often highly independent cantonal parties. Some parties have existed in only one or two cantons. The policy positions of the Swiss Socialist Party, with a nationwide presence, have diverged widely at the cantonal level. The PSS/SPS has never aggregated or articulated the interests of the Swiss working class in any real sense (Sigg 1985, pp. 47–52).

Trade unions, on the other hand, have been an important social partner, since the constitution expressly requires the government to consult labor organizations when formulating and implementing policy. Still, Switzerland's industrialization was a very decentralized process; regional particularities caused an uneven development of the workers' movement across the country. Trade unions, correspondingly, took on a decentralized cast, and weak national labor federations have resulted. Besides the dominant USS/SGB there are the Federation of Swiss Christian Unions (Confédération des Syndicats Chrétiens de la Suisse/ Christlicher Gewerkschaftsbund der Schweiz—CSC/CGB), allied with the Christian Democrats, and several other smaller unions.[4]

Solidarity with immigrant workers did not come easily. From 1896 until World War I, working-class riots broke out in Zurich and other industrial centers to protest employers' use of foreign labor to break strikes and reduce wages.[5] In the immediate aftermath of the war and the Russian Revolution, however, immigrants played a leading role as worker agitation reached its highest levels ever in Switzerland. The

General Strike of 1918 shattered social tranquility and broke with the prevailing pattern of peaceful and consensual conflict resolution. Terrified Swiss business and political leaders tended to make a causal link between the strike and the presence and participation of foreigners: "Foreign elements infiltrated the cities, especially German deserters and Communist agents . . . Political fanatics wanted to institute the 'Dictatorship of the Proletariat,' using the model of Russia" (quoted in Halter 1972, p. 152). Officials deported many immigrant workers active in the labor movement.

The unrest convinced Swiss officialdom that a more extensive federal role in immigration matters was imperative. A heated campaign against foreign "infiltration" led to constitutional changes in 1925. Then, in 1931, the legislature enacted the Federal Law of Abode and Settlement of Foreigners (Bundesgesetz über Aufenthalt und Niederlassung für Ausländer—ANAG), which remains in force with only minor modifications today. It stipulated that authorities would take into consideration the nation's cultural and economic interests, the situation of the labor market, and popular sentiment against *Überfremdung* (overforeignization) when determining the desired level of immigration (Hofstetter and Moor 1982, p. 29).

The ANAG confirmed that Switzerland would view its immigrants in a strictly economic light. It established a three-tiered categorization of foreigners: those with a permanent residency permit, those with a permit of abode, and those with a seasonal permit. No foreigner had any express right to any of these permits, whose issuance was completely at the discretion of Swiss officials. Unlike its French equivalent, the permit of abode was to incorporate permission both to reside and to work. In reality the ANAG contained only rules of procedure, and great discretionary powers thus accrued to the specially constituted Foreigners' Police.[6] Through this permit system and the institution of varying provisions for the entry and treatment of immigrants of different nationalities, the Swiss government created a highly differentiated hierarchy of foreigners (Castelnuovo-Frigessi 1978, pp. 20–21; see also Hoffmann-Nowotny and Hondrich 1982, p. 578).

In the 1930s economic crisis and the spread of fascism to the north and south of Switzerland caused great trepidation among the populace and public officials.[7] The Swiss labor movement consequently softened its demands on employers and the state. In a spirit of solidarity against the external threats, the largest of the federations in the USS/SGB, the

Metal- and Clockworkers' Union (Fédération des Travailleurs de la Métallurgie et de l'Horlogerie/Schweizerischer Metall- und Uhren-arbeitnehmerverband—FTMH/SMUV), signed a "labor peace" agreement with factory owners in 1937. In it trade unionists agreed to renounce use of the labor strike; employers, the lockout. The pact's major institutional instrument was collective bargaining at regular intervals, complemented by constant consultation on social problems. Similar accords quickly spread to other industrial sectors. As a result the strike wave of 1918 proved to be a rather isolated instance of labor activism in Switzerland.

Immigration after World War II

THE "ROTATION MODEL"

After World War II authorities attached several ordinances and regulations to the 1931 ANAG. These modifications enforced—more sharply than in France—divisions in the foreign population according to nationality and the type of permit held. Like West Germany but unlike France, Switzerland in the postwar period aimed explicitly at a "rotation model" of immigration: immigration was to involve only short-term stays in the host society, after which foreign workers would return to their homelands to impart their newly acquired industrial skills; new foreigners would replace them. As "cushions for the economy" *(Konjunkturpuffer)*, foreign workers would be breathed in and out of Switzerland in accordance with cycles of economic growth and stagnation. The special statute for seasonal workers, who suffered an exceptionally precarious and demeaning existence, served this function well.[8] For decades the government struggled mightily to present all importation of foreign labor in purely economic terms. Authorities studiously avoided even the term *immigration* (Hoffmann-Nowotny 1973).

The foreign workers were to remain on the margins of Swiss public life. According to Article 10 of the ANAG, a foreigner faced deportation if he or she committed a crime or troubled the undefined "public order of the country that offers him its hospitality" (Nicod 1983, p. 112). A 1948 federal ordinance stipulated that only foreigners possessing a permanent residency permit could express publicly their political opinions, and even then they were not to "mix themselves in internal Swiss affairs" (Arta 1983, p. 83; Thürer 1990, p. 30).

In contrast with France, the civic incorporation of noncitizens in

Switzerland has never been a favored means of resolving the "foreigner problem." Citizenship and the institutions structured around it—a citizen army, assembly democracy at the cantonal and local levels, and so on—have performed the functions that representative political parties have elsewhere. Citizenship flows from the communal to the cantonal and federal levels, with long local residency requirements (normally twice as long as in France) and fees of up to the equivalent of $50,000 for naturalization (the process being free in France for those with low incomes) (Etienne 1989, annexe III). In the end, this long "filtering" process hinges on the community's decision whether the applicant is of suitable moral timbre and has been "sufficiently Swissified." Rolf Lyssy's film *Schweizermacher* has shown just how difficult and humiliating the naturalization process can be (see also Hoffmann-Nowotny 1985, p. 222; Barber 1988).

Only through the destruction of their own cultural identity and specificity, then, have the immigrants been able to join Swiss society fully. As might be expected, such a procedure has not encouraged numerous applications for naturalization: barely over 1 percent of the immigrant population has attempted to attain Swiss citizenship in any given year since World War II.[9] That rate was far lower than the comparable French one—almost 3.5 percent on average—and contributed to the nation's higher ratio of foreign citizens to total resident population (Lempen 1985, p. 79).

Switzerland is alone among European nations in having a nationality law based solely on *jus sanguinis;* it accords no advantages or privileges in conferring Swiss citizenship on second- or even third-generation immigrants (Thürer 1990; Brubaker 1992, chap. 1). It has not been uncommon to find three and four generations of foreigners born in Switzerland retaining the nationality of their "homeland." This condition has severely reduced the basis for the kind of autonomous, collective organizing in which France's second-generation immigrants have engaged (Brühwiler-Ewig 1970).

Postwar Swiss governments, in general, seriously neglected the infrastructural investments necessitated by the large immigrant presence. The growing numbers of foreigners overburdened hospitals and schools that had been geared toward servicing the stable native Swiss population. Switzerland's economic wealth and the absence of wartime destruction made it unnecessary to undertake large public housing projects after 1945. No urban or suburban slums formed in Switzerland;

the *bidonvilles* of France, which incubated group organization among the immigrants, had few Swiss counterparts.

The market for apartments tightened severely after the war, however, especially in the nation's largest urban areas. Formal and informal discrimination added to immigrants' difficulties in finding an adequate place to live. On the whole, the immigrants enjoyed better, less segregated housing and living conditions than their counterparts in France; but Switzerland's foreign workers lived in far poorer conditions overall than the native population. Every major Swiss city had shabby neighborhoods and HLM complexes with heavy immigrant concentrations near their industrial zones: "Too clean and orderly to allow *bidonvilles* to develop, Switzerland has really only kept up a good appearance. The reality of the *bidonvilles* is hidden in the HLM of Zurich's suburbs, in the makeshift *cités* on the outskirts of Basel, in the ancient buildings doomed to demolition west of Lausanne. It is there that the last colonies of cockroaches have taken refuge, where the electricity has been cut, where the landlord refuses to fix the shower until the rent has been paid" (Rebeaud 1978, p. 15).[10]

The ideology of the welfare state, moreover, never took hold in Switzerland. Health insurance and—until 1977—unemployment insurance remained voluntary. Private savings have always played a central role in social-welfare programs, and public spending for them has been minimal. Severe, intentional discrimination has attended the immigrants' inclusion in what programs do exist. Foreigners' rights and protections in this regard have tended to grow with the length of time spent in the country. The modesty of the Swiss social-welfare response to the immigrants has had the important effect of encouraging sending-country governments to set up far more extensive networks of official and fraternal homeland organizations than in France in order to provide for their nationals' material needs ("Considérations" 1977; Tschudi 1978; and Segalman 1986).

Pressed by employers anxious to take advantage of Switzerland's favorable market position immediately after the war, the government concluded a labor-recruitment agreement with Italy in 1948. Competition for unskilled workers from other Western European labor importers soon caused Swiss employers to search for more distant sources. Agreements followed with Spain in 1961, and later with Turkey, Yugoslavia, and Portugal. These accords specified the homeland governments' responsibilities for their nationals (de Rham 1985, pp. 6–7).

Homeland-oriented participation never lost its salience to foreigners in Switzerland to the same degree as in France. The dense organizational network of the sending-country governments in Switzerland, along with the Swiss institutional "nonresponse" and the draconian naturalization process, helped sustain immigrants' interest in homeland politics. The Italian, Spanish, and—somewhat later—Portuguese Catholic Missions received financial support from homeland religious entities and from the "ecclesiastical tax" levied on all Swiss residents professing a religion. The strength of these organizations limited the reach of the left-wing Catholic social action movement, which found nowhere near the echo that it did on the other side of the Jura Mountains (Castelnuovo-Frigessi 1978, pp. 280–281).

Immigrants could not engage in activities that threatened foreign governments or compromised the confederation's foreign relations, and they could not vote in homeland elections at consulates or elsewhere on Swiss territory.[11] But the Swiss government provided them with free rail transportation to the nation's frontiers to allow them to vote back home. This assistance was in keeping with the government's express intention to maintain foreigners' identification with "their" cultures (Girod 1975).

POLITICAL MOBILIZATION

Such efforts, part of Swiss authorities' campaign to implement a rotation model, largely explain why immigration into that delicately balanced, multiethnic society did not appear to have any social or political fallout for a long time. While seeming to produce less overt social conflict, however, Swiss policy did generate its own tensions. It was about Swiss immigration policy, after all, that Max Frisch uttered his famous aphorism: "We asked for laborers, and human beings came" (quoted in Hoffmann-Nowotny 1985, p. 224). Foreign workers did not "rotate" as effectively as the Swiss would have liked. On average they stayed longer and longer in the country, and the resident foreign population grew.

After World War II the Swiss left responded to the massive influx of foreign workers with customary indifference, if not animosity, demonstrating significantly less consistent solidarity with the immigrants than the French left during the same period. The introduction of the very small social-welfare state apparatus after the war had pacified most Socialists, and the party adopted a mildly social democratic line. In the

1959 election the PSS/SPS won its second seat on the seven-member Federal Council. This yielded the so-called magic formula: the Socialists held two seats on the body, as did each of the two largest center-right, "bourgeois" parties, the Radicals/Free Democrats and the Christian Democrats; their smaller ally, the agrarian Swiss People's Party, had one. Minor fluctuations in the parties' strength notwithstanding, the magic formula has been followed to the present day. With it the Socialists became an integral part of the institutional order and, in the process, cocreators and codefenders of federal immigration policies (*Revue syndicale suisse*, Nov. 1960, p. 314).

The "labor peace" remained in force, as the social partners renewed the accord every five years. The central labor federation, the USS/SGB, held to its reformist, social democratic line. It invited foreign workers to join the ranks of its member unions, yet it made no real efforts to organize them or to fight for their interests. It argued for a reduction in the immigrant presence and the job competition and depressive effects on wage scales that it allegedly represented. Trade union leaders and most Socialist Party officials favored restrictions on new immigration (Heintz and Hoffmann-Nowotny 1970; Calvaruso 1974, p. 80).

Seeing the immigrants exclusively as workers, Swiss officials, like French authorities, accepted immigrant participation in the workplace, determining that it did not constitute an unwarranted intrusion into host-society political life. In the factory, in fact, foreigners stood on equal legal footing with Swiss workers. The modified ANAG did not prohibit noncitizens from joining Swiss political parties or trade unions. Immigrants could vote and run in elections to employee institutions, and there were no restrictions on their participation in trade union activities or their management. Swiss labor law never mentioned any right to strike, but it was regularly granted in practice to Swiss workers and their foreign co-workers both before and after World War II. It was actually the ambivalence toward the immigrants demonstrated by the mainstream Swiss left, with its great stake in the consensual labor peace, that robbed these participatory rights of much of their potential force (CFE/EKA 1976c, pp. 278–279; Wertenschlag 1980, pp. 342–343).

Even so, not everyone on the Swiss left saw the immigrants as a threat. Though belonging to the USS/SGB, the Construction Workers' Union Federation (Fédération des Ouvriers du Bâtiment et du Bois/Gewerkschaft Bau und Holz—FOBB/GBH), most notably, came out very early for the abolition of the seasonal worker statute and demanded full social and political rights for all workers, regardless of nationality. With a high proportion of foreigner members, the FOBB/ GBH tended to take noticeably more progressive and pro-immigrant positions.[12] Additionally, many Southern Europeans were active in the Christian trade union movement (CSC/CGB), which championed their workplace and human rights but discouraged them from engaging in any form of militant, nonconsensual activity.

The small Labor (Communist) Party had no qualms on that score. It, too, demonstrated greater solidarity with the foreign workers than the bulk of the Swiss left. To Swiss Communists the immigrants represented an integral part of the Swiss working class. Their internationalist outlook resembled that of the French Communist Party. But the Labor Party did not sign any agreements with its "brother" parties in the immigrants' homelands. It did not insist on the large-scale membership of foreigners in the Swiss organization; the foreign parties were free to maintain a separate organizational existence.[13]

Communists suffered much harassment in resolutely capitalistic Switzerland up through the 1960s, and authorities deported many foreign activists. Despite the suppression and the generally lukewarm support of the Swiss left for immigrant interests, Italian and Spanish labor unions and political parties—particularly the Communists—encouraged their members to join forces with the indigenous labor movement for their own protection. By the late 1960s, its fears calmed by a relaxed superpower relationship, the Swiss government loosened its control over foreign Communists. The homeland Socialist parties, too, slowly built up a working relationship with the PSS/SPS. In the most prominent instance, the Spanish Socialist General Workers' Union (Unión General de Trabajadores) often stepped in directly to make demands on behalf of resident Spaniards, even as it encouraged its members to join forces with the local labor movement (Vercellino 1971; Parti du Travail 1974, pp. 8–9; Wihtol de Wenden 1978, p. 97).

Furthermore, though certainly not possessing the same political resources as Swiss citizens, the immigrants were not without legal channels of access to Swiss politics outside the factory. In fact those channels were more numerous and significant than in France. In sharp contrast with the pre-1981 situation there, importantly, resident foreigners in Switzerland could form their own associations. They merely had to inform local authorities of their presence and the sources of their funding. Immigrant associations could even make a formal appeal to public officials for procedural or policy reform *(das Vernehmlassungsrecht)*.[14]

Immigrants of all nationalities made early use of available opportunities to organize. They quickly developed their own associational presence in Switzerland. Such activity proceeded along ethnic lines for the most part, responding both to the stratifying effects of Swiss immigration policies and to the presence of homeland government institutions that nurtured ethnic identities.

Italian antifascists had been active in Switzerland since the late 1920s, with Zurich becoming one of the main hotbeds of such activity outside Italy itself. Branches of the so-called Italian Free Colony (Colonia Libera Italiana—CLI) formed in almost every canton to counter the work of official diplomatic and consular authorities tied to Rome. Those associations built on the foundations of the network of mutual assistance organizations that Italian workers, like those of other nationalities, had established during earlier migratory phases. In 1943 representatives of twelve branches of the CLI met to form the Federation of Italian Free Colonies in Switzerland (Federazione delle Colonie Libere Italiane in Svizzera—FCLIS) (Monnier, de Rham, and Martin 1976, pp. 54–55).

A year after the Federazione was founded, the Christian Associations of Italian Workers (Associazioni Cristiane dei Lavoratori Italiani) came into being. The Italian Catholic church, the Christian trade unions, and the Christian Democratic Party provided the driving force behind the ACLI. Though inspired by different political visions, the ACLI and the FCLIS kept up a constant dialogue. As the years passed, they began to cooperate more frequently on matters pertaining to the postwar Italian experience in Switzerland and jointly formulated demands on Swiss and Italian authorities (Wihtol de Wenden 1978, p. 96).

In the late 1950s Spanish immigrants began arriving in Switzerland in large numbers. Under Madrid's aegis they founded cultural centers in the major areas of settlement. In 1968 the more active of those centers in Zurich and Lausanne decided that the community needed a more developed national structure separate from the Francoist embassy and consulates. Modeled directly upon the FCLIS—and, like it, close to the Communist movement in its homeland—the Association of Emigrant Spanish Workers in Switzerland (Asociación de Trabajadores

Emigrantes Españoles en Suiza—ATEES) consisted of a network of local organizations that formulated demands on authorities in both Switzerland and Spain. In the early stages the ATEES—like the FCLIS —geared its efforts much more toward the homeland and presented the expatriate workers as part of the struggle of the Spanish working class (Castelnuovo-Frigessi 1978, pp. 267–293).

More and more, however, the homeland had to compete with the host society for the immigrants' interest and concern. Much of the FCLIS leadership, for example, had returned to Italy after the war, and the organization began to stress immigrant-worker issues to a greater degree than before. FCLIS leaders sat as the representatives of Switzerland's Italian immigrants at the bargaining table during the bilateral discussions that produced new Italo-Swiss accords in the 1960s and 1970s.[15]

Swiss law, in addition, has permitted immigrants to draw up and distribute petitions to officials at any level of government. Noncitizens cannot participate directly in popular consultations, but they can campaign for and against them. Their own petitions are not binding on Swiss officials, but the consensual nature of Swiss policymaking and the fact that such petitions often bear the signatures of sympathetic, enfranchised Swiss citizens have often caused authorities to take them seriously. Both individually and collectively, the FCLIS and the ATEES organized and supported a number of petition drives that drew the attention of governmental officials and sometimes won substantive policy gains (Annoni, Chitvanni, and Richards 1976).

In the late 1960s immigrants increased their political activity. Waves of unrest washed over Switzerland as they did the rest of Europe: universities seethed, farmers expressed their anxieties about the future of agriculture, French-speaking separatists in the Jura region of Canton Bern stepped up their fight to establish their own canton, and the women's movement pushed for suffrage at the cantonal and federal levels.[16] Swiss progressives and foreign workers launched demonstrations against the Franco and Salazar/Caetano regimes in Iberia. Foreigners' living and working conditions in Switzerland also began to attract attention. In 1970 the FCLIS called for a rally against the seasonal worker statute in Bern, and thousands heeded the call (Autorengruppe 1980, p. 231; Deriaz, del Curto, and Maeder 1981).

Shortly thereafter the struggle reached the workplace. Immigrant workers, with no real alternative outlets for their frustrations under the labor peace, launched spontaneous strikes that shook the Swiss system of labor relations to its core. The events began in April 1970 with a three-day work stoppage by Spanish seasonal workers at the Murer construction company in Geneva. A mass demonstration of support, Switzerland's largest since the 1950s, drew more than 5,000 foreign and Swiss workers. It was the first time in the postwar period that the immigrants' class-based mobilization had gone beyond marching in the May Day parade. "For normally staid Geneva," Mark J. Miller observes, "this was an event that bordered on the sensational" (1981, p. 116).

The strikes spread across French- and Italian-speaking Switzerland and to parts of the traditionally less militant German-speaking areas. There were a dozen strikes in 1971 alone, even more in 1972. Often they centered on economic demands such as salary increases, opposition to layoffs, and job security; but wider issues usually came into play as well: housing conditions, opposition to the labor peace and the seasonal worker statute, and human dignity. Some strikes involved only immigrant workers; others brought foreigners and Swiss together in a united effort. Usually, Italian and Spanish workers were the primary foreign participants in these wildcat job actions—as opposed to the situation in France, where less-established and more-threatened immigrants often took the lead ("La grève des pianos" 1974).

Also unlike in France, where the entire left awoke to the immigrants' cause after similar strikes, in Switzerland it was normally only the most progressive elements in the trade unions and on the political left who came to the foreign strikers' defense.[17] Dismayed by the strikes, the mainstream USS/SGB and the Socialist Party aligned themselves with the employers, making maintenance of the imperiled labor peace the paramount issue. Even the normally sympathetic FOBB/GBH local reacted with horror to the first strikes in Geneva: the foreign workers were behaving like "savages"; they simply "were not familiar with Swiss ways" (quoted in Castelnuovo-Frigessi 1978, p. 318; see also Ligue Marxiste Révolutionnaire 1974). In several instances unionists negotiated over the heads of the striking employees and assisted employers in their efforts to play foreign and Swiss workers against each other. The federal and cantonal governments repressed many strikes outright and deported a number of immigrant leaders. Several homeland governments reacted bitterly to such moves and lodged official protests (Miller 1981, p. 77).

THE EARLY 1970S: XENOPHOBIA
AND THE IMMIGRANT RESPONSE

Officials warned protesting workers that their "radicalism" threatened to exacerbate a growing xenophobic reaction. Of course, anti-immigrant feeling was nothing new in Switzerland; the term *Überfremdung* had first come into usage before World War I. By the 1960s, however, the forces of xenophobia were organizing politically. In 1965 the small Democratic Party of Canton Zurich launched a constitutional popular initiative against *Überfremdung*.

Private institutions and interests wield considerable power in Swiss politics, and the role of the central state has been far more restricted than in other European liberal democracies. It is not just that Swiss federalism, consensual policymaking processes, and institutions of direct democracy create "veto points" in the "chain of representation" into which interests can insinuate themselves (Immergut 1991; see also Gourevitch 1980). In fact the gulf that has separated people from the loci of political decisionmaking in the centralized, executive-driven French Fifth Republic disappears in Switzerland. There politics thoroughly permeates society: "In Switzerland it is the people and not the courts who are to be the judge of constitutionality" (Bogdanor 1988, p. 79).

They have done so in part by means of the highly developed Swiss practice of semidirect democracy. Swiss citizens may initiate a vote to introduce or modify a constitutional article *(initiative)*. At least 100,000 (formerly 50,000) people must sign a petition to that effect within an eighteen-month period, after which the legislature may offer up a counterproposal that it finds preferable. The Federal Council determines when to submit the initiative to a popular vote, and its results become part of the federal constitution. A majority of the voters and of the cantons must accept the proposed amendment for it to become law. As a result, very few initiatives have been successful, but a close defeat has usually led the government to take preventive reforms. The initiative has thus acted as a source of dynamism in Swiss politics, a real catalyst. The right of *referendum*, obversely, has given the electorate veto power and has slowed down the political process. It allows the Swiss electorate to accept or reject a law passed by the federal legislature. The legislatures of eight cantons or 50,000 Swiss citizens can call for this form of popular consultation (see Heller 1992).

The Zurich Democratic Party's initiative in the mid-1960s demanded that authorities limit the total number of foreigners with permits of abode and of permanent residency to 10 percent of the total population of Switzerland. The federal government had moved tentatively in that direction as early as 1962 by instituting job-sector quotas. When authorities took measures to restrict the admission of immigrants, supporters of the initiative retracted it. The foreign presence continued to swell, however, and the immigrants' heightened activism was alarming many on the far right. Soon a new, even more extreme initiative emerged. A right-wing federal deputy from Zurich, James Schwarzenbach, had left the Democratic Party to join the National Action against Overforeignization of the People and the Homeland (Action Nationale/Nationale Aktion gegen die Üeberfremdung von Volk und Heimat—NA). The NA had taken form in Winterthur in 1961. Under Schwarzenbach, it organized a drive to limit the foreign population in every canton to 10 percent of the total *Swiss* population there, with the exception of "international" Geneva. The presence of so many foreigners, Schwarzenbach argued, "makes our country dependent on the outside; internally, it . . . diminishes the rights of Swiss citizens and our general welfare" (quoted in *Züri-Lieu,* Feb. 2, 1969).

The initiative would have necessitated an immediate 44 percent reduction in the number of foreigners. Fearing disastrous economic ramifications, the federal and cantonal governments and the *Vorort* harshly criticized the initiative. Save for the NA, all the Swiss political parties, trade unions, churches, and employers' associations rejected it as well. The initiative was defeated at the polls in June 1970, but the margin was narrow: 54 percent against, versus 46 percent in favor.[18]

The near miss rocked the political establishment. The legislature and the Federal Council responded at once by instituting a "global ceiling," which, in conjunction with a spate of ordinances and laws between 1970 and 1974, wound up having the same result as a general immigration stoppage. Only when immigrants had obtained a permit of permanent residency (after an average of ten years in Switzerland) did they gain the right to occupational and geographic mobility.[19] With that permit, a foreign citizen enjoyed the same rights as Swiss citizens except for the rights to vote and to take up certain professions reserved for citizens.

In the early 1970s officials also established a national quota for seasonal workers, who could not bring their spouses or other family members into the country, receive social-welfare benefits of any kind, or even rent an apartment. They had to live in expensive, employer-provided dwellings; the "barracks" *(baraques)* in which they were housed on or near factory grounds often resembled the tawdry shacks of America's migrant farm workers. Immigrant associations, human rights organizations, and churches regularly called for the abolition of the discriminatory seasonal statute, unique in Europe (Calvaruso 1971, p. 46; *Tribune de Genève,* March 28–29, 1981).

The Federal Council took a more constructive step to defuse anti-immigrant sentiment in December 1970, when it established the Federal Consultative Commission for the Foreigners Problem (Commission Fédérale Consultative pour le Problème des Etrangers/Eidgenössische Konsultativkommission für das Ausländerproblem—CFE/EKA). Representatives of the federal government, the cantons, the churches, trade unions, political parties, and employers sat on the new advisory body. The presence of National Action on the CFE/EKA, combined with the absence of the immigrants themselves, indicated that its goal was to reduce political tensions and not to "emancipate" the immigrants or even to represent their interests (Autorengruppe 1980, pp. 235–237).

Such governmental efforts failed to satisfy the NA. The movement had begun to win seats in municipal and cantonal councils scattered across German Switzerland and was spreading to the French-speaking cantons. Earlier in 1970 it had undertaken another initiative campaign to limit the number of foreigners to 550,000 by 1 January 1978. Like the previous initiative, the new petition called for a limit on the number of naturalizations permitted. This drastic proposal split the xenophobic movement. Its most prominent leader, James Schwarzenbach, left to found his own party, the Swiss Republican Movement (Mouvement National d'Action Républicaine/Schweizerische Republikanische Bewegung).[20] In 1973 the NA deposited yet another initiative, one demanding that the federal government submit all international treaties to a popular referendum. It clearly aimed at revoking the revised Italo-Swiss labor recruitment agreement. The initiative thus continued to serve as a ready institutional outlet for the expression of xenophobic sentiment. The plebiscitary element of the

Swiss political system played a vital role in shaping immigration policy (Ebel and Fiala 1983, pp. 24–27).

Shaken by the xenophobic upswing, the immigrant communities shifted their focus away from the homelands and more toward Switzerland. In the most noteworthy instance, autonomous Italian associations joined those with official homeland ties to form the National Committee for Understanding (Comitato Nazionale d'Intesa), an institutional structure through which the community could present a united front to Swiss society and authorities.[21]

Before 1974, in short, the immigrants utilized those ethnic-based associational and class-based institutional channels (trade union and political party membership) that were open to them. When the Swiss left exhibited unwillingness to facilitate their use of such channels, effectively blocking them in many respects, the immigrants began "overflowing" them. Their wildcat strikes and public demonstrations shattered the tranquility of postwar labor and social relations in Switzerland. By the early 1970s these actions had become the immigrants' participatory form of choice. Homeland-oriented participation declined, but it remained far more conspicuous than in France.

At this time, parts of the Swiss labor movement were starting to follow the immigrants' example. Economic troubles were reducing the appeal of traditionally consensual labor relations. Rather gingerly at first, Swiss workers undertook their own actions and eventually added the immigrants' demands to their own. Swiss trade union leaders began to talk of "limiting" the labor peace and employing the strike weapon "when all other attempts at conciliation have failed" (quoted in *Schweizerische Handelszeitung*, May 17, 1973). The renewal of collective conventions was growing more prolonged and contentious than before. At the 1973 May Day celebration, USS/SGB and FOBB/GBH president Ezio Canonica denounced "the insufficiency of our solidarity with workers from other countries. That lack of generosity is fertile ground for temptations to xenophobia and apartheid" ("Extrait du discours" 1973).

The major Swiss labor federation and the Swiss Socialist Party began to make overtures to their underappreciated immigrant constituency. Informal barriers to foreigners' professional advancement and election to positions of authority in the trade union and employee-institution hierarchies fell. The immigrant workers had won greater respect for their efforts, and a basis for further cooperation and consultation had been laid. A trend toward solidarity was evident. The advances were uneven, however, and varied from sector to sector and from locality to locality. Within the left, tensions between the pro-immigrant and xenophobic forces were building.[22]

Earlier than their counterparts in France, Switzerland's immigrants were braving an organized extreme-rightist reaction. National Action went on gathering signatures for its newest anti-immigrant initiatives in the early 1970s. It and the Republican Movement reacted shrilly to the immigrants' political advances, which they saw as a real danger to the Swiss polity. The federal government, caught in the middle, tried to walk a tightrope and worked to stabilize immigration and, less energetically, to integrate the foreigners already resident in the country.

5

Switzerland, 1974–1992

The early manifestation and strength of anti-immigrant movements in Switzerland contrast strikingly with the situation in France, where, despite a far larger population of non-European immigrants, the National Front did not emerge as a political force until the 1980s. But the precocity of Swiss xenophobia, as Hoffmann-Nowotny (1973) observed, had more to do with the particularities of the Swiss political system than with exceptionally virulent anti-immigrant sentiment.

Political negotiations take place at all levels of Swiss society all the time. The availability and widespread use of the initiative and the referendum complete the blurring of the distinction between civil society and the political realm. Weak and fragmented as a political party and hardly a bona fide social movement, National Action and similar groups have nonetheless managed to affect public policy profoundly with the tools of direct democracy. Conversely, the boundary determining the Swiss "in-group" has taken on particular salience, and organized groups of outsiders with political demands can threaten the legitimacy and integrity of the entire system. As noncitizens, immigrants did not break into that charmed circle any more easily after the immigration stoppage in the early 1970s than they had before.

The Swiss experience with postwar immigration, as a result, seemed far more placid and more successful than in France. In the long run, however, the ability of dominant groups to freeze out a minority can leave them unable to cope with a world over which they lack arbitrary control (March and Olsen 1989, p. 47). Diversity is one of the central elements of Swiss identity. But the geographic concentration of

Switzerland's ethnic, linguistic, and religious components—coming together as highly autonomous cantons in a weak federalist system—has permitted each to protect and maintain itself. Immigrant workers are different. Overall, they swell the country's Catholic and Italian population, but they are spread out over the national territory. Thus although Switzerland has largely avoided the "ghetto" phenomenon found in a number of French suburbs, its huge resident immigrant population challenges it to its sociopolitical foundations (K. Müller 1992).

By the mid-1970s immigration had clearly become the pivot of Swiss political discourse. As one left-wing critic remarked, "put crassly, foreign workers have become our 'nigger' problem" (Hubacher 1974, p. 18). For all that, Switzerland never did adopt a true immigration policy. Conditions varied wildly among cantons and even among communities within a single canton. Yet as much as possible, the Swiss left immigration, like most policy areas, to the mechanisms of self-regulation.

Swiss officials refused to alter the "immigrants = workers" equation. At most, they were prepared to see them as a collection of individuals, so many imported potatoes in a sack. The recession of the mid-1970s merely reinforced this perception. The economic turmoil forced many immigrants out of work and thus out of the country once their initial, modest benefits had run out. Seasonal workers had no recourse to assistance at all. From June 1974 to June 1975, overall employment in Switzerland fell by 7 percent, or some 180,000 jobs; yet that drop produced only 10,000 unemployed workers. Domestic and international critics charged Switzerland with "exporting" the problem. Over 300,000 immigrant and seasonal workers left the country between 1974 and the end of 1976 alone. Had they not departed, unemployment would have reached 10 percent (Katzenstein 1984, p. 104).[1]

Switzerland did not have to issue a formal halt in immigration like the French stoppage in 1974: the quantitative limits on seasonal workers, quotas, institutionalized preferences for native Swiss workers over foreigners, and other policies to reduce the foreign presence had had the same outcome. All the same, federal officials were losing their margin of maneuver, for the share of foreign workers holding permits of permanent residency ("C" permits), and thereby enjoying extensive protections against administrative fiat, climbed steadily. Table 16 shows that by the mid-1970s almost two-thirds of immigrants held that coveted permit; and by the early 1980s the proportion climbed to over

Table 16 Percentage of foreign residents in Switzerland by permit of stay, 1960–1991

Year	Permit of abode	Permit of permanent residency ("C")
1960	76.5	23.5
1965	75.1	24.9
1970	62.8	37.2
1975	35.4	64.6
1980	23.4	76.6
1982	23.5	76.5
1986	22.0	78.0
1991	23.7	76.3

Sources: Hoffmann-Nowotny (1985), p. 219; Hammar (1990), pp. 80–81; and *Statistisches Jahrbuch der Schweiz* (1993), p. 75.

three-quarters. The lion's share of immigrants (70–80 percent) were still manual workers, despite the increasingly settled and familial nature of the resident foreign population. Switzerland had acquired the resident proletariat that its form of industrial development had not created (Rossi 1985).

Immigrants showed few signs of becoming collective social actors; certainly, no immigrant social movement developed. "Capitalist states," Jane Jenson reminds us, "have varied across time and place in their contribution to the creation of gender, regional, and ethnic identities" (1985, p. 9). Those states have even determined whether or not any collective identities develop at all.

By the early 1980s in France, the legal status of immigrants of all nationalities was converging. Swiss law and Swiss authorities, in contrast, continued to divide immigrants according to their national origins and their length of stay in the host society. Homeland ties remained strong. For immigrants with "C" permits, officials gradually lifted many restrictions on choice of employment and internal mobility. At the same time, seasonal and commuting "frontier" workers continued to enter (and leave) Switzerland in accordance with the needs of Swiss agriculture and the construction and tourist industries. The constant turnover of that most precarious stratum allowed established immigrants to improve their status. Finding themselves always between a less and a more advantageous legal position, they tended to opt for strategies aimed at individual advancement. Second-generation immigrants, too, opted for mobility over group organizing, and they developed no French-style social movement (Bolzman, Fibbi, and Garcia 1987).

The Enduring Hold of the Homelands

Swiss officials persistently asserted that the foreign workers "regarded their stay as mainly for working purposes, returning home if and when the circumstances made it desirable or necessary" (quoted in Hoffmann-Nowotny and Hondrich 1982, p. 212). After 1974 the Swiss government continued to pressure homeland governments and homeland fraternal associations to assist their nationals. Sympathetic Swiss trade unions and solidarity groups provided some support; but unlike their counterparts in other Western European nations, private "Swiss welfare organizations and even churches remained aloof from any formal involvement with the . . . immigrants" for a long time (Schmitter Heisler 1980, pp. 186–187).

Swiss public-sector involvement was minimal. The modest Swiss social-welfare state was geared toward meeting the limited needs of a generally very affluent, self-sufficient indigenous population, and it made few provisions for a foreign-born proletariat. What aid the Swiss system did provide for noncitizens fell mostly to the cantons, thereby ensuring great variance in coverage across the confederation (CFE/ EKA 1977a; "La politique sociale" 1985).

Foreigners of certain nationalities, moreover, received benefits not available to others. Swiss officials still insisted on meeting their economy's foreign labor needs by means of bilateral agreements with each of the labor-sending countries. Each component of the social-welfare package had to be haggled over in the bilateral talks. Many of the most significant improvements in the immigrants' legal position were owing to homeland-government pressures. Pursuant to talks between Italian and Swiss delegations, for example, the waiting period for Italian immigrants to convert a permit of abode into a permit of permanent residency fell from ten years to five. A similar reduction soon applied to the French and Germans. A boon for the national groups so favored, such changes widened discrepancies in the treatment of different national groups (Nicod 1983, pp. 96–97).

Immigrants could campaign for elections in their homelands, and the Swiss government continued to help them return there to cast their votes. In 1977 the Federal Council affirmed that the activity of Iberian and Italian Communists on Swiss soil did not pose a threat to the nation. Such positions fitted well with the preferred official vision of immigrant workers as foreign nationals only temporarily resident in Switzerland and with no sociopolitical claims on it. Hence immigrants did not loosen their homeland ties even as they gradually developed a deeper interest in host-society politics (Foschi 1977; Willi 1977).

The umbrella Italian National Committee for Understanding (CNI) illustrates well the evolving nature of homeland-directed participation. The CNI sought to articulate the demands of the Italian community in Switzerland to both Italian and Swiss officials. Political and ideological differences sometimes hobbled its efforts, yet more successfully than not it brought together homeland organizations—Italian trade unions, political parties, religious groups, and consular organizations—and several prominent autonomous Italian associations in the host society.[2] The consultative consular bodies that Italian officials had established earlier steadily gained in confidence and influence after 1974. Rome, moreover, was forming regional consultative councils attached to the consulates that gave the emigrants a limited say in the socioeconomic development of their home provinces (Fratini 1979; "Ausländervereinigungen" 1981, pp. 21–22).

Some observers have attributed the high overall level of homeland-directed immigrant political activity in Switzerland to the numerical predominance of Italians, since their government has played an exceptionally dynamic role in representing foreign-worker interests in several Western European host societies (see Miller 1981, pp. 113–115). And indeed—and even more so than in France—Italians in Switzerland had a tight, vigorous homeland organizational network that included the consulates, the church, trade unions, and political parties.

But high levels of homeland-directed participation and collaboration also characterized other national groups. After the arrival of democracy in the mid-1970s, the Spanish government converted consular offices and the "Spanish Houses" established by the Franco regime from instruments of surveillance and control over its nationals into Italian-style organizational clearinghouses for the entire Spanish community. Government-backed Spanish organizations, homeland political parties and trade unions, and the Catholic missions began to mount unified actions to change Swiss policy, and they made overtures to autonomous Spanish associations in the country. Although no overarching, coordinating body resembling the Italian CNI was formed, all Spaniards in Switzerland shared a common lot, and their associations followed the spirit of the Italian example in large measure, harmonizing their actions to an ever-greater degree (Unión General de Trabajadores–Federación Suiza 1977).

Spaniards in Switzerland demonstrated the same concern as in France over transmitting the language and culture of the homeland to their children. Thus Switzerland in 1976 gained its own version of France's Spanish parent-teacher federation. Both consisted of a loose collection of local-level associations already in operation. But whereas the French federation lobbied governments of both the homelands and the host society shortly after 1974, its Swiss counterpart illustrated the greater importance of homeland-directed participation in that host society: it concentrated on authorities in Spain for a longer time and united a more disparate collection of ideologies and political leanings (Schaller 1984).

Smaller and less settled than its French counterpart, the Portuguese community in Switzerland had an even more intense attachment to Portugal. The government in Lisbon created the catchall Council of Portuguese Communities in Switzerland (Conselho da Comunidade Portuguesa em Suíça), a companion organization to France's CCPF, in 1982.[3] Resembling the fraternal homeland organizations of other national groups, the Portuguese organizations active in Switzerland kept their focus on Portugal, while only gradually being drawn into Swiss affairs after 1974 (Tosato 1985).

The same was true of other more recent immigrant groups. For example, Turks—a national community present in both host societies in comparable numbers and for similar lengths of times—exhibited a greater tendency in Switzerland to remain steeped in the politics of the homeland. All the major political currents active in Turkey had their organizational manifestation, from Maoists to the fascist Gray Wolves. The Turkish embassy and consulates set up an extensive web of "Turkish Houses" and other "apolitical, secular" associations in an attempt to control the community. Islamic fundamentalists opposed to

Turkey's official secularism organized slowly but surely (Köppel 1982, p. 5).

In Switzerland, to sum up, the interaction effects created by home-country organizational efforts and the noninvolvement of host-country organizations kept the immigrants there enmeshed in a network of familiar, nationality-specific institutions. This pattern slowly changed after 1974 as the host society took on more importance for an increasingly sedentary foreign population, wedged between the homeland and Switzerland. Immigrants were making more demands on the Swiss political system.

The Decline in Confrontational Participation

By cultivating the immigrants' ties with their countries of origin, Swiss immigration policies accentuated divisions between national groups and categories of foreign workers. Like their French counterparts, the immigrants found at first that without the assistance of Swiss organizations their demands often remained unanswered in the host society. Immigrants were highly vulnerable to the job losses produced by worldwide economic troubles. Upset both at the layoffs and at the failure of Swiss leftists to defend them, foreign workers had launched wildcat labor strikes in the early 1970s.

The movement escalated decisively after the immigration slowdown of the mid-1970s. It affected many areas of the country, but especially those plants and cities in French-speaking Switzerland with more of a tradition of labor agitation: Murer in Geneva (construction—1974), Burger and Jacobi in Biel (pianos—1974), Walo et Bertschinger near Lausanne (construction—1974), and Béton Bau in Geneva (construction—1974). All told, there were half a dozen strikes in 1974, more in 1975. Immigrant workers instigated most of them, and over half involved foreigners exclusively.

In France a strong separation between central decisionmakers and legitimate political actors has incited French leftists to ally themselves with such protesters and to serve as mediators between them and the political system. In Switzerland, however, solidarity has not been a natural response. The superposition of the political and decisionmaking realms has meant that when forces expressing "uncontrollable" social demands emerge, those actors deemed responsible for controlling them get blamed.

In the case of foreign workers, that usually meant the Swiss Socialist Party (PSS/SPS) and, especially, the Swiss Syndicalist Union Federation (USS/SGB). Almost three-quarters of unionized workers (about 500,000 people) belonged to the USS/SGB in the mid-1970s. The Federation of Swiss Christian Unions (CSC/CGB), its closest rival, counted 100,000 members; and a pair of smaller Protestant and right-wing nationalist unions were also present. The USS/SGB was close to the Socialist Party and, like it, was highly decentralized, with cantonal organizations rarely presenting a unified front on divisive issues. Swiss trade unionists were in general agreement only that extrainstitutional forms of participation were less legitimate and less effective than plebiscitary and other institutional means (Castelnuovo-Frigessi 1978, pp. 320–362; Bolzman, Fibbi, and Garcia 1987; compare also Riedo 1976).

The immigrants, however, were obtaining much of what they wanted. Their aggressive strikes yielded some concrete improvements, including more favorable terms in their employment contracts, better housing, greater freedom of mobility, and amnesty for strikers. The confrontational participation also provoked much media and official attention. These results changed the attitudes and policies of segments of the Swiss left. For the first time since the 1930s, some Swiss labor leaders questioned the wisdom and value of the vaunted labor peace. The president of the USS/SGB stated publicly that the Swiss labor federation had misconstrued the labor peace, taking it for a "blank check" (quoted in CFE/EKA 1976c, p. 293).

Starting with the 1976 strikes at the Bulova Watch Company in Neuchâtel and the Matisa Metalworks in Renens, Swiss and immigrant workers began to protest together. A more harmonious relationship between them thus resulted from the foreign workers' unconventional, militant activity. As the decade wore on, many Swiss trade unions further democratized their institutional structures, opening them more completely to nonnative workers. Foreign-worker membership in Swiss trade unions rose markedly. By the early 1980s almost 30 percent of immigrants belonged to a Swiss trade union, nearly as high as the share of autochthonous Swiss workers (35–40 percent) and a significantly higher share than in France.[4]

Swiss employee institutions (company and employees' commissions) were purely advisory and quite weak, involving only about 45 percent of workers. Formal and informal barriers had long barred noncitizens' full participation in them. Restrictive clauses limited the eligibility of certain categories of foreign workers. Those limitations gradually disappeared after 1974, partially under pressure from federal government officials. They had decided that workplace-based participatory outlets were acceptable forums for Swiss-immigrant interaction. The immigrants named to them would "exert a positive influence on their countrymen" (CFE/EKA 1977b, pp. 51–60).

Swiss and immigrant workers participated in sporadic strike activity in factories in French Switzerland, Zurich, and Bern from 1974 to 1979 to protest the restructuring of Swiss industry and the attendant loss of jobs. In most of the strikes, foreign and Swiss workers formed picket lines, occupied factories, and mounted demonstrations side by side. Employers' efforts to split workers of different nationalities and disparate skill classifications encountered more effective resistance than before (Miller 1981, p. 164).

The immigrant workers' militancy also radicalized several other segments of the native Swiss population: a new wave of protest swept through the ranks of the unemployed, Jura separatists, farmers, environmentalists, and renters' organizations. Still, those isolated actions, all rather short-lived and limited in scope, never developed into a sustained strike movement. Social relations in Switzerland appeared positively serene by comparison with those in France, where in any given month in the 1970s there were more strikes than the Swiss experienced during the entire decade.

The Tenacity of Xenophobia

As elements in the mainstream Swiss left began to adopt the demands and tactics of the more established immigrants, the latter found it more fruitful to adopt institutional forms of participation under the aegis of the left. As in France, it was those foreigners in the most precarious legal situation who found it necessary to take to the streets and launch colorful and unorthodox protests. From the late 1970s on, illegal immigrants, refugees, and seasonal workers vociferously protested the policies of the Turkish and Swiss governments (Deriaz, del Curto, and Maeder 1981).

During the same period, however, the labor unrest had aroused business groups, which feared disruption. Their alarm fueled the anti-immigrant initiative campaigns already in progress and gave impetus to new ones. National Action and the Republicans linked strikes and homeland-directed immigrant participation. James Schwarzenbach argued that "Switzerland ought not to become an arena for foreign agitators who from our soil foment revolution in their homelands and ours" (1974, pp. 69–70).

Swiss voters rejected the string of xenophobic initiatives in the 1970s by steadily larger margins. The drastic National Action initiative launched in 1972 (No. 3) won support from only 34 percent of voters in October 1974. That same year two additional "overforeignization" initiatives—one proposed by the Republican movement (No. 4) and one by National Action (No. 5)—took shape. Both suffered sizable defeats in March 1977, receiving support of 29.1 percent and 35.1 percent, respectively. On the same day voters repelled the NA's attack against the 1964 Italo-Swiss bilateral treaty. Throughout the period the NA and the Republicans were losing seats in national and cantonal elections.

Those electoral setbacks notwithstanding, anti-immigrant sentiment remained widespread. In typically Swiss fashion, authorities took into consideration what was a substantial minority position. To control that potential threat and still meet the economy's labor demands, authorities formulated policies that attempted to balance industries' needs with deep fears of *Überfremdung* (Windisch, Jaeggi, and de Rham 1978).

Anti-immigrant sentiment was nothing new among working-class voters, and the xenophobic initiatives of the 1970s drove a larger wedge into the Swiss labor movement. The Swiss Syndicalist Union (USS/SGB), rent by internecine bickering, embraced the Federal Office of Labor's directives to give employment priority to Swiss workers over foreigners. The organizations of the mainstream Swiss left "essentially . . . continue[d] to uphold the overall immigration policy of federal authorities" (Castles and Kosack 1973, p. 147; see also USS 1974). The Socialist Party was part of the federal governing coalition that devised those policies.

Formations further to the left were more critical of the government. The Trotskyist Socialist Workers' Party (Parti Socialiste Ouvrier/Sozialistische Arbeiterpartei—PSO/SAP) and, in German Switzerland, the Progressive Organizations (Progressive Organisationen der Schweiz) rarely garnered more than a small percentage of votes in any election.

But like the PSU in France, the far left often pricked the conscience of mainstream leftists with its criticisms of the policies devised and supported by them and the government (Ebel and Fiala 1983, pp. 127–135). The Labor (Communist) Party, which also stood on the fringes of Swiss political life, declared that the fight against the xenophobic initiatives represented "only the first, albeit important, step in the fight to raise workers' consciousness with respect to their position in capitalist society."[5] Instead of trying to supplant the Communist parties of the immigrants' homelands, like the French Communists, it continued to cooperate with them and thus encouraged their organizing on Swiss territory (*Neue Zürcher Zeitung*, May 13, 1970).

The Communists and the far left had pockets of electoral strength in certain larger cities and heavily industrial regions. They were too weak overall to sway the majority of the Swiss left, which eventually fell into bitter disunity over the immigration issue. The breach within the labor movement widened so far that by the late 1970s, separate May Day parades for each faction threaded through different sections of Switzerland's major industrial centers. One proclaimed solidarity with the immigrants, while the other defended the position of native Swiss workers above all others (Deriaz, del Curto, and Maeder 1981, pp. 79–107).

Then, on November 1, 1980, more than 20,000 Swiss and immigrant workers assembled in front of the Federal Palace in Bern to demand the abolition of the discriminatory seasonal workers' statute. The Construction Workers' Union (FOBB/GBH), which had more foreign members than any other USS/SGB member federation, masterminded that "largest mass demonstration in Swiss history." Several USS/SGB officials spoke at the rally. In the throng were militants and leaders of the FOBB/GBH, the public employees' and textile workers' unions, and several Christian Democratic trade unions. On the other hand, the more reformist branch of the Swiss labor movement, particularly strong in the Metal- and Clockworkers' Union (FTMH/SMUV) in most cantons, was lukewarm toward the 1980 rally (FOBB 1980).

Split in two over immigration, the Swiss labor movement and Socialist Party had reached an impasse that solidified the status quo. Strike activity declined markedly, and the agitation of the mid-1970s came to seem in retrospect a mere blip hardly troubling the placidity of Swiss labor relations. In the end, the Swiss left was overall "too integrated into the Swiss government to resort to disruptive tactics in defense of foreign workers" (Miller 1981, p. 164). Switzerland's trade unions and political parties had never gone as far as France's in their defense of the immigrants. Paralyzed, they were now unable to take any unified actions in favor of their foreign members.

A Wide Range of Institutional Participatory Channels

Switzerland's foreign workers had found that wildcat strikes could sometimes yield important gains, but at the cost of isolating them and provoking a dangerous xenophobic reaction and costly referendum campaigns. Participation through reformist Swiss working-class organizations, on the other hand, soon led to a dead end when the latter divided and stalemated over the immigration issue. And yet immigrants did not turn to collective forms of unconventional behavior as in France.

The multiplicity and diversity of institutional channels available for the expression of their demands—more numerous than in France—was the major reason. The existence of alternative participatory outlets reduced the viability of the type of noninstitutional strategies that social movements often favor, at least at the outset (Bolzman, Fibbi, and Garcia 1987, p. 67).

Notable in this regard were the associational rights that, unrecognized in France from 1939 to 1981, traditionally lay open to foreigners in Switzerland. The Swiss government's hierarchization of immigrants according to nationality and the maintenance of ties with the countries of origin that Swiss and homeland officials cultivated through their policies and nonpolicies contributed to the development of ethnic-based associations among the immigrant communities. After the mid-1970s, immigrant associational activity took on a new dimension: as Hans-Joachim Hoffmann-Nowotny has noted, "the foreigners' associations, which at first organized themselves in a fashion analogous to political organizations in their home countries, [had] come to understand the special features of Switzerland's political system and . . . adapted accordingly" (1985, pp. 232–233).

After 1974, most prominently, the leftist Federation of Italian Free Colonies in Switzerland (FCLIS) labored to unify the various political and ideological strands present in the Italian community. With more than 10,000 members, it was the largest immigrant organization in Switzerland. The FCLIS served as de facto mouthpiece for the homeland-backed National Committee for Understanding (CNI), which united most of the organized Italian community; and it took to articulating the sociopolitical demands of the entire foreign population. The Janus-faced character of the FCLIS' interests held firm: "In Italy we die physically; here in Switzerland, we die socially and politically," one of its tracts proclaimed in the 1970s.[6]

The FCLIS enjoyed great prestige among all the immigrant communities in Switzerland. The kindred Association of Emigrant Spanish Workers in Switzerland (Asociación de Trabajadores Emigrantes Españoles en Suiza—ATEES) likewise began to turn toward the problems of Spaniards in the host society. Easily the most important autonomous Spanish association in the country, its central office outside Geneva and thirty-odd local branches in all areas of significant Spanish concentration represented about the same percentage of its national group (10 percent) as the FCLIS (and the Algerian Amicale in France). Like the FCLIS, it remained close to homeland and host-society Communist movements. The more conservative and culturally oriented associations rejected its political leanings and agenda but often collaborated with it (CFE/EKA 1981a, pp. 27–33).

Even relatively new immigrant communities displayed important traits in organization and in their choice of political strategies that set them apart from their counterparts in France. Switzerland's small Portuguese and Turkish communities, for instance, manifested surprisingly early on the same trend toward organizational streamlining and coordination as the Italians and Spaniards there. The left-wing Portuguese Democratic Association (Association Démocratique Portugaise) in Geneva and the Federation of Turkish Workers' Organizations in Switzerland (Verband Türkischer Arbeiter-Vereine der Schweiz) in Zurich, both founded in the early 1980s, each seemed intent on replicating the central role of the FCLIS and ATEES for its community.[7]

Neither had the reach of those federations. Among the more recent immigrants the political divisions of the homeland retained much of their acuity. The Portuguese and Turkish "umbrella" associations had difficulty forging a working relationship with conservatives and official homeland representatives. All the same, cooperation was slowly building by the mid-1980s in the Portuguese community under the influence of the Lisbon-backed Council of the Portuguese Community in Switzerland, of which the Portuguese Democratic Association was a pillar. A trend in that direction was also evident among the Turks after the exit of the military junta in Ankara in 1983 ("Merhaba" 1985; "Dossier: Les associations" 1987, pp. 6–7).

In general, relations between autonomous immigrant associations

178 · The Policy Challenge of Ethnic Diversity

and the homeland fraternal organizations of all political flavors held firm. Associations were permeable, with many immigrants belonging to more than one. That interconnectedness facilitated coordinated action within each national group. Compelled by Swiss policies to take an active interest in Swiss social and political life, homeland-oriented organizations were accordingly able to relate to associations rooted more deeply in the immigrants' daily experience in Switzerland (Piñero 1982).

Ethnic associations not only articulated the immigrants' demands to Swiss society but also absorbed and rechanneled much of their disappointment with Swiss policies and institutions. Hoping to effect change from within Swiss working-class organizations, left-leaning immigrant associations like the FCLIS and the ATEES urged their members and all foreigners to participate actively in them. In 1976 they formulated an ultimately unsuccessful joint petition with the USS/SGB for a forty-hour work week (Autorengruppe 1980, pp. 230–231). In fact the FCLIS and ATEES had undertaken several joint actions even before the immigration halt of the mid-1970s.[8] Interethnic cooperation became the norm thereafter. The two immigrant associational federations were among the driving forces behind opposition to the "overforeignization" initiatives and formation of the Committee for the Abolition of the Seasonal Workers' Statute (Comité pour l'Abolition du Statut du Saisonnier—CASS) ("Presa di posizione della CLI" 1976; CASS 1979).

By dividing the immigrants according to their national background and nurturing their homeland ties, the Swiss government influenced the nature of this collaboration. When working together, immigrants of various nationalities maintained their ethnic and national integrity. They never became unified, truly multiethnic actors, as occurred in France after 1981 in immigrant women's associations, private radio stations, and the like.

Consultative structures, some of which dated to the 1960s, proliferated in the 1970s. In dealing with any contentious issue, the Swiss have always held great stock in bringing together, in an institutionalized, consultative fashion, all recognized social actors affected. Extensive negotiating on advisory commissions has been the ideal Swiss strategy for working out problems and misunderstandings without open conflict (see Centre Social Protestant 1974). Consultative bodies for the "foreigners problem" offered the immigrants additional institutional channels of political access and at the same time further reinforced the political structuring of the immigrant communities along ethnic lines. Varied in their nature and scope, those bodies designed to deal with immigration operated at the neighborhood, communal, regional, and cantonal level. Some were private; others, publicly sponsored. Their primary function was to reduce social tensions and xenophobic pressures. Not nearly as developed as in Belgium or West Germany, the Swiss network of consultative bodies nonetheless far surpassed that which was slowly developing in France (Olmos 1983, p. 10; "Dossier: Commissions des immigrés" 1984).

A loose umbrella organization, the Community of Contact and Information Centers (Communauté des Centres d'Information et de Contact Suisses-Etrangers/Interessengemeinschaft der Beratungs- und Kontaktstellen Schweizer-Ausländer—IGSA), brought together the heads of the various consultative bodies and official homeland organizations present in Switzerland to discuss common problems, exchange information and skills, and instill Swiss-style consensus-building. The IGSA board of directors acted as a liaison with the Federal Consultative Commission for the Foreigners Problem (CFE/EKA). It kept the lines of communication open and ensured that federal and subfederal developments remained in sync.[9]

A majority of the local and cantonal bodies allowed for direct immigrant representation. The CFE/EKA finally followed suit in 1980, with the seating of five (out of twenty-seven) foreign members. On the CFE/EKA, as on most other commissions, Swiss officials selected the immigrants' delegates, normally on the basis of nationality. Most often, the foreign representatives chosen were not "foreign" to the Swiss political system: they were uniformly respectable, moderate pillars of their respective communities. The xenophobic movements and employers' groups with representation on the CFE/EKA refused to deal face to face with the "Communist" FCLIS or ATEES (CFE/EKA 1976b).

Because the Swiss system relied heavily on such consultative structures and encouraged the venting of all opinions on a subject before final decisions were rendered, the immigrants' involvement could be of some consequence. Consultative participation resulted in some substantive policy gains at the local and national levels. Seeing the foreigners employ institutional means of pressure that the Swiss could understand and appreciate seemed to alleviate the anxiety of many in the general populace to a degree that should not be slighted or underestimated. Crossing the line that separated social action from political involvement, some of the more assertive consultative institutions participated actively in the antixenophobic movement ("Dossier: CFE" 1984).

Since the immigrants could not actually vote against the anti-immigrant referenda or sanction officials electorally in most instances, however, they could not constitute a true pressure group. As separate associations acting jointly in 1979, the FCLIS and the ATEES initiated identical cantonal petitions across the nation, calling for local- and cantonal-level voting rights and eligibility for all immigrants who had spent at least five years in Switzerland and one year in the canton in question. In several cantons Swiss trade unionists, left-wing extremists, and Socialist Party activists worked with the immigrant associations to gather signatures. By 1980 they collected over 100,000 in fifteen cantons. Even though the petitions did not achieve their primary goal in any canton, they did wring several lesser concessions out of federal and cantonal officials. These authorities were used to accommodating or at least pacifying minority views that were sincerely expressed through institutional channels.[10]

As for suffrage, the government argued that it could not be separated from several obligations incumbent upon citizens, most importantly military service. An additional complexity was, of course, the semi-direct nature of Swiss democracy: since citizens, as the "sovereign," regularly decide on the acceptance or rejection of constitutional amendments, voting rights are part and parcel of membership in the political community. Yet the picture was more mixed in the cantons, which were free to determine who could vote at the cantonal and communal levels. The canton of Neuchâtel had allowed foreigners meeting certain residency requirements to take part in communal elections ever since 1849. The new canton of Jura went even further, permitting certain immigrants to vote in cantonal and communal elections and making them eligible to sit on several commissions at both levels (CFE/EKA 1976c and 1982).[11]

The "Togetherness" Initiative and the Proposed ANAG Reform

Far from full members of the host-society polity, Switzerland's *Gastarbeiter* (guest-workers) had discovered at an early date that their use of institutional avenues of participation often depended on the actions of the left-wing Swiss trade unions and political parties that controlled access to them. Swiss churches and progressive voluntary associations (the "solidarity groups") also loomed critical. Their pressure was often instrumental in convincing governments to set up consultative bodies and to open additional political opportunities for immigrants. They, like the rest of the Swiss left, truly woke to their social and political needs only after the foreign-worker militancy of the early 1970s.[12]

Solidarity groups were soon mobilizing in defense of the immigrants' political rights. It was they and not the trade unions or even the immigrants themselves who during this period initiated the most ambitious effort to improve the immigrant condition to date. In 1974 the small Catholic Workers' Movement (Katholische Arbeiterbewegung) in German Switzerland drew up a "Togetherness Initiative" (Initiative Etre Solidaires/Mitenand Initiative). This carefully worded popular initiative would have eliminated the seasonal workers' statute and guaranteed the immigrants freedom of choice in employment, family reunification, equal social security coverage, and the right to renew their permits automatically. Only federal judges acting in cases in which a foreigner had been convicted of a crime would have been able to issue deportation orders. As for political rights, "Togetherness" diplomatically called only for consulting the immigrants on all decisions concerning them (C. Farine 1981; *La Suisse,* March 29, 1981).

The reformist bent of the initiative's proposals gave away its Christian Socialist pedigree. The Catholic Workers' Movement and its counterpart in French Switzerland, Catholic Workers' Action (Action Catholique Ouvrière—ACO), along with the Protestant Social Centers, all preached on behalf of "Togetherness." They were instrumental in the development in the late 1970s of the Togetherness Committee, the nonprofit umbrella organization for local and cantonal groups lobbying for the initiative. In 1980 it organized a meeting of immigrant associational activists in Bern, where for the first time officially some 600 representatives from the Italian, Spanish, Portuguese, Greek, Turkish, and Yugoslavian communities discussed together the problems facing Switzerland's foreign population (Mitenand-Initiative 1980).

The Swiss left split over the initiative, with progressive trade unions like the FOBB/GBH unable to convince the rest of the USS/SGB to support the measure. The USS/SGB recommended neither acceptance nor rejection, allowing each member to make up his or her own mind. The Socialist Party endorsed the initiative but balked at campaigning for its passage.[13]

The mainline Protestant Swiss churches in quite a few cantons eventually backed away from the Togetherness Initiative, too. They buckled under the weight of pressures from the government and from conservatives in their congregations. Many Swiss churches thus divided into pro- and anti-immigrant factions in much the same way as the major trade unions and leftist political parties (Conseil de la Fédération des Eglises Protestantes 1974; ACO 1981).

National Action and the Republican movement accused the immigrants and their "Communist" sympathizers of trying to destabilize Swiss society. What had started as a humanitarian reform, designed to shift the discourse on immigration away from economics and onto human rights, became a very bitter political controversy. Organizers encountered major difficulties gathering the requisite 50,000 signatures to have the initiative come to a vote (Communauté de Travail "Etre solidaires" 1980, p. 3).

Federal authorities opposed the Togetherness Initiative. Hoping to prevent its passage and to blunt the growing force of the xenophobic movement, they decided to update and revise the 1931 general immigration law (ANAG), which continued to guide Swiss policy. Discussions opened in 1974. Immigrant associations participated on an informal consultative basis only.

In 1980 policymakers reached a compromise solution that would have harmonized Swiss law with prevailing international treaties concerning immigrant labor and elaborated the immigrants' legal rights and protection. Legislators did not revoke the seasonal workers' statute. Immigrants would gain greater protection against arbitrary deportation orders, but administrative expulsions could continue. Although the 1948 restriction on foreigners' political discourses would disappear, officials could invoke the nation's internal and external security and the public order—still undefined—to silence or deport them (Département Fédéral de Justice et Police 1976). The Federal Council scheduled the plebiscite on the Togetherness Initiative just before the final parliamentary vote on the ANAG reform, which it marketed as a reasonable counterproposal ("'Etre solidaires'" 1981).

In the April 1981 vote on the Togetherness Initiative, the immigrants and their allies suffered a massive defeat. Some 84 percent of voters and every canton disallowed the proposed constitutional amendment. Turnout was a low 39.5 percent of eligible electors. Federal Councillor Kurt Furgler interpreted the verdict as a "clear and precise mandate in favor of the government's policy of maintaining an equilibrium between the foreign and Swiss populations and its immigration stabilization program" (quoted in *Tribune de Genève,* April 6, 1981).

That June, less than two months after the crushing rejection of the Togetherness Initiative, the Federal Assembly overwhelmingly approved the government's amended version of ANAG. But the legislation had not included enough restrictions on immigration to satisfy the xenophobes. The government, they felt, had subordinated protection of Switzerland's national identity to certain employers' needs. In just three months, National Action mounted a successful referendum campaign to recall the legislation. That is exactly what happened in June 1982, when a close majority of 50.4 percent voted against the reform.[14]

The ringing defeat of the Togetherness Initiative and the narrower but more stunning one of the ANAG reform demoralized a broad spectrum of immigrant political leaders and their Swiss allies. Even a crushed Togetherness Initiative, however, was enough to provoke meaningful improvements in the immigrants' political-legal status; and it generated further support from many solidarity groups. The initiative played a role in the federal government's willingness in 1982 to reduce Italians' residency requirement for a permit of permanent residency from ten years to five. "Goliath" had beaten "David," several immigrant activists acknowledged, but "at least debate had opened over the immigrants' place in Swiss society" (Sanchez 1981).

Swiss militants gradually convinced their disillusioned foreign friends that a sustained, united effort was necessary to foster a climate propitious to the immigrants' integration. The local Togetherness Committees that had formed to champion the initiative transformed themselves into the "Swiss-Immigrant Committees," with a coordinating headquarters maintained in Basel. Instead of dealing with the immigration issue as a specific set of problems, the new committees sought to incorporate them into the program of a united progressive movement (Zuppinger 1981; Congrès Etre Solidaires 1982). In 1982 the movement organized a new multiethnic meeting in Bern: the "Swiss-Immigrant Forum '82." Regrouping after the demise of their initiative, the conference delegates reaffirmed the need to work closely with the Swiss labor movement: "syndical action is in itself the best school for collaboration between the Swiss and the immigrants, men and women, young and old" (Forum '82 Suisses-Immigrés 1982, p. 2). The FCLIS, the ATEES, and the Portuguese Democratic Association soon joined Swiss trade unions in a new petition campaign for a forty-hour work week. Turks, Yugoslavs, and Greeks participated in the effort on an individual basis ("Gemeinsam" 1984).

These groups blew on the activist embers for a while. But participatory exhaustion had set in. The string of defeats that the immigrants encountered using institutional participatory forms wore down all but the most committed militants. By the mid-1980s regional associations multiplied among the resident immigrant communities, particularly the Italians and Iberians. They forsook an active political role for a celebration of provincial cultures. Even the FCLIS and the ATEES began to devote more time to solving the immigrants' problems more on a personal, concrete level than on an overarching ideological one. In addition to job and educational counseling, dances, food festivals, and folk concerts took up greater shares of funding and time. Though lively, such local-level activities did not connect up with developments elsewhere in the country or contribute to social-movement formation (Deike 1984).

Public officials tried to juggle the concerns of the xenophobic movements, employers, and the government's own stabilization and integration policies. This arduous task left very little room for innovation. Caught between denunciations from right and left, the federal government argued that the Swiss people had closed off further moves to integrate foreigners (CFE/EKA 1976c, p. 276).

By the early 1980s, any move toward widening the channels for immigrant political expression seemed sure to incur the wrath of the anti-immigrant movement. Switzerland was operating under the same basic legal framework that it had introduced before World War II. Barbara Schmitter Heisler points out that the rejections of the Togetherness Initiative and the ANAG reform served as a "reminder that although the 'foreigners question' has lost much of its bite, the majority of the Swiss people are not ready to embrace fundamental changes that would permit the legal recognition of immigration rather than prolonged labour migration" (1988, p. 694; see CFE/EKA 1977c, p. 4).

The immigrants did not seem to be conforming to the Swiss pattern of political organization so much as developing the most logical strategies for themselves in the Swiss context. The increase in regionally based associations seemed to reflect many immigrants' conclusion that more explicitly political actions had proved ineffectual. Facing the immigrants were a constant stream of xenophobic challenges, twenty-six different cantonal political contexts, and a myriad of regulations and procedures governing their behavior in Switzerland and dividing them along ethnic and socioprofessional lines. By maintaining the discriminatory seasonal workers' statute, the Swiss made clear their determination to split already segregated national groups into even smaller segments.

The immigrants had at their disposal a multitude of institutional political outlets. These were so numerous that even when challenged on many fronts, the immigrants felt little temptation to embrace confrontational or more broadly collective strategies. Their political mobilization suffered a sort of death by a thousand cuts. The regular defeats they suffered when they availed themselves of this array of institutional channels resulted in an ineffectual dribbling away of their political energies. The Swiss left—decentralized and susceptible to infighting in the best of times—and the solidarity groups did not freeze the immigrants out of institutional channels; but internally divided as they were over immigration, neither were they in a position to advance the immigrants' cause. It is hardly surprising that the organized immigrant movements in Switzerland lost their momentum far more than in France.

The Second Generation

Despite clear similarities in their social and cultural predicament, the second generations of France and Switzerland adopted very different patterns of political participation. The effective combination of institutional and confrontational tactics that the *Beurs* and other second-generation youth adopted in France had no Swiss equivalent; the children of Switzerland's foreign-worker population remained almost entirely passive and politically invisible. There emerged nothing resembling France's second-generation civic rights and voter registration campaigns, and few signs of an incipient social movement.

Stricter regulations on family immigration in Switzerland produced a smaller second-generation immigrant population than in France. This population, however, grew rapidly even after the immigration slowdown of the mid-1970s as family reunification became one component of the federal government's effort to encourage the integration of the resident foreigner population. By 1979, numbering more than 275,000, second-generation immigrants accounted for one-third of the total foreign population (de Rham et al. 1980; "Les jeunes étrangers" 1980; Thürer 1990, p. 27).

Nicknamed the "neither-nor" generation *(die Weder-Noch-Generation)* by German-Swiss journalists, the foreign workers' children were caught between two cultures even more awkwardly than their French counterparts. French and Swiss institutions and laws nurtured different social identities among the second immigrant generations. A common disadvantaged residential and socioeconomic condition, in conjunction with inclusive French citizenship laws and the encouragement of some important institutional actors, propelled the second generation's conflicts in France. In Switzerland, by contrast, the trend was away from an aligning of immigrants' legal and political status. Policies balkanized the immigrant children, like their parents, into a series of ethnically and functionally defined categories ("Frankreich" 1984). Many felt Swiss, but they remained locked into their identity as immigrants because of strict Swiss citizenship laws and naturalization procedures.[15]

The second generation accounted for a disproportionately large share of Switzerland's unemployed workers (27 percent by 1983). In France the discrepancy between the second generation's ability to improve its legal (that is, citizenship) status and its inability to improve its social status has favored the emergence of a social movement. Yet in Switzerland's highly stratified labor market, those with jobs often managed to make some ostensible professional advances on their parents' bottom-rung classifications. However meager, opportunities for individual socioprofessional advancement—"exit"—seemed to compare favorably with opportunities for political "voice." Also, like other immigrants, young noncitizens in Switzerland have enjoyed access to a number of institutional political channels. It was along them that the basis for a collective political identity and confrontational protests drained away, leaving Swiss political life unthreatened (Bolzman, Fibbi, and Garcia 1987, pp. 62–68; see also Baggio and Pozzi 1978).

As in France, though, the sheer number of second-generation immigrants made them a highly visible source of misunderstandings and social tensions in the schools of a nation with an aging, stabilizing native population. Noncitizens' low levels of academic achievement became a major focus of concern for Swiss and homeland authorities.

Federal officials could only suggest and cajole in the area of education. Local and cantonal governments were responsible for elementary and secondary education, and some of them instituted special bilingual programs, kindergartens, and remedial courses for the children of the foreign workers. Wide gaps persisted, and financial outlays were generally paltry (Fibbi and de Rham 1985; see "L'Inserimento sociale" 1982).

True to form, Swiss officials argued that it was the duty of homeland officials to "nurture a positive attitude toward our social and economic system" among the children. Immigrant parents also received a large share of the blame for the atmosphere of mistrust and incomprehension that typified their relations with school officials ("Appréciation" 1981). To make up for the modesty of the efforts undertaken by the host society, homeland governments sent teachers and established schools and professional training centers in the host society in conjunction with Swiss organizations.

Except for certain sports clubs, the children of Switzerland's foreign workers largely avoided structured activities organized by indigenous, immigrant, and homeland associations. These youngsters turned in on themselves and developed their own social life. Fewer than 3 percent of even second-generation Italians—supposed to be better integrated than others into Swiss society—belonged to a political organization as late as the mid-1980s. Bands of youth formed, hanging around on street corners and shunning contacts with the Swiss population and foreign adults (Lorenzi-Cioldi and Meyer 1986).

Criminality rates for second-generation immigrants were no higher than for Swiss youth of similar socioeconomic straits. However, policymakers' anxiety about them rose in the wake of the "events" of 1980–1982. Hundreds of loosely connected demonstrations by young people turned Zurich and then other major Swiss cities into circuses of social conflict. The violence of the protests shocked Switzerland and reminded many observers of France's "hot summer" of 1981. The two phenomena, however, diverged in key, telling respects—particularly regarding the role of the second immigrant generation.

Zurich, like other Western European cities, had spawned a counterculture during the 1970s whose guiding spirits introduced new forms of cultural and political action. Rock music became the vehicle by which many alienated young people in this "scene" expressed their feelings. Influenced by Britain's "Rock against Police" and presaging France's movement of the same name, "Rock as Revolt" ("Rock als

Revolte") was born at a Zurich rock music festival in 1979 (Kriesi 1982; see Morin 1975; Haller 1981; and Hollstein 1981).

What concerned the Swiss rockers was not racism, as in France, but the need for a place of their own to enjoy their music. Ironically, it was the departure of immigrant workers, forced out by economic circumstances in the 1970s, that had freed up space in the working-class neighborhoods for the counterculture to flourish. When urban renewal and gentrification in Zurich later threatened that space, the youthful protests erupted (Deriaz, del Curto, and Maeder 1981, pp. 175–189). Most of those involved in the Zurich movement were well educated, but many were from working-class backgrounds. Just over one participant in ten was a foreigner, far less than their 20 percent share in the city's overall population. Half of those foreigners who were active were members of the extremely well-integrated minority of the second generation already involved in Swiss youth organizations or attending the University of Zurich. Immigrant workers were only one group among "marginals" of all stripes—including homosexuals, prisoners, drug users, and street people—whose daily problems served as themes for the movement. It was, in the end, an evanescent, postmaterialist outburst of rebels with a very eclectic cause (Kriesi 1982, p. 216).

Even so, the uproar shook Swiss society profoundly, producing panicky responses from the Swiss media, government officials, and public opinion. A conservative backlash ensued. Instead of opening up Swiss society to cultural diversity, the protesters had frightened mainstream Swiss opinion. Policymakers now recoiled from any ideas of granting the second generation easier access to Swiss citizenship, let alone voting rights as immigrants.

Officials feared that the youth movements that rocked Zurich and other cities had given dangerous ideas to the second generation of immigrants, described in one federal report as a "social time bomb" (Eidgenössische Kommission für Jugendfragen 1981). Several deportations of noncitizen participants followed. Citing the potential disruptiveness of the "neither-nor generation," the government imparted a new sense of urgency to projects designed to effect its integration. In December 1984 two second-generation immigrants were appointed to the CFE/EKA, which advocated the formation of immigrant parents' associations at the communal and cantonal levels to "troubleshoot" with school boards (CFE/EKA 1986).

After the Zurich "events" there were few signs of significant political mobilization among second-generation immigrants. Of course, many of them did closely monitor the March of 1983, Convergence '84, the activities of SOS-Racisme, and the other more spectacular forms of second-generation participation in France. By the mid-1980s several cities in French Switzerland were home to small, copycat SOS-Racisme organizations. Their badges and posters, however, bore a different message: a palm with crossed fore- and middle fingers and the words "I'll love whom I like." That slogan bespoke a more eclectic membership than the French group's, with a focus less on generational differences than on society's outcasts—young immigrants, homosexuals, and the fringe left ("Mach meinen Kumpel nicht an!" 1985). The movement remained very tentative and with virtually no public presence, attesting to the difficulty for immigrants of any generation of developing into a collective political force in Switzerland.[16]

A Policy Stalemate?

Swiss officialdom's newfound concern about advancing the second generation's integration into the host society soon encountered intransigent resistance. Stoked by National Action and the Republicans, fears grew among the electorate that immigrants, especially the younger generation, posed a serious threat to the social order. The xenophobic movement was supposed to melt away, rendered superfluous by the government's acceptance of most of its agenda. But it persisted, using the weapons of direct democracy to thwart any amelioration of the foreigners' situation. The successes of the National Front in France energized Swiss xenophobes even in French Switzerland. In those previously rather hostile environs, National Action and the Republicans scored significant gains at the cantonal level; Geneva even had its own xenophobic party, Vigilance (Vuillomenet 1986).

In 1983 National Action submitted another initiative intended to restrict immigration by refusing to allow more immigrants to enter than to leave Switzerland and by limiting numbers of border commuters and refugees. Xenophobic petitions also began circulating in the cantons. In the 1983 federal election, NA/Vigilance increased its parliamentary representation to five seats. The Socialists and the Labor Party lost seats and were further discouraged from taking high-profile positions in defense of the immigrants (Lohneis 1984).

The immigrants and their fragmented allies on the Swiss left barely managed to resist the onslaught of xenophobic efforts at limiting immigration, political asylum, and immigrant rights. The repeated defeats of their efforts sapped their energy to mobilize (Thürer 1990). Organized immigrant political activity in Switzerland, never as boisterous and rambunctious as in France, slumped further. Folkloric celebrations became more than ever the privileged arena for community affirmation and inevitably hardened the lines of ethnicity separating the national groups.[17]

THE DEBATE OVER REFUGEES
AND ILLEGAL IMMIGRANTS

Years of National Action propaganda made the nation extremely sensitive to demographic influxes of any nature. Switzerland's reservoir of xenophobia and cultural defensiveness made the refugee issue and illegal immigration the nation's major political preoccupations in the late 1980s. As in France, these two issues presented a different complex of problems from that of migrant workers turned immigrants (Schmitter Heisler 1988, p. 684). But the Swiss institutional system responded to both in similar fashion.

Efforts to stem illegal immigration were notably unsuccessful. The estimated number of "clandestines" rose from 50,000 in the mid-1980s to more than 100,000 by decade's end. In addition, by 1986 Switzerland sheltered more than 30,000 refugees, one for each 150 native Swiss, one of the highest concentrations in Europe. Bureaucrats could not keep up with applications for asylum. Petitioners filled shabby, makeshift detention centers throughout the country (Gesú 1990). The presence of these foreigners prompted the xenophobes' shrillest call to arms. Employing terms reminiscent of Jean-Marie Le Pen, young NA parliamentarian Markus Ruf warned that each refugee and undocumented alien was a "potential assassin, thief, schizophrenic, drug trafficker, AIDS or syphilis carrier" (quoted in Jaccoud 1987b).

Quickly, to avoid an initiative campaign, the federal government instituted a series of administrative changes that slashed the approval rate on applications for asylum (which was over 80 percent in 1981) to around 10 percent. In 1986, after months of stormy debate, the Federal Assembly passed a revision of the laws covering asylum. The text maintained the existing legislative framework but added new restrictions designed to weed out "true" political refugees from "mere" economic ones. Greater responsibility for managing applications for asylum would fall to the cantons, which were deemed better able than Bern to gauge their absorptive capacity. Deportations would become easier to execute, and a French-style *aide au retour* would be introduced.

The extensive legislative change required voter approval. The Socialists, Communists, churches, and immigrant associations squared off against the "bourgeois" right over what the government touted as a reasonable compromise between the extreme positions of the xenophobes and of well-meaning but unrealistic humanitarians. The campaign further frayed nerves that had suffered under the previous xenophobic initiatives and dredged up painful recollections of Switzerland's refusal to grant asylum to German Jews during World War II. Slightly over two-thirds of Swiss voters approved the new law in April 1987, with francophone Neuchâtel, Geneva, and the Jura the only cantons to register a positive response of less than 60 percent (*Le Monde*, April 4, 1987).

The xenophobic movement seized on the unrelieved frustration with the refugee and immigration issues. In 1988 it brought yet another initiative to a federal vote, the sixth since 1965. This one proposed a "gentle" reduction in the foreign population of some 300,000 over fifteen years and the introduction of quotas on the numbers of seasonal workers, refugees, and other "unassimilable" aliens (*Corriere del Ticino*, Oct. 29, 1988; *Tribune de Genève*, Dec. 5, 1988). In an atmosphere of general indifference, every canton rebuffed the latest National Action offering that December. The Federal Council saw the vote as further confirmation of its immigration policies.

Many refugees and illegal immigrants were upset by those policies. Virtually alone in their militancy, they mounted hunger strikes across Switzerland throughout the late 1980s. One group of Tamils dropped their pants on the tarmac at Geneva's Cointrin Airport to symbolize the stripping of their human rights. Others engaged in violent actions: a band of radical Kurds occupied the German consulate in Basel in 1988 to demand the release of fourteen compatriots in German jails (see "Dossier: Le spectre" 1989). These actions unsettled many of the Swiss, who had seen their resident immigrant communities settle into institutional channels of participation.[18]

But these causes aroused the major immigrant associations and some solidarity groups and churches. The same Swiss active in the Swiss-Immigrant Committees were at the forefront of efforts to defend refugees. Religious groups stitched together a network of safe-houses for illegal refugees, directly inspired by the Sanctuary movement in the United States (Caloz 1982; Huber and Trossmann 1987). The new outburst of protests, as in France, reflected the precarious legal situation of refugees and undocumented immigrants. But in the prevailing political impasse, the more militantly a solidarity group defended the refugees, the more likely it was to be a marginal group, itself outside the political consensus.[19]

THE RACIST UPSURGE AND THREATS
TO SYSTEM STABILITY

Switzerland had avoided the social conflicts and racial violence that afflicted France in the early 1980s. But as the refugee and illegals "crisis" grafted itself onto the still-smoldering foreign-worker question, that example of Swiss exceptionalism was vanishing. Looking across their borders at the serious racial problems in France and West Germany, Swiss political leaders—and not only the xenophobes—worried about the delicately balanced nature of Swiss society (Nicod 1983, pp. 155–157). Swiss identity, rooted in the canton and village *Heimat* and defined as much by whom it excludes as by who belongs, can easily degenerate into aggressive provincialism with unmistakably militant undertones (Schworck 1991, p. 748). The Swiss institutional system inevitably weighed heaviest on non-Europeans.

But discrimination among national groups in the foreign population had never translated into expressly ethnic or racial hostility. Rather, it was the distinction between "citizen" and "foreigner" that mattered the most. Even when Swiss xenophobes attacked the "foreign presence," they did not designate a particular category of immigrants. "It is not because one is an Italian or a Spaniard that one faces discrimination," Bolzman, Fibbi, and Garcia conclude, "but because one is a foreigner" (1987, p. 66). Discrimination grew out of differences in legal status. Non-Europeans, who had arrived in Switzerland most recently, and seasonal workers performed the most menial and least secure jobs.

By the late 1980s, Switzerland's channeling mechanisms were showing signs of inadequacy, even failure. Racially motivated crimes were becoming more common. Refugee centers were burned, foreigners were beaten and killed, and discrimination in housing and employment occurred with alarming frequency. Neo-Nazi skinheads roamed the streets of several German-Swiss cities. Outwardly typical young Swiss boys informed news reporters that "we wouldn't have these foreign shits around if there were another Hitler" (*Der Spiegel*, Feb. 13, 1989, pp. 34–35; see Just, Niethammer, and Meyer 1989). Extremist groups like the Patriotic Front, the Swiss Democrats, and Action for Independent and Neutral Switzerland sprouted and demanded that federal officials take emergency measures to stem the influx of asylum seekers and clandestine immigrants from North Africa and Turkey (Meyer 1991, p. 100).

The increasingly exotic origins of Switzerland's foreign population clearly contributed to social tensions. The presence of Turkish laborers and of North and sub-Saharan African and Asian refugees was raising fears of the "danger of Islamization." Mosques, prayer rooms, and Koranic schools (many financed from abroad) had sprung up across Switzerland since 1974. But Muslims in Switzerland were adopting participatory patterns that more closely resembled those of Southern European immigrants there than those of Muslims in other host societies like France. Formal Islamic associations were rare. The ones that were active tended to concentrate on religious matters and to direct their political interests toward the homeland (Köppel 1982, pp. 3–5).

The new racial violence drew its real force from the evolving relationship between immigrants and the Swiss political system. On the surface that system seemed generally rather stable. One government minister described it as "the comfort that chloroforms" (quoted in Church 1989, p. 117). Ominously, however, the apparent tranquility resulted largely from the electorate's alienation from the political system. Voter abstention worsened steadily: turnout fell to 45.6 percent in the 1987 federal parliamentary elections—the lowest since the inception of proportional representation voting in 1919. One observer described the "alliance of the abstainers" as the country's only party "with a broadening electoral base" (Papadopoulos 1988, p. 146).

Swiss voters expressed their political frustrations by forming new movements and parties. Ecologists, who did not make their presence felt in France until the 1989 legislative elections, used the instruments of direct democracy and arrived on the Swiss political scene in the early 1970s.[20] Single-minded, most Swiss environmentalist groups disregarded the immigrants. Less indifferent were the "super-Greens," fiercely xenophobic activists who saw immigrants as a heavy burden on the country's fragile ecosystem (see *Tages-Anzeiger*, April 3, 1987; Ingold 1988).

The ecological movement quickly generated a political reaction: the formation of antiecological parties. One of these, the equally anti-immigrant Swiss Auto Party, with its stronghold in German-speaking cantons, elected two federal parliamentary deputies in 1987—motorists have since had better representation in Bern than Communists—and challenged National Action on the far right of the political spectrum. On the far left the militant Movement for an Open, Democratic, and Fraternal Switzerland (known by its exclamatory acronyms, MODS!/BODS!) tried to fuse working-class interests and the counterculture around the immigration question into a revolutionary force.

None of these movements altered fundamentally the Swiss pattern of party competition or of consensual bargaining. It proved too difficult for new, "outsider" groups to gain a real degree of legitimacy, despite their ability to effect change through initiatives and referenda and their electoral success at the cantonal level. After 1987 National Action itself could no longer form a parliamentary group (of five members) on its own at the federal level (Church 1989).

The spread of racist violence and attitudes spurred immigrants to action once again. On the eve of the 1987 federal elections the "Togetherness" movement published a list of demands, countersigned by several immigrant associations, including the Italian FCLIS, the Spanish ATEES, the Portuguese Democratic Association, and the Federation of Turkish Workers' Organizations. These and other organizations reissued their call for stepped-up governmental and police efforts to combat all manifestations of racism and discrimination and to encourage cross-cultural contacts (Thévenaz 1989).

Immigrants in a number of cities and cantons drew up a new battery of petitions demanding voting rights and consultative bodies, and they asked their Swiss allies to undertake similar initiatives. The response varied across the cantons. The petitions did heighten the sensitivity of local officials to the political demands of the immigrants. In Zurich the municipal commission charged with considering the immigrant associations' voting-rights petition publicly interviewed their leaders to learn more about the motives behind their initiative ("Aktive Politik" 1990; *Neue Zürcher Zeitung,* April 30, 1987; *Corriere del Ticino,* April 29, 1987).

But these efforts bore few concrete results. Authorities argued that the immigrants already enjoyed enough opportunities for political integration and that any further opening would generate a dangerous reaction from the far right. Basically, the Swiss government still preferred the rotation model of immigration. It refused to debate immigration except in terms involving numbers and their stabilization (Thévenaz 1989).

Officials still stressed the responsibilities of homeland governments for the education and welfare of the second as well as the first immigrant generation in Switzerland. True, the Federal Insurance Court (Eidgenössisches Versicherungsgericht) in Lucerne consistently confirmed even illegal foreign workers' rights to at least the level of social insurance protection provided for in bilateral accords between their homelands and the Swiss government (*Neue Zürcher Zeitung*, July 29, 1992). But the Swiss welfare state remained puny. In December 1987 voters overwhelmingly repudiated federal proposals to expand medical insurance and to provide maternity allowances (*Neue Zürcher Zeitung*, Aug. 7, 1992).

Not surprisingly, then, homeland-oriented immigrant participation did not subside. Foreigners resident in Switzerland continued to lobby their homeland governments to exert pressure on Swiss authorities. They and their associations persisted in operating within a dense network of relations with homeland and host-society institutions (Grossi 1989; *Neue Zürcher Zeitung*, June 25, 1991).

It remained difficult for immigrants to involve themselves in class-based militancy. Few strikes or other forms of unrest troubled the Swiss labor scene. A 1987 Organization for Economic Cooperation and Development (OECD) study indicated that from 1970 through 1985 Switzerland experienced lower strike rates than any other member nation. The initiative for a forty-hour work week championed by the major immigrant associations went down to defeat in 1988. The immigrants, who argued that more free time would mean more chances for sociopolitical integration, had played a very important role in the signature-gathering campaign for the proposal (Grossi 1988; *Le Monde*, Dec. 6, 1988).

Meanwhile, May Day marches attracted fewer and fewer militants, and environmental and quality-of-life concerns began to figure most prominently in speeches. Immigrant and refugee leaders did take to the podium in most cities, addressing crowds that had become increasingly foreign in makeup. With the decline in the size of the traditional working class, the immigrant share of trade union membership climbed, to 31 percent of the FTMH/SMUV and 75 percent of the FOBB/GBH. The long-standing divisions within left-wing parties and trade unions remained, even if they lost some of their acuity (*Tages-Anzeiger*, May 2, 1987).[21]

The second generation of immigrants remained disconnected from Swiss society and politically passive. Switzerland's naturalization laws remained among the most restrictive in Europe. New proposals to facilitate naturalization procedures for the children of immigrant workers met with voter disapproval several times in the 1980s. A 1983 survey among second-generation immigrants (aged twenty-five and over) in French Switzerland found that only 9.2 percent were considering eventual naturalization.[22] This and other related institutional factors, including the long reach of sending-country consular officials and fraternal homeland organizations, kept working to dampen second-generation immigrants' political mobilization. SOS-Racisme established small outposts throughout Switzerland, but young people did not participate in any form of associational life to a significant degree (SOS-Racisme 1988). Low unemployment rates and limited possibilities for individual professional advancement diffused their organizational energies even while institutional forces kept them socially marginalized (see de Rham 1990).

An important event in 1987—the first "Festival of Young Emigrants" in Lausanne—illustrated the second generation's contradictory situation. The multiethnic celebration of traditional cultures involved the progeny of Switzerland's foreign workers and refugees—Turks, Antilleans, Spaniards, Greeks, Africans, Portuguese, and Yugoslavs. Like most others of their generation, the participants experienced no small measure of discomfort from their dual cultural background. For teenagers who "preferred 'The Cure' to bouzouki and the flamenco," it was decidedly strange to don the folkloric garb of their parents', and sometimes only their grandparents', birthplace (Jaccoud 1987a).

Summary: *Fin de Régime?*

Swiss institutional channeling, to sum up, continued to prevent immigrants from posing a challenge to the host-society political system. They did broaden both the "repertoire of democratic participation" and the policy agenda in the mid-1970s (see Tarrow 1989), at least until Swiss authorities and trade unionists reasserted their authority and successfully directed the immigrants' protests into institutional channels. From the early 1980s on, their level of activity and influence ebbed, although their participatory potential built in the face of intensifying anti-immigrant sentiment.

Xenophobia had by then developed into a serious menace. Even so, with the Swiss labor market "as dry as the Sahara," the government came under intense pressure from businesses to raise the cantonal immigration quotas. Although people with specialized skills were needed in a number of sectors, federal officials continued to turn to unskilled foreign workers, whom they could "export" whenever demand slackened.[23] "Like no other country Switzerland afforded itself the luxury of permitting more immigration of lesser-skilled foreigners," according to Saint-Gallen economist Peter Moser, "while erecting barriers to qualified ones" (quoted in Müller von Blumencron 1991, p. 43). Squeezed between the interests of the far right and Swiss business, federal policymakers lost manuevering room.

By the start of the 1990s, the threat to the system's resiliency had reached a dangerous new level. The country was confronting more problems than outsiders and even the Swiss themselves often realized. Switzerland's decades-long special role as Europe's model country was playing itself out.

In 1989 a money-laundering scandal involving Justice Minister Elisabeth Kopp stunned the political establishment. The uproar forced her resignation and raised damning questions about the solicitous attitudes adopted toward foreigners with money, even when it came from drugs. Kopp had been a controversial minister, detested by the left and the immigrants for her hard-line policy on immigration and asylum seekers (*New York Times*, Aug. 11, 1991).

Rising unemployment was also generating concern. After reaching what for the Swiss was already an upsetting 1.3 percent on average in 1991, the rate would climb to 3.1 percent in December 1992—the highest such figure since 1939. In French Switzerland the figures were up to twice as high as the national average, and workers under age twenty-nine were the hardest hit. Foreigners, over 16 percent of the gainfully employed population, accounted for a disproportionately high 23 percent of the unemployed (*Neue Zürcher Zeitung*, July 19–20, 23, and 30, 1992; Dec. 6–7, 1992).

Studies undertaken by Swiss economists and the federal government have dispelled widespread fears of the country's becoming a "paradise without a future," but its economy will have to undergo significant, rapid restructuring if unemployment and socioeconomic disparities are not to increase precipitously (*Neue Zürcher Zeitung*, Nov. 13, 1992). Poverty rates are already approaching American levels in some Swiss cities (15 percent of the total population in Basel, for example, with another 10 percent teetering on the edge) (Müller von Blumencron 1991, p. 44). Switzerland has Europe's biggest per-capita drug abuse and AIDS problems, the end of the Cold War has cast doubts on its traditional policy of neutrality, and foreign pressures have forced a loosening of its banking secrecy laws. As Zurich banker Hans Bär told the German magazine *Wirtschafts Woche* (May 1, 1992), "We no longer have anything special to offer" (p. 40).

No issue in Switzerland has generated more anxiety and heat than immigration, which is bound up with all the nation's other crises (*Neue Zürcher Zeitung*, July 26–27, 1992). By the end of 1989 there were 1,040,325 alien residents, fully 15.6 percent of the total population of 6.67 million.[24] Almost 80 percent of resident noncitizens held permanent residency permits, which, apart from the area of political rights, gave them rights and protections equal to those of the Swiss (see Table 16).

The effects of previous waves of immigration, combined with Europe's highest rate of marriages between citizens and noncitizens and the increased mobility of the native Swiss, had made Switzerland a truly pluricultural society (*La Suisse*, April 13, 1987; Hoesli 1988). At the same time, however, fewer and fewer of Switzerland's foreigners were aspiring to Swiss citizenship: from 1980 to 1990 the number of approved applications fell by almost half, to 9,000. Interest dropped even among those noncitizens born and raised in the country. Only business executives hoping for a local edge and aging foreign workers not wanting to spend their retirement in their now-foreign homeland continued to naturalize at steady rates (*Neue Zürcher Zeitung*, July 24, 1992).

The trend upset officials, since it did not augur well for the the integration or assimilation of foreigners into Swiss society. Accordingly, in 1992 the Federal Assembly made naturalization easier in several respects. Foreign husbands of Swiss citizens won claim to Swiss citizenship after three years of marriage. (Women marrying Swiss citizens, conversely, no longer received Swiss citizenship automatically.) More significantly, it was no longer necessary for anyone to give up his or her original citizenship when receiving the Swiss, provided that the homeland permitted this arrangement. A rush of applications was expected from Italians, who received the right to hold dual citizenship in August 1992 (*Der Spiegel*, 34, 1992, pp. 152–153). The status of second-generation immigrants did not change.

Nor did noncitizens receive any new openings into the host-society political system. The cantonal government of Zug and voters in the canton of Vaud, for example, refused to grant foreigners local-level voting rights (*Neue Zürcher Zeitung*, July 22, 1992; *Informations européennes*, Oct. 1992, p. 12). Despite the general realization that the "foreigners problem" had long since become a consummately Swiss problem, the public and policymakers alike appeared bewildered and unable to act decisively.

The voters' alienation and fragmentation were manifest in parliamentary elections in 1991. In the upper house (Ständerat), the liberal Free Democrats were the big winners, adding four seats to their fourteen, while the Social Democrats lost two of their five seats. In the lower house (Nationalrat), in contrast, most of the main parties lost ground to the Swiss Auto Party (a gain of six seats for a total of eight), the Greens (a gain of five seats to fourteen), and fringe parties on the left and right. The Socialists held their ground, largely because the party had successfully "rid itself of its working-class image" (Ladner 1992, p. 530). The "magic formula" balancing the four major parties in the executive suffered no serious challenge (Church 1992).

Antiforeigner violence, meanwhile, spread apace. Accommodation centers for asylum seekers became targets of many attacks (*Journal de Genève*, Jan. 11, 1993). A large, diverse antiracist front formed at the initiative of the Evangelical Ecclesiastical Federation in October 1991 to condemn both the assaults and the government's weak-kneed policy response. Including churches, left-wing political parties, and trade unions, the new group urged politicians to refrain from electoral appeals playing on racism and xenophobia (*Informations européennes*, Nov. 1991, p. 11). Alone among Western European host societies, Switzerland had failed to enact an antiracism law after World War II. In December 1992 the National Council finally voted in favor of ratifying the International Convention against All Forms of Racial Discrimination, adopted a revision of the penal code, and approved the establishment of a mediating body to combat racial discrimination.[25]

In the interim, the escalating social conflicts impelled the federal government to issue vague calls for "openness to 'interculturality,'" understood as the "interaction of different cultures under conditions of mutual respect." What that meant in practical terms became the subject of fierce, sometimes panicked debate, exacerbated by the need to decide Switzerland's response to European integration (K. Müller 1992).

Uncertainty about Switzerland's future in a new Europe has brought tensions to a boil. Many Swiss feel that their nation, delicately balanced as it is along linguistic and religious lines, has much to fear from European integration; and not least among their worries is the prospect of losing control over immigration into Switzerland. The immigration debate thus flows into and sharpens a deeper national identity crisis, which first rose to the surface in the form of bitter polemics during preparations for the celebration of the Confederation's 700th anniversary on August 1, 1991 (Grossi 1989; Reich 1991).[26]

The political leadership has largely determined that the Swiss polity must adapt in order to survive. After Swiss voters approved the country's application to join the World Bank and the International Monetary Fund in a May 1992 referendum, the federal government made plans to seek early membership in the European Community (*New York Times*, May 19, 1992).[27] That December it called the electorate back to the polls to decide whether Switzerland should participate in the European Economic Area, a nineteen-country trading bloc encompassing the European Community (EC) and the European Free Trade Association.[28]

Concerned about the loss of national autonomy and the institutions of direct democracy as well as an influx of Europe's unemployed, the Swiss People's Party, the Auto Party, the far right, and the Greens mobilized to defeat the proposal. The other mainstream parties and employers' and trade union confederations, especially the central USS/SGB, worked actively to convince Swiss voters to accept entry into the EEA. Whether or not closer association with the rest of Europe would jeopardize Switzerland's strict immigration laws and complex permit system was a central issue animating the very heated discussion over the proposal (*Neue Zürcher Zeitung*, Aug. 7, 1992; *Der Spiegel*, 48, 1992, pp. 189–191).[29]

To address both the immigration-related worries of the Swiss electorate and the labor demands of Swiss business, in October 1992 the Federal Council adopted a new regulation on foreign labor.[30] Citizens of EC and EFTA countries came to constitute the "first circle" of recruitment sources. A second circle, consisting of citizens of the United States, Canada, and the former Communist nations of Eastern and Central Europe, would be subject to a quota system. Immigration from citizens of the third circle of countries—including Turkey and former Yugoslavia—would be practically prohibited (*Tribune de Genève*, Sept. 24, 1991; *La Suisse*, Sept. 24, and Oct. 24, 1991).

Already angered by these restrictions, the immigrant associations watched in horror as once-liberal asylum laws were also tightened and border patrols were expanded. Applicants now had to present an acceptable identity document, and anyone from what was deemed a "safe country" (where persecution supposedly does not exist) was rebuffed out of hand. Together with the effects of the war in the former Yugoslavia (which blocked off the so-called Balkan route to Switzerland), these measures reduced the number of applications by more than half from 1991 to 1992 (*La Suisse*, Sept. 16, 1992). Officials examined some 37,000 cases in 1992, accepting 4.5 percent.[31]

The entry into force of the EEA would have prevented foreign nationals of any of the nineteen member states from recovering their obligatory social security contributions when they left Switzerland. Many immigrant activists decried that scenario, as well as the absence of a coherent social dimension to the European integration process in general (Adank 1990). The Swiss government, hoping to avoid an exodus of cheap Southern European workers, obtained permission from the EC to permit repatriation of the pension funds for five more years. Fear of nevertheless losing their contributions prompted large numbers of affected immigrants, especially Spaniards, to leave (*Informations européennes*, Nov. 1992, p. 2).

To the chagrin of the government, just over half of the electorate (50.3 percent) rejected membership in the EEA on December 6. Voter turnout was 78.3 percent, the highest since 1947 (*Le Monde/hebdomadaire*, December 3–9, 1992). Instead of providing solutions, the election made it more essential than ever for the Swiss to reconsider the underpinnings of their traditionally peaceful and prosperous society. The result of the voting caused dismay in the immigrant communities. It also pointed out another sign of major strain in the Swiss Confederation, the widening division between German and French Switzerland: save for the two Basel half-cantons, all eight cantons that voted "yes" to the EEA were in French Switzerland, where disappointment and anger were palpable.[32]

Switzerland's immigrant communities are likely to be actively involved in the resolution of its European challenge. At the core of the EC, the French have experienced external pressures as strong as any of those now acting on Switzerland. Yet France's immigrant communities produced a social movement that—through either explicitly political or symbolic cultural means—forced the host society into a sustained dialogue with them. In Switzerland, instances of potentially instructive and thus valuable political conflicts have been rare. In the absence of a meaningful if contentious dialogue between the immigrants and the host society, the Swiss have not learned as much as the French. They have been able to perpetuate the myth of temporary postwar labor migration. Now pressed from without and within, the Swiss system is proving itself to be more vulnerable in the long run to the effects of permanent immigration.

Nevertheless, France and Switzerland do share some similarities. In both, immigrant political participation has demonstrated the powerful effects of host-society institutional channeling since World War II. As supposedly temporary foreign workers, the immigrants first encountered political opportunities that lay open to them more or less unintentionally, opportunities that reflected traditional ways of dealing with demands on the political system in each society and initial assumptions about the foreign workers' status there. The evolution of the immigrants' political role in and impact on the host society resulted from their interaction with French and Swiss authorities and the forces that developed to oppose the immigrant presence.

What influence has federalism had on the nature and evolution of that interaction in Switzerland? A complex system of financial and administrative links has made all levels of government interdependent in many fields, but cantonal and local-level variations have been great in the area of immigration. Some observers have even tied the high degree of decentralization in Switzerland directly to its poor record of extending industrial, social, civil, and political rights to postwar immigrants and their families (Layton-Henry 1990, pp. 186–195). More so than in France, therefore, local-level comparison becomes necessary to informed conclusions about the relationship between immigrants and politics in Switzerland.

6

The Local Swiss Cases: Schlieren and La Chaux-de-Fonds

In France political centralization has until very recently limited local variations in immigrants' political opportunity structure and otherwise influenced their participation. In Switzerland decentralization has been the rule. The cantons have always enjoyed significant powers, and "there is no such animal as a 'typical' canton" (see Bogdanor 1988). Each has had its own political and institutional setup.

The cantons have varied widely in their openness to immigrant political involvement. Federal officials are responsible for the quantitative aspects of immigration policy and the immigrants' access to federal-level political rights. Cantonal authorities play the same gatekeeping role at their level. They have an influential voice in setting the quotas of immigrant and seasonal workers allowed into their canton. They also share decisionmaking and implementation responsibilities with the federal government in the areas of education, religious life, health and unemployment insurance, incentives for housing construction, and the naturalization of foreigners (Urio and Markov 1986). Throughout Switzerland, local-level governments have also had far greater latitude than French municipalities, even after the Mitterrand-Mauroy administration introduced its decentralization legislative package (CFE/EKA 1977c, p. 6).

Controlling for the intervening variables of total population and its immigrant percentage, I have selected two Swiss localities, Schlieren and La Chaux-de-Fonds, that permit an effective comparison with La Courneuve and Roubaix in France. Because controls on class and ethnic variables are possible in all four cities, it becomes clear that immigrant participatory strategies have owed less to those factors than to the influence of very divergent institutional linking processes—including the independent effects of positive actions by political parties, trade unions, and voluntary associations.

Schlieren

Schlieren resembles La Courneuve in many respects socioeconomically. In terms of its politics and the political incorporation of its immigrants, though, it is a polar opposite. Instead of developing a Communist mobilization system, the small, conservative Swiss city sealed itself off from its foreign population.

Schlieren is one of Switzerland's most industrialized cities, lying in the Limmat River Valley (Limmattal) in the canton of Zurich, which extends from Lake Zurich into the canton of Aargau. Although the region bears little superficial resemblance to the dreary industrial wastelands of Seine-Saint-Denis, its industrial might has earned it a reputation as "Switzerland's *Ruhrgebiet*" (Fortuna 1975). The Limmattal's economic well-being has depended on the manufacture of export-dependent heavy machines and appliances.

Schlieren has long been a working-class city. In 1970, 55 percent of the 12,000 Schliermers were economically active, and two-thirds of those with employment held blue-collar jobs (Statistische Mitteilungen des Kantons Zürich 1978, pp. 30–31). Just as the Mécano plant's operations determined the rhythm of the working day in La Courneuve for decades, the Schweizerische Wagons- und Aufzügefabrik AG played a central role in the life of Schlieren. "D'Wagi," as the factory was known to Schliermers, carried the city's name around the world on its locomotives, streetcars, and elevators. The largest industrial operation in the Limmattal, d'Wagi established itself in Schlieren in 1895, after the first wave of industrialization. It provided for much of the city's employee housing and other social infrastructural needs, underwrote many cultural activities, and was the source of great civic pride (Baumgartner 1986).

D'Wagi was not the only factory in Schlieren. More than a dozen large and medium-sized firms set up operations there in the 1890s. Even so, the sheer size and influence of d'Wagi tended to govern the tenor of labor relations throughout the city. Strikes hit the factory in 1906—the year that the Socialist Party of Schlieren formed—and again in 1912 and 1918. That last job action added to the General Strike wave that rolled across Switzerland and so terrified its Communist-fearing leaders. A handful of short job stoppages and slowdowns marked the ensuing years, but the Schliermer labor peace held firm by the 1930s. D'Wagi management cultivated a close relationship with the local government. At least one of the firm's upper-level managers normally sat on city executive bodies (Baumgartner 1986, pp. 53–54, 73–75).

In the canton of Zurich three types of legally defined, though not necessarily coterminous, "communities" *(Gemeinden)* coexist: church communities, school communities, and political communities. Not until 1973 did Schlieren acquire status as a jurisdiction uniting the three, thus becoming a completely independently functioning political entity with its own executive, the City Council (Stadtrat), and legislature, the Communal Council (Gemeinderat). Schlieren duplicated the federal collegial system at the local level: all the major political parties had at least one representative on each body *(GB* 1974, pp. 1–4).

Like La Courneuve, Schlieren became an immigration center only after World War II. Employers there recruited their first sizable contingents of Italian workers in 1945, as Switzerland got the jump on its war-ravaged neighbors and geared up its labor-short economy to meet booming demand worldwide. Spaniards, then Yugoslavs, Greeks, and Turks arrived in successive waves. From the late 1960s through the early 1990s, around one Schlieren resident in four was an immigrant *(GB* 1974, p. 59; 1982, pp. 103–106; *DL,* Nov. 14, 1990).

A CLOSED POLITICAL SYSTEM

Again like La Courneuve, Schlieren lacked institutional structures for the articulation of immigrant interests. But in that Red-Belt Parisian suburb the municipal government and its allies did their utmost to direct immigrant residents' political mobilization into class-based channels controlled by the French Communist Party. Schlieren offers the contrasting case of an almost complete institutional freezing out of noncitizens at the local level.

Schlieren's municipal government made no institutional provisions for its immigrant communities. Noncitizens could contact city officials whenever a problem arose, but there was no institutionalized consultation. The municipality had commissions and commissioners for a wide variety of issue areas, such as social welfare, regional planning, the handicapped, hospitals, and education. The city council even named delegate to handle all matters pertaining to horses. Yet there was no official appointed to act as an intermediary for foreign workers and their families. Nor was there a formal body for immigrants. Conservative politicians and trade unionists feared that such an institution would offer a forum to radical foreign workers and usher in ethnic political party formation detrimental to the social and labor peace.[1]

The importance of direct citizen participation helps to explain why political rights were seen as the exclusive province of citizens. Because only 5,000 signatures were needed to place an initiative or referendum on the ballot in the canton, each voter constituted an integral component of the collective sovereign.[2] Naturalization, it follows, was exceedingly difficult to obtain. A special commission of the Communal Council examined the dossiers of the foreigners concerned, paying particular attention to the degree to which they had adopted Swiss manners and values. Political militants need not have applied.[3] Not surprisingly, immigrants showed little interest in obtaining Swiss citizenship, painfully aware that the Swiss intended for them to be guest-workers. As one put it, adding an ironic twist to Max Frisch's aphorism, "they asked for a labor force, and we *are* a labor force" (*DL*, Sept. 3, 1976).

Schliermer politics involved local branches of the major Swiss political parties, plus the Independents (Landesring der Unabhängigen), who were interested above all in consumer issues. By the early 1970s three political blocs had developed: the Socialists, the three major center-right "bourgeois" parties (which merged their slates of candidates in local elections), and the Independents and neighborhood groups. Among the last were small new political groupings concerned with quality-of-life issues.[4] The Socialists were the largest single party, consistently winning just under one-third of the vote. They and the bourgeois parties, which won around half, held their strength throughout the decade (*GB* 1975, p. 3; 1978, p. 4; 1982, p. 6).

Schliermer political elites stressed the overriding virtue of compromise and collective decisionmaking in local governmental bodies. The Socialists (SPS) and the bourgeois parties rotated in the positions of Communal Council president and heads of municipal commissions. A representative of the agrarian Swiss People's Party (Schweizerische Volkspartei) presided over meetings of the City Council after the SPS relinquished its hold on this largely symbolic post in the late 1960s.

Immigrants rarely figured in Communal or City Council meetings. Quality-of-life issues—airplane noise, traffic, pollution, gentrification, a new city park, even public toilet facilities for dogs—preoccupied politicians responsive to a comfortable electorate concerned above all with its immediate environment. Also explaining that focus in part were divisions within the ranks of the immigrants' would-be allies on the left. Ever since the initial full city elections of 1974, the two trade union locals had banded together in an electoral alliance with the Socialist Party. But the left had few muscles to flex in Schlieren, and the immigration issue rendered them weaker. The Socialists divided into pro- and anti-immigrant factions. The Metal- and Clockworkers' Union (FTMH/SMUV), which represented laborers in d'Wagi and other large factories in town, accused the immigrants of pushing down wages and competing for jobs, although it had several immigrant directors and secretaries. The smaller Construction Workers' Union (FOBB/GBH) counted more foreign workers than native Swiss as members. It offered them a far more extensive and meaningful role in the union hierarchy. Its policy positions showed consistent support for the immigrants' interests.[5]

For most municipal officials, the immigrants were no more than a cheap, transitory labor force, even if many of them spent a good number of years in the city and raised their families there. The city government, following the federal example, had never provided much in the way of social welfare. It offered a skimpy, "à la carte" public assistance system. Residents paid for most services, with only scant public aid. The recessionary 1970s did change that minimalist posture somewhat, as particularly overburdened large families began to receive rental assistance.[6]

Proposals from progressive Socialists to provide heating assistance to impoverished households and to construct low- and moderate-income public housing failed to win passage, however. Very few communal housing units existed. Up through the 1960s, employers had housed most of the foreign workers whom they brought to Schlieren. The dwellings amounted to no more than rustic barracks that offered very little in the way of comfort or amenities. Somewhat less spartan "foreign workers' houses" replaced the barracks, which seasonal workers then occupied. Eventually immigrants and their families also began to move into private apartments. The market's invisible hand then largely determined where people lived. Immigrants clustered in the lower-income areas next to Swiss citizens with the same economic resources. An acute housing crisis heightened anti-immigrant sentiment and anxiety over the area's "overdevelopment" more than it encouraged public housing programs (*DL,* June 30, 1976).

The social outlays that did exist were rarely adequate for the immigrants, who were legally barred from receiving certain forms of assistance. Moreover, federal and cantonal law made immigrant associations ineligible for public funds. Organizations of Swiss citizens that assisted immigrants and refugees in Schlieren received small municipal grants. Above all, though, local officials expected the immigrants' homeland governments to take care of their nationals' interests and problems during their stay in the area. Likewise, local trade unions saw foreign labor organizations as the legitimate representatives of immigrant workers' interests (see *GB* 1978, pp. 84–87; *DL,* Jan. 3, 1978).

The dearth of effective institutional connections to local centers of power discouraged the immigrants from orienting themselves toward host-society politics. The municipality's impermeability to their demands and its refusal to take responsibility for their material and social needs directed immigrant political mobilization away from Schliermer affairs. Schlieren immigrants' avid engagement in homeland-oriented activities suggested that they had no lack of interest in politics.

International cooperation took precedence over local efforts to integrate or consult with the immigrants. When city officials had an immigration-related problem, they turned to consular officials in Zurich for a solution. The consulates' proximity made it convenient for them to monitor and attempt to mobilize their nationals in Schlieren and throughout the Limmattal (see, for example, *DL,* Feb. 6, 1974). The Italian and Iberian governments ran job-training and language institutes in nearby Dietikon and Zurich, several in conjunction with Swiss trade unions or left-wing political parties; more than a few of their students lived in Schlieren (*DL,* Jan. 22, 1974; Jan. 21, 1978). The Italian and Spanish Catholic missions worked out of local parishes and their national headquarters in Zurich, ministering to Catholic immigrants in their native languages and helping immigrant children with their school lessons.

Such an institutional framework lent durability to immigrants' political and cultural ties with the homelands. Newer immigrants such as the Turks exhibited the most internecine divisions ("Schlieren—Sulla casa" 1984). Iberians, Greeks, and especially the Italians presented a diverse but loosely united organizational front.[7]

True to the Swiss model, homeland-oriented participation was closely linked with the foreigners' gradual development of their own associational networks. These never grew very strong, however. The local government and other Swiss institutions were not supportive of any association that was not at least a quasi-official emanation of a homeland government. High local rents made it almost impossible to find a meeting place; La Courneuve's publicly financed meeting house had no counterpart in Schlieren.[8]

The largest immigrant community in Schlieren, with the longest history of settlement in the city, the Italians enjoyed the strongest organization. The Italian Recreational and Workers' Association (Associazione Recreativa e Lavoratori—ARLI) was the only immigrant association in town with its own headquarters, thanks to its status as an ostensibly apolitical association officially supported by the Italian government. In reality close to the Italian Christian Democrats, the ARLI existed first and foremost to facilitate the immigrants' relations with the homeland. "We cannot do much more here than provide translation services and handle paperwork for Italian nationals," activists shrugged.[9] ARLI leaders did not hesitate to contact local officials when a major difficulty arose. Otherwise, however, few ties bound the association to a generally indifferent city hall. Though not looking for a direct political role, ARLI did work with other Italian groups in the area, including the leftist Federation of Italian Free Colonies in Switzerland (FCLIS), based in Zurich ("ARLI-Schlieren" 1983).

Schlieren's public officials expressed great fear that the Southern Europeans' alleged propensity for communism and labor militancy would manifest itself in their city. The FCLIS did not organize overtly in Schlieren. It had established a "Colony" in 1964 in next-door Dietikon, where officials were less resistant to its activism. Only major causes and issues would occasionally coax it into the open in Schlieren. The far less threatening Christian Association of Italian Workers (ACLI) also had a regional branch in Dietikon and members in Schlieren.[10]

Other immigrant communities had even less of an organizational presence there. A Turkish association with close ties to consular officials in Zurich began operating in Schlieren in 1970. It focused on cultural events and on teaching the children of Turkish workers the language and cultural traditions of their homeland. The group's studied avoidance of political issues made it acceptable to parents with leftist beliefs as well. Relations with local governmental officials were cordial, if low-key. The Turks did not have their own meeting place, but a Catholic charity arranged for the group to use the local parish hall on occasion.[11]

Neither the Spaniards nor the Portuguese produced their usual pattern of flourishing associational life in Schlieren. A small, informal Spanish recreational group met in a Schliermer coffeehouse and planned cultural events.[12] But no local association existed for Portuguese immigrants, one of the newest, smallest immigrant communities in Schlieren (*DL,* Sept. 1, 1978).

Immigrant associational life in Schlieren, in sum, proceeded at low frequency. Cultural events dominated the agendas of the few associations there. The local newspaper, *Der Limmattaler,* covered these and included regular foreign-language columns (such as the monthly "Angolo italiano") and occasional special feature articles. At best, though, immigrants played an indirect political role. Routes of access to city policymakers were practically nonexistent, and the immigrants' would-be leftist allies were either so divided in their regard or so outnumbered that positive action proved impossible. Islam never grew into the focus for multiethnic cooperation in Schlieren that it was in French cities: Schlieren's Turkish association, reflecting the secularism of the Ankara regime, did not promote it. Neither did immigrant women form any organizations of their own in Schlieren.

Schlieren's immigrants did not resort to confrontational forms of participation, since opportunities to exercise their political voice existed at the cantonal and federal levels. The Spanish and Portuguese Communist and Socialist political parties and trade unions, the Catholic Missions, and the Christian Democrats in Zurich all had members who lived in Schlieren. And the more independent Portuguese Association of Zurich, the Federation of Turkish Workers' Organizations, several large Spanish associations, and the very vigorous national headquarters of the FCLIS there attracted immigrants from the entire Limmattal.[13] In addition, a Contact Center (*Kontaktstelle*) established in Zurich in 1968 acted as a smaller version of the Federal Consultative Commission for the Foreigners Problem, and it encouraged foreigners throughout the canton to participate (CFE/EKA 1980, pp. 47–56, 107–109; Tosato 1985).[14]

Zurich was a hotbed of activity for immigrants of all nationalities. The organizational ferment there did not spill over into the hostile territory of Schlieren. But then, it did not need to. It was far easier for that city's immigrants to venture into Zurich to take part in associational activities, petition drives, and other events that would most certainly have panicked Schliermer officialdom. Since militancy seemed to guarantee further retrenchment among native-born Schliermers, the immigrants' relative inactivity in the city itself was logical.

THE XENOPHOBIC REACTION

Although Schlieren officials usually denied that any social tensions existed, xenophobic sentiment had long been rife in the Limmattal. Immigrants from Germany and Austria had never posed problems in this German-speaking area, but Italian workers met with widespread prejudice and suspicion after World War II. Older Italians recalled the signs found throughout the city in the 1950s: "Rooms for rent—but not to Italians."

Resentment increased with the arrival of other Southern Europeans and Turks. The region, after all, had spawned Schwarzenbach. Workers in the canton of Zurich feared job competition from the immigrants. Years of trade union diatribes against employers' use of cheaper alien labor to reduce their wage bills did nothing to foster solidarity, just as it retarded unified action among French and immigrant workers in La Courneuve and Roubaix (Ebel and Fiala 1983, pp. 273–276).

The xenophobes found a ready audience in Schlieren. Although the canton defeated National Action's second initiative in 1970 by a margin of 53 to 47 percent, 52 percent of Schliermers, voting in record numbers, said yes to it. Schlieren was the only city in the entire Limmattal to approve the initiative.[15]

Further stoking xenophobic reactions were the economic troubles that hit Schlieren, like all of Western Europe, in the early and mid-1970s. Many local factories scaled down their operations, laying off workers. Though tame by comparison with the turbulent French labor scene, several labor strikes and factory occupations during these years did endanger the revered labor peace accords in Schlieren. Public officials and the local media began to speak ominously of the "crisis." The City Council reactivated its employment assistance office (*GB* 1974, p. 52; 1975, pp. 57–58; *DL*, June 15, 1975). For all that, the unemployment rate never surpassed 1 percent. Most European cities—and certainly La Courneuve and Roubaix—would have envied Schlieren's position. Foreign workers suffered the brunt of the contraction of employment, and the local economy "breathed them out" with remarkable ease. "We export not only cheese and clocks," one local Socialist Party leader remarked, "but also unemployment" (*DL*, Aug. 29, 1975). The city's economic base was thereby largely protected from severe shocks.

But many Schliermers' perception ran counter to the objective situation. Xenophobic initiatives continued to do very well in Schlieren, much to the embarrassment of city fathers (see Table 17). In elections to the Communal Council and cantonal legislature, however, party organizations and loyalties came into play to a greater degree, making it harder to cast a xenophobic vote in a fit of pique at the "system." In Schlieren, National Action and Democratic Party candidates achieved only meager support. The same institutional factors that prevented the formation of a collective immigrant political movement thus hurt the xenophobes as well.[16]

The mainstream center and right backed the federal government's stabilization policy and opposed the xenophobes on economic grounds: the economy had to have access to all the alien labor it required, even at the cost of large numbers of immigrants who resisted assimilation. Members of the working class tended to be the most susceptible to appeals by National Action and its allies. There was no outright support among the leftist leadership for xenophobic initiatives or positions, but

Table 17 Percentage of votes supporting xenophobic initiatives in Schlieren, 1974–1988

Year	Initiative	Result in Schlieren	Cantonal result
1974	Third xenophobic initiative	43.0	35.3
1975	Scholarship aid to Czech and Hungarian refugee university students (cantonal)	58.1	56.8
1977	Fourth xenophobic initiative	40.0	30.1[a]
1977	Fifth xenophobic initiative	45.6	35.8[a]
1984	Against the "sell-out" of the homeland	57.3	59.2
1988	Sixth xenophobic initiative	39.5	36.2

Sources: Fortuna (1974–1988), entry for April 1984; *DL*, Oct. 22, 1974; Sept. 9, 1975; March 15, 1977; and *Neue Zürcher Zeitung*, Dec. 5, 1988.
a. Regional-level support in Limmattal.

the split in the Socialist Party and the trade unions weakened their effectiveness in combatting them.[17]

Quality-of-life concerns combined with economic fears to keep anti-immigrant feeling high in Schlieren. In the Limmattal the National Action emphasized the ecological aspects of its anti-immigrant position with the slogan "The valley is full." As opposed to French ecologists, a prominent segment of the antigrowth and proenvironment movement embraced drastic limitations on the size of the foreign population as one way of "reducing the burden on the ecosystem" of the Limmattal (*DL*, April 19 and Oct. 27, 1975). Communal festivals and neighborhood groups were playing an important role in the increasingly inward-looking city. An ad hoc "Working Group for a Livable Schlieren" brought together concerned citizens from the entire political spectrum to consider ways to reduce the isolation and anomie of the industrial suburbs (*DL*, June 2, 1981; *GB* 1979, p. 13).

THE TOGETHERNESS INITIATIVE

As the 1980s began, it was the churches that seemed to exhibit the greatest concern for Schlieren's immigrants. The home of Zwingli, the canton of Zurich had a long history as a center of Calvinist Protestantism. Most of the immigrants from the Swiss mountains, Bavaria, Austria, and Southern Europe who had settled there were Catholics, and Schlieren's first Catholic church had opened in 1923. Both branches of Christianity had enjoyed equal status in the canton since 1963 (*GB* 1984, p. 95).

Churches in the canton of Zurich determine their own internal affairs; yet they are public entities, receiving tax money from the government. Both politically unaffiliated and party representatives run in elections to the municipal church board. These elections have generated extensive discussions between political leaders and religious congregations over social policy. In contrast to many other parts of Switzerland, the cantonal electorate consistently voted down proposals to allow foreigners to participate fully in internal church management and church elections (*DL*, March 13 and April 3, 1974; Dec. 6, 1977; April 20, 1978; Jan. 31, 1979; Sept. 28, 1982).

Nevertheless, churches were at the forefront of local efforts to improve the immigrant condition. Their positions sometimes grew out of a "brotherly love" that smacked of charity. But they gradually embraced as their goal the immigrants' empowerment and not just the meeting of their needs. Irrespective of the internal divisiveness over the correct social role for a Swiss church, pastors and laymen spoke out against housing and job discrimination against foreigners; they organized get-togethers and potluck suppers to reduce ignorance and encourage friendships among the native and foreign populations. Schlieren had a branch of the Catholic Workers' Movement, and the local Catholic parish contributed to the operation of the small Italian Catholic Mission (*DL*, Aug. 27, 1974; June 23, 1979).

In 1981 the Catholic Workers' Movement and the Catholic and Protestant churches organized a local campaign in favor of the federal Togetherness Initiative, which would have brought improvements in the immigrant condition. The Evangelical Reformed church took the most active role in promoting the issue. It held an annual "Peace Week" *(Friedenswoche)*, a series of nightly conferences, discussions, and parties centering on a set of salient social or foreign policy issues. That year, one evening was given over to a debate and exposition on the Togetherness Initiative. Immigrant associational leaders, trade union and Socialist Party leaders, and other Swiss citizens and public officials discussed what the immigrants and the host society could do to increase the integration of the former and to avoid xenophobic reactions in the latter. The discussion was a first for Schlieren. It represented real progress, but "a chasm still stretched between the Swiss and the foreigners" (*DL*, March 30, 1981).

The 1981 Peace Week celebration was important, but it was a one-time occurrence. Street theater, rallies, and door-to-door neighborhood canvassing marked the campaign for the Togetherness Initiative in Zurich proper. In Schlieren no such colorful or overt campaigning by foreigners was advisable. Immigrants tried to win over their Swiss co-workers in the factories. More assertive behavior seemed likely to win them more enemies than friends. The Socialist Party and the local Construction Workers' Union quietly backed the Togetherness Initiative but organized no activities in Schlieren.

In the end the initiative did worse in the city than nationwide: 85.4 percent of Schliermers voted against it, compared with an 80 percent negative response overall. A year later the bourgeois parties joined the Socialists in supporting the government's proposed reform of the ANAG immigration law. Only National Action and the Democrats called for its rejection in a 1982 referendum. Yet 54.5 percent of Schlieren voters, a higher percentage than in the canton or the Confederation as a whole, sided with the xenophobes. Schlieren, in fact, was one of only three communities in the canton to endorse the xenophobic referendum (*DL*, March 3 and June 8, 1981; "Die Zürcher Kontaktstelle" 1980).

FACTORY CLOSINGS AND XENOPHOBIC GAINS

Meanwhile, the city's economic woes had not abated. Factories laid off workers or closed entirely throughout the late 1970s and early 1980s. Job-related disruptions peppered the period. The strikes and demonstrations were not impressive by non-Swiss standards. In a city that had not seen a strike of any significance since 1918–19, however, the events were big news indeed.

Foreign workers, active in the interwar strikes, were highly visible participants in those sixty years later. In the course of a bitter conflict in the Schlieren dyeworks in 1976 and 1977, Heinrich Meier, the president of the Company Commission that was to arbitrate the dispute— he was also the president of the city—publicly attributed that "threat to the labor peace" to the "southerly temperament" of "extreme-leftist foreign participants." He prayed that cooler (presumably Swiss) heads would prevail (quoted in *DL*, Nov. 3, 1976; see also May 5, 1977). But the immigrants never adopted confrontational, "un-Swiss" tactics. Nor did they instigate job actions themselves or attempt to escalate one into a major clash.

In May 1983 Schlieren sustained the biggest blow ever to its economy and collective psyche: after several years of paring down its labor force, the Schindler Company announced that it would close d'Wagi. The very soul of the city for ninety years, the factory would release its remaining 740 workers. The city government and the Metal- and Clockworkers' Union pleaded with the plant's owners to keep some of its operations in the city. Concerned people from throughout the Limmattal joined d'Wagi's employees in a series of massive street demonstrations, boycotts, and petitions to protest the closing. The local administration bestowed its blessings on all but the most provocative actions, putting aside its fears of encouraging class divisions (*DL*, June 1, 1983).

Schlieren's typical, consensual style of crisis resolution soon reasserted itself: d'Wagi owners formed the Open Planning Work Group, which brought together the "social partners" to find ways to bring new industries and jobs to the area being abandoned. Local officials extracted a few promises of retraining and employment counseling, but the negotiations produced no change in the final outcome (see the comments of Heinrich Meier in *GB*, 1983, p. 1).

Angry workers had collected enough signatures to place on the ballot a proposal to have the city take over the factory. Heeding authorities' warnings, nearly 80 percent of Schliermers turned down the "Let's Save d'Wagi" initiative, and the plant shut its doors shortly thereafter.[18] Virtually all the Swiss former employees soon found jobs in factories in or near Schlieren. The abandoned plant became home to a healthily diversified collection of small and medium-sized companies. Unemployment never rose much over 1 percent ("Schlieren: A votazione" 1984).

The heavy involvement of immigrant workers in the struggle earned its share of attention. The Swiss trade unions and workers appreciated the participation of their noncitizen comrades, praising their solidarity. But they did not lift a finger to help when the closing of d'Wagi and the meagerness of Swiss unemployment benefits forced many immigrant laborers to return to their homelands.[19] As "inhuman" as that forced departure might have been,[20] Schliermers reacted to the turmoil not with greater compassion for the foreigners in their midst but with intensified zeal to defend the quality of their lives. There were no calls for more complete integration of immigrants into the local host society. The fickleness of the Swiss left in particular disheartened many immigrant activists. "We've been frozen out politically," one immigrant in the FOBB/GBH leadership complained. "There is no true right to strike in this country . . . and there are really no unions in Switzerland."[21]

The closing of d'Wagi and the defeat of both the Togetherness Initiative and the proposed reform of the federal immigration law doused what sparks of immigrant political activity still smoldered in Schlieren. Divisions over immigration widened in both the churches and the trade unions. Schlieren's immigrants had a limited group of sincerely committed allies, in most cases a tiny minority even within their own organizations. Afraid for themselves as well as for the immigrants, these solidarity-group activists advised the immigrants to avoid provocative actions (see Fröhlich 1985).

Apart from appealing to the governments of their homelands to press for the improvements in their condition that they could not effect themselves, the immigrants found only the cultural outlet open to them as a way to advance understanding and tolerance of their traditions without antagonizing the autochthons. Such was the motivation for the annual International Family Festivals that six immigrant communities—Turks, Italians, Spaniards, Portuguese, Yugoslavs, and Greeks—first organized in 1982. Swiss folk groups also participated. Concerts, dancing exhibitions, and food stands offered a range of entertainment possibilities. The immigrant participants hoped to contribute to understanding between peoples and to heighten the sensitivity of their Swiss "guests" to the problems of foreign workers. City officials welcomed the festivals, boasting of Schlieren's "cosmopolitanism" (*DL*, May 21, 1982; see also "Festa internazionale" 1983).

The local administration and politicians turned their attention to the postmaterialist concerns of voters. In 1984 one-third of all motions at Communal Council meetings related to traffic problems, one-quarter to the environment, and most of the rest to housing and employment. Simultaneously, voter participation was falling off precipitously, as increasingly disaffected electors opted not to take time out from their pursuit of the good life to involve themselves in the solution of what were coming to look like insoluble problems. Schlieren's rates of voter participation were low even for Switzerland: from one-third to 40 percent for most federal parliamentary elections, and not infrequently down to single digits for votes on local-level initiatives dealing with less vital issues.[22]

The xenophobes were arousing fewer passions in the city, but they managed to score impressive political gains. The Democratic Party, the environmentalist and xenophobic movement that had initiated the anti-immigrant initiatives of the late 1960s, won representation on the Communal Council in 1982. And the voices of xenophobia carried the day once more in 1983, when 57.9 percent of Schliermers declined the federal government's proposal to ease regulations on the naturalization of certain categories of foreigners. Foreigners applying for Schliermer citizenship met with ever-greater reluctance from the municipal authorities. They suspended the requests of more and more applicants, particularly non-Europeans, until they could demonstrate a "better knowledge of Swiss civics" (*DL*, Dec. 1, 1982).

THE SECOND GENERATION

Even the second generation of foreigners and Europeans had to satisfy local officials as to their full assimilation into Swiss society. In fact one of the few issues that still aroused the interest and involvement of first-generation immigrants in Schlieren was the difficult socio-economic position of their progeny. All the difficulties that they faced coalesced in local schools. The exceedingly low Swiss birthrate, combined with the more familial nature of the immigrant presence in the nation after the early 1970s, produced large numbers of second-generation immigrant schoolchildren in the Limmattal. The recession of the mid-1970s initially reduced their presence slightly, but the overall trend thereafter was a steady rise. Foreign students occupied up to 70 percent of the desks in some schools. Officials complained that they "burdened" *(belasteten)* the educational system (see, for example, *GB* 1981, p. 79).

Educational matters came under the jurisdiction of both the canton and the community, with the boundaries between the competencies of each shifting and occasioning spirited turf wars. Because members of the local school board *(Schulpflege)* ran for election under party labels, debates over the schools unavoidably took on broader political overtones. Although authorities introduced "special" remedial German-language courses, they expected the immigrants' homeland governments and their own autonomous associations to set up bilingual programs and professional training centers for the immigrants and their children.

Homeland officials, working through the Italian consulate and the Italian Catholic Mission in Zurich, felt compelled to act. The Limmattal had an Italian school in Dietikon, and Schlieren itself was home to the region's only Italian preschool, sponsored by the government in Rome. In interviews, immigrant associational leaders of all nationalities tended to criticize officials in the homeland more than those in Switzerland for the paltriness of the programs in place (see Barili and Rovetta 1982).

In 1978 the Italian Recreational and Workers' Association had formed a parents' committee *(comitato genitori)* that worked with the consulate in Zurich to develop courses in Italian language and culture in Schlieren for second-generation immigrant children. Swiss school officials gradually accepted those courses as supplements to the regular educational curriculum ("Schlieren—I corsi" 1982; *DL,* Oct. 5, 1977). Other national groups soon followed the Italians' lead, all of them with a significant degree of official homeland assistance. No other nationality quite matched the Italian network in extensiveness or the close collaboration between consular officials and autonomous immigrant associations. Nevertheless, there were soon courses in language, culture, and religion throughout the canton, several of them in Schlieren. Loosely constructed Spanish, Turkish, and Yugoslav parents' associations appeared. Generally they constituted the only organizational manifestation of immigrants of those nationalities in the city.

Even these immigrant parents' associations never left the limited domain of problem resolution. Their function was to familiarize the immigrant communities with the Swiss educational system and to help their children fit into it more readily. They contacted local school officials to reduce misunderstandings. Administrators valued their input but refused to grant them any form of privileged or institutionalized access. The parents' groups had no noticeable effect on any actions taken by the school board: "They have allowed for an exchange of ideas, that's all."[23]

Churches and local humanitarian groups did work closely with these associations. Aside from the Construction Workers' Union, in fact, they offered the only real forum for contacts between the immigrants and members of the Socialist Party of Schlieren. Concerned about their children's cultural identity, the parents' groups also took part in the annual International Family Festivals after 1982. Among the Italians and Iberians, the absence of militant, leftist immigrant associations like the FCLIS and the ATEES rendered the parents' organization less combative and assertive than in Dietikon, where such organizations were active (*DL,* May 21, 1982; April 7, 1983).

Adolescent Schliermers were mostly a passive lot, although several youth associations engaged in a full slate of social and recreational activities. The municipal government encouraged them to coordinate their activities and to include young and second-generation immigrants in their activities. Schlieren never experienced the sporadic youthful unrest that afflicted Zurich in the early 1980s (*DL,* Jan. 31 and Feb. 6, 1974).

Nevertheless, the city did undergo a nearly decade-long struggle over its "Youth House" (Jugendhaus), a sort of clubhouse in which all youth associations and activities with the blessings of local officials could hold their meetings and parties. The Youth House had opened in 1972 under the auspices of the municipal Youth Department (Jugendarbeit). Repeated drug busts and cases of petty delinquency had forced its doors closed the next year. In the mid-1970s, calls for its reopening grew louder. The "Ju Hu People," an extreme leftist organization active throughout the region, organized boycotts of official events for young people.[24]

The municipality set up a youth counseling center to deal with drug, employment, and the generation's other problems in 1975 and named a new Youth House Commission in 1976. Worried about the growing alienation of its young people, with some trepidation Schlieren officials permitted the Youth House to reopen in 1979. Quiet prevailed thereafter. Under the city's watchful eye, youth organizers could mount no unruly or unorthodox projects on the premises. Radical and politically active youth associations bypassed Schlieren (DL, Feb. 2, 1978; Feb. 8, 1980; April 20, 1982).

Foreign workers' children proved even less politically involved than other youth. They developed no collective identity or political mobilization. They struggled to improve their individual socioeconomic condition and wrestled with their confused, divided cultural and ethnic identities. Authorities encouraged them to participate in the activities of the Youth House, where special events designed to valorize the homeland cultures of Schlieren's workers took shape. The municipal counseling center sponsored special workshops for young Iberian and Turkish immigrants, seriously affected by unemployment and discrimination. Cantonal authorities also provided job counseling services and underwrote extensive bilingual educational programs (GB 1984, p. 59; Tages-Anzeiger, June 24, 1987).

THE IMMIGRATION POLICY DEADLOCK

By the mid-1980s Schlieren's immigrant population had stabilized, with births and family reunification balancing departures. Owing to a stagnant native Swiss birthrate, the percentage of foreigners in the total population, already 26 percent by 1985, crept inexorably upward. A record high 83.3 percent of the city's foreign population then held permits of permanent residency. Even in the newer Portuguese community, the figure had more than doubled in a decade to 43 percent (GB 1984, p. 68).

Especially from the early 1980s on, Turkish, Kurdish, and South and Southeast Asian refugees settled in Schlieren, unsettling the uneasy native-born population in the process. As elsewhere in the country, refugees and illegal immigrants came to preoccupy the immigrant associations, solidarity groups, and xenophobes alike. The sight of Cambodians, Tamils, and sub-Saharan Africans on city sidewalks did not provoke overt signs of racism, but local café chatter resounded with it. Debate over the fate of these newest arrivals threatened the local Socialist Party-trade union political alliance (*Tages-Anzeiger*, July 1, 1987).

True to form, Schliermers responded more favorably than other Swiss to National Action's 1988 initiative: 39.5 percent approved the sixth xenophobic initiative since 1970, compared with 36.2 percent in the canton and 32.7 percent nationwide (*Neue Zürcher Zeitung*, Dec. 5, 1988). The campaign provoked little interest and no political demonstrations in Schlieren, however. Indeed, although xenophobia precluded any policy changes to improve the immigrant condition, neither did greater restrictive practices ensue. The political status quo ante held.

Voter participation continued to slide. In elections in the late 1980s the major parties held their own—the Socialists and the consumerist Independents actually gained lost ground—but the xenophobic Democrats lost the Communal Council seat they had won in 1982. Seemingly in compensation, several newcomers entered the Communal Council from the lists of Environmental Defense of the Limmattal (Umweltschutz Limmattal), which subscribed to the "immigrants as polluters" school of thought, and the free-thinking Humanist Party (*Tages-Anzeiger*, April 6, 1987).

Channeled away from local political involvement, the immigrants remained a cipher. Some activists championed the initiative for a forty-hour work week. Several immigrant associations held meetings with the Construction Workers' Union to discuss the initiative, and disappointment was great when it went down to defeat in December 1988. Immigrant associations then shifted their focus to facilitating peaceful coexistence between citizen and noncitizen Schliermers, which they judged a necessary precondition for meaningful strides toward integration.

No new immigrant or second-generation associations had sprouted by decade's end. The annual International Family Festivals went on without fail, as did other cultural events. Local-level petitions for voting rights circulated in a half-dozen communities in the canton in the late 1980s. Schlieren's immigrant associations gave their verbal and moral support, but overt efforts to gather signatures would have been too inflammatory. Only where the local Swiss left stood united in support were such campaigns feasible ("Les expériences dans le canton de Zürich" 1988).

The immigrants, in short, "have not really played a political role at all" in Schlieren.[25] Their political marginalization in the city, combined with their continuing strong attachment to their homelands, contrasts with the participatory patterns evident in La Courneuve and Roubaix. Schlieren's immigrants managed to wield some small influence within like-minded church groups, and somewhat more within the Construction Workers' union local. They sometimes had a minor grievance redressed. Yet those local channels of political access open to the immigrants stimulated individual rather than collective mobilization.

These points of access became obstructed to a large degree as divisions proliferated and deepened within the Schliermer left. Instead of adopting confrontational tactics, immigrant activists responded by turning to more readily accessible levels of government. But xenophobic sentiment remained strong in the canton of Zurich. The constant stream of anti-immigrant initiatives and referenda at both the federal and cantonal levels wore down the capacity of the Limmattal's immigrants and their remaining allies to mount an effective counteroffensive.

By the early 1990s economic conditions were making matters worse. Local joblessness, which had stuck at unbelievably low levels, began to rise (*Neue Zürcher Zeitung,* July 21, 1992). Just as the reverberations of the closing of d'Wagi were slowly dying away, several large plants that had been in difficulty for years finally closed. Chastened, the city council no longer spoke of the "fundamental resiliency of Schlieren's economy, one of the strongest in the Confederation" (Fortuna 1974–1988, entry for Dec. 1985). When roughly two-thirds of Schliermers voted against Swiss entry into the European Economic Area in December 1992, fear of economic dislocation and of immigrants came together in a vote against confronting the city's and Switzerland's future (*Neue Zürcher Zeitung,* Dec. 8, 1992).

La Chaux-de-Fonds

In a clear counterpoint to "closed" Schlieren, as well as to "mobilizational" La Courneuve, La Chaux-de-Fonds provided wide political access to noncitizens. As in Roubaix, the local network of left-wing and solidarity-group militants was dense, attuned to immigrants' interests, and effective in working toward their empowerment at the local level. Nevertheless, specifically Swiss institutional factors were also at work in La Chaux-de-Fonds, and their effect on immigrant political behavior was undeniable.

The structure of political opportunities in the city resulted from its unique history. Nestled in the Jura Mountains in the canton of Neuchâtel near the French border, La Chaux-de-Fonds and its environs belonged successively to the counts of Neuchâtel, the princes of Baden, and the Orléans-Longueville family. When that dynasty died out in the eighteenth century, the citizens of the canton chose to have the kaiser of Prussia rule over them. Long allied militarily with the Swiss cantons, Neuchâtel became an affiliated member of the Confederation in 1814, even while it remained a Prussian duchy. That curious dual identity lasted until 1848, when a mountaineer-led rebellion proclaimed the Neuchâtelois Republic. After an abortive counterrevolution and a threatened declaration of war from Berlin, Napoleon III of France mediated an end to Prussia's ties to the canton, which officially joined the Swiss Confederation (Pichard 1978, pp. 49–63).

The canton's "ferociously Protestant" religious tradition (Picard 1978, p. 54) and the distance that separated it from Berlin had allowed for the emergence of progressive social and political organization. As early as the mid-1800s workers initiated a broad network of self-help associations and consumer cooperatives. In the 1880s the Socialist Party of Neuchâtel (Parti Socialiste Neuchâtelois—PSN) appeared (Oppliger 1980, pp. 7–8). The party won control of La-Chaux-de-Fonds in 1912, one of its first breakthroughs in Switzerland. After World War I the PSN gained a permanent majority. Thus began the city's lasting reputation as "La Chaux-de-Fonds the Red." Soup kitchens, municipal butchers' shops, communal housing, public works projects, workshops for the unemployed, and the other trappings of municipal socialism familiar in Socialist-led French cities like Roubaix materialized in the ensuing decades.

Socialism in La Chaux-de-Fonds rarely went beyond the bounds of mild social democracy, and the consensualism and collegiality that characterized its political life were uniquely Swiss. The president of the legislative General Council (Conseil Général) was always a Socialist. But municipal commissions reflected proportionally the political makeup of the executive Communal Council (Conseil Communal), whose presidency rotated annually among all parties represented.

To receive representation in the local legislature, a party or movement had to garner at least 10 percent of the vote. That high barrier weakened the kind of minor, fringe parties that enlivened Schlieren's politics. Direct democracy, similarly, was not as easy to practice as in the canton of Zurich: fully 15 percent of a community's voters had to sign a petition for an initiative or referendum to appear on the local ballot.[26]

The Socialists retained their hold over the city, although after 1944 they had to share the reins of local power with the Communists. Cantonal authorities had banned the latter party, established in 1921, under the pretext that it was inciting political violence. It underwent several reincarnations before becoming the gentle, reformist Popular Workers' Party (Parti Ouvrier et Populaire—POP). The city thus became one of the few in Switzerland with a truly influential, "electable" Communist Party. On the other hand, neither the Christian Democrats (Parti Démocrate Chrétien) nor the Swiss People's Party—two important center-right parties nationwide—had any presence in Canton Neuchâtel (LI, June 19, 1981).

La Chaux-de-Fonds's pioneering left-wing tradition owed much to the nature of its economic development: it was one of Switzerland's first and most industrialized cities. Like Roubaix it had a long history of monoindustrialism. Whereas Roubaix had become synonymous with textiles, La Chaux-de-Fonds had been the "Watch City" since the Middle Ages, the capital of a clockmaking region stretching from Basel along the spine of the Jura to Geneva. Luxury gold watches were a speciality of the area's early craft industry. The city turned to the mass production of cheap "watches for the proletariat" when the national railroad linked La Chaux-de-Fonds with the rest of the nation in the mid-1800s and cleared the way for full-scale industrialization (Landes 1983, pp. 257, 271–272).

Because of its location and industrial base, La Chaux-de-Fonds had as long a history as Roubaix of welcoming immigrants, refugees, and foreign workers. The revocation of the Edict of Nantes in 1685 sent a flood of French Protestants into La Chaux-de-Fonds. Other refugees followed over the years: French counter-Revolutionaries and *Communards*, German Anabaptists and Mennonites, Catholics from central Switzerland, Alsatian Jews, and German and Italian antifascists (Osterwald 1913).

Foreign labor offered an ideal solution to the fluctuating labor demands of the export-dependent, boom-and-bust watchmaking industry. Immigrants from German-speaking areas of Switzerland long manned the city's workshops. By 1860 non-Neuchâtelois Swiss represented just under half of resident Chaux-de-Fonniers; non-Swiss, between 12 and 16 percent. In 1880 a full third of Chaux-de-Fonniers spoke German, not French (Cop 1980, pp. 109, 198).

Like the Flemings in Roubaix, the newcomers were not long in having a political impact. The Berners and Germans brought with them the Socialist ideas that came to dominate the political life of La Chaux-de-Fonds and neighboring Le Locle. In the nineteenth century the Socialist movement drew its most ardent proponents from the immigrant ranks (Cop 1980, pp. 229–289).

After World War II immigration produced much of La Chaux-de-Fonds's growth. From 10 percent of the total resident population in 1960, immigrants came to make up over 20 percent by 1982 (Service Cantonal de Statistique 1982, p. 52). Italians formed the largest postwar contingent, but their share of the foreign population gradually declined in favor of Iberian, Yugoslav (Slovenian and Croatian), and Turkish workers.[27]

AN OPEN, NURTURING POLITICAL OPPORTUNITY STRUCTURE

La Chaux-de-Fonds's experience demonstrates the positive impact of indigenous institutions on the evolution of immigrant politics. The city's political and economic development established both a tradition of democratic communal socialism and a tight network of progressive militants in the trade unions, political parties, voluntary associations, and churches. The institutional response to immigrants' needs achieved a high degree of effectiveness and inclusiveness.

Even though the municipality could not by itself compensate entirely for the inadequacies of the Swiss welfare state, social services in La Chaux-de-Fonds were relatively well developed (see "Considérations" 1977). Moreover, the city contained far more public housing units than any other in the country. Since 1918 it had constructed municipal housing and, in collaboration with cantonal authorities, French-style low-rent housing projects (HLM) in the 1950s (LI, Jan. 7, 1974). Immigrants lived there and in other housing that ran the gamut from squalid to fairly comfortable. Employer-provided apartments and barracks for seasonal workers presented the same cramped spaces and lack of amenities typical of their ilk nationwide.

Because the local housing market offered greater possibilities to lower-income people, there were proportionately fewer such units in La Chaux-de-Fonds. The private housing stock in working-class neighborhoods left a lot to be desired by normal Swiss standards. Buildings often dated from the mid-1800s, and many landlords failed to keep their properties up to code. Even so, a 1974 solidarity-group study found fewer egregious instances of substandard lodging in La Chaux-de-Fonds than anywhere else in the canton. Costs there ran among the lowest in the nation (CASS 1974).

As a result of these factors, the immigrants' homeland governments stepped in less frequently than in Schlieren, though more than in France. When they did, city officials exhibited great tolerance and support for all democratic regimes. The result was a high level of cooperation between homeland and Swiss officials in La Chaux-de-Fonds, with both focusing on the immigrants' lot in the host society. The immigrants' homeland-oriented political involvement did not so much slacken as become more pragmatic and issue oriented, geared toward prying resources out of governments there in order to improve life in the host society.

Homeland organizations and officials had an impressive track record of interest in La Chaux-de-Fonds's foreigners. From the beginning, the large, active Italian community had attracted notice back home: King Umberto I visited the city in 1890; Benito Mussolini, then a Socialist, in 1904. In later years antifascists found a safe haven in the city. So, too, did Iberians opposed to the Franco and Salazar/Caetano regimes until democracy arrived on the peninsula in the mid-1970s (*LI*, Oct. 10, 1975).

Such objects of intense concern diminished thereafter. The immigrants' focus shifted toward La Chaux-de-Fonds, where a choice of institutional outlets was at hand to employ in voicing grievances. Homeland officials interested in maintaining foreign workers' loyalties turned toward filling the gaps in Swiss social-welfare coverage and meeting their nationals' cultural and religious needs in the host society. More than in the other case cities, foreigners in La Chaux-de-Fonds identified with their host city and lobbied their homeland governments as permanent emigrant communities and not as temporary expatriates.[28]

In the mid-1970s, for example, the Italian government reorganized the Consular Coordinating Committees that linked Italian officialdom and local expatriate communities. The first balloting under new electoral rules occurred in 1978. The Italian community in La Chaux-de-Fonds, wanting to ensure the city's influence in the European-wide organization headquartered in Rome, put aside internal ideological squabbles and presented a single list of candidates. Participation in the consular elections reached higher levels in La Chaux-de-Fonds than anywhere else in Switzerland (*LI*, June 7, 1978).

Homeland officials also cooperated extensively with foreign and Swiss trade unions and political parties. Both the Italian and Spanish governments set up schools and professional training institutes in the La Chaux-de-Fonds/Le Locle area with the help of trade unionists and the Socialist Party. Municipal authorities granted regular financial support to these institutions, which they saw as providing essential services that complemented municipal programs. The smaller numbers of Turks, Portuguese, and other more recent groups did not generate a major homeland organizational presence; but the Swiss, Italian, and Spanish institutions served those foreigners too (CFE/EKA 1986).

The Chaux-de-Fonds Inhabitants (not "Foreigners") Police tolerated the activities of homeland organizations. The Italian, Spanish, Portuguese, Turkish, and Chilean Communist and Socialist parties all organized in the city. Foreign Catholic missions were also very active and did not shrink from an overtly political role. The Italian Catholic Mission's influential monthly, *L'Amico*, published particularly sharp analyses of events in the host society. Consular officials and homeland leftist groups were on good terms with each other and with city and cantonal officials (Menghini 1984a).

Newer groups like the Turks agitated openly against the regimes in their homelands. They were less fearful of retaliation in La Chaux-de-Fonds than in German Switzerland, where disapproving local authorities and squads of Turkish terrorists operating from Germany could readily silence dissenting voices. But gradually even the more recent emigrants devoted more interest to host-society affairs. Immigrant groups learned from one another's experiences which tactics produced positive results in La Chaux-de-Fonds (Menghini 1984b).

The worldwide economic crisis of the 1970s and early 1980s hit La Chaux-de-Fonds harder than Schlieren or any other area in the country. Clockmaking suffered a 36 percent loss of jobs from 1966 through 1975. The canton lost fully 10 percent of its jobs overall in 1974 alone, La Chaux-de-Fonds even more. Like Switzerland's other labor markets, the city "exhaled" foreign workers, more than 600 in the first half of the 1970s. As a result, unemployment never affected more than 2 or 3 percent of the labor force—negligible by French standards, but high enough to make the city the most afflicted in Switzerland (*LI*, Oct. 15, 1975).

Unlike in Schlieren and despite severe economic problems, the municipal and cantonal governments refused to abandon their cultural, health, and educational programs. Indeed, they launched new ones facilitating job retraining and language instruction for immigrants and refugees. Large shares of communal spending were going to immigrants and native Chaux-de-Fonniers in need of welfare assistance, rental supplements, and unemployment benefits. Though more modest than the centralized French effort, this social assistance continued to reduce pressures on official homeland organizations to assist their nationals (*LI*, March 6 and Oct. 10, 1974).

Chaux-de-Fonnier leftists remained true to their combative reputation (for Switzerland). Starting in the mid-1970s, they took to the streets to decry the loss of jobs. Organized labor was robust in La Chaux-de-Fonds. In 1974 a higher proportion of workers in the canton of Neuchâtel, 31 percent, belonged to a trade union than in any other Swiss canton. The percentage climbed even higher in industrial centers like La Chaux-de-Fonds. The Metal- and Clockworkers' Union (FTMH/ SMUV) was the single largest union, with the Construction Workers' Union (FOBB/GBH) and the Christian trade unions strong as well. Unionized to roughly the same degree as their native-born counterparts, foreign workers made up over half of La Chaux-de-Fonds's local FOBB/GBH and a good portion of the FTMH/SMUV.[29]

La Chaux-de-Fonds's Trade Union Cartel, part of the Swiss Syndical Union (USS/SGB), brought together the major elements of the labor movement in the city and was a progressive force to be reckoned with. The Construction Workers took a leading role in advancing the immigrants' cause within the Cartel and the allied Socialist Party, and it opened up its own organization to noncitizens on an equal basis with the native-born. In fact by the late 1970s the leader of the local branch of the Spanish Socialist Workers' Party headed both that trade union and the Trade Union Cartel. Even the FTMH/SMUV, whose local in Schlieren was so deaf to immigrant demands, welcomed immigrants warmly throughout its ranks in La Chaux-de-Fonds.[30]

Left-wing political parties demonstrated similar inclusiveness. Many had close ties with their "brother" parties from the immigrants' homelands. As with the trade unions, dual membership was common among foreign workers. The bourgeois parties did not exclude foreigners, but they won few new recruits from what was almost entirely a working-class constituency.[31]

The two largest left-wing political parties—the ideologically moderate POP and the Socialists—worked closely in running the city. One bourgeois party leader astutely declared that the POP's policies "owed more to the Salvation Army than to Marx."[32] The trade unions' connections with the local Socialist-Communist administration were extensive. Hence immigrant labor activists enjoyed direct access to municipal decisionmaking. This thoroughgoing, genuine unity of the local left went a long way toward ensuring its durability. By the mid-1970s La Chaux-de-Fonds and Le Locle were Switzerland's only cities under the political control of the left ("Economie locale" 1982, p. 371).

Because of the accepted presence and activity of foreign trade unions and political parties on Swiss soil, working-class mobilization in La Chaux-de-Fonds grew to take the form of loosely coordinated action by an array of ethnic-based labor movements. Immigrant workers participated heavily in the strike activity that hit La Chaux-de-Fonds throughout the middle and late 1970s. The Swiss took their presence at rallies and meetings as a matter of course. The working-class organizations saw immigrants as Chaux-de-Fonniers with the right to express demands, and trade unions and left-wing political parties actively courted them. The sheer size of the foreign worker population, the local economy's dependency on their labor, and the extent of their rights in and outside the workplace made it important for the local left to incorporate them—even if the political competition that pluralism fostered in the French left did not exist to the same degree.[33]

Just as they had earlier taken up the causes of antiauthoritarian Iberians, Swiss leftists in the city offered financial and moral backing for Turkish, Chilean, Southeast Asian, and other refugees and immigrants in their opposition to homeland regimes. Solidarity also held firm whenever an incident arose involving discrimination against foreign laborers. Local trade unionists organized debates that addressed both the general interests of the working class and the specific concerns of its immigrant component. Militancy also spread beyond the factories, with renters' associations in the HLM demanding rent freezes during the difficult economic times (*LI*, Oct. 3, 1975).

The local government endorsed the protesters' actions. It cautioned them against resorting to illegal or otherwise "aggressive" demonstrations, calling instead for "dialogue and reason." Favored were tried-and-true Swiss methods: petitions, round-table discussions, and officially authorized marches (*LI*, Feb. 1 and May 9, 1974; Oct. 24, 1975). Even the secular decline of the clockmaking industry failed to devalue such institutional forms of participation.[34]

Indeed, La Chaux-de-Fonds experienced no more confrontational immigrant political participation than Schlieren. The most serious offense committed by foreigners was the unauthorized posting of political signs and notices on city walls *(l'affichage sauvage)*. Confrontation lost the importance that it had where all institutional participatory channels were blocked, as in mid-1970s France. In La Chaux-de-Fonds local-level opportunities for effective institutional participation by the immigrants were abundant and support from the indigenous left consistent.

Such circumstances limited the impact of possible losses on any one particular front. They also worked against the rise of xenophobia in the city and the canton. Though not free from isolated xenophobic incidents, La Chaux-de-Fonds was easily the most "anti-anti-immigrant" of the four case cities in this study.[35] Accustomed to and structurally dependent on foreign labor, it heeded those political and trade union leaders who warned against "cutting off the branch on which our economy sits" (*LI*, Feb. 20, 1974). Economic interest groups lobbied long and hard against the series of anti-immigrant initiatives in the 1970s. The 1970 National Action initiative attracted support from 38.6 percent of the city's voters—compared with 46 percent nationwide—and the xenophobes fared even worse thereafter (see Table 18). Xenophobic candidates rarely received more than a handful of votes from La Chaux-de-Fonds in cantonal and federal elections (see *LI*, May 9, 1972; Oct. 7, 1974; March 11, 1977).

ETHNIC ASSOCIATIONAL ACTIVITY AND THE COMMUNAUTÉ NEUCHÂTELOISE DE TRAVAIL SUISSES-ETRANGERS

The immigrants themselves were in fact far more dynamic than the xenophobes in La Chaux-de-Fonds. The fact that city authorities and political and trade union activists welcomed the immigrants' homeland political and labor organizations helped make class and eth-

Table 18 Percentage of votes for xenophobic initiatives in
La Chaux-de-Fonds, 1970–1988

Year	Result in La Chaux-de-Fonds	Cantonal result	Swiss result
1970	38.6	39.1	46.0
1974	28.6	26.3	34.2
1977	27.1	25.3	29.4
1977	29.4	27.3	33.8
1988	34.2	33.6	32.7

Sources: L'Impartial June 8, 1970; October 21, 1974; March 14, 1977; and *Neue Zürcher Zeitung,* Dec. 5, 1988.

nicity and the homeland and host society separate but clearly complementary bases and targets for immigrant identity and mobilization.

Not hampered in Switzerland by legal restrictions like the ones in force in France until 1981, autonomous immigrant associations of all kinds had an easier time in La Chaux-de-Fonds than in Schlieren. Authorities nurtured the development of viable, representative interlocutors in the immigrant communities. The city could not by law offer public monies to foreigners' associations, but it charged them only modest sums for the use of public rooms.[36]

All modes of immigrant associational activity operated at a relatively high level in La Chaux-de-Fonds. The left-leaning Italian Free Colony (CLI) organization there was French Switzerland's most active and aggressive. The National Committee for Understanding (CNI) unified the Italian immigrant community at the national level in Switzerland. La Chaux-de-Fonds had an effective local version: the Italian Citizen Committee (Comitato Cittadino Italiano—CCI) brought together the CLI, the Italian Catholic Mission, the Italian Socialist and Communist parties, and other Italian recreational and cultural associations ("CLI–La Chaux-de-Fonds" 1983; "Festa organizzata" 1983). The CCI heightened the effectiveness of La Chaux-de-Fonds's Italians with both homeland and host-society officials.[37]

The Portuguese community also had an associational life that in its vibrancy resembled that of their compatriots in France more than those in Schlieren. More typically of the pattern in Switzerland, though, it created only one formal organization, the Association of Portuguese Workers (Associação dos Trabahaldores Portugueses—ATP), which welcomed immigrants of all political persuasions. Autonomous, it was nonetheless on cordial terms with consular officials in Geneva.[38]

Other communities could not match the Italians or Portuguese in intraethnic cohesion. Still, local Spaniards did achieve a degree of coordination. The culturally oriented People of Spain (Pueblos de España) maintained a local version of the Spanish Houses established by Madrid throughout the Western European host societies. A Coordination Committee of Spanish Associations (Comitado de Coordinación de las Asociaciones Españoles—CCAE) embraced the Pueblos and most of the non-Communist local parents' and cultural associations. The Association of Emigrant Spanish Workers in Switzerland (ATEES), close to the Spanish and Swiss Communists, had an extremely active group in the city and its own headquarters. The Spanish Communist Party likewise maintained a visible organizational presence. It had close ties to the ATEES leadership. Relations with the CCAE were slightly strained, yet by comparison with the more divided Spanish communities in many other cities and the organizationally dormant or co-opted Spaniards of Schlieren and La Courneuve, those in La Chaux-de-Fonds seemed quite unified and spirited.[39]

For Turks, the political picture was more complex. Through their ties with local Communists in the POP, Turkish Communists took an especially intense interest in local politics. By the mid-1970s an autonomous, left-leaning Turkish association had formed. Kurdish refugees also organized with the help of a group of sympathetic Swiss activists. Turks and Kurds distrusted each other; but as nowhere else in Western Europe, representatives of the two groups cooperated to an unheard-of degree in La Chaux-de-Fonds. They even participated in parallel if uncoordinated fashion in particularly important activities sponsored by local Swiss leftists. Such amazingly peaceful coexistence attested to the unifying forces at work in the city.[40]

Generally speaking, the other national groups present in La Chaux-de-Fonds modeled their forms of organization on those pioneered by the earlier, more numerous Italians. And again, Italian immigrants organized in often strikingly different ways in the Swiss and French case cities. Similar divergences were also evident among the Iberian and Turkish communities, suggesting that more was going on than merely the adoption by all active immigrants of the participatory pattern set by the predominant national group.

A crucial factor was the strong, well-connected network of solidarity-group activists in La Chaux-de-Fonds. In Roubaix a long tradition of Catholic socialism and humanitarian associational activity produced a greater independent participatory thrust for immigrants than did the co-optation-minded, Communist-dominated militants of La Cour-neuve and the ambivalent, heavily outnumbered activists of Schlieren. Of the four cities, La Chaux-de-Fonds was home to the most unified, sympathetic network of local and regional militants.

Besides the political parties and trade unions, religious groups were particularly crucial. Notions of social action imbued the Protestant So-cial Center in town, which forged many pro-immigrant actions. Also, Southern Europeans made up a large share of the sizable Catholic mi-nority (about one-third of churchgoers by 1980), and Catholic Work-ers' Action (ACO) enjoyed a higher profile in La Chaux-de-Fonds than was customary in Protestant cantons. The viable Christian trade union local, similarly, espoused more militant positions in the canton than in most Swiss regions. The immigrants had real clout within those congre-gations, since they enjoyed full religious voting rights in the canton (*LI*, Sept. 23–24, 1978; May 12, 1980; June 9, 1981).

The municipal government depended heavily on the input of reli-gious and other humanitarian organizations when formulating policy, and implementation fell to them in many instances. Feeding that cozy local state-society relationship were the bonds of friendship and family that bound political, trade union, and associational militants. Ties be-tween the solidarity groups in the canton's largest cities were also close. The crazy-quilt of connections assured immigrants allied with one or more key solidarity groups of a direct line of contact with city hall and the Château—the seat of cantonal power—in Neuchâtel.

Solidarity groups provided immigrant associations with much-needed financial wherewithal and moral support, which their own members' dues could not alone provide. The most vulnerable of foreign groups were able to profit from the umbrella provided by stronger, well-connected Swiss patrons. Antixenophobic committees formed seemingly spontaneously whenever National Action or the Republi-cans launched initiatives.

On a more permanent basis, several solidarity-group coalitions served as nerve centers for sustained local efforts promoting the immigrants' causes. The Committee against the Seasonal Workers' Statute (CASS) had a very active section in La Chaux-de-Fonds, bringing together immigrant associations and virtually the entire non-Communist left in collaborative efforts (CASS 1976).

In 1975 CASS and other solidarity-group activists were instrumental in the creation of a consultative structure for the immigrants: the Neuchâtel Swiss-Foreigners Work Community (Communauté Neuchâteloise de Travail Suisses-Etrangers—CNTSE) included solidarity-group representatives, immigrant associations, trade union leaders, employers, and local and cantonal political leaders. Swiss nationals outnumbered immigrants. Most were *Chaux-de-Fonniers,* but the CNTSE operated at the cantonal level because there were participants from across the region (CNTSE 1975).

The CNTSE received a small subsidy from the Communal Council of La Chaux-de-Fonds, but otherwise it depended on private funds and members' dues to advance its agenda. Its efforts focused on the immigrants' educational and training problems, discrimination cases, and administrative imbroglios. Every year the CNTSE organized a multicultural festival that resembled Schlieren's International Family Festival and Roubaix's Festival of Friendship.[41] The organization sent a delegate to the national umbrella group for consultative bodies, the Community of Contact and Information Centers (IGSA), and had close ties with the Federal Consultative Commission for the Foreigners Problem in Bern (CNTSE 1978, 1979, 1980).

The CNTSE contributed to the ethnic-based organizational structuring of the immigrant communities and strengthened solidarity among them. As in Roubaix the consultative body organized along ethnic lines. Although more than one delegate could stand for each of the canton's immigrant communities, each *nationality* had equal weight on it. That setup had a consolidating effect on organization. It "brought the Italians closer together, and the other nationalities squabbled less among themselves as well."[42] Because of the mutual suspicions poisoning relations between business leaders and Swiss and foreign Communists, however, the CNTSE did not welcome foreign Communist activists or the POP—which opposed such "alibi institutions" anyway. With the Italian CLI, Spanish ATEES, and Portuguese ATP on the CNTSE, however, Communists did have close friends inside the institution.[43]

When the city's economy failed to recover in the late 1970s, the left came in for sharp attacks from the bourgeois parties. The traditional practice of rotating top municipal offices among the left remained inviolate, nevertheless, and consultation and discussion remained the rule. A POP councillor even acceded to the city presidency in 1976 (*LI*, May 16, 1980). Local political discourse and General Council debates were growing more heated, however.

The campaign for the Togetherness Initiative in the late 1970s and early 1980s caused tempers to flare. Internal conflicts in the CNTSE burst into the open: the immigrant associations, the political left, the trade unions, and the churches strongly endorsed the proposal to improve the immigrant condition; the bourgeois parties and employers, fearing higher labor costs, called for its defeat. They grew upset with the CNTSE's open politicking in favor of "Togetherness." Business leaders withdrew their funding from the consultative body, and the Employers' Union (Union Patronale) withdrew its membership altogether in 1980 (CNTSE 1984). That move doomed a body whose legitimacy in the Swiss context necessitated the participation of all social partners.[44]

Over 38 percent of voters in La Chaux-de-Fonds approved the Togetherness Initiative in 1981, in contrast to 16 percent nationwide. A year later, while the Swiss electorate rejected the proposed relaxing of the federal immigration law (ANAG), 55 percent of Chaux-de-Fonnier voters accepted that modest federal project (*LI*, April 6, 1981; May 28 and June 7, 1982).

The defeat of the Togetherness Initiative and the revised ANAG in 1982, though less crushing in La Chaux-de-Fonds than in almost any other Swiss community, sapped many activists' energies. A small core of committed local leftists refused to give up. A Swiss-Immigrant Committee (Comité Suisses-Immigrés) tried to pick up the pieces of the Togetherness movement. Consciousness raising took the form of "Swiss-Immigrant Days" that combined food and folklore with policy debates and speechmaking (*LI*, Oct. 8, 1974; April 28, 1975).

THE IMMIGRANT VOTE

Despite the setbacks and challenges of these years, many immigrants in La Chaux-de-Fonds were able to exercise a political right to which few foreigners in Western Europe had access: since 1849, immigrants at least twenty years old who met certain residency requirements could vote in municipal elections in the canton.[45] The legal quirk was a legacy of the confused period during which the canton of Neuchâtel led a dual existence as both a Prussian duchy and a Swiss canton. Several modifications over the years notwithstanding, the fundamental right of resident foreigners to participate in local political contests survived after World War II (Bois 1973, p. 23).

Still, immigrants actively lobbied for wider suffrage. In 1979 the Italian Free Colony, the Spanish ATEES, the Portuguese ATP, and allied groups organized a petition campaign in favor of immigrant eligibility for local elected office and cantonal-level voting rights. All immigrant associations in the canton worked for the reforms; even consular officials expressed their support. In October 1980 a parade of more than 100 activists and sympathizers marched through the Jura passes from La Chaux-de-Fonds to Neuchâtel, banners flying, to deposit the signed petitions at the Château (*LI*, Oct. 6, 1980).

In direct response, and to make up for the immigrants' disappointment over the defeat of the Togetherness Initiative, their Socialist, Communist, and Swiss solidarity-group allies proposed in 1981 that immigrants be allowed to vote in local matters if they had a permit of permanent residency and had spent one year (down from five) in the city. In the face of some cranky but not intense opposition in the ranks of the bourgeois parties, the canton's Grand Council approved the reduction in the waiting period (*LI*, Dec. 3, 1980; June 24, 1981).

The potential immigrant electorate expanded yet again in 1982, this time as a result of Swiss diplomacy. Negotiators working out a renewal of the official Italo-Swiss immigration accord that year included modifications that further cut the wait for the permit for the largest immigrant contingent in Switzerland and La Chaux-de-Fonds. As a result, like the French and Germans, Italians would have to spend only five years instead of the usual ten before acquiring a permit of permanent residency. In 1984 the cantonal legislature decided to require that immigrants simply possess such a permit and live in the canton (not in a specific community) before they could cast a local ballot. Noncitizens represented 2 percent of the potential electorate in La Chaux-de-Fonds in 1960; they constituted a full 15 percent in 1984. More than half of the city's foreign population (57 percent) could vote (Débely 1986, pp. 12–17; Ville de La Chaux-de-Fonds 1984, pp. 379–380, 504–505).

This growing electoral clout heightened the interest that solidarity groups, political parties, and trade unions showed in the immigrants and the issues of special concern to them. By 1984 the left's hold on the municipal government was wavering. The immigrants became the crucial factor in the balance of local political power. The POP, worried that it might fall below the high 10 percent threshold necessary to retain communal political representation, formed the "POP-Socialist Unity" (POP/Unité Socialiste) with the small, previously snubbed, extreme-leftist Socialist Workers' Party (PSO/SAP). Neither the Socialists nor the POP had deigned to deal with the small, highly intellectualized movement.[46] Like the PSU in France, it had called attention to the immigrants and their problems throughout Switzerland since the 1960s, under its earlier manifestation as the Revolutionary Marxist League. In La Chaux-de-Fonds the mainstream left's receptivity to the immigrants had long made the minuscule PSO less useful to them. In 1984 the new POP-PSO alliance emphasized immigration-related issues. It promised the immigrant communities that in return for their support, they would receive several of its seats on municipal commissions (G. Berger 1986).

The campaign witnessed outright lobbying of noncitizen voters by all the major local political parties. The Socialists underscored the advances made by immigrants under their leadership. Even the Liberals (Parti Libéral), pillars of the bourgeois opposition, ran advertisements in Italian and Spanish in the local media. The Radicals (Parti Radical-Démocratique) issued appeals in French because "we know that you electors from other countries have mastered our language" (see Débely 1986, appendix).

Homeland consular officials, the autonomous immigrant associations, and the Catholic Missions all urged the immigrants to vote. Most immigrant community leaders, even Italian and Iberian priests and nuns, supported the left, which had consistently defended immigrant interests. The foreign political parties and trade unions, of course, campaigned for their "brother" political formations.[47]

In the canton of Neuchâtel each political party draws up and mails to electors its own ballot—traditionally in Switzerland's three official languages: French, German, and Italian. Several changes in 1984 reflected the immigrants' new electoral strength. The Socialists replaced the explanation in German with one in Spanish. The POP went even further, dropping German and adding Spanish and Portuguese (Débely 1986, p. 25).

The May vote produced some surprising results. The center-right bourgeois parties picked up five seats. The Independents, who had made their political breakthrough in 1976, lost all five of theirs. But the Socialists lost only a single seat, and the POP surpassed the 10 percent barrier and kept its six General Councillors. The PSO profited from its alliance with the POP, seating its first councillor and joining the governing majority (*LI*, May 21 and 23, 1984).

The immigrants made the biggest splash in the 1984 municipal voting. Twelve percent of eligible foreigners, or over 37 percent of those registered, voted; though hardly overwhelming, that percentage of voters had grown from less than one-quarter in 1972. (Among registered Swiss voters, 50.1 percent participated.) Local and national commentators acknowledged that the electoral contribution of noncitizens kept La Chaux-de-Fonds under left-wing control. That was the most noteworthy impact that immigrant political participation won in Switzerland or France ("Le poids des immigrés" 1984; "A sinistra, ma . . ." 1984).

The left kept its promise to the immigrants. The Italian Citizen Committee (CCI) chose an Italian to sit on the Education Commission, a Spaniard allied with the POP became a member of the Library Commission, and a Portuguese Socialist joined the Socialist Unity delegation on the Economic Commission. Tellingly, when a family crisis compelled the Education Commission member to return to her country of origin in 1984, the CCI replaced that Christian Democrat with a Communist. The immigrant communities found a united front to be their best weapon (de Rham 1987).

Thus through institutional participatory channels the city's foreign population won greater political access, as well as the fulfillment of several concrete demands. The immigrants' political activities also received extensive media coverage. Local newspapers offered the immigrants a crucial soapbox.[48] The Neuchâtel Cantonal Radio-Television Society, an officially sponsored media advisory board, had appointed an immigrant to its board in 1980 to keep the group abreast of the foreign communities' needs ("Economie locale" 1982).

Not surprisingly, perhaps, naturalization was an easier process in La Chaux-de-Fonds than in Schlieren. With Swiss nationality law based on *jus sanguinis*, the number of applicants remained relatively modest. Few of them, however, failed to obtain a positive response from the General Council. No applicant was ever told to brush up on his or her knowledge of Swiss civics. In a stark departure from Schliermer practice, La Chaux-de-Fonds by the mid-1980s welcomed as citizens a number of Turkish, sub-Saharan African, and Asian immigrants and refugees, in addition to the more common Western and Southern Europeans.[49]

THE SECOND GENERATION

Like their parents, the children of foreign workers enjoyed more institutional channels of political participation in La Chaux-de-Fonds than in any other Swiss city. Their naturalization rates, while not overwhelming, were higher than elsewhere in the country. Then again, they had greater difficulty finding employment than in most Swiss cantons. Their chances of improving on the low-paying, low-status jobs that their parents performed were also somewhat lower (albeit higher than in France).

The second generation was most visible in the city's public schools. A privately funded 1978 study indicated that about one-third of primary-school students were foreigners. That percentage dropped for the upper grades and the nonvocational schools, reflecting their high dropout rates. Two-thirds of the students that the school system considered educationally lagging were non-Swiss (Sammali 1978).

La Chaux-de-Fonds had always taken the lead on preschool programs, bilingual education, homework supervision and assistance services, and vocational training for citizen and noncitizen residents. Homeland governments and fraternal associations, local Swiss labor organizations, and solidarity groups acted aggressively, both individually and in tandem. A Swiss educational advisory body observed: "It is certainly not a coincidence that it has been in a canton where political rights are guaranteed to foreigners on the communal level that the second generation's scholastic problems have been recognized and acted on so progressively" (Centre Suisse en Matière de Documentation et d'Education 1985).[50]

Most second-generation immigrants eluded the determined efforts of left-wing Swiss and foreign groups to attract them into their organizational orbits. Some foreign-origin youngsters did join in the various political actions undertaken by some of their parents and native Chaux-de-Fonniers. In addition, La Chaux-de-Fonds was home to one of French Switzerland's few chapters of SOS-Racisme.[51]

Overall, though, the institutional forces that defused most organized second-generation mobilization in Switzerland at the federal level operated even in progressive La Chaux-de-Fonds. Immigrants of the second and third generations, including those born and educated in Switzerland, remained above all foreign laborers. The system denied them automatic naturalization and a wider collective social identity. Access to multiple institutional political channels discouraged them from adopting aggressive, confrontational tactics. La Chaux-de-Fonds experienced little of the protest and violence among native-born youths that so startled Zurich and other cities in the early 1980s, and juvenile delinquency was far less of an issue.[52]

THE IMMIGRANTS AS A PRESSURE GROUP

La Chaux-de-Fonds's political system faced new challenges in the latter half of the 1980s, and so did the relationship between immigrants and local authorities. Economic worries persisted. Yet municipal and cantonal authorities lured investment into the area, and the unemployment rate dropped. Outmigration more than balanced job losses. Labor shortages even developed in certain unskilled and semiskilled sectors (Jeannet 1986).

As in Schlieren, quality-of-life issues filled the local political agenda almost as much as economic concerns. Living in a picturesque mountainous region, Chaux-de-Fonniers of all political stripes had joined the environmentalist movement at an early date. That general consensus, combined with the 10 percent hurdle to representation in local government, had long kept environmentalism from providing the basis for a new political cleavage (*LI*, Feb. 22 and June 18, 1974). The situation changed in the 1980s, when a new green party appeared in the canton: Ecology and Liberty (Ecologie et Liberté) argued that a separate political movement was necessary to draw the proper intensity of attention to environmental issues. The movement resembled the French Greens more than those in Schlieren, aligning itself with the antixenophobic camp.

Ecology and Liberty joined with the other local political formations in calling on voters to approve easier naturalization procedures for foreigners in a 1983 federal ballot. The electorate heeded the counsel, supporting the reform by a 57 to 43 percent margin; nationally, again, voters turned it aside. The federal government's more restrictive new asylum law in 1987, backed by the business community and the small local National Action organization, won approval in the city, but by one of the scantest margins in Switzerland (*Tages-Anzeiger*, April 6, 1987).

Such reaffirmations of La Chaux-de-Fonds's relative tolerance came as refugees from Southeast Asia and Latin America and illegal immigrants from Turkey were arriving in significant proportions. Local immigrants, Socialists, *POPistes*, the Socialist Workers' Party, churches, and the rest of the local humanitarian militant network banded together to provide assistance (*LI*, May 11, 1984). In 1987, in a particularly colorful gesture, an illegal Kurdish refugee covered his head with a bag and spoke at a meeting of the local Unemployed Workers' Association. He fielded several questions from unemployed Southern European workers in attendance, in an attempt to calm fears that the newest immigrants would "steal" their jobs (*LI*, March 6, 1987).

In autumn 1988 these same solidarity-group activists formed a "unified committee" *(comité unitaire)* to fight the sixth xenophobic initiative. The major immigrant associations organized their own campaign against the proposed immigration restriction, arguing that it violated the "solidarity made necessary by the European and international context within which Switzerland must work" (*LI*, Nov. 3, 1988; *Tribune de Genève*, Oct. 26, 1988). More voters in La Chaux-de-Fonds rejected National Action's latest initiative that December than in Schlieren, but the percentage accepting it (33.6 percent) was higher than the average nationwide. Observers attributed the anomalous outcome to rising concern in the canton over drug smuggling across its frontier with France (*Neue Zürcher Zeitung*, Dec. 5, 1988).

Nevertheless, that outcome worried the church-inspired solidarity groups. They argued strongly that the immigrants could best improve their lot by keeping a low political profile and by buying into the Swiss consensual policymaking system. Those active in extreme-leftist organizations were more likely to rail against the "passivity" that limited suffrage created among the once-militant immigrants. "It's dead here," others complained.[53] Working-class rallies remained more numerous and animated than in other regions, however, and the immigrants made themselves heard at them (see *LI*, March 21–22 and May 2–3, 1987).

And certainly, the immigrants' political star in La Chaux-de-Fonds had been rising ever since their key role in the 1984 elections. Their votes again saved the city's left-wing majority in the 1988 communal elections. Some 16 percent of all eligible foreigners cast a ballot.[54]

There was talk among cantonal Socialists about resurrecting the CNTSE. But the immigrants were developing into an essential swing constituency possibly no longer in need of special political structures.

Buoyed by their political advances, the local immigrant communities worked for new rights. In 1988 the Italian Free Colony, acting in the name of the CCI, petitioned cantonal officials to allow immigrants with a permit of permanent residency to run for municipal legislative and executive offices. All the Italian, Spanish, Portuguese, Turkish, and refugee associations in La Chaux-de-Fonds endorsed the petition, which appeared in four languages. Local leftist and religious activists lent their backing (Menghini 1988). Though ultimately unsuccessful, the initiative did keep immigrants' demands on the municipal policy agenda.

In La Chaux-de-Fonds, then, the foreign population worked within the system and accepted the rules of the local political game. Institutional channels sufficed. Through their combination of institutional and confrontational and symbolic participatory forms, immigrant militants in France attained greater influence on national and local political discourse. The effective use of institutional political opportunities in La Chaux-de-Fonds, however, yielded more procedural and concrete, "bankable" rewards.

Second-generation immigrants, it is true, exerted little pressure on local officials in La Chaux-de-Fonds. The "neither-nor" children focused on the daunting challenge of socioprofessional integration and gains. Only a fraction of those eligible voted in local elections, and their associational involvement was modest. Irrespective of the impediments, the local branch of SOS-Racisme pursued its activities. In September 1987 a squad of mopeds rolled from La Chaux-de-Fonds to Bern, part of a national "Roll against Racism" demonstration that concluded with a mass concert in front of the Federal Palace. The Swiss *potes'* concerns still reflected the particularities of the immigrant condition in La Chaux-de-Fonds: "Money Can't Buy Us Love" and "The Boat Is Far from Full" were among the slogans decorating wall posters in La Chaux-de-Fonds that Harlem Désir and his French allies would hardly have recognized.

Even in the relatively free political context in La Chaux-de-Fonds, the repeated defeats of their cause in federal ballotings chipped away at the immigrants' energy and resolve. Although the canton of Neuchâtel usually turned a deaf ear to the federal initiatives and referenda of the National Action and the Republicans, each of them had to be fought. Like a fortress under siege, the immigrants and their allies in La Chaux-de-Fonds found it ever harder to mobilize for costly battles simply to maintain the status quo. Local and cantonal political advances had to compete with a gloomy national scenario that threatened to rob them of much of their import.[55] By the early 1990s unemployment rates in the canton, at just under 6 percent, were almost twice as high as the national average (*Neue Zürcher Zeitung*, July 21, 1992). Chaux-de-Fonniers still resisted closing themselves off from the immigrants and Europe: at the end of 1992 they joined voters across the *Jura neuchâtelois* in producing the most resounding tally in favor of the European Economic Area—80 percent—in Switzerland (*Neue Zürcher Zeitung*, Dec. 8, 1992).

Summary

La Chaux-de-Fonds, like Schlieren, did not face the urban unrest and confrontations with immigrant youth that plagued French cities by the late 1980s. Authorities' efforts to institute a rotation model of immigration had a "depressurizing" effect on social tensions. Added to that, difficult naturalization procedures and multiple routes of political access discouraged immigrants in Swiss cities from evolving into a collective political force utilizing confrontational tactics.

As in France, the importance of native-born political actors on the left, the source of most host-society support for the immigrants, was a critical factor determining the mode, form, and impact of immigrant participation. Would-be allies blocked their political opportunities in Schlieren or, at best, failed to be in a position to offer effective tactical or moral backing. In La Chaux-de-Fonds, in clear contrast, an effective network of sympathetic militants made it possible for the immigrant communities to proceed remarkably well along institutional channels at the local and cantonal levels.

Federal immigration policies aimed to deny foreign workers everything but a functional, economic identity; to do so, they stressed the workers' non-Swiss nationality and the supposedly temporary nature of the foreign-worker phenomenon. Together with traditional tolerance of foreign political organizations and immigrant associations and the meagerness of the Swiss welfare state—tempered by important municipal social programs in La Chaux-de-Fonds—they favored homeland-oriented and ethnic-based immigrant political organizing. Neuchâtel's cantonal CNTSE also toed the ethnic line. Even in Socialist-run La Chaux-de-Fonds, where working-class solidarity prevailed, ethnic and regional identity maintained its salience and viability within class-based mobilization.

Each national group in La Chaux-de-Fonds followed a pattern of political mobilization closer to that of other immigrants there than to that of their compatriots in Schlieren. That was even truer in comparison with their counterparts in France, irrespective of superficial similarities in the ways that immigrants of each nationality organized in both countries and in all four case cities. Patterns of participation specific to each host society and, particularly, each host city are clearly visible. The institutional frameworks within which the immigrants found themselves at both the national and local levels conditioned their political activism more than their ethnic background or class status.

Conclusion

If the preceding analysis has proved anything, it is that immigrant workers and their families, those seemingly most marginal components of European societies, have engaged in a multitude of political activities, often with some real effect on host-society political life and culture in France and Switzerland. Perceptive scholars on both sides of the Atlantic have made this general point at least since the late 1970s, yet it bears repeating. Too often the policy discourse on immigrants still ignores the autonomous, dynamic political role that they have created for themselves.

Of course, the immigrants in France and Switzerland have not operated within a political vacuum. Increasingly since the mid-1970s, the ways in which foreigners plug into politics at the national and local levels in host societies have revealed themselves to be the result of the interplay of immigrants, institutions, and public authorities. Each institutional context has produced its own evolving pattern of participatory forms and demands and, consequently, different types and levels of impact.

Perspectives on the Evolution of Immigrant Politics

The two country and four city cases presented in earlier chapters have illuminated the different ways in which the policy challenge of ethnic diversity has played out. The cases have shown how the immigrants have organized to express their political demands and how host-society institutions have both conditioned and responded to them. It seems clear from these cases that institutional channeling, rather than class or ethnicity/race, has been the crucial element in their varying degrees of success.

There has been a common underlying direction to developments in both of the capitalist democracies examined here. "Capitalists never want people," Robert Miles and Annie Phizacklea argue, "only their capacity to labor" (1984, p. 19). Pressure from employers, who saw in foreign workers a source of cheap labor and market growth, led French and Swiss governments to permit, even organize the recruitment of immigrant labor. During the economic difficulties of the early 1970s, business interests applauded official moves to restrict new inflows. While sensitive to the social tensions that the presence of settled immigrant communities generated, however, they exhibited little interest in supporting programs to integrate the immigrants resident in the host societies. Greater social and political rights, after all, reduced their value as low-cost workers.

The immigrants' common social-class characteristics, meanwhile, influenced their choice of political strategies. It was their difficult position within the indigenous working class that spawned many of their demands. The workplace witnessed their first signs of political assertiveness and host-society-oriented mobilization. Yet the preceding chapters have shown that significant differences have distinguished the foreign workers' participatory patterns across the national and local cases. Such a finding argues directly against the theory that the immigrants' working-class status ultimately explains their interaction with host-society politics. If most immigrants, regardless of nationality, performed backbreaking manual labor, why should their participatory strategies have differed?

Part of the answer lies with the particular place that class and class-based participation in general occupy in each institutional setting. Trying to explain waves of political turbulence in Italy, Sidney Tarrow has argued that the "structural problems of advanced capitalism" generate the potential for protest, but that the forms that it ultimately takes depends on the "particular political institutions and opportunities of each country and social sector" (1989, p. 4). For immigrants, specifically, legal access to class-based strategies like involvement in strikes and membership in labor organizations has varied over time and across localities. Just as critically, the immigrants' class position has put them in contact with indigenous left-wing political parties, trade unions, and other progressive—albeit often religious—solidarity-group allies.

Through their organizational support, indifference, or outright hostility, the actions of those host-society institutions have had a clear intervening effect on the immigrants' differential employment of class-based participatory channels. All these institutional factors help to explain why foreign workers in Roubaix's textile mills, La Chaux-de-Fonds's watch factories, and the heavy industrial plants of Schlieren and La Courneuve did not produce identical patterns of class-based mobilization.

Institutional channeling has played a similarly important role in determining the frequency and importance of immigrant participation along ethnic lines. Immigration has produced a polyglot, multiethnic working class in France and Switzerland. Certain nationality-specific organizational traits have retained their salience: Spaniards in each host society and case city focused especially on the bilingual education of the second generation; Italians achieved more intraethnic coherence than other national groups; and Portuguese cultivated their homeland culture and Turks their homeland blood feuds with particular insistence irrespective of the host society in which they have settled.

Still, immigrants of the same national background have not organized in the same way across the cases. Different ethnic-based associations have appeared, and local branches of the same associational federations have often mobilized in different ways and with distinctive objectives. Institutional forces in the host countries have determined what political forms such special concerns would take and, more than any intrinsically ethnic particularities, whether immigrant mobilization would occur along ethnic lines. Legal and institutional discrimination against particular groups has incited such organizing. National and local authorities have sometimes instituted consultative structures for immigrants, almost always organized on the basis of national origin, thereby actively contributing to the creation of ethnic minority communities and ethnic conflict (Miles and Phizacklea 1980, pp. 26–28). Host-society officials and social-welfare programs, furthermore, have encouraged or discouraged immigrant political identification with their homelands. They have largely determined the role of homeland governments, whose policies explain many of the lingering differences between immigrant groups.

Hans-Joachim Hoffmann-Nowotny and Karl-Otto Hondrich (1982) have found that Italians in Switzerland and West Germany present patterns of social integration most similar to those of other immigrant communities in each nation. With class characteristics controlled for,

I have isolated essentially the same phenomenon in the evolution of immigrant politics in France and Switzerland. After the immigration bans of the mid-1970s, the political organization of even the newer immigrant groups and the less comparable Portuguese began to dovetail with that of other nationalities in the same host society. The immigrants adopted forms of participation—whether class or ethnicity based, and homeland oriented, institutional, or confrontational in form—resembling those adopted by other immigrants in the same host society more closely than those adopted by immigrants of the same ethnic origin in another host society. In other words, whatever their national origin or the mix of nationalities present, immigrants in both France and Switzerland developed participatory forms that reflected the political opportunity structures they faced.

Significantly, this assessment has held for second-generation immigrants. They underwent a different socialization process from their parents, often faced a different legal and institutional position, and rejected a class-based political identity. At the same time, they developed very diverse modes of political activity across the cases. Again, these varied organizational responses reflected the different institutional frameworks and pressures experienced in each.

In both France and Switzerland, in fact, the very content and focus of first- and second-generation immigrants' demands on the host society varied with the nature of the political opportunity structure, further evidence of its impact on their political behavior. Some concerns were common ones: human dignity, higher wages, and an end to discrimination. Most of the demands articulated by the immigrants, however, were related to the legislation and procedures specific to the national/federal and local political contexts. The immigrants responded to the institutions and the issues they encountered most directly in their day-to-day existence. In the words of Frances Fox Piven and Richard A. Cloward, "the opportunities for defiance are structured by the features of institutional life" (1979, p. 23).

Explaining Patterns of Immigrant Action and Institutional Response

If we accept that institutional channeling has become increasingly more important than class and ethnic factors in shaping immigrant political participation in France and Switzerland, the evidence presented here can tell us much about why the immigrants adopted certain forms of political participation at various times and in various settings and what policy responses and policy gains they wrested from French and Swiss officials and institutions. In short, we can deduce much about why the politics of ethnic diversity developed in some directions and not others in each nation and city.

THE ORIGINAL PARTICIPATORY CHANNELS

Essential to understanding this evolution is the network of participatory channels that the immigrants first found open to them. France and Switzerland, like other capitalist democracies, are, as Ira Katznelson has already observed, "defined politically by their country-specific systems of political and social 'trenches' which delineate what is special about class and politics in each society and which help to shape its rules of conflict" (1981, p. 19). Before World War II, immigrants to France and Switzerland had either assimilated completely as individuals or had eventually returned to their homelands. The more numerous and structurally more necessary foreign workers who built Western Europe's postwar prosperity emigrated under different conditions and faced a different set of economic, social, and political conditions. As they settled more or less permanently in countries like France and Switzerland, establishing veritable minority communities, they formulated demands on the political systems there. Like Suzanne Berger's French peasants, the immigrants discovered that "in order to move their demands up to the centers of national decision, they [were] forced to employ relays fashioned for other issues" and groups (1972, pp. 236–237). The immigrants thus flowed into the channels of participation that the earlier struggles of the indigenous working class and previous policy decisions had—in many respects unwittingly—left available to them.

Immigrants in France initially had fewer political opportunities than their counterparts in Switzerland. The Ministry of the Interior had to authorize all immigrant associations and could deport anyone who disturbed the political order. Authorities tolerated nonthreatening home-land-directed activities, but the law forbade foreign parties and unions from operating in France. French social-welfare programs were fairly well developed, and they grew steadily more inclusive of the immigrants. These factors reduced the need for an extensive network of homeland-sponsored organizations on French soil and diminished the homeland as a focus of immigrant political concern.

French governments squeezed immigrant participation into a narrow class-based channel. It was in the workplace that immigrants most nearly reached legal parity with the French. As workers, the foreigners could take part in trade union activities, including strike actions, provided they left leadership positions to the native-born.

Immigrants fashioned forms of political participation that responded in large measure to the national political opportunity structure. Like other workers in France, they tended to target Paris and representatives of the central administration at the departmental and communal levels. The political centralization of France has long made it necessary for interest groups to aim for the national level if they hope to acquire any degree of power (S. Berger 1972; Cerny 1982).

Differences in the institutional setup at the local level did not completely alter that calculus. Still, even within that potent national framework, local-level institutional channeling had noticeable effects on immigrant politics. Thus in Roubaix, which had a long history of incorporating immigrants and their organizations into more typically French class-based mobilization, municipal authorities actively encouraged immigrant associational activity. In La Courneuve, by contrast, the Communist-run municipal government pushed immigrants to work within the PCF and local CGT cells. The local Communist leadership co-opted autonomous immigrant protests, directing them against the forces of capital and the state.

The situation in Switzerland differed from that in France in several important respects. Not only could immigrants join Swiss trade unions and political parties; they could also form their own associations, circulate petitions for constitutional amendments, and participate in consultative structures that jibed well with prevailing decisionmaking processes. Restrictive Swiss labor policies distinguished between immigrants according to their socioprofessional status and strove to maintain a "rotation model" of immigration. Accordingly, the immigrants were not likely to stray from available participatory channels, nor did they forge a truly separate, collective identity.

Public and private welfare organizations and churches in Switzerland also fulfilled a key function. They failed for years to take much interest in the immigrants. They did not introduce any special services or training for them or particularly welcome immigrant members or administrators. This unresponsiveness of major Swiss organizations led homeland consulates and official homeland organizations to step in to provide for their nationals' social, economic, and political needs. Given that high profile, the immigrants' political involvement with their homelands proved more intense and persistent than in France, leading some conservative critics to warn of the "state within the state" (see Schmitter Heisler 1983).

Switzerland has had a strong tradition of communal and cantonal autonomy, and as a political entity it is far smaller than France. Accordingly, immigrants aimed many of their political efforts at the subfederal level. In both Schlieren and La Chaux-de-Fonds, the patterns of immigrant politics reflected the confluence of national and often highly divergent local institutional forces. In Schlieren, where the three center and center-right "bourgeois" parties dominated local politics, immigrants did not have much of an organized political presence. They formed cultural, parents', and homeland-sponsored associations but had only occasional, case-by-case contacts with city officials.

Many of the immigrants lapsed into inactivity or cultivated a regional identity (that is, as Friulians, Sicilians, Andalusians, and the like) that imposed less of a choice between Swiss and homeland identity (Bolzman, Fibbi, and Garcia 1987). Still others turned to alternative points and levels of political access. They spent their political energies participating in cantonal and federal petition drives and in the activities of immigrant associations based in next-door Zurich. City officials there tolerated the presence of foreign political parties and unions, and participation oriented toward influencing homeland policies was far higher than in the French cities.

In La Chaux-de-Fonds immigrants enjoyed more political opportunities than in the other three case cities, including a limited local franchise. The political channeling process there generated high levels of institutional participation, based on a unique constellation of modes that blended class and ethnicity. Homeland-oriented participation among immigrants in La Chaux-de-Fonds was greater than in France but less than in Schlieren: the Socialist-Communist municipality filled some of the holes in the Swiss social-welfare net, although enough remained to justify the activity of homeland-sponsored organizations. Chaux-de-Fonnier and cantonal officials cooperated with the latter in the immigrants' and their own financial interests, a trend that reduced distinctions between immigrant participation geared toward the homelands and toward the host society.

INSTITUTIONAL GATEKEEPERS AND POLITICAL PARTICIPATION

Just as crucial as the political and legal environments in which the immigrants acted was the nature of the support provided by local left-wing militants in trade unions, political parties, and solidarity groups. These institutions, straddling the participatory trenches along which the immigrants initially mobilized, influenced their choice of strategies and the effectiveness of their participation. They served as indispensable political midwives for the immigrant communities.

Such a conclusion supports those scholars who have maintained that institutional arrangements and actions significantly structure political participation. In many ways my findings here complement those of Sidney Verba, Jae-On Kim, and Norman Nie (1978). In their seven-nation comparison of the forms and social sources of citizen participation, they argue that "[g]roup-based forces embodied in institutions such as parties and organizations can modify the participation patterns that one would have if only individual forces were operating" (p. 19). By their own admission, though, they "lump together the effects of all institutions in each nation" and "pay no attention to differences among institutions within each nation," nor to the "differences in which institutions affect the different modes of participation" (p. 81).

The findings presented in the preceding chapters suggest that both sorts of differences can be important. For a long time French trade unions and political parties insisted that immigrants not form separate organizations. At the national level the French Communist and Socialist parties and the trade unions largely ignored the specific concerns of foreign workers up through the early 1970s, leaving them with only minuscule, extreme-leftist organizations as dependable allies. In La Courneuve the French Communist Party and the General Labor Confederation brooked little class-based organizing outside of their aegis. But in Roubaix, where organized labor and the left owed much to Flemish immigrants, Socialists and Communists in the political parties and trade union locals demonstrated sensitivity toward the immigrants' interests and involvement fairly early.

What accounted for these disparate institutional dispositions? The bipolarization of the French political system under the presidential Fifth Republic has had definite effects on left-wing institutions' receptivity toward the immigrants. A large bloc on the left squared off against a right-wing bloc, with a very small swing vote deciding electoral outcomes. The pluralistic nature of the French left could create a situation in which Communists and Socialists vied for the tactical support of even the foreign component of the working class (see Miller 1982). Such rivalry did not occur in Communist-dominated La Courneuve, but it was keen in more competitive Roubaix.

That phenomenon did not exist in Switzerland, where open hostility, as opposed to competition, between clearly defined pro-immigrant and xenophobic camps often paralyzed the left. A neocorporatist "labor peace" had prevailed since the 1930s. Strike activity was minimal. Owing to the decentralized structure of the Swiss Socialist Party and loosely confederated trade unions, debates over immigration shifted decidedly toward the cantonal and local levels. Thus in Schlieren immigrants participated indirectly in politics through their leadership of the local branch of the Construction Workers' Federation (FOBB/GBH), which together with the Metal- and Clockworkers' Union (FTMH/ SMUV) formed an electoral partnership with the Socialist Party of Schlieren. However, the xenophobia of the FTMH/SMUV crippled that alliance. In La Chaux-de-Fonds, by contrast, large numbers of immigrants joined the local branches of the FOBB/GBH and the FTMH/ SMUV and had real influence on the local Trade Union Cartel, an important social partner in local policymaking. Solidarity between the indigenous left and the immigrants was consistent.

Only in Roubaix and La Chaux-de-Fonds, then, were indigenous institutions assisting immigrants in undertaking as much class-based participation as was possible. Far less so in those cities than elsewhere, existing participatory channels were proving inadequate by the early 1970s. In France immigrants of several nationalities, disappointed and bereft of adequate legal political outlets, banded together *as workers* to launch wildcat strikes, hunger strikes, and factory occupations to protest their working and living conditions and their precarious legal status. The protests upset the national government and the mainstream French left.

In the early 1970s severe socioeconomic strains in several areas of Switzerland provoked a temporary break from characteristic participation patterns, manifested in a rash of immigrant strike activity. As in

France, the foreign workers' labor militancy in this period at first prompted sharp negative reactions from employers, public officials, and trade unions alike.

THE INSTITUTIONAL RESPONSE

The immigrants' political militancy and the social ill will that crystallized around their presence during a period of economic slow-down forced governments to act. If host-society officials hoped to prevent a dangerous escalation of resentment and alienation, they had to respond to the immigrants' outrage. "Elites," Tarrow tells us, "can re-knit the fabric of hegemony by repression, by press campaigns against violence, as well as by selective reform" (1989, p. 343). French and Swiss officials opted for both repressive and facilitative strategies in the mid-1970s. First, they prohibited new immigration, beefed up police forces and border controls, and reiterated their right to expel noncitizens deemed threatening to the public order. Simultaneously they pledged to integrate the immigrants already resident in their countries.

Political learning, Hugh Heclo's "phenomenon of adaptation through politics" (1974, p. 319), occurred on both sides. Immigrants adapted to policies quite rapidly, and the experience of more established immigrant communities benefited later arrivals: the Turks, a relatively new community in both France and Switzerland, showed signs of political acclimation quite soon.

French and Swiss policymakers and the institutions of the left, likewise, learned from the immigrant protests. In the beginning, they reacted from within the prevailing institutional context. As Piven and Cloward have observed, reforms are "drawn from a repertoire provided by existing institutions" (1979, p. 33): the participatory channels that the immigrants had overflowed were cleared of obstacles and widened, but no new ones were established. Trade union rights expanded in both France and Switzerland in the mid-1970s, Swiss officials stepped up their efforts to maintain the immigrants' homeland ties, and the French welfare state became more inclusive.

The confrontational forms of immigrant political participation in the early and mid-1970s also produced changes in the attitudes of Swiss and French left-wing political parties, solidarity groups, and trade unions. They awoke to the immigrants and their needs. The impact was greater in France, since its more closed, centralized political system generated higher levels of protest, and competition within the left there accentuated the importance of immigrant labor in a declining working class. The left responded with grudging acceptance of the immigrants' special socioeconomic situation and helped them exercise their expanded rights in the workplace.

In 1981 the Mitterrand-Mauroy government capped the move toward greater political rights for immigrants by permitting noncitizens to form their own associations without severe restrictions. Almost immediately, associations grouping immigrants of one or more nationalities flourished. Once legally recognized, these associations began to compete with each other and with their French allies for government subsidies and for the right to represent the immigrant communities.

The mainstream French left struggled to incorporate the newly invigorated ethnic identities—further complicated by the rise of Islam in the workplace and suburban housing projects—into its class projects without alienating indigenous working-class constituencies. In La Courneuve, the local Communist administration was still strong enough to co-opt immigrant struggles. But where political control was less monolithic, concessions were often forthcoming. Cities with longer experience welcoming immigrants and adjusting to their presence—for example, Roubaix—tended to be more flexible and innovative. New kinds of institutions and rights soon made their appearance.

Katznelson (1981) and Piven and Cloward (1979) have noted that poor people's protests can press officials to create new institutions to contain and defuse challenges, to absorb participants' energies and render them harmless. In Roubaix the Socialist-dominated Union of the Left municipal government established the Extra-Municipal Commission (CEM) in 1977 to deal with immigrants and their integration. Organized along ethnic lines, the CEM even inspired some previously unorganized national communities to form their own associations. Thereafter the CEM became the instrument by which the immigrants made their political demands known. Confrontational tactics became rarer.

In Switzerland, similarly, federal, cantonal, and local authorities responded to the immigrants' growing assertiveness by instituting more consultative structures organized on the basis of national origin. One of these was the semipublic Swiss-Foreigners Work Community (CNTSE) in the canton of Neuchâtel, which like Roubaix had had long experience with immigration. The CNTSE stimulated ethnic-based participation and encouraged cooperation between the immigrant communities and local left-wing political, trade union, and solidarity-group activists.

In both host societies there was a connection between the forms of immigrant participation and the type and level of impact that they won. When the immigrants adopted participatory forms that departed from conventional behavior in the host society—marching in the streets to denounce homeland governments, mounting wildcat strikes, going on hunger strikes—they registered their greatest impact on media coverage and public opinion. Unorthodox participation often shocked host-society institutions and political actors into improving the immigrants' social and political-legal status.

Much of the literature on marginal groups' participation (for example, Piven and Cloward 1979; and Offe 1985) sees such confrontational strategies as the only effective ones. More in line with the analysis of Rufus P. Browning, Dale Rogers Marshall, and David H. Tabb (1984) and contributors to Russell J. Dalton and Manfred Kuechler's volume (1990), my findings indicate that the immigrants were most potent when they employed both conventional and unconventional political tactics. Sometimes institutional participation fulfilled their concrete policy demands and increased their political and social rights and acceptance within the political system.

In France the threat of more confrontational tactics added to the force of institutional participation. The lack of access points that originally caused immigrants in France to adopt unconventional tactics had been the root cause of their receiving much attention from the media, the public, and other political actors. Pierre Grémion has stressed how difficult it can be for outsider groups in France "to avoid either the straitjacket of being absorbed or tamed by the 'bureaucratic-notable system' on the one hand, or being marginalized by exclusion from the system and thereby reduced to impotent if vociferous dissent" (1976, p. 413). In effect, the essential political vulnerability of noncitizens, the sheer power differential between ordinary French citizens and the immigrants, drew attention to their protests and heightened awareness of their demands.

And that was an important advantage. It allowed the immigrants to resist both political absorption and marginalization. When later governments eventually opened additional avenues of political participation to them, the immigrants used them. They did not totally abandon or forget the familiar out-of-channel forms, however. The threat of vociferous, confrontational modes of participation, together with their increasingly assimilative strategies, produced policy gains. Once governments and other indigenous institutions had witnessed the immigrant workers' militancy of the mid-1970s, they tended to react more readily to their in-channel mobilization.

The immigrants' militancy in Switzerland was more limited and shorter lived. The official nurturing of foreign workers' homeland-oriented participation steered pressures away from the Swiss political system more forcefully and longer than in France. In Schlieren, for example, officials never came under strong, organized pressure to integrate the city's immigrants into local politics. Foreign-worker activists could turn to alternative political channels or a different level of government "whose biases [were] more favorable to their cause," or at least "different" (Crenson 1971, p. 183). Those additional institutional arenas drained away out-of-channel participation.

The appearance, if not the reality, of greater socioeconomic mobility in Switzerland was another critical factor in generating less confrontational participation—in fact less collective political activity overall—than in France. The Swiss rotation model of immigration forced many out-of-work foreigners to return home. As their legal status and employment security advanced in tandem the longer they were able to stay in the country, the foreign workers who remained usually concentrated on individual advancement.

Such a relationship substantiates Samuel P. Huntington and Joan Nelson's contention that individual socioeconomic mobility and group organization are "practically, if not logically, exclusive" (1976, p. 95). This finding, in turn, meshes well with Albert O. Hirschman's (1970) discussion of the complex interrelationship among the concepts of exit, voice, and loyalty. Hirschman argues that both the level and organization of resources in a system affect the relative availability of exit and voice. He points to the importance of the structural context, in which participation stands as but one possible course of action (see Ross 1988).

Emigration, in this optic, is itself a political act. Emigrants, after all, have already "chosen exit" once: instead of working to improve conditions in their homeland, they have left in the hope of finding individual solutions abroad, opting for "modernity" (see Schnapper 1974). Therefore, as Ko-Chih Tung (1981) and others have pointed out, it is logical to expect immigrants to display low levels of efficacy and loyalty, and thus low levels of political activity, in the host societies. Like Miles and Phizacklea (1984), however, I have argued here that economic factors and long-term settlement in the host society can make exit—in the form of either a return home or individual socioeconomic betterment—a less viable option for foreign workers.

THE SECOND GENERATION: A SOCIAL MOVEMENT?

Logically, one might then expect exit to be even less open to second-generation immigrants born in Western Europe. Most of them occupy the same undesirable occupational niches, the same marginalized class position, as their parents. For these youths, though, the host society is also the homeland; they have a greater claim on and loyalty (in Hirschman's sense) to it. By the early 1980s in France the embryo of a bona fide social movement was discernible in the participation of the second immigrant generation. This movement developed even as the first generation settled into institutional channels. In Switzerland, conversely, the voice of the foreign workers' children was not heard: they proved more docile than their parents.

Why has the second immigrant generation produced a social movement in France but not in Switzerland? Neo-Marxists have considered such movements to be part of the painful process through which native- and foreign-origin workers of all generations discover their common class interests. Presumably, therefore, capitalism and the labor movement in France have for some reason simply reached that stage earlier than in Switzerland (see Castles, Booth, and Wallace 1984; and Cerny 1982). Why most second-generation immigrants stubbornly refuse to identify with the French or Swiss working class remains a mystery.

Searching for the causes and contours of popular social and political protests in general since the events of 1968, other students of Western European society have focused on the role of personality, values, and other psychological factors in generating and shaping group-based behavior. They have seen recent social movements as an expression of collective identity. In its most prominent form, this perspective has highlighted an intergenerational change in values, a shift from "materialism" to quality-of-life issues, that has incited a "silent revolution" in Western Europe: postwar economic prosperity has freed younger Europeans from material concerns, and they have turned away from class-based formations and toward environmentalist and peace movements that speak to their "postmaterial" values (see Inglehart 1977; Messina 1987).

As applied to the immigrants, such an approach might illuminate why the foreign workers' children have chosen their particular participatory strategies. Those born and raised in the host society have undergone different processes of political socialization from the first generation. Perhaps an intergenerational shift in values has occurred: buying into the affluence and consumerism to which they have been exposed in Western Europe, they reject all ties to class-based organizations and ideologies. What remains to be explained is why they have formed a social movement, postmaterialist or otherwise, in France but not in generally more prosperous Switzerland.

Indeed, just as Klaus Boehnke and his colleagues (1987) have determined in Germany, there has been scant evidence of a "silent revolution" among either immigrant generation in France and Switzerland. Neither does the deepening alienation of France's antiracist movement from traditional working-class organizations offer support for the argument that it has grown out of the basic conflicts of capitalist development. Instead, the particular evolution of immigrant politics in those two nations shows that such institutional factors better account for the organizational discrepancies observed.

Since the late 1950s and the 1960s, scholars have zeroed in on specific regime characteristics that "shape the channels of access through which groups press their claims" (S. Berger 1981, p. 9).[1] Gary T. Marx and James L. Wood (1975), Richard J. Evans (1977), Charles Tilly (1978), Frances Fox Piven and Richard A. Cloward (1979), Philip G. Cerny (1982), Doug McAdam (1982), Sidney Tarrow (1982 and 1989), Jane Jenson (1985), Herbert P. Kitschelt (1986), and others working in the field have found that the general rules of government and institutional arrangements do not only trigger social movements. They actually create country-specific templates for interest organization. In the process they mold movements' political tactics and groups' collective identities and shape the terms in which they understand and couch their demands, as well as how elites respond to them (Tarrow 1989, p. 4; see also S. Berger 1972 and 1981).[2]

The analysis here has effectively united a resource mobilization perspective on social movements with one that stresses the importance of the available network of political opportunities for immigrant participation. Developed by Anthony Oberschall (1973), William A. Gamson

(1975), John D. McCarthy and Mayer N. Zald (1977), and others, re-source mobilization "conceives of social movements as collective and rational decision-makers that mobilize their followers and promote their causes with the best available strategies given limited cognitive and material resources" (Kitschelt 1986, p. 59). And yet the prevailing institutional context in a society or city has determined the best avail-able strategies and the resources available to immigrants for actualizing them.

Exit, in a word, has not been blocked by institutions to the same extent or with the same consequences in every host society. In France second-generation immigrants could not readily choose exit: their soci-oprofessional possibilities were severely limited. But since their legal status was not—they could or would acquire citizenship in France—it makes sense that what was once a mere "social category" (a group of individuals sharing recognized common traits) would evolve into a "social actor" (a group having a collective identity on the basis of which it intervenes in the sociopolitical realm) (Bolzman, Fibbi, and Garcia 1987, p. 57).

France's second immigrant generation thus gave birth to a range of collective confrontational and symbolic actions that host-society insti-tutions struggled to co-opt and convert into institutional participation. Although legal discrimination fell after 1974, racism continued to tar-get North African and other non-European immigrants. Thus a minor-ity of the *Beurs* tried on occasion to form a movement excluding French youth and the children of European immigrants. Even so, the youth movements typically included both of those groups, largely as a result of the way in which the French state oversaw the creation of suburban housing projects that mixed ethnic groups and implemented a univer-salistic system of education.

The second-generation social movement took on different contours depending on the institutional context. In a "Red" city like La Cour-neuve, the young people's refusal to see any common purpose with the working class caused consternation. Confrontational, often violent actions like the 1980 "Rock against Police" concert broke out until the National Front's successes prompted changes in Communist positions on immigration. In Roubaix and other areas of France outside such tight PCF control, second-generation immigrants utilized an effective amalgam of institutional (voter drives) and confrontational (violence, marches, hunger strikes) modes of participation.

In Switzerland no social movement formed at all. Immigrants and their progeny there faced a ladder of narrow functional and bilaterally determined distinctions that legitimated individual strategies for socio-professional advancement in their eyes. What is more, a "forced" exit loomed as a very real threat during economic downturns. Enjoying no special access to Swiss citizenship, immigrant children remained no more than a social category. The political marginalization and passivity of this "neither-nor" generation was nearly complete. Some mimicking of the French second generation's SOS-Racisme and *Beur* movements took place in French-speaking Switzerland, where socio-economic mobility was particularly problematic and where supportive left-wing activists eagerly encouraged political organizing. But such actions were highly exceptional.

THE RACIST/XENOPHOBIC COUNTEROFFENSIVE

The immigrant presence, as well as any and all forms of political participation and the institutional concessions that it sometimes won, fueled a hostile reaction in France and Switzerland. Pressures from the anti-immigrant extreme right eventually boxed in policymakers in both nations and divided and weakened the immigrants' allies.

The counterattack materialized first in Switzerland, in part because of the greater number of foreigners there. But neither the sheer size of the immigrant population nor its particular ethnic composition was as important as institutional factors. The xenophobic movement availed itself easily and quickly of Switzerland's vaunted instruments of direct democracy. The proposed series of anti-immigrant federal initiatives in the 1970s and 1980s split the newly aroused Swiss left and soon left it unable to advance any of the immigrants' interests. Though permitted to circulate and campaign for petitions, the foreigners themselves could not vote on them. The immigrants and their allies were at all levels battling opponents who, with more resources at their disposal, regularly defeated them.

The result was a wearing down of the immigrants' political energies. Huntington and Nelson have noted that political participation may create "feelings of relevance and efficacy with respect to politics" (1976, p. 158; see Edelman 1971). By the same token, repeated setbacks can produce the opposite effect. By the mid-1980s there was ample evidence of what John Gaventa has termed "deferral of action" and a "sense of powerlessness" (1980, p. 255).

The knife of direct democracy cut both ways, however. The xenophobic National Action and Republican parties created powerful reverberations in cities like Schlieren and found many sympathizers for their constitutional initiative campaigns. But they were unable to elect candidates there and encountered little success elsewhere. What Claudio Bolzman, Rosita Fibbi, and Carlos Garcia (1987) have argued about the initiative and referendum applies to the xenophobes as well: "the formal (guaranteed by the constitution), real (widely practiced) and ideological (foundation of the consensual Helvetic political discourse) possibility to employ a channel that concerns the 'individual-citizen' constitutes a brake on the development of new social actors" (p. 64). The xenophobes splintered along the traditional fault lines of Swiss politics and did not endanger the four-party centrist coalition in power since 1959 (*New York Times,* Oct. 27, 1991). The "establishment" parties mobilized to respond to the xenophobic threat, encapsulating it and inserting it into the traditional political game.[3]

In the early 1980s, more than a decade later than in Switzerland, immigrants in France found themselves confronted by supporters of Jean-Marie Le Pen and his National Front. They fed on the atmosphere of social and economic crisis and found convenient scapegoats in the immigrants. One might well wonder why their political breakthrough took longer. After all, France had far higher levels of unemployment than Switzerland and a much larger non-European immigrant population, and even anti-European immigrant sentiment ran high (Messina 1990, pp. 42–43).

Like the second-generation immigrants' movement, ironically, *lepénisme* did fail to make political headway for years as it careened between Grémion's (1976) Charybdis of absorption and Scylla of marginalization. France's two-ballot, absolute-majority electoral system acted as a firebreak that kept the National Front out of French party politics. Whereas in Switzerland politics thoroughly penetrated society, the distance that separated French outsider groups from the center of political power in Paris could be wide indeed. They gained in cohesion and organization but risked remaining on the political sidelines.

That situation changed significantly as a result of the decentralization program pursued by the Socialists from 1981 through 1983. These policies, "relocating substantial decision-making and revenue-gathering powers to subnational units," focused attention on local politics (Safran 1991, p. 233). It was at that level that the political struggle over immigration was most intense and that the National Front—again, like the immigrants—was able to achieve its first political successes. As a result of the Socialists' decision to change the electoral system to one based on proportional representation, legislative elections in 1986 gave the National Front enough strength to constitute a parliamentary group. Its fortunes have fluctuated since then, and mainstream politicians have adopted some of its rhetoric and policy positions. But the Front's status as a major political party in its own right has not wavered.

The rise of the far right pushed the French Communists, including those running La Courneuve, to rediscover their solidarity with the immigrant communities. But in Roubaix a surprisingly strong showing by the anti-immigrant forces upset the local political balance enough to allow a coalition between the center and mainstream right to snatch victory from the left for the first time since 1912. The new administration allowed the "Knights of Roubaix," a *posse comitatus*, to patrol the streets and sharply limited the activities of the Extra-Municipal Commission for Immigrants. Once an important linking mechanism between Roubaix's immigrant communities and local officials, it degenerated into a demobilizing "racial buffer" (Katznelson 1973).

Immigrants, Politics, and Democracy

Clearly, the evolution of immigrant politics in France and Switzerland can tell us much about the causes, nature, and impact of participation and social movements in those two nations in general. But my findings also have wider implications for the functioning of democracy there. The ways in which host societies have linked immigrants—the most politically vulnerable of minorities—to politics or excluded them say much about the organization of power in them and the access of all outsider groups and underprivileged to their political systems. The immigrants have fulfilled a mirror function: discourse on them refers ultimately to the functioning of the host-society political system itself (see Gamson 1975, p. 5; Allal et al. 1977). Like no other issue since World War II, immigration illuminates for the citizens of the host societies, sometimes painfully, the underlying power relations at work in Western Europe.

Scholars like E. E. Schattschneider (1960), Stein Rokkan (1966), Martin O. Heisler (1986), Grant Jordan and Jeremy J. Richardson (1987), and Heisler and Barbara Schmitter Heisler (1990) have demonstrated that political participation in liberal democracies can take place through both group-based and electoral channels, both of which are legitimate. These two avenues of political access can compete with or complement each other. Noncitizens have had the franchise in a restricted sense at the local level (La Chaux-de-Fonds) and as second-generation immigrants (France). This book has demonstrated that group-based participation, both of an autonomous kind and through indigenous mediating organizations, also provided immigrants with effective mechanisms for pursuing their interests across the cases.

To varying degrees immigrant participation has left what Piven and Cloward (1979) have termed a "residue of reform": greater trade union and social rights, greater sensitivity from politicians and the media, and more consistent support from many host-society institutions. Converting themselves from wards into autonomous social and political actors, they breathed new life and demands into institutions like trade unions that indigenous workers had been abandoning; they widened the "repertoire of participation" in the host societies; and, at least in France, they affirmed new collective identities—all important kinds of impact for an outsider group to realize (Tarrow 1989).

It is clear that the French and Swiss polities have not proved impermeable even to those suffering from the most extreme "political poverty" (Rokkan 1966). Variations on a common pas de deux between immigrants and host-society authorities and institutions have played out in France and Switzerland. The choreography has been different and impromptu in each case, making for varying patterns of immigrant political incorporation and thus of ethnic politics. But the forces of the anti-immigrant reaction have tried to "cut in" since the mid-1970s, and the range of options available to policymakers has narrowed. Cycles of action and response like those between immigrants and host-society institutions "shape patterns of class and group formation" that differ across societies and that constitute important mechanisms of social control, "a crucible of interaction and struggle" (Katznelson 1981, p. 209). Seen in this light, France today faces a severe crisis of control in its decaying suburbs. Like the African-Americans who challenged the "city trenches" in the 1960s, France's second-generation immigrants threaten to "explode the community boundaries" (Katznelson 1981, p. 115). Segments of the second generation, their social integration stalled, have turned once more to militant cultural and violent political action in suburban streets.

In Switzerland, the prototype of consensual democracy (Lijphart 1984), different ethnic and cultural groups have long lived in peaceful but segregated coexistence. The Swiss maintained longer than the French the fiction that the immigrant presence was only provisional, and they have insisted on the complete assimilation of those foreigners remaining in the country. Democratic but not very liberal, the decentralized Swiss system has managed to deflect many of the tensions arising from the large-scale importation of foreign labor. The problems, just as real as in France, have rested in suspension.

Nelson W. Polsby (1963), Robert A. Dahl (1967), and others have drawn on a tradition going back to Madison and Tocqueville to argue that federalism contributes to democratic stability by dispersing political power and thereby providing multiple access points at which influence might be exerted. Gaventa, on the other hand, has found that where they occur, multiple "levels of power maximize the capacity of the holders of power to lie beyond challenge, and minimize the ability of the relatively powerless subjects of power to formulate or act upon the full extent of their interests" (1980, p. 259). And Peter A. Gourevitch (1980) and Ellen Immergut (1991) remind us that access points are *ipso facto* "veto points" that can (but do not have to) make it easier for the same actors' goals to be blocked (Gourevitch 1980, p. 236).

The immigrants found many apparent points of access to the Swiss political system. In a city like La Chaux-de-Fonds, a solidaristic indigenous left aided them in utilizing these points effectively. As a result the immigrants had significant impact on host-society politics. In Schlieren and much of the rest of the country, however, xenophobic movements could take advantage of those institutional openings—not to mention those offered by the institutions of direct democracy—more successfully than the disfranchised immigrants. In many cities and cantons the left, crippled by disagreements over immigration, could not offer them meaningful assistance. Immigrant activists often targeted cantonal and federal officials, yet it was not clear that they gained true entree into the Swiss system as a result. The playing field remained decidedly uneven everywhere.

A biased political market existed in France as well, of course, but Swiss federalism (and semidirect democracy) exacerbated its effects. Such an institutional arrangement protected political stability up to a point but most decidedly did not ensure greater political efficacy for outsiders. Hence, what mattered seemed not to be decentralization per se but rather the rules governing immigrant political participation and the nature of institutional responses. Federalism may be "one institutional mechanism designed to secure the sharing of power"; but "it is rarely a sufficient means" to that end (Bogdanor 1988, p. 89).

The immigrants, to sum up, built a very real political presence in both France and Switzerland, where institutions channeled their energies in a variety of directions, with different, important consequences for those host-society polities. Such contrasts notwithstanding, both of those capitalist democracies have come to harbor an anachronistic "Fourth World," one directly challenging their progressive, egalitarian self-images. Policy responses to the economic and technological upheavals of the 1970s and early 1980s have contributed to the emergence of an unsettling new population of marginals in all the industrial democracies of the West. Poverty and regional disparities have spread in France and Switzerland to the point that governments can no longer simply ignore the problem. Very different from the *clochards* and mentally disturbed war veterans that have long prowled the streets of major European cities without drawing much notice or concern, the "new" poor consist largely of young people and families unable to find any or adequate work, along with people suffering from some form of substance abuse. Far from accounting for the whole of this problem population, the immigrants have been a highly visible component of it (see, for example, *Le Monde*, Jan. 11–12, 1987; and *Basler Zeitung*, May 4, 1987).

As the living by-product of the postwar evolution of industrial capitalism, disposable only with great economic and moral difficulty, the immigrants have embodied perfectly the democratic turbulence of recent years. By settling and forming minority communities, those "guests come to stay" (Rogers 1985) have caused great upset. Heisler (1986), stressing that the formation of foreign minorities is not a reversible process, argues that they undermine the governing power of Western democracies. Gary P. Freeman carries this line of reasoning further: he contends that the immigrant presence has "reduced the political clout of those social strata that have traditionally been the chief source of support for welfare state development"; specifically, they have "diminished the power of organized labor by dividing the working class into national and immigrant camps, by easing the tight labor market conditions that would have enhanced labor's strategic resources, and by provoking a resurgence of right-wing and nativist political movements" (1986, p. 61).

With justification Anthony M. Messina (1990) retorts that this thesis of the "Americanization of European welfare politics" amounts to blaming the victim (see Carens 1988, pp. 208–213). He reminds us that it was the broad policy consensus reigning among economic and political elites that made mass migration possible in the decades following World War II. And as Freeman (1986) himself acknowledges, politics has determined in large measure whether or not a nation's labor supplies are adequate. Subservience to the logic or whims of the market in Switzerland, no less than ad hoc immigration and housing policies in France, has represented a policy choice with undeniable effects on the immigrants' living conditions and political organizing.

As several prominent social theorists have argued, moreover, the modern welfare state is "based ultimately upon the liberal premise of the moral equality of all humans" (Carens 1988, p. 208). For T. H. Marshall (1973) it represented the expansion of the rights of citizenship in Britain to include social rights, in addition to the "bundles" of first civil and then political rights that had each served "as a kind of step or platform for the others" (Held 1988, p. 191). Even in Switzerland the trend since World War II and especially since 1974 has been toward according welfare-state provisions to people largely on the basis of their legal residence and employment, thus encompassing a steadily growing majority of immigrants. If most of them still cling to the bottom rungs of the socioeconomic ladder, "even at the bottom there is a modicum of well-being that would not have been available before the advent of the new citizenship" (Heisler and Schmitter Heisler 1990, p. 10).

Several battles for social rights remain to be fought in Switzerland. Yet there, as in France, it is more for civil rights like complete freedom of speech and association and explicitly political rights that organized immigrant groups are now fighting. Whether in La Courneuve, Roubaix, Schlieren, or even La Chaux-de-Fonds, the immigrant communities have not completely integrated with the host-society political system. On the whole Ralf Dahrendorf's observation (1963) remains valid: the immigrants have enjoyed something of a "secondary citizenship," whereby participation in the more limited sphere of work or school has acted as a substitute for formal political citizenship. Through their group-based mobilization in those arenas, they have used claims to political rights that the bourgeoisie once employed in its struggle against the aristocracy (Turner 1986, p. 136). The immigrants have thus juggled the sequence of Marshall's threefold, staged process.

Explicitly and implicitly, they have pushed for new forms of citizenship. As Held observes, "Citizenship is about involvement of people in the community in which they live" (1988, p. 199). The question becomes one of who can and should belong and participate, and more than just the social-class dimension must come into play. Marshall's formulations—as well as those of political theorists who tie the extension of citizenship more tightly to class conflict itself (for example, Giddens 1981 and 1985)—fail to take into consideration such movements as the immigrants', since they have operated on different bases and along different axes. They are posing new sorts of questions about citizenship and participation in Western democracies.

What the immigrants have been challenging are no less than traditional conceptions of membership in the democratic polity. They are raising the "boundary problem": who constitutes the " 'people' or unit within which democratic governance is to be practiced" in nations like France and Switzerland (Whelan 1983)? Like women and the other excluded groups who struggled before them, politically active immigrants have been widening the prevailing definition of the "people."

The result has been heated debate over issues of legitimacy and representativeness in France and Switzerland. In each a large number of residents who have contributed to society through their work and their taxes, raising and educating their children there and using public services, cannot participate fully in the determination of public policy. Whether one deems that exclusion justified or not, it has certainly resulted in a "distortion of preferences" and thus of the public agenda (see Verba, Kim, and Nie 1978, pp. 301–309); herein lies one major reason for the lack of a comprehensive, adequate policy response to immigration. Zig Layton-Henry argues that this situation "challenges the liberal democratic values and institutional procedures so greatly prized in these multi-party democracies" (1990, p. 186). It means that "representative government is no longer representative" (p. 24). Joined by Tomas Hammar (1985), Peter H. Schuck and Rogers M. Smith (1989), and others, he worries as well that failure to incorporate immigrant communities politically could result in serious internal unrest. This demand is a revolutionary and not a reformist proposal, for Western European states could not meet it without profoundly altering the structure of their economies and their polities (André Gorz, cited in Freeman 1979, p. 255).

France has started down that rocky road, largely in spite of itself. Writing in *Libération* (Oct. 15, 1990), French philosopher Jean-Paul Dolle has repeated the warnings issued in general terms by Michael Walzer (1983) and Barber (1988): "Our political system resembles more and more that of the ancient Greek city-states: fully democratic for full citizens (that is, 'native' French); tolerant toward the 'metics' (rich foreigners); closed toward the 'barbarians' (poor foreigners)." It follows, Dolle argues, that the question of "the troubled suburbs is not a simple issue of urban policy or even a social issue. It is an issue that concerns French society in its entirety—its coherence, unity, and even its integrity" (p. 8).

Truly, it is the Jacobin model of the nation-state itself that faces a severe test. Since the Revolution, membership in the French national community has involved a voluntary commitment to the republic and to its values. The republic has imposed a process of socialization and national integration entailing the eradication of peripheral cultures and any special treatment of cultural differences. This Jacobin vision has insisted on a direct relationship between each citizen and a strong state, which defines the nation. Intermediate groups and identities— political, economic, ethnic, religious, or regional—have been suspect.[4]

Many factors have contributed to a decline of Jacobinism since 1945, including the erosion of traditional authority structures as a result of postwar modernization, the Socialist government's decentralization program in the early 1980s, and its recognition of cultural differences and loosening of associational laws. Because of France's failure to integrate its immigrant communities, as well as institutional encouragement of ethnic identity among them, the immigrants have sharpened and propelled the continuing debate over France's increasingly pluralist society. They have "reethnicized" older, seemingly assimilated immigrants and national minorities: Jews, Poles, Bretons, and Italians. H. Giordan (1982), William Safran (1985 and 1991), and other academics and politicians have applauded signs of a more pluralist France and the immigrants' role in bringing it about. Meanwhile, loyal Jacobins on the right (for example, Debré 1984) and the left (for example, Dumont 1990; Weil 1991a) have warned of the alleged dangers and inapplicability of the "American" model (see Pinto 1988).

France has entered a difficult period of profound change, and anti-immigrant feelings and violence have intensified. Yet the immigrants have made use of a potent mixture of institutional and confrontational tactics to compel French society to confront their dire situation. The French institution of citizenship, which has so far resisted all challenges, is slowly but surely inserting the immigrant communities into the French polity (see Brubaker 1992).[5] Authorities have had no choice but to persist in searching for ways to reassert control, integrate the immigrant communities, and fend off the extremist challenge that endangers social harmony. The growing electoral clout of both indigenous and immigrant ethnics has been of no small consequence here (Safran 1991, p. 229). The immigrants have forced a painful but necessary process of institutional adaptation that, in the long run, may well revitalize and strengthen French democracy, "producing stability by way of change" (Dalton and Kuechler 1990, p. 298; see Leveau and Wihtol de Wenden 1988). Thus do democracies often expand, absorb, and deal with "problems of their own making" (Tarrow 1989, pp. 344–348).

Switzerland has avoided much of France's social torment over immigration. Swiss political institutions, at most levels and in most instances, have channeled away the immigrants' protest potential, fragmenting their political energies and neutralizing their threatening aspects. Citizenship laws based on *jus sanguinis* and tortuous naturalization procedures have made the Swiss system resemble Walzer's "tyranny" at most levels: "it is the exercise of power . . . over men and women who resemble citizens in every respect that counts in the host country, but are nevertheless barred from citizenship" (1983, p. 59). The immigrants and their children have remained "live-in servants" (p. 62).

Effective as they have been, such "tyrannical" institutional arrangements are brittle. They have come under attack from the inside: the percentage of immigrants with permanent residency permits continues to climb. And they have come under attack from the outside: the European Community has been specifying rights and duties that transcend Swiss borders, the type of international rules that "whilst they may lack coercive powers of enforcement, have far-reaching consequences" (Held 1988, p. 202). Europe has adopted many of the defining political values of Jacobin France, such as human rights, equality, and *laïcité* (secularism). European integration threatens to erode France's specific identity as well as the political sovereignty of its strong state. However, both of these changes work in a direction eventually favorable to the immigrants, whose references to "universalistic" French values have in any event added legitimacy to their struggles.

Switzerland has no such defining ideology, not even a declining one. European integration has challenged its system in even more unsettling and unfamiliar ways. Its strict immigration policies, uncompromising hierarchization of foreign workers (including the seasonal workers' statute), and institutions of direct democracy are all out of sync with Europe. Should the prevailing institutional framework erode, thoroughgoing change and a shattering crisis of social control might well ensue, given the proven strength of xenophobic feeling and the potential for a forceful response from a very large, settled, and less constrained foreign population—whose labor is even more structurally essential to the economy than in France. Immigrant associations in Switzerland have seen the European question as providing them with a political opening, a means to spur improvements in their social and political situation in a nation that must bring its policies in line with the more generous ones that the European Community has been developing (Grossi 1989; *New York Times,* Aug. 11, 1991).

By the early 1990s it was virtually impossible for authorities and institutions in either host society or any case city figuring here to deal with immigration and the new ethnic minority communities in an honest, thoroughgoing manner. The anti-immigrant reaction was too strong. Authorities in France and Switzerland—like their counterparts across Western Europe—so misread the true nature and implications of postwar labor immigration that their policy response has been reactive from the start. The immigrants did not play the victim. Instead, participating in ways and on bases that reflected the institutional frameworks within which they had to operate, they defended their interests and addressed demands to the governments and institutions of France and Switzerland as well as their homelands. In light of their fundamental political vulnerability, it was not surprising that the Le Pens and the Schwarzenbachs of those host societies managed to shift political discourse to the right.

French and Swiss officials stand at a crucial crossroads. They find themselves caught between growing pressures from European integration, anti-immigrant forces and sentiment, employers demanding more cheap labor, and increasingly "permanent" immigrant/ethnic communities unwilling to accept passively their social and political marginalization. Whatever governments choose to do, they are certain to incur the wrath of important segments of society. Yet, as William Wallace has argued in the *New Statesman and Society* (May 17, 1991), "the political risks of undirected drift are also great." If this volume has a positive message, it relates to the power of French and Swiss institutions to bring about a solution, arduous and convulsive though such a reactive process might be. Institutional channeling, rather than more intractable ethnic and class factors, created the current challenge of ethnic diversity in France and Switzerland. Pressured from without and within, those societies might yet effect the institutional changes necessary to meet and resolve that challenge.

Notes
References
Index

Notes

Introduction

1. I use the terms *foreign workers* and *immigrant workers* interchangeably to denote this labor force. *Foreigners, foreign population, foreign-origin population,* and *immigrants* refer to these workers and their families in general. Illegal immigrants and political refugees constitute separate categories.
2. For an application of this concept to African-American migrants to the American North, see Katznelson (1981, chap. 4). Compare Thomas Sowell's emphasis on human capital (1978 and 1981).
3. This goes further than the class theory's vision of the organizations of indigenous labor movements as arenas for and simple stimuli or barriers to immigrant participation.
4. It might appear tempting to compare Turks in Germany with Algerians in France. But although the two populations are of similar proportions, their disparate immigration histories and ethnoreligious and national backgrounds preclude such a comparison. One would have to assume from the start that the two populations' overwhelming adherence to Islam counted more than any other factors (see Kastoryano 1987). The British case, too, is inappropriate here, being unique among the major European host societies: ex-colonial migrants, who at least initially enjoyed *de jure* equality, make up almost all the "foreign" population in the United Kingdom, whereas in France ex-colonials account for only part of that population (see Rath and Saggar 1987).
5. In each the so-called threshold of tolerance has been met or surpassed. This term refers to a widespread, albeit completely unsubstantiated, working assumption in Western Europe that once the foreign population reaches a designated critical level—set variously at anywhere from 5 percent to 20 percent of the total population—social conflict becomes likely (V. de Rudder 1984). Working with four cities with even greater shares of immigrants, I ignore the entire acrimonious debate over this *idée reçue*.

6. The slightly smaller Spanish presence in the French cities has arisen in part from higher rates of naturalization among that older national community.

7. Reliable statistics are hard to come by, but municipal officials in my four case cities corroborated this assessment.

8. Formal and informal polls have suggested that only about 10 percent of immigrants ever join a foreigners' or indigenous association of any kind in the Western European host societies, similar to the percentage among the indigenous populations (Schmitter Heisler 1983, p. 309).

9. McAdam (1982) and Tilly (1978) are among the scholars who have stressed the value of newspapers in providing the kind of data central to my project.

10. Huntington and Nelson provide a concise definition of political participation that applies here: "activity by private citizens designed to influence government decision-making. Participation may be individual or collective, organized or spontaneous, sustained or sporadic, peaceful or violent, legal or illegal, effective or ineffective" (1976, p. 3). Participation thereby becomes an umbrella concept that resists a simplistic indexing of "total participation" and welcomes a richer, more nuanced discussion of its levels, forms, bases, and impact. This does not exclude or ignore the type of nonelectoral or confrontational modes of participation that immigrants have sometimes employed.

11. Taking a cue from Maurice Jackson (1969), I define a social movement as the "more or less continuous interaction of conscious human beings in an emergent collectivity striving toward a goal" (p. 8).

1. France before 1974

1. Schor (1985b) demonstrates that Catholic religious practices could serve as either an integrating or an isolating factor in the workplace, depending on the nature of those practices and the trade union response to them.

2. Although Algerians were also present in France by the nineteenth century, the French labor movement long perceived the problem of "foreign competition" as one involving Europeans (see Mouriaux and Wihtol de Wenden 1987).

3. This xenophobic law was reactivated under Marshal Pétain's *Etat Français* in 1940, laying the basis for Vichy to promulgate its harsh anti-Semitic laws (see Guillaume 1985, p. 125).

4. The CGT, for example, which had counted around 25,000 foreign members in the mid-1920s and around 50,000 in the mid-1930s, included between 350,000 and 400,000 by 1937 (Gani 1972; Noiriel 1980; Schor 1985a, p. 3).

5. The French government did not hesitate to deport striking foreign workers guilty of "showing a lack of appropriate respect for local authorities" (*Le Peuple*, May 14, 1936, p. 17, cited in Schor 1985a, p. 4).

6. The 1901 association law reserved to the president the right to dissolve by decree associations that had foreign administrators, a noncitizen membership of more than one-quarter, or its headquarters outside France and that he deemed a threat to the nation's internal or external security. Under Daladier's 1939 decree those three features qualified an association as "foreign"; thus

the minister of the interior could theoretically have outlawed both the French Communist Party and Catholic associations, since he could easily have seen them as controlled from abroad (that is, from Moscow and the Vatican).

7. For more on the political economy of postwar immigration into France, see Hollifield (1992).

8. These two kinds of permits were seldom of equal duration, because both the Ministry of the Interior and the Ministry of Employment were involved in their issuance (see Verbunt 1985a, pp. 138–139). Legislation in 1926 first made it a requirement that foreign workers obtain special identification cards (Wihtol de Wenden 1988, pp. 38–39).

9. The ONI became the Office of International Migrations (Office des Migrations Internationales—OMI) in 1985.

10. Migrants from Algeria—then an integral part of the republic—gained the right to enter and work freely in metropolitan France in 1947 (Tapinos 1975, p. 28).

11. French law obliged by allowing immigrants to vote at consulates in homeland elections; candidates for office in the countries of emigration could campaign discreetly in France. Italy (at first), Greece, and Turkey insisted that their citizens return home to vote, whereas Algeria permitted consular voting.

12. Many of the Algerians in postwar France are not Arabs but Berbers from peripheral, largely rural regions, a situation that has contributed to organizational rivalries.

13. Personal interview with militants of the Colectivo de Estudos e Dinamização da Emigração Portuguesa (CEDEP), Paris.

14. The French Communists allowed the AAE its autonomous existence, however, out of deference for the party's intimate relations with the FLN in Algiers.

15. *Le Monde* provided extensive coverage of a particularly tragic event in Aubervilliers between January 3 and 30, 1971.

16. Extreme leftist movements exhibited genuine support for the immigrants' autonomy, but their lack of real political influence reduced their appeal as allies (see Gani 1972).

2. France, 1974–1992

1. Only the public meetings of Lotta Continua, the neofascist Movimento Soziale Italiano, and other extremist groups were prohibited.

2. The "Franco-Algerian exchange of letters" in 1980 exemplified the continuing bilateral desire to bring order to the flow of migrant labor (Wihtol de Wenden 1988, pp. 250–251; compare Sayad 1979).

3. The Gray Wolves, right-wing extremists so active in terrorizing left-wing Turks in West Germany, were less organized but not absent from France (see Pekin 1979; Legrain 1985).

4. Among these were the Organization of African Communists, the Antillean Workers' League, and the Federation of Black African Students in France.

5. The number of foreigners serving in such a capacity could not exceed one-

third of the total number of trade union administrators. For more details on French employee institutions, see Minet (1984).

6. It was at least in part in response to this demand for attention that a secretary of state for immigrant workers *(secrétaire d'état aux travailleurs immigrés)*, the first since World War II, was named soon after Valéry Giscard d'Estaing's victory in the presidential election in 1974 (Wihtol de Wenden 1988, p. 193).

7. For the government's position, see "Nouvelle politique de l'immigration" 1977.

8. Personal interview with militants of the CEDEP, Paris.

9. Brought up on the trade unions' earlier opposition to the introduction of foreign labor, many rank-and-file members bitterly opposed any special concessions to their foreign co-workers (CGT 1981, pp. 72–73; see Mouriaux 1982, pp. 161–164).

10. See the criticisms of these tactics in *Journal officiel—Assemblée Nationale* 42, June 8, 1978.

11. For an overview see "Statistiques relatives" 1981.

12. French Communists usually opposed consultative bodies, favoring noninstitutionalized consultation with the official organizational representatives of emigration countries friendly with the PCF and CGT (for instance, Algeria).

13. For details on French immigration policy after 1981, see C. Bruschi (1985).

14. Some 140,000 "paperless" *(sans-papiers)* took advantage of the program, which lasted until 1983 (see Valentin 1983).

15. For more on the Auroux laws, see Gallie (1985) and Bodin (1987).

16. The FAS, the "prototypical immigrant welfare organization" dating from 1958, concerned itself first only with Algerian workers. Gradually, however, it has expanded to cover all immigrants and their families. Its funding comes from the money that the government withholds from family assistance grants to foreign workers whose families do not reside in France.

17. Personal interview with Moussa Raballi, president, CTA, Paris.

18. Personal interview with militants of the ATAF, Paris.

19. By 1989 the FAEEF encompassed some 128 associations across France.

20. See the declaration reprinted in *Presse et immigrés en France* 129 (April 1985), p. 18.

21. Personal interview with M. Ferreire, CCPF. See Cordeiro (1985b).

22. Personal interview with militants of the Front de Libération Nationale du Kurdistan, Paris.

23. Personal interview with militants of the UTT and with Yalnaz Hamdan, UCTT, Paris.

24. Personal interview with Urel Bektas, Democratic Association of Turkish Workers (Association Démocratique des Travailleurs Turcs—ADTT), and with militants of the Association of Turkish Workers (Association des Travailleurs Turcs—ATT), Paris.

25. Personal interview with Abderrazak Bouazizi, CAIF.

26. Appointed immigrant representatives, trade unionists, bureaucrats, and French human rights activists sit on the CNPI (see CAIF 1986).

27. Personal interview with Abderrazak Bouazizi, CAIF.

28. The *harkis* were native Algerians who had served in the French colonial military forces and remained loyal to France, where they withdrew en masse after independence in 1962. For political reasons, some prefer the term *French Muslims* to *harkis*.

29. Reflecting the heightened sensitivity of solidarity groups in general, Catholic churches offered significant support for the construction of mosques in many localities and often provided temporary space for Islamic prayer rooms.

30. For their complete comments, see the front page of *Le Monde*, Feb. 11, 1983.

31. His foreign minister, Claude Cheysson, did reignite the debate, however, when he declared in Algiers in the summer of 1981 that the government would have liked to allow immigrants to participate in the 1983 elections (*Le Matin*, Aug. 12, 1981). The Socialists quickly backed away from the project when opposition to the idea flared (see Le Pen 1985, p. 232).

32. By the 1980s the service sector was employing more youth of both sexes; however, low-paying jobs in fast-food restaurants, hotels, and the like accounted for much of it (see Lebon 1981; Wihtol de Wenden 1990).

33. If both parents have been born in France, the acquisition of citizenship under this article is "definitive and unconditional" (Brubaker 1992, p. 141).

34. Georgina Dufoix, more sympathetic to the cultural pluralists, served as secretary of state for the family, population, and immigrants *(secrétaire d'état chargé de la famille, de la population et des immigrés)* from the summer of 1983 to March 1986.

35. One playwright of Algerian descent poked fun at the situation in a piece that he called "A Star Is *Beur*" (see *Le Matin*, Sept. 5, 1986).

36. See the comments made by this faction's leader, Farida Belghoul, at the concluding ceremonies of Convergence '84, in Belghoul (1984).

37. Personal interview with SOS-Racisme leaders, Paris.

38. Personal interview with SOS-Racisme leaders, Paris.

39. Personal interview with CAIF officials, Paris.

40. See the comments of Manuel Dias, regional delegate of the Social Action Fund for Aquitaine and Poitou-Charentes, in *Migrations-société* 4 (Jan.–Feb. 1992): 23–33.

41. Personal interview with Eric Montes, SOS-Racisme/93, Saint-Denis.

42. For detailed coverage, see *Libération* and *Le Monde* from late December 1986 to mid-January 1987.

43. Spanish authorities, for example, turned the Casa de España in Paris into a "window" on Spanish culture (with no room for the "popular" activities of the traditional associations and their working-class membership) in 1987, created a Council of Spanish Residents in France in 1988, and instigated the formation of a new association close to the Socialist Party and the UGT trade union. Upset by Madrid's "abandonment" of them, the two major associational federations, the FAEEF and the APFEEF, merged early in 1992. The integration of Spanish immigrants in French society has become their prime area of concern (see "El CRE" 1990; Dianteill 1992).

44. The new rector, Cheikh Abbas, also improved relations between Algerians and the *harki* community (Kepel 1987, p. 325).

45. The Conseil d'Etat issued an ambiguous ruling in late November that students may wear religious symbols in schools, provided that they do not interfere with the secular educational program (see Beriss 1990). In November 1992 the Council definitively annulled the restriction imposed by the *collège* (*Le Monde*, Dec. 3, 1992). The "scarf affair" put the spotlight on the Muslim woman and gave rise to organizations of second-generation North Africans—who call themselves *Nanas-Beurs* instead of the more common but demeaning *Beurettes*. Among its highest-profile members are the second-generation immigrants (overwhelmingly female) who have won local elected office in recent years in Lyons, Marseilles, Limoges, and elsewhere (Barbara 1992; compare Sebbar 1991).

46. See the dossier on events in Mantes and their aftermath in *Panorama de la presse* (1991).

47. Robert Solé made these comments in *Le Monde*, Feb. 19, 1992. See the set of articles on the HCI in *Migrations-société* 4 (March–April 1992): 54–68.

48. In a thinly veiled allusion to Napoleon's famous dismissal of Talleyrand as "a shit in silk stockings" ("une merde dans un bas de soie"), Prime Minister Cresson called the former president "a Le Pen in silk stockings" (Perotti 1991, p. 44). The leader of the National Front expressed satisfaction at seeing mainstream politicians adopt his positions and vocabulary, as well as confidence that the voters would in the end "prefer the original to a copy" (*Le Figaro*, June 21, 1991).

49. See Gilles Verbunt's review of Patrick Weil's book in *Migrations-société* 4 (March–April 1992): 71–73.

50. EC citizens residing anywhere in the Community would be able to participate like natives in elections for municipal councils and the European Parliament; non-Europeans' rights went unmentioned.

51. Désir's Mouvement has since flopped, and he has dissolved it, joining Génération Ecologie, one branch of France's divided Greens, as its vice president (personal interview with Antonio Cruz, editor-in-chief, *Migration News Sheet*, Brussels).

3. The Local French Cases

1. Political shenanigans robbed the PCF of its rightful victory immediately after World War II. A woman voted onto the city council on the PCF list in 1947 revealed herself after the election to be a member of the opposition center-right coalition, tilting the balance of power in its favor (personal interview with Pascal Gaillard, archivist, Ville de La Courneuve).

2. Personal interview with Mayor James Marson (PCF), La Courneuve.

3. Some of this information comes from a letter from Mayor James Marson to the residents of La Courneuve, dated Feb. 18, 1976, found in the municipal archives of La Courneuve.

4. The protests elicited a reprieve from the owners, but in the end the plant shut its doors. Police stormed the factory in August 1977, expelling the French and foreign workers who had occupied it (personal interview with Pascal Gaillard, municipal archivist).

5. Noncitizen residents could vote in all elections that took place in public housing complexes (*JA*, Nov. 11, 1976; May 5, 1977; April 17, 1980).
6. Personal interview with Jean Durand, PSU, La Courneuve.
7. Personal interview with M. Salah, president, AAE, La Courneuve.
8. Personal interview with militants of the AOP, Bobigny.
9. Personal interview with Mayor James Marson.
10. Personal interview with Jean Durand, PSU.
11. Personal interview with members of the Association Portugaise de Culture, Saint-Denis; personal interview with members of Rancho Folklorico Português, Aulnay-sous-Bois.
12. The moderate CGT/Force Ouvrière (Workers' Force) came in a distant second with 11.5 percent. Figures and CGT reaction provided by the Municipal Archives of La Courneuve.
13. Text of the "Déclaration des maires communistes de la Seine-Saint-Denis" (1980) from the Municipal Archives of La Courneuve.
14. Some of this information comes from a "Rock against Police" bulletin provided by the Municipal Archives of La Courneuve.
15. Personal interview with Jean Durand, PSU.
16. Personal interview with Jimmy Kiavué.
17. Before year's end, the national government would allocate some 56 million francs in a two-year emergency plan designed to effect the most urgently needed repairs and improvements (*BM*, April 1984).
18. Personal interview with Jean Durand, PSU.
19. Personal interview with Kenan Oz Turk, Association Culturelle de la Turquie, La Courneuve.
20. Personal interview with Imam Besscübia, Mosquée Sidi Ibrahim El-Khalil, La Courneuve.
21. Personal interview with members of the Comité Justice Abdel Benyahia, La Courneuve.
22. Personal interview with Jimmy Kiavué and associates. See the series of articles "Le coup des jeunes," in Ville de La Courneuve, *Regards*, Jan. 1987.
23. The rate of abstentionism reached a stunning 55.2 percent (*Le Monde*, March 14 and June 20, 1989; Bouamama 1989, p. 44).
24. Quoted in Congrès CGT (1906), p. 153. For the development of Guesdism in Roubaix and the Nord, see Willard (1981).
25. Bringing their food with them for the coming week of work in France, they earned the derisive nickname *"les pots à beurre"* (the butter crocks) (Marty 1982, pp. 71–78).
26. Not integrated but scarcely noticed was a small community of Algerian workers who had drifted up from the mines of the Houillères (Salah 1973, pp. 10, 63–64).
27. Personal interviews with M. Lakhdar, regional head of the AAE, Roubaix; and militants of the Union des Syndicats des Travailleurs Algériens, Roubaix.
28. Personal interview with Marc Vandewynckèle, former president of the CEM, Roubaix.
29. For several instances, see *VN*, June 30–July 1, 1974; Sept. 9, 1976; Feb. 17, 1977.

30. See the comments by Councillors Faba and Coisne (PSU) in *BC,* April 18 and Oct. 3, 1977; April 9, 1979. See also the comments of Councillor Jacques Fontaine (PSU) in *VN,* June 3, 1983.
31. Personal interview with Thierry Delattre, municipal archivist, Roubaix.
32. Official homeland and fraternal organizations did not normally benefit from such funding, since it was assumed that their governments should cover their costs.
33. Legal restrictions made it impossible to have the immigrants directly elect their own representatives to the body (personal interview with Marc Vandewynckèle, CEM).
34. Personal interviews with Marc Vandewynckèle, CEM; M. Lakhdar, AAE; and Moussa Raballi, president of the Comité des Travailleurs Algériens, Paris.
35. Personal interview with Marc Vandewynckèle, CEM.
36. Personal interview with Jacques Fontaine, PSU municipal councillor, Roubaix. For an example, see the letter to the editor, *VN,* Dec. 1, 1983.
37. Personal interviews with Ahmed Zahri, Association Culturelle des Ressortissants Ivoiriens de Roubaix; and Adolphe Eyango-Elimbi, Association des Camerounais de Roubaix et Environs.
38. Personal interviews with Marc Vandewynckèle and Fikret Kaynar, president of the Association Culturelle Islamique des Turcs, Roubaix.
39. Personal interviews with Marc Vandewynckèle.
40. Personal interview with Jacques Fontaine, PSU.
41. Personal interview with the imam at the Abbou Bakr mosque, Roubaix.
42. Lecluse had actually done even better, but his photo appeared on 500 of the ballots distributed by his campaign, which invalidated them (*NE,* March 19, 1983).
43. Personal interviews with Thérèse Constans, president of the CEM; and Jacques Fontaine, PSU.
44. Mayor Diligent, quoted in "Discours prononcé par le sénateur-maire," press release, May 13, 1984.
45. Personal interview with Eric Barth, SOS-Racisme/Association Texture, Lille.
46. Consider, for example, the comments of Gérard Follin, producer, "De bonne source," French Television Channel One (TF1), Feb. 11, 1987, 9:35–11:05 P.M.
47. Personal interview with André Coornaert, Ligue des Droits de l'Homme, Lille.
48. In 1985 it created a national stir by organizing a registration concert headlined by the *Beur* supergroup "Carte de Séjour."
49. See *VN* and *NE* in late November and early December 1986 for excellent, detailed coverage.

4. Switzerland before 1974

1. Only the mass media and the army (in which every adult male from age eighteen to sixty-five must serve) act as "uniformizing" national-level institutions (see de Rham 1976, p. 6). On the nature of Swiss multiculturalism, compare Steiner (1974) with Schmid (1981).

2. Swiss schoolchildren still sing, "Mother dear, give me 100 lire, I want to go to America" (Meyer 1991, p. 98).

3. German minister-president Otto von Bismarck was so concerned that he had spies infiltrate the expatriate community in Switzerland and pressured federal officials into appointing a special prosecutor to monitor alien inhabitants (Meyer 1991, p. 98).

4. Centralized in the financial capital of Zurich, the business community (known as the *Vorort*) has been better organized and more effective (see Höplinger 1976; and Schmitter Heisler 1981).

5. To Lenin, "the characteristic trait of imperialism in Switzerland is the growing exploitation of foreign workers deprived of rights by the bourgeoisie of that country, whose hopes rest with the division between [native and foreign] workers" (Revolutionäre Marxistische Liga 1974, p. 80).

6. Article 19 of the ANAG did state, though, that cantonal law had to provide foreigners with the right to appeal decisions rendered against them.

7. Fascism also produced a new wave of refugees, especially Jews, during the 1930s and 1940s. Swiss fascist groups stirred up xenophobia and anti-Semitism and convinced the federal government to prohibit the classification of people fleeing for "racial reasons" as "political asylum seekers." In 1938 Swiss officials cooperated with the Nazis, agreeing to mark expatriate German Jews' passports with a special stamp (Meyer 1991, p. 98). For more on Switzerland during World War II, see Mauroux (1968).

8. These workers are supposed to work and live in Switzerland for a maximum of nine months in any one year. Yet their true function is to relieve labor shortages in the construction, agricultural, and catering sectors, which offer low-paying positions and are not fully integrated into the labor market. Seasonal workers have extremely limited rights to change their jobs and none at all to have their families join them or to draw unemployment benefits. Few manage to qualify for an annual residence permit, attainable after thirty-six months of work within four consecutive years with no gaps in their employment period (Meyer 1991, pp. 99–100).

9. Importantly, the most politically militant immigrants are the least likely to envision such assimilation.

10. For details on the immigrants' housing problems in Switzerland, see CFE/EKA 1976a; V. de Rudder 1976.

11. Neither foreigners nor Swiss citizens could engage in revolutionary propaganda or incite violence. In 1966, the government singled out Communism, right-wing extremism, and anarchism as three political ideologies whose espousal could pose a threat to Swiss democracy.

12. Foreigners accounted for over half of the FOBB/GBH membership by the early 1970s (Castelnuovo-Frigessi 1978, pp. 73, 278).

13. Personal interview with Gérard Berger, Parti Ouvrier et Populaire (POP/Communist), La Chaux-de-Fonds.

14. In practice, the lower the status of the permit held by an immigrant, the greater were the effective barriers to his or her active political involvement (Commission Protestante Suisse-Immigrés 1980, pp. 6–7).

15. Personal interview with Guglielmo Grossi, president, FCLIS, Zurich, June 25, 1987.
16. Women won the federal vote in 1971. Many cantons, especially in French-speaking Switzerland, had earlier granted cantonal- and communal-level suffrage.
17. The agitation overwhelmed the typically docile employee committees—organizations elected by all workers in a plant, unionized or not, and responsible for the application of labor conventions. The committees had little choice but to go along with the movement (Castelnuovo-Frigessi 1978, pp. 286–287).
18. Eight cantons accepted the initiative: Bern, Luzern, Uri, Schwyz, Obwalden, Nidwalden, Fribourg, and Solothurn (Ebel and Fiala 1983, p. 9).
19. The length of the waiting period depended on an immigrant's nationality and was included in the provisions of the treaties between Switzerland and the various homeland governments.
20. Schwarzenbach wanted to create a more structured political force and to broaden its message to encompass other issues (such as opposition to Swiss membership in the United Nations) besides the fear of *Üeberfremdung*, which had become the sole obsession of the NA.
21. Personal interview with Guglielmo Grossi, FCLIS.
22. Personal interview with Anjuska Weil, Mitenand-Komitee and Partei der Arbeit, Zurich.

5. Switzerland, 1974–1992

1. For the government's apologetics, see "Conséquences" 1977.
2. See the comments of Giampiero Camurati, president of the CNI, in Passamonte (1984).
3. Personal interview with M. Ferreire, president, CCPF, Paris.
4. Disparities did remain across cantons, industrial sectors, and trade union federations (Hoffmann-Nowotny and Hondrich 1982, p. 626; compare Minet 1984, pp. 5–6).
5. Personal interview with Gérard Berger, Parti Ouvrier et Populaire (POP), La Chaux-de-Fonds.
6. Tract provided by Jacqueline Sammali, Comité Suisses-Immigrés, La Chaux-de-Fonds.
7. Personal interview with Francisco Belo, Associação dos Trabahaldores Portugueses (ATP), La Chaux-de-Fonds.
8. Personal interview with Guglielmo Grossi, FCLIS.
9. Personal interviews with Léon Hoyas, Pueblos de España; and André Sandoz, Communauté Neuchâteloise de Travail Suisses-Etrangers (CNTSE), La Chaux-de-Fonds.
10. Personal interviews with Jacqueline Sammali, Comité Suisses-Immigrés; Guglielmo Grossi, FCLIS; and Léon Hoyas, ATEES. The Labor Party, though "sympathetic," disparaged the "nationalistic, delusory" nature of electoral participation (personal interview with Gérard Berger, POP, La Chaux-de-Fonds).
11. Variations existed on that theme: thus in the canton of Fribourg foreign taxpayers could appoint a Swiss citizen of their choice to represent them at local

meetings to decide the disposition of public revenues. For a concise overview of the debate about granting the immigrants local-level voting rights in Switzerland, see Grisel (1982).

12. Personal interview with Fr. Esteban, Misión Católica Española, Zurich.

13. Personal interview with Professor Denis Maillat, Université de Neuchâtel.

14. For the xenophobic position, see Valentin Oehen's comments in *Volk und Heimat,* Feb. and Sept. 1978.

15. Swiss voters turned down government-sponsored naturalization reforms in 1983. They thereby ruled out federal officials' plan to defuse anti-immigrant sentiment by reducing the noncitizen population and to facilitate its integration (*La vie économique,* April 1986, p. 168).

16. Personal interview with militants of SOS-Racisme, La Chaux-de-Fonds.

17. Information gleaned from participation in the "Journée Suisses-Immigrés," University of Geneva, Switzerland, July 4, 1987.

18. Also unsettling the placid Swiss conscience was the occasional public suicide or freezing to death of would-be clandestine immigrants and refugees in the Alpine passes leading from Italy.

19. Personal interviews at the Regionalzentrum der 3.-Welt Läden and the headquarters of SOS-Flüchtlinge, Zurich.

20. It was partially a matter of urgent need, since groundwater pollution, high ozone concentrations, and acid rain afflicted the small, densely populated, mountainous nation early on.

21. The once-significant Labor (Communist) Party has become in a sense the tiny left wing of the Swiss Socialist Party, lobbying for the interests of the poor, the elderly, and the marginalized (compare Maillard 1991). The FOBB/GBH recently merged with the Gewerkschaft Textil, Chemie und Papier to form the Gewerkschaft Bau und Industrie. With some 350,000 affiliated workers, it became Switzerland's largest single trade union (*Neue Zürcher Zeitung,* Sept. 8, 1992).

22. Still, nine out of ten expressed a very Swiss aversion to strikes as an acceptable means of solving labor disputes.

23. There were no corresponding moves toward greater labor mobility within the country (Gesú 1989).

24. Added to that number were some 156,725 seasonal workers (Meyer 1991, p. 99). By 1992 more than 1,200,000 foreigners lived in the country (*Tribune de Genève,* Jan. 23–24, 1993).

25. The Swiss Democrats immediately launched a referendum campaign against such an antidiscrimination office (*Neue Zürcher Zeitung,* Dec. 18, 1992; *Informations européennes,* Jan. 1993, p. 11).

26. Switzerland, said Max Frisch on that occasion, "is a putrefied state." "It's a prison," said Friedrich Dürenmatt, "an abscess, even, that could burst at any moment." Given these reactions it is little wonder that the president of the National Council, Ulrich Bremi, offered the terse diagnosis: "Switzerland is running a fever" (quoted in Müller von Blumencron 1991, p. 38).

27. Although the May vote was 55.8 percent in favor of the government's policies, turnout was a low 37.7 percent.

28. Under the EEA agreement—which was to take effect on January 1, 1993—

the members of EFTA (Switzerland, Austria, Sweden, Liechtenstein, Norway, Finland, and Iceland) would join the EC's existing plan to establish a single market in which goods, services, and (eventually) people circulate freely.

29. The Federal Council had to issue an appeal for tolerance when verbal exchanges between proponents and opponents grew bitter, with some politicians even receiving death threats (*Neue Zürcher Zeitung*, Nov. 13, 1992).

30. Also, applications for Swiss naturalization from the preferred European immigrants were declining, since they hesitated to give up their nationality when a wider European citizenship seemed to be forming. If Switzerland joined the EC in the future, Italians, Iberians, Germans, French, and Greeks would have no reason to trade their passports for a Swiss one.

31. That acceptance rate, up slightly from 3 percent the year before, was highest for Turks and Kurds (12.1 percent) (*Journal de Genève*, Jan. 16–17, 1993).

32. For approval a majority of the voters and the cantons would have been necessary. Italian-speaking Ticino, bearing witness to the influence of the federalist Lombard League just south of the border, also rejected Swiss entry into the EEA.

6. The Local Swiss Cases

1. Personal interview with Pastor Hansrüdi Guyer, Reformierte Kirchgemeinde, Schlieren.
2. Personal interview with M. Baumann and W. Roth, Stadtkanzlei, Schlieren.
3. Once Schliermer officials had bestowed communal citizenship upon a postulant, cantonal officials usually added citizenship at that level as well, although Zurich was not among the most obliging cantons.
4. The Mülligen Neighborhood Association (Quartierverein Mülligen), for instance, worked to protect its section of Schlieren from further industrial development.
5. Personal interview with Luigi Stara, FOBB/GBH, Schlieren.
6. See the comments of President Heinrich Meier (SVP) in *DL*, March 20, 1974.
7. Personal interview with Pastor Hansrüdi Guyer.
8. Personal interview with Anjuska Weil, Mitenand-Komitee and Partei der Arbeit, Zurich.
9. Personal interview with activists at ARLI, Schlieren.
10. Personal interview with Guglielmo Grossi, president, FCLIS, Zurich.
11. Personal interview with Rafet Kaymaz, president, Turkish association of Schlieren (no official name), Schlieren.
12. Personal interview with António Altisent, Spanish immigrant leader, Schlieren.
13. Personal interview with António Antunes, president, ATP, Zurich.
14. Predictably, the far right reacted angrily: "To those Swiss who fear *Ueberfremdung*," such activities amounted to the "closest, most obvious proof of foreign interference in Swiss affairs" (Miller 1981, p. 140).
15. Unfortunately, the fact that voting did not take place by set precincts precludes even "ecological" anaylsis (*DL*, Oct. 22, 1974).
16. Personal interviews with Anjuska Weil, PdA; and Luigi Stara, GBH.

17. Personal interview with Pastor Hansrüdi Guyer.
18. For details on these events, see Fortuna (1974–1988), entries throughout the period from May 1982 to December 1983.
19. Personal interview with Luigi Stara, GBH.
20. The adjective is Pastor Hansrüdi Guyer's.
21. Personal interview with Luigi Stara, GBH.
22. The administration even reduced the number of polling places in the city because of the shrinking numbers of voters (see Fortuna 1974–1988, entries from April 1983 and December 1983).
23. Personal interview with Daniel Kolb, secretary, Schulpflege, Schlieren.
24. Personal interview with organizers at the Jugendhaus, Schlieren.
25. Personal interview with Luigi Stara, FOBB/GBH. A few years later, Zurich's cantonal Council of State announced its opposition to the facultative right to vote for foreigners in local elections. At the same time, it declared itself firmly in favor of fully integrating foreigners, especially in the area of easing naturalization procedures (*Informations européennes*, Oct. 1992, p. 12).
26. Despite that hurdle, a steady stream of proposals on a wide range of issues attracted enough backers (*LI*, April 17, 1974).
27. Personal interview with Gérard Stehlin, Police des Habitants, La Chaux-de-Fonds.
28. Personal interviews with Ginetta Stucchi, Missione Cattolica Italiana; directors of the Misión Católica Española; and Francisco Belo, ATP, La Chaux-de-Fonds.
29. Personal interview with André Sandoz, former president of the General Council and of the CNTSE, La Chaux-de-Fonds.
30. Personal interview with André Sandoz, CNTSE.
31. Personal interview with Gérard Berger, POP, La Chaux-de-Fonds.
32. See the comments of André Brandt (Radical), in *PV*, Dec. 21, 1976, p. 317.
33. Personal interview with Gérard Berger, POP.
34. Personal interview with Francisco Belo, ATP.
35. On this point see the discussions in *PV*, April 28, 1976, pp. 1744–45; Jan. 31, 1979, pp. 1663–64.
36. Personal interview with André Sandoz, CNTSE.
37. Personal interview with Guglielmo Grossi, president, FCLIS, Zurich.
38. Personal interview with Francisco Belo, ATP.
39. Personal interview with Leon Hoyas, Pueblos de España, La Chaux-de-Fonds.
40. Personal interviews with Jacqueline Sammali, Comité Suisses-Immigrés; and activists of the Comité Suisse-Kurdistan, La Chaux-de-Fonds.
41. This information came from materials provided by André Sandoz: CNTSE *Procès-verbaux* from Sept. 3, 1976; Jan. 13, Feb. 22, March 16, and April 16, 1978; and a letter from the Union Patronale Neuchâteloise to J.-C. Perrinjaquet of the CNTSE, June 12, 1975.
42. Personal interview with André Sandoz, CNTSE.
43. Personal interview with Gérard Berger, POP.
44. This argument is found in a letter, furnished by André Sandoz, from Claude Borel (PSN) to the Département de l'Industrie/Conseil d'Etat, Neuchâtel, April 10, 1981.

45. Outside the canton of Neuchâtel noncitizens have enjoyed voting rights (mostly at the local level) only in Ireland, Scandinavia, the Netherlands, and, in Switzerland, the canton of Jura.
46. Personal interview with Philippe Kunzi, PSO, La Chaux-de-Fonds.
47. Personal interviews with Gérard Berger, POP; and Ginetta Stucchi, Missione Cattolica Italiana.
48. See, for example, the letter to the editor written by Gabriel Bonfanti, an Italian worker, *LI*, Oct. 9, 1980.
49. See the comments of Claude Robert (Independent), *PV*, Sept. 28, 1978, p. 1421; and the "Naturalisations" sections in the same source from 1974 through 1984.
50. On municipal efforts to assist second-generation immigrants, see Kohler (1982).
51. Personal interviews with militants of SOS-Racisme; and Jacqueline Sammali, Comité Suisses-Immigrés.
52. See the comments of Francis Matthey, president, Conseil Communal, *PV*, Nov. 29, 1983.
53. Personal interview with Jacqueline Sammali, Comité Suisses-Immigrés.
54. Exact figures on the immigrant vote in the 1988 communal elections were not available during my last visit to La Chaux-de-Fonds. See Pauchard (1988).
55. Personal interview with Jacqueline Sammali, Comité Suisses-Immigrés.

Conclusion

1. Alexis de Tocqueville, in fact, in his analytical brilliance captured well the interplay between institutional forces and both group activity and the overall content of political conflict (Zysman 1977, pp. 295–298).
2. In his effort to explain the nonparticipation of poor people in Appalachia, Gaventa (1980) refers to this type of process as the "third dimension" of power.
3. There has been continuing debate over whether Switzerland should strengthen the instruments of direct democracy or weaken them (see *Neue Zürcher Zeitung*, July 24 and 26–27, 1992).
4. Safran (1991) has argued persuasively that there always remained alongside the Jacobin vision "an organic conception which much of the Right never abandoned, according to which non-Europeans, Jews, and other non-Christians could not be considered fully French" (p. 221). And the cases of Roubaix and the Nord suggests that some regions of France have experienced much associational activity. As a general paradigm, however, the Jacobin model has long dominated France.
5. The situation may change under Edouard Balladur's Conservative government, which was voted into power in the spring of 1993 (*Libération*, June 3, 1993).

References

Newspapers and Newsletters

L'Algérien en Europe. Paris: AAE.
L'Amico. La Chaux-de-Fonds: Missione Cattolica Italiana.
Bulletin der Zürcher Kontaktstelle für Ausländer.
CAIF Infos. Paris.
CFE/EKA Information. Bern.
La Croix. Paris.
Emigrazione italiana. Zurich: FCLIS.
FONDA lettre d'information. Paris.
Hommes et migrations. Paris.
L'Impartial. La Chaux-de-Fonds.
Le Journal d'Aubervilliers. Aubervilliers/La Courneuve.
Libération. Paris.
Der Limmattaler. Dietikon/Schlieren.
Migrations-société. Paris: CIEMI.
Minute. Paris.
Mitenand/Etre solidaires/Essere solidali—Bulletin. Basel.
Le Monde. Paris.
Neue Zürcher Zeitung.
Le Nord-éclair. Lille/Roubaix.
Piazza. Basel: Komittee "Mitenand."
Presse et immigrés en France. Paris: CIEMI.
Revue syndicale suisse. Bern: USS/SGB.
Sans frontière. Paris.
La Suisse. Geneva.
Der Tages-Anzeiger. Zurich.
La Tribune de Genève.

La Voix du Nord. Lille/Roubaix.
Volk und Heimat. Winterthur.

Municipal Documents, 1974–1988

Stadt Schlieren. *Geschäftsberichte.*
—— *Jahresberichte.*
—— *Jahrhefte von Schlieren.*
Ville de La Chaux-de-Fonds, Conseil Général. *Procès-verbaux.*
—— *Rapports du Conseil Communal.*
Ville de La Courneuve. *Bulletins d'information municipale.*
—— *Bulletins municipaux.*
—— *Comptes-rendus du Conseil Municipal.*
—— *Regards.*
Ville de Roubaix. *Bulletins municipaux.*
—— *Comptes-rendus des réunions de la CEM.*

Books and Articles

Abdallah, Mogniss H. 1989–90. "La communauté portugaise a été protégée jusqu'ici par le paratonnerre maghrébin" (conversation with Albano Cordeiro). *L'Europe multicommunautaire,* special issue of *Plein droit,* pp. 115–118.
Abou-Sada, Georges, et al. 1981. *L'immigration dans le Nord-Pas-de-Calais.* Lille: OMINOR.
ACO. 1981. *L'ACO soutient l'initiative "Etre solidaires."* Fribourg.
Adank, Felix. 1990. "Ja zu Europa; Nein zu diesem Binnenmarkt!" *Piazza,* no. 25 (March):13.
ADRI. 1991. *Panorama de la presse* (Paris), May 27–June 17.
Aissou, Abdel. 1989. "Exercice de solidarité communautaire." *Migrations-société* 1, no. 5–6 (Oct.–Dec.):43–44.
Akkacha, M. 1973. "La participation des travailleurs algériens aux institutions représentatives dans les entreprises françaises." *Revue algérienne des sciences juridiques,* June.
"Aktive Politik gegen Rassismus." 1990. *Piazza,* no. 25 (March):5.
Allal, Tewfik, et al. 1977. *Situations migratoires.* Paris: Galilée.
ANGI. 1984. *Les cahiers de la nouvelle génération.* Vol. 1. Gennevilliers.
Anido, Nayade, and Rubens Freire. 1978. *L'émigration portugaise.* Paris: Presses Universitaires de France.
Annoni, Mario, Patricia Chitvanni, and Martina Richards. 1976. "La Colonie Libre Italienne." In Laurent Monnier, Gérard de Rham, and Sophie Martin, eds., *Pour une recherche sur l'immigration—Bilan d'un séminaire.* Lausanne: Institut de Science Politique, Université de Lausanne, pp. 55–64.
Annuaire statistique du Canton de Neuchâtel. 1982. Neuchâtel: Service Cantonal de Statistique.
"Appréciation de l'activité déployée par la commission de mai 1977 à décembre 1980." 1981. *CFE Information* 13 (March):11–16.

"ARLI-Schlieren." 1983. *Emigrazione italiana,* Feb. 9, p. 10.

Arroteia, Jorge. 1981. "Portugal e a emigração." In Maria Beatriz Rocha Trindade, ed., *Estudos sobre a emigração portuguesa.* Lisbon: Sá Da Costa Editoria, pp. 8–69.

Arta, Hans-Rudolph. 1983. *Die Vereins-, Versammlungs- und Meinungsäusserungsfreiheit der Ausländer.* Diss. St. Gallen.

"A sinistra, ma . . ." 1984. *L'Amico,* no. 156–157 (June–July):4–5.

Atelier d'Art Urbain. 1982. *Roubaix Alma-Gare: Lutte urbaine et architecture.* Roubaix: Editions de l'Atelier d'Art Urbain.

Ath-Messaoud, Malik, and Alain Gillette. 1976. *L'immigration algérienne en France.* Paris: Entente.

"Ausländervereinigungen in der Schweiz." 1981. *EKA Information* 13 (March).

Autorengruppe für eine fortschrittliche Ausländerpolitik. 1980. *Basta!* Zurich: Limmat Verlag.

Avagliano, Lucio. 1976. *L'emigrazione italiana.* Napoli: Editrice Ferraro.

Baggio, Gildo, and Tarcisio Pozzi. 1978. *Die zweite Generation der Ausländer in der Schweiz.* Lausanne: Katholische Komitee für Innereuropäische Wanderung, Jan.

Baklanoff, Eric N. 1978. *The Economic Transformation of Spain and Portugal.* New York: Praeger.

Balibar, Etienne, and Immanuel Wallerstein. 1988. *Race, nation, classe: Les identités ambiguës.* Paris: La Découverte.

Banton, M. 1985. *Promoting Racial Harmony.* Cambridge: Cambridge University Press.

Barbara, Augustin. 1992. "Représentation de la femme musulman." *Migrations-société* 4, no. 19 (Jan.–Feb.):11–22.

Barber, Benjamin. 1988. "Participation and Swiss Democracy." *Government and Opposition* 23, no. 1 (Winter):31–50.

Barili, R., and M. Rovetta. 1982. "Scuola materna di Schlieren: L'ARLI contesta il nuovo comitato di gestione." *Emigrazione italiana,* Feb. 24, p. 8.

Barou, Jacques. 1985. "L'Islam, facteur de régulation sociale." *Esprit,* no. 6 (June):207–215.

Barth, Fredrik, ed. 1969. *Ethnic Groups and Boundaries: The Social Organization of Cultural Difference.* London: Allen & Unwin.

Battegay, Alain. 1985. "Les 'Beurs' dans l'espace public." *Esprit,* no. 6 (June):113–119.

Baumgartner, Georges. 1986. *D'Wagi, 1895–1985.* Schlieren: U. Stolz und G. Baumgartner.

Bayet, Albert. 1945. *Le problème des immigrés dans la France libérée.* Paris: Comité d'Aide et de Défense des Immigrés.

Belghoul, Farida. 1984. "Lettre ouverte aux gens convaincus." Reprinted in *Presse et immigrés en France,* no. 125 (Dec.):1–6.

Bendix, John. 1990. *Importing Foreign Workers.* New York: Peter Lang.

Benoît, Floriane. 1982. *Le printemps de la dignité.* Paris: Editions Sociales.

Ben Tahar, Mekki. 1979. *Les Arabes en France.* Rabat: Société Marocaine des Editeurs Réunis.

Ben-Tovin, G., and J. Gabriel. 1982. "The Politics of Race in Britain, 1962–79: A Review of Major Trends and of Recent Debates." In C. Husband, ed., *Race in Britain: Continuity and Change*. London: Hutchinson, pp. 145–171.

Berger, Gérard. 1986. "Des élus et des actes." *Unité d'action—Bulletin d'information politique du Parti Ouvrier et Populaire*, Dec.

Berger, Suzanne. 1972. *Peasants against Politics*. Cambridge, Mass.: Harvard University Press.

—— 1981. *Organizing Interests in Western Europe*. New York: Cambridge University Press.

Beriss, David. 1990. "Scarves, Schools, and Segregation: The *Foulard* Affair." *French Politics and Society* 8, no. 1 (Winter):1–13.

"La 'Beur' génération." 1985. *Sans frontière*, no. 92–93 (April–May):13.

Beylier, Anne-Françoise. 1978. "L'action législative et réglementaire récente concernant les étrangers." *Revue française des affaires sociales*, special issue, April–June, pp. 147–157.

Birenbaum, Guy. 1987. "Les stratégies du Front National." *Vingtième siècle* 16 (Oct.–Dec.):3–20.

Blanc, Albert. 1901. *L'immigration en France et le travail national*. Lyons: Faculté de Droit.

Bodin, Raymond-Pierre. 1987. *Les lois Auroux dans les PME*. Paris: La Documentation Française.

Body-Gendrot, Sophie. 1988. "Les immigrants dans la vie politique aux Etats-Unis et en France." *Revue européenne des migrations internationales* 4, no. 3:7–22.

—— 1989. "Migration and the Racialisation of Urban Space in France." Paper presented at the Conference on Racism and the Postmodern City, University of Warwick, Coventry, March 28–31.

Boehnke, Klaus, et al. 1987. "Ausländer und Wertwandel." *Kölner Zeitschrift für Soziologie und Sozialpsychologie* 39, no. 2:330–346.

Bogdanor, Vernon. 1988. "Federalism in Switzerland." *Government and Opposition* 23, no. 1 (Winter):69–90.

Bois, Philippe. 1973. "Une particularité du droit public neuchâtelois: Le droit de vote des étrangers en matière communale." *Extrait du Musée Neuchâtelois* 1.

Bolzman, Claudio, Rosita Fibbi, and Carlos Garcia. 1987. "La deuxième génération d'immigrés en Suisse: Catégorie ou acteur social?" *Revue européenne des migrations internationales* 3, 1st–3d trimesters:55–71.

Bonacich, Edna, and J. Modell. 1980. *The Economic Basis of Ethnic Solidarity*. Berkeley: University of California Press.

Bonnet, Jean-Charles. 1976. *Les pouvoirs publics français et l'immigration dans l'entre-deux-guerres*. Paris: Presses Universitaires de Lyon.

Bonvin, F., and E. Thery. 1977. *Les associations d'aide aux travailleurs immigrés*. Paris: Fondation pour la Recherche Sociale.

Bouamama, Saïd. 1989. "Elections municipales et immigration: Essai de bilan." *Migrations-société* 1, no. 3 (June):22–45.

Boulot, Serge, and Danièle Fradet. 1982. "Statistiques et échec scolaire des enfants étrangers: Mythe ou réalité?" *Dossiers migrations*, Jan.–Feb.

Boumaza, Nadir. 1985. *Générations issues de l'immigration*. Paris: CIEMI.

———— 1988. *Actes du séminaire: Banlieues, immigration, gestion urbaine*. Grenoble: Université Joseph Fourier–Grenoble I.

Bourdieu, Pierre, and Abdelmalek Sayad. 1964. *Le déracinement: La crise de l'agriculture en Algérie*. Paris: Editions de Minuit.

Bouzid. 1984. *La marche: Traversée de la France profonde*. Paris: Editions Sinbad.

Breton, Emile. 1983. *Rencontres à La Courneuve*. Paris: Temps Actuels.

Briot, Françoise, and Gilles Verbunt. 1981. *Les immigrés dans la crise*. Paris: Editions Ouvrières.

Browning, Rufus P., Dale Rogers Marshall, and David H. Tabb. 1984. *Protest Is Not Enough*. Berkeley: University of California Press.

Brubaker, W. Rogers, ed. 1989. *Immigration and the Politics of Citizenship in Europe and America*. New York: University Press of America.

Brubaker, W. Rogers. 1992. *Citizenship and Nationhood*. Cambridge, Mass.: Harvard University Press.

Brühwiler-Ewig, Edith. 1970. "Zur Frage der Einbürgerung italienischer Jugendlichen in Grenchen." In Viktor J. Willi, ed., *Denkanstösse zur Ausländerpolitik*. Zurich: Orell Füssli Verlag, pp. 46–84.

Bruschi, Christian. 1985. "Le droit et l'insertion des immigrés." *Esprit*, no. 6 (June):49–63.

Bruschi, Myrto, and Christian Bruschi. 1985. "Le pouvoir des guichets." In *L'immigration maghrébine en France: Dossier de la revue "Les Temps modernes."* Paris: Editions Denoël.

CAIF. 1986. *Etude sur la vie associative immigrée: "Quel bilan, quel avenir?"* Paris.

Caloz, Marie-Claude. 1982. *Le tamis helvétique: Des réfugiés politiques aux nouveaux réfugiés*. Lausanne: Editions d'En-Bas.

Calvaruso, Claudio. 1971. *Sottoproletario in Svizzera*. Rome: Coines.

———— 1974. *Emigrazione e sindicati*. Rome: Coines.

Campani, Giovanni. 1983. "Les réseaux italiens en France et en famille." *Peuples méditerranéens* 24 (July–Sept.):13–23.

———— 1985. "Les réseaux associatifs italiens en France." In Michel Oriol and Marie-Antoinette Hily, eds., *Les réseaux associatifs des immigrés en Europe occidental*. Paris: CNRS/GRECO 13, pp. 19–41.

Carens, Joseph H. 1988. "Immigration and the Welfare State." In Amy Gutmann, ed., *Democracy and the Welfare State*. Princeton: Princeton University Press, pp. 207–230.

Cases Méndez, José Ignacio. 1979. "The Migrant's Participation in the Political Life of His Country of Origin in the Context of His Integration." *International Migration* 17, no. 1/2:209–225.

CASS. 1974. *Les migrants: Une enquête sur leur logement dans le Canton de Neuchâtel*. Neuchâtel.

———— 1976. *Bref résumé des dernières activités du groupe*. La Chaux-de-Fonds.

———— 1979. *Compte-rendu de la 28e réunion*. Bern.

Castelnuovo-Frigessi, Delia. 1978. *La condition immigrée*. Lausanne: Editions d'En Bas.

Castles, Stephen. 1992. "The Australian Model of Immigration and Multiculturalism: Is It Applicable to Europe?" *International Migration Review* 26, no. 2 (Summer):549–567.

Castles, Stephen, with Heather Booth and Tina Wallace. 1984. *Here for Good.* London: Pluto Press.

Castles, Stephen, and Godula Kosack. 1973. *Immigrant Workers and Class Structure in Western Europe.* Oxford: Oxford University Press.

—— 1974. "How the Trade Unions Try to Control and Integrate Immigrant Workers in the German Federal Republic." *Race* 15, no. 4:497–514.

—— 1985. *Immigrant Workers and Class Structure in Western Europe.* 2d ed. Oxford: Oxford University Press.

Castles, Stephen, et al. 1990. *Mistaken Identity: Multiculturalism and the Demise of Nationalism in Australia.* 2d ed. Sydney: Pluto Press.

Castro-Almeida, Carlos. 1979. "Consultative Participation and the Role of Immigrants' Associations in Relation to the Country of Origin." *International Migration* 17, no. 1/2:189–208.

CEDEP. 1983. "O financiamento e poio das associaçoes portuguesas." *Dossier de informação* 3:3–6.

CEDETIM. 1975. *Les immigrés.* Paris: Editions Stock.

Centre Social Protestant. 1974. *Etude sur les conseils consultatifs des immigrés.* Lausanne.

Centre Suisse en Matière de Documentation et d'Education. 1985. "Quelle formation pour les enseignants suisses?" *Piazza,* no. 6 (March):7.

Cerny, Philip G. 1982. *Social Movements and Protest in France.* London: Frances Pinter.

CFDT. 1974. *Le Racisme.* Paris.

—— 1978. *Positions et orientations de la CFDT.* Paris.

CFE/EKA. 1976a. "Incidence de la présence des étrangers sur le marché du logement et l'infrastructure de la Suisse." *La vie économique,* Jan.

—— 1976b. *Modell einer regionalen, kantonalen oder städtischen Arbeitsgemeinschaft für die Ausländerfrage.* Bern.

—— 1976c. *Die Stellung der Ausländer im politischen Leben der Schweiz.* Bern.

—— 1977a. *Conséquences de la récession sur les étrangers.* Bern.

—— 1977b. *Considérations sur la condition des étrangers dans le système de sécurité sociale en Suisse.* Bern.

—— 1977c. *Förderung der gesellschaftlichen Eingliederung der ausländischen Arbeitnehmer durch die Sozialpartner.* Bern.

—— 1977d. *Die gesellschaftlichen Eingliederung der Ausländer in den Städten und Gemeinden.* Bern.

—— 1980. "Tätigkeit der kantonalen, regionalen und kommunalen Arbeitsgemeinschaften, Koordinationsstellen, Kontaktstellen." *EKA Information* 10 (Feb.), special edition.

—— 1981a. "Ausländervereinigungen in der Schweiz." *EKA Information* 13 (March).

—— 1981b. *Ausländische Jugendliche in der Verbandsjugendarbeit.* Bern.

—— 1982. "Participation des étrangers à la vie publique du pays d'accueil." *CFE information* 14:51–60.

——— 1986. "Gemischte kantonale Kommissionen für die berufliche Aus- und Weiterbildung." *EKA Information* 16 (Aug.):1–21.

CGT. 1981. *Questions de l'immigration et syndicat.* Paris.

Charef, Mehdi. 1983. *Le thé au harem d'Archi Ahmed.* Paris: Mercure de France.

Charlot, Martine. 1978. *La participation des immigrés à la vie communale en France depuis mars 1977.* Paris: CNDP Migrants.

Church, Clive. 1989. "The Swiss Way of Change." *The World Today,* July: pp. 117–121.

——— 1992. "The Swiss Election of 1991: Stability, Not Stasis." *West European Politics* 15, no. 4 (Oct.):184–188.

CLAP (Comité de Liaison pour l'Alphabétisation et la Promotion). 1981. "La participation des immigrés à la vie municipale." *Alphabétisation et promotion,* no. 105/106 (July–Aug.):8–9.

Clark, Gardner. 1983. "The Swiss Experience with Foreign Workers." *Industrial and Labor Relations Review* 36:607–623.

Clément, Jean-François. 1985. "Après la marche." *Esprit,* no. 6 (June):111–112.

Clévy, Jean. 1976. *La scolarisation des enfants de travailleurs migrants.* Paris: ESF.

"CLI–La Chaux-de-Fonds." 1983. *Emigrazione italiana,* March 10, p. 8.

CNTSE. 1975. *Pour une commission neuchâteloise consultative pour le problème des étrangers.*

——— 1978, 1979, 1980, 1984. *Manifestes de la Communauté Neuchâteloise de Travail Suisses-Etrangers.* La Chaux-de-Fonds.

Coeuret, Alain. 1974. "La participation des étrangers aux institutions représentatives des salariés en France." Paper presented at the colloquium Les Travailleurs Etrangers en Europe Occidentale, IRERP, Université de Paris X, June.

Cohen, Gaynor. 1982. "Alliance and Conflict among Mexican Americans." *Ethnic and Racial Studies* 5, no. 2 (April):175–195.

Coleman, David A. 1992. "Does Europe Need Immigrants?" *International Migration Review* 26, no. 2 (Summer):413–461.

Comité d'Etudes et de Liaison "Etrangers." 1983. "Les associations immigrées." *FONDA lettre d'information* 19, special issue, Nov. 16.

Commission Nationale Consultative des Droits de l'Homme, 1991. 1992. *La lutte contre le racisme et la xénophobie.* Paris: La Documentation Française.

Commission Protestante Suisse-Immigrés. 1980. *Droit de vote des étrangers dans la commune et le canton.* Lausanne.

Communauté de Travail "Etre solidaires," Groupe de Travail pour la Préparation de la Campagne de Votation. 1980. *Projet d'un concept pour la campagne de votation.* Bern.

Congrès CGT. 1906. *Compte-rendu officiel.* Paris: CGT.

Congrès Etre Solidaires. 1982. *Projet d'organisation.* Basel.

Conseil de la Fédération des Eglises Protestantes de la Suisse and Conférence des Evêques Catholiques Romains de la Suisse. 1974. *Les sept thèses des Eglises sur la politique à l'égard des étrangers.* Bern and Sion.

"Conséquences de la récession sur les étrangers." 1977. *La vie économique,* special issue, Oct.

"Considérations sur la condition des étrangers dans le système de sécurité sociale en Suisse." 1977. *La vie économique*, special issue, Oct.

"Contrôle des étrangers." 1984. In *Rapport du Conseil Communal au Conseil Général*. La Chaux-de-Fonds: Ville de La Chaux-de-Fonds.

Coordination: Immigrés. 1983. *Bilan sommaire de la journée du 25/11/83*. Roubaix.

Cop, Raoul. 1980. *Histoire de La Chaux-de-Fonds*. La Chaux-de-Fonds: Conseil Communal.

Cordeiro, Albano. 1985a. "La grande communauté 'invisible' de France: Les Portugais." *Travail* 2, no. 7:34–41.

———— 1985b. "Mouvements associatifs et communautés issues de l'immigration." Manuscript, Grenoble.

Cordeiro, Albano, and Manuel Dias. 1985. "Quarante députés pour les immigrés." *Presse et immigrés en France* 19 (April):9–12.

Costa-Lascoux, Jacqueline. 1980. "Une législation pour une nouvelle politique de l'immigration." *Pluriel* 21:7–31.

———— 1982. "Les droits d'expression et de participation des immigrés au sein d'une nouvelle 'solidarité nationale.'" In *Les droits politiques des immigrés: Compte rendu du colloque des 5 et 6 décembre 1981*. Paris: Etudes, pp. 47–52.

———— 1987. "Nationaux seulement ou vraiment citoyens?" *Projet* 204 (March–April):45–57.

———— 1990. "Le droit contre le racisme." *Migrations-société* 2, no. 11 (Sept.–Oct.):21–36.

Costa-Lascoux, Jacqueline, and Catherine Wihtol de Wenden. 1981. "Les travailleurs immigrés clandestins en France." *Studi emigrazione* 63:7–28.

"Le coup des jeunes." 1987. *Regards* (Ville de La Courneuve), Jan. 10.

Courtois, Stéphane, and Gilles Kepel. 1987. "Musulmans et prolétaires." *Revue française de science politique* 37, no. 6 (Dec.):782–793.

"Les 'Craignos' contre l'abstention." 1990. *Accueillir* (Service Social d'Aide aux Emigrants), no. 169–170 (May–June):17.

"El CRE no tiene local." 1990. *Boletín informativo del CRE de Paris*, no. 4 (Dec.):1.

Crenson, Matthew A. 1971. *The Un-Politics of Air Pollution*. Cambridge, Mass: Harvard University Press.

Cross, Gary S. 1983. *Immigrant Workers in Industrial France*. Philadelphia: Temple University Press.

Cunha, M. 1988. *Portugais de France*. Paris: Editions CIEMI/L'Harmattan.

Dahl, Robert A. 1967. *Pluralist Democracy in the United States*. Chicago: Rand-McNally.

Dahrendorf, Ralf. 1963. "Recent Changes in the Class Structure of Western European Countries." In Stephen Graubard, ed., *A New Europe?* Boston: Beacon Press, pp. 291–336.

Dalton, Russell J., and Manfred Kuechler, eds. 1990. *Challenging the Political Order*. New York: Oxford University Press.

Débely, Martial. 1986. *Droit de vote des étrangers dans la commune de La Chaux-de-Fonds*. Diss. Institut d'Etudes Sociales, Université de Genève.

Debré, Michel. 1984. "La nation répudiée." *Le Figaro*, Dec. 5.

Deike, Jorge. 1984. "Y ahora, ¿que pasa con los extranjeros en Suiza?" *Etre solidaires bulletin,* no. 21 (Oct.):6–7.

Delorme, Christian. 1984a. "L'envie de pleurer et de tout casser." *Sans frontière,* no. 85–86 (April):22–23.

—— 1984b. "Le mouvement 'Beur' a une histoire." In ANGI, *Les cahiers de la nouvelle génération.* Vol. 1. Gennevilliers, pp. 18–46.

Département Fédéral de Justice et Police. 1976. *Projet de nouvelle loi sur les étrangers.* Bern.

de Rham, Gérard. 1976. *La fonction socio-politique du "pluralisme": Le cas de la Suisse.* Collection Travaux de Science Politique, no. 1. Lausanne: Institut de Science Politique.

—— 1985. "La législation sur les étrangers comme processus symbolique de légitimation de l'état-nation." Paper presented at the Thirteenth World Congress of the International Political Science Association, Paris, July.

—— 1987. "La Chaux-de-Fonds: Une expérience à imiter." *Piazza,* no. 14 (March), special section, pp. 7–8.

—— 1990. "Naturalisation: The Politics of Citizenship Acquisition." In Zig Layton-Henry, ed., *The Political Rights of Migrant Workers in Western Europe.* London: Sage, pp. 158–185.

de Rham, Gérard, et al. 1980. *Qui sont-ils: Suisses et/ou espagnols? (Enquête JOC/E).* Mémoires et documents, no. 13. Lausanne: Institut de Science Politique.

Deriaz, Armand, Mario del Curto, and Philippe Maeder. 1981. *Suisse en mouvement/Schweiz in Bewegung.* Lausanne: Editions d'En Bas.

de Rudder, Chantal. 1989. "Immigrés: La soft révolution." *Le Nouvel Observateur,* Jan. 5–11, pp. 30–31.

de Rudder, Véronique. 1976. "Le logement des travailleurs immigrés: La situation actuelle et leurs aspirations." In Philippe J. Bernard, ed., *Les travailleurs étrangers en Europe occidentale.* Paris/The Hague: Mouton.

—— 1984. "Seuil de tolérance et cohabitation." *Différences et réalités: Actes du colloque du 10 décembre 1983, Palais du Luxembourg.* Paris: Editions Différences.

Dianteill, Erwan. 1992. "L'état espagnol et les associations d'émigrés en France: Une relation structurante." *Migrations-société* 4, no. 19 (Jan.–Feb.):35–43.

Dias, Manuel. 1983. "Ils ont fait marche arrière—Faisons un pas en avant." *Sans frontière,* no. 73 (Feb.):8–9.

—— 1986. "Evolution du mouvement associatif issu de l'immigration." *FONDA lettre d'information,* no. 37 (Feb.):11–15.

Di Meo, Isabelle. 1986. "La présence italienne en France aujourd'hui." *Dossier: Migrations* 34 (Sept.–Oct.).

Dittrich, Eckhard J., and Frank-Olaf Radtke, eds. 1990. *Ethnizität.* Opladen: Westdeutscher Verlag.

Dolle, Jean-Paul. 1990. "L'intifada des banlieues." *Libération,* Oct. 15, p. 8.

"Dossier: Les associations issues de l'immigration en Europe." 1987. *CAIF infos,* June, special supplement.

"Dossier: CFE." 1984. *Piazza* no. 2 (March), special supplement.

"Dossier: Commissions des immigrés." 1984. *Piazza* no. 3 (June), special supplement.

"Dossier: Le spectre de la 'criminalité des étrangers/ères.' " 1989. *Piazza* no. 24 (Sept.), special supplement.

Dumont, G. F. 1986. *La France ridée*. Paris: Editions Pluriel.

Dumont, L. 1990. "Sur l'idéologie politique française: Une perspective comparative." *Le Débat*, no. 58:128–158.

Dupeux, Georges. 1980. *L'immigration en France de la fin du XVIIIème siècle à nos jours*. Paris: Editions du CNRS.

Ebel, Marianne, and Pierre Fiala. 1983. *Langages xénophobes et consensus national en Suisse (1960–1980)*. Neuchâtel: Université de Neuchâtel.

"Economie locale." 1982. In *Rapport du Conseil Communal au Conseil Général*. La Chaux-de-Fonds: Ville de La Chaux-de-Fonds.

"L'écrivain public est un médiateur." 1989. *Hommes et migrations*, no. 1121 (April):40–42.

Edelman, Murray. 1971. *Politics as Symbolic Action: Mass Arousal and Quiescence*. Chicago: Markham.

Edmond-Smith, Joyce. 1972. "France's New Law." *Race Today* 4, no. 9:304 ff.

Eidgenössische Kommission für Jugendfragen. 1981. *Ausländische Jugendliche in der Verbandsjugendarbeit*. Bern.

Entzinger, H. B. 1984. *Het Minderhedenbeleid*. Meppel: Boom.

Erie, Steven P. 1985. "Rainbow's End: From the Old to the New Urban Ethnic Politics." In Lionel Maldonado and Joan Moore, eds., *Urban Ethnicity in the United States*. Beverly Hills: Sage.

Esman, Milton J. 1985. "Two Dimensions of Ethnic Politics." *Ethnic and Racial Studies* 8, no. 3 (July):438–440.

Etchebarne, Serge. 1983. "L'urne et le xénophobe: A propos des élections municipales à Roubaix en mars 1983." *Espace, population, société* 2:133–138.

Etienne, Bruno. 1989. *La France et l'Islam*. Paris: Hachette.

" 'Etre solidaires': La votation est avancée!" 1981. *Etre solidaires bulletin*, no. 19 (Feb.):2.

L'Europe multicommunautaire. 1989–90. Special issue of *Plein droit*.

Evans, Richard J. 1977. *The Feminists*. London: Croom Helm.

Evrensel, Ayse Y. 1984. *Ausländische Arbeiter in der Einwanderungsgesellschaft am Beispiel Türkischer Arbeiter in der Stadt Zürich*. Diss. Universität Zürich.

"Les expériences dans le canton de Zürich." 1988. *Piazza*, no. 18 (March), special section.

"Extrait du discours d'Ezio Canonica." 1973. *Correspondance syndicale suisse*, May 2.

Fagnen, Yanne. 1981. "A La Courneuve, le Yuro." *Actuel*, Nov., pp. 6–7.

Farine, Claude. 1981. "Votations sur les étrangers." *Tribune de Genève*, March 31.

Farine, Philippe. 1991. "Le rapport du Haut Conseil à l'Intégration." *Migrations-société* 3, no. 14 (March–April):61–64.

"Festa internazionale." 1983. *Emigrazione italiana*, Sept. 14, p. 8.

"Festa organizzata in occasione del quarantesimo di fondazione della FCLIS." 1983. *Emigrazione italiana,* June 29, p. 8.

Fibbi, Rosita, and Gérard de Rham. 1985. "Formation et insertion professionnelle des jeunes étrangers en Suisse." *Bulletin BVA,* no. 10.

Fiévet, Michel. 1984. *S.O.S.-Racisme: Enfants et jeunes réagissent.* Paris: Les Editions Ouvrières.

FOBB. 1980. "Tous les salariés à la manifestation de Berne: Fin de la discrimination envers nos collègues de travail—solidarité avec les travailleurs immigrés." *FOBB Information,* Oct.

FONDA. 1983. "Les associations d'immigrés." *FONDA lettre d'information* 19 (Nov. 16).

Foner, Nancy. 1979. "West Indians in New York City and London." *International Migration Review* 13, no. 2:284–297.

Fornacciari, Marc. 1986. "Les étrangers, les droits et le droit." *Revue catholique internationale: Communio* 11, no. 2 (March–April):88–97.

Fortuna, Ursula. 1974–1988. *Chronik von Schlieren.* Schlieren: Stadt Schlieren.

——— 1975. "Zur Bedeutung der Industrie für Schlieren." In *Jahrheft von Schlieren.* Schlieren: Stadt Schlieren, pp. 3–5.

Forum '82 Suisses-Immigrés. 1982. *Projet de plateforme d'action.* Bern.

Foschi, Franco. 1977. "Svizzera ancora ostile ai nostri emigrati." *Il Popolo,* Oct. 15.

——— 1979. "Elezioni europei: Il voto degli emigrati." *Dossier Europa emigrazione,* no. 7–8 (July–Aug.):6–7.

Fourcaut, Annie. 1986. *Bobigny, Banlieue rouge.* Paris: Presses de la Fondation Nationale des Sciences Politiques.

"Frankreich: Für gleiche Rechte—gegen Rassismus." 1984. *Piazza,* no. 2 (March):25.

Fratini, Maurizio. 1979. "Nuove forme associative dell'emigrazione italiana in Svizzera: I comitati cittadini e cantonali d'intesa." *Affari sociali internazionali* 7, no. 4:173–178.

Freeman, Gary P. 1979. *Immigrant Labor and Racial Conflict in Industrial Societies.* Princeton: Princeton University Press.

——— 1986. "Migration and the Political Economy of the Welfare State." *Annals* 485 (May):51–63.

Fröhlich, Hans U. 1985. "Ausländerpolitik in schwieriger Zeit." *Piazza,* no. 6 (March):10.

Gallie, Duncan. 1978. *In Search of the New Working Class.* Cambridge: Cambridge University Press.

——— 1985. "Les lois Auroux: The Reform of French Industrial Relations?" In Howard Machin and Vincent Wright, eds., *Economic Policy and Policy-Making under the Mitterrand Presidency.* New York: St. Martin's Press, pp. 205–221.

Gamson, William A. 1975. *The Strategy of Social Protest.* Homewood, Ill.: Dorsey Press.

Gani, Léon. 1972. *Syndicats et travailleurs immigrés.* Paris: Les Editions Ouvrières.

Gans, Herbert. 1962. *The Urban Villagers.* New York: Free Press.

Garache, Jean-Baptiste. 1984. "6 février 1933. Explosion à l'atelier 17." *Revue d'histoire des usines Renault* 5, no. 28 (June):151–157.

Gaudemar, Jean-Paul. 1982. *L'ordre et la production.* Paris: Dunod.

Gaventa, John. 1980. *Power and Powerlessness.* Urbana: University of Illinois Press.

"Gemeinsam für die Reduktion der Arbeitszeit." 1984. *Piazza*, no. 2 (March): 8.

Gesú, Remo. 1989. "Kritik am Entwurf zur neuen Ausländer-Regelung." *Piazza*, no. 24 (Sept.):4–5.

—— 1990. "Schwarz ist die Arbeit, dunkel die Zipfern." *Piazza*, no. 25 (March):10–11.

Giddens, Anthony. 1981. *A Contemporary Critique of Historical Materialism.* London: Macmillan.

—— 1985. *The Nation-State and Violence.* London: Macmillan.

Ginioux, Georges, and Juliette Minces. 1983. *L'implantation des Centres d'Information sur les Droits des Femmes dans cinq 'îlots sensibles' nationaux de la région Ile-de-France.* Paris: Centre National d'Information sur les Droits des Femmes.

Giordan, H. 1982. *Démocratie culturelle et droit à la différence.* Paris: La Documentation Française.

Girod, Roger. 1972. "Les travailleurs immigrés: Renfort du salariat intégré ou ferment de révolution?" In *Table-ronde sur "Les ouvriers et la politique en Europe occidentale," November 3–4.* Paris: Association Française de Science Politique.

—— 1975. "Les travailleurs étrangers en Suisse: Ouverture et domination." *Année sociologique* 26:21–42.

Glazer, Nathan. 1954. "Ethnic Groups in America: From National Culture to Ideology." In Morroe Berger, Theodore Abel, and Charles H. Page, eds., *Freedom and Control in Modern Society.* New York: Van Nostrand, pp. 158–173.

Glazer, Nathan, and Daniel P. Moynihan. 1963. *Beyond the Melting Pot.* Cambridge, Mass.: MIT Press.

Gonçalves, José J. 1971. *Portugueses dispersos pelo mundo.* Lisbon: Agência-Geral do Ultramar.

González-Anleo, Juan. 1981. "Una aventura solitaria: La emigración española a Suiza." In José A. Garmendía, ed., *La emigración española en la encrucijada.* Madrid: Centro de Investigaciones Sociológicas, pp. 343–388.

González Hernándes, M. 1977. "El proceso electoral portugués." *Revista española de la opinión pública* 48 (April–June):205–270.

Gorz, André, and Philippe Grani. 1970. "La bataille d'Ivry." *Les Temps modernes*, March, pp. 1388–89.

Gourevitch, Peter A. 1980. *Paris and the Provinces.* Berkeley: University of California Press.

Granotier, Bernard. 1976. *Les travailleurs immigrés en France.* Paris: François Maspéro.

Grémion, Pierre. 1976. *Le pouvoir périphérique.* Paris: Seuil.

—— 1980. "Crispation et déclin du jacobinisme." In Henri Mendras, ed., *La sagesse et le désordre.* Paris: Gallimard, pp. 329–350.

"La grève des pianos." 1974. *Tout va bien,* Sept.

Grillo, R. D. 1985. *Ideologies and Institutions in Urban France.* Cambridge: Cambridge University Press.

Griotteray, Alain. 1984. *Les immigrés: Le choc.* Paris: Plon.

Grisel, Etienne. 1982. "Les droits politiques des étrangers en Suisse." In *Les étrangers en Suisse: Recueil de travaux.* Lausanne: Faculté de Droit, Université de Lausanne, pp. 71–82.

Grossi, Guglielmo. 1988. "Ja zur 40-Stunden-Woche." *Piazza,* no. 20 (Sept.):3–5.

—— 1989. "Etrangers en Suisse et immigrés dans la CEE." *Piazza,* no. 23 (June):9.

—— 1990. "Intégration en Europe et vote par correspondance." *Piazza,* no. 24 (Sept.):6.

Guillaume, Pierre. 1985. "Du bon usage des immigrés en temps de crise et de guerre, 1932–1940." *Vingtième siècle* 7 (July–Sept.):117–125.

Guillon, Michèle, Véronique de Rudder-Paurd, and Gildas Simon. 1977. *La population étrangère dans le département de la Seine-Saint-Denis.* Paris: CNRS-ERMI.

Hall, Peter A. 1986. *Governing the Economy.* New York: Oxford University Press.

Haller, M., ed. 1981. *Aussteigen oder Rebellieren.* Hamburg: Rororo.

Halter, Eugen. 1972. *Vom Strom der Zeiten.* Vol. 1. St. Gallen: Fehr'sche Buchhandlung.

Hammar, Tomas, ed. 1985. *European Immigration Policy.* Cambridge: Cambridge University Press.

Hammar, Tomas. 1990. "The Civil Rights of Aliens." In Zig Layton-Henry, ed., *The Political Rights of Migrant Workers in Western Europe.* Newbury Park, Calif.: Sage, pp. 74–93.

Harbi, Chérif. 1977. "Le logement des travailleurs immigrés en 1976: Une prise de conscience collective." *Hommes et migrations,* no. 927 (May 15):14–20.

Heclo, Hugh. 1974. *Modern Social Politics in Britain and Sweden.* New Haven: Yale University Press.

Heintz, Peter, and Hans-Joachim Hoffmann-Nowotny. 1970. *Bericht über eine Survey Analyse des Fremdarbeiterproblems,* pt. 1. Zurich: Soziologisches Institut, pp. 1–120.

Heisler, Martin O. 1990. "Ethnicity and Ethnic Relations in the Modern West." In Joseph V. Montville, ed., *Conflict and Peacemaking in Multiethnic Societies.* Lexington, Mass.: D. C. Heath.

—— 1986. "Transnational Migration as a Small Window on the Diminished Autonomy of the Modern Democratic State." *Annals* 485 (May):153–166.

Heisler, Martin O., and Barbara Schmitter Heisler. 1986. "Transnational Migration and the Modern Democratic State: Familiar Problems in New Form or a New Problem?" *Annals* 485 (May):12–22.

—— 1990. "Citizenship: Old, New, and Changing." Paper presented at the

Workshop on Dominant National Cultures and Ethnic Identities, Free University of Berlin, June 11–14.

Held, David. 1988. *Political Theory and the Modern State*. Stanford: Stanford University Press.

Heller, Daniel. 1992. "Für eine qualitative Stärkung der direkten Demokratie." *Neue Zürcher Zeitung,* July 24, p. 21.

Hervo, Monique, and Marie-Ange Charras. 1971. *Bidonvilles*. Paris: François Maspéro.

" 'Hierher kommen keine Flüchtlinge': Fremdenhass und Ausländerfeindlichkeit in Westeuropa." 1989. *Der Spiegel,* Feb. 13, pp. 34–35.

Hifi, Belkacem. 1985. *L'immigration algérienne en France*. Paris: L'Harmattan/ CIEM.

Hilaire, Yves-Marie, ed. 1984. *Histoire de Roubaix*. Dunkerque: Editions des Beffrois.

Hirschman, Albert O. 1970. *Exit, Voice, and Loyalty*. Cambridge, Mass.: Harvard University Press.

Hochet, Agnès. 1988. "L'immigration dans le débat politique français de 1981 à 1988." *Pouvoirs* 47:27–30.

Hoesli, Eric. 1988. "Le cauchemar de l'asile." *L'Hebdo,* Sept. 29, pp. 12–15.

Hoffmann-Nowotny, Hans-Joachim. 1973. *Soziologie des Fremdarbeiterproblems*. Stuttgart: Enke.

——— 1974. "Immigrant Minorities in Switzerland: Sociological, Legal, and Political Aspects." Paper presented at the Eighth World Congress of Sociology, The Hague.

——— 1985. "Switzerland." In Tomas Hammar, ed., *European Immigration Policy*. Cambridge: Cambridge University Press, pp. 206–236.

Hoffmann-Nowotny, Hans-Joachim, and Karl-Otto Hondrich, eds. 1982. *Ausländer in der BRD und in der Schweiz*. Frankfurt: Campus Verlag.

Hofstetter, Yves, and Pierre Moor. 1982. "Les autorisations et décisions de police des étrangers." In *Les étrangers en Suisse: Recueil de travaux*. Lausanne: Faculté de Droit, Université de Lausanne.

Holden, Barry. 1974. *The Nature of Democracy*. London: Thomas Nelson & Sons.

Hollifield, James F. 1992. *Immigrants, Markets, and States*. Cambridge, Mass.: Harvard University Press.

Hollstein, W. 1981. *Die Gegengesellschaft*. Hamburg: Rororo.

Holmes, Madelyn. 1988. *Forgotten Migrants*. Rutherford, N.J.: Fairleigh Dickinson University Press.

Höplinger, François. 1976. *Industriegewerkschaften in der Schweiz*. Zurich: Limmat Verlag.

Hoppe, A., and C. Arends. 1986. "The Politics and Policy Dynamics of Ethnicity in the Netherlands." Paper presented at the ECPR Workshop on Migration as a National and International Challenge in European Immigration Countries, Göteberg, April 1–6.

Hubacher, Helmut. 1974. "Wirtschaftsaspekte der Ausländerfrage." In Dieter Zeller, ed., *Ausländische Arbeitnehmer*. Basel: Z-Verlag.

Huber, Ahmed, and Max Trossmann. 1987. "Tamilien Sollen Bleiben." *Schweizer Illustrierte,* Jan. 19, pp. 12–16.

Humblot, Catherine. 1989. "Les émissions spécifiques." *Migrations-société* 1, no. 4 (Aug.):7–14.

Huntington, Samuel P., and Joan Nelson. 1976. *No Easy Choice.* Cambridge, Mass.: Belknap Press of Harvard University Press.

Immergut, Ellen. 1991. "Institutions, Veto Points, and Policy Results: A Comparative Analysis of Health Care." *Journal of Public Policy* 10, no. 4:391–416.

Inglehart, Ronald. 1977. *The Silent Revolution.* Princeton: Princeton University Press.

Ingold, Jean-Luc. 1988. "Les super-verts." *L'Hebdo,* Feb. 4.

"L'inserimento sociale dei giovani immigrati di seconda generazione." 1982. In *Rapport semestrali.* Vol. 1. Lugano: Dipartimento dell'Economiche Pubblica, Cantone Ticino.

Ireland, Patrick R. 1989. "The State and the Political Participation of the 'New' Immigrants in France and the United States." *Revue française d'études américaines* 41 (July):315–328.

——— 1991. "Facing the True 'Fortress Europe': Immigrants and Politics in the EC." *Journal of Common Market Studies* 24, no. 5 (Sept.):457–480.

Jaccoud, Antoine. 1987a. " 'Echanger nos cultures,' mais lesquelles?" *L'Hebdo,* Sept. 10, pp. 49–50.

——— 1987b. "L'extrême droite souffre d'avoir déjà gagné." *L'Hebdo,* March 19, p. 32.

Jackson, Maurice. 1969. "The Civil Rights Movement and Social Change." *American Behavioral Scientist,* March–April, pp. 8–17.

Jaffré, Jérôme. 1986. "Front national: La relève protestataire." In Elisabeth Dupoirier and Gérard Grunberg, eds., *Mars 1986: La drôle de défaite de la gauche.* Paris: Presses Universitaires de France, pp. 211–229.

Jakubowicz, A., M. Morrissey, and J. Palser. 1984. *Ethnicity, Class, and Social Welfare in Australia.* Sydney: Social Welfare Research Center, University of New South Wales.

Jazouli, Adil. 1986. *L'action collective des jeunes maghrébins en France.* Paris: CIEMI/L'Harmattan.

——— 1991. "Les bandes de jeunes en France." *Migrations-société* 3, no. 14 (March–April):53–60.

Jean, Martin. 1981. "Combien sont-ils?" In Martine Charlot, comp., *Des jeunes Algériens en France: Leurs voix et les nôtres.* Paris: CIEMI, pp. 251–259.

Jeannet, Alain. 1986. "Les mousquetaires de la relance." *L'Hebdo,* April 17, pp. 34–39.

Jenson, Jane. 1985. "Struggling for Identity." *West European Politics* 8, no. 4 (Oct.):5–18.

"Les jeunes étrangers—La deuxième génération—Problèmes et solutions possibles." 1980. *EKA Information* 12 (Sept.):1–73.

Johnson, Signe-Lou, and Andrea Czepek. 1992. "Die 'Ruhrpolen.' " *Die Mitbestimmung,* Aug.–Sept., pp. 45–48.

Jordan, Grant, and Jeremy J. Richardson. 1987. *Government and Pressure Groups in Britain.* Oxford: Clarendon Press.

Just, Carl, Nik Niethammer, and Charles Meyer. 1989. "Racistes et fiers de l'être." *L'Hebdo,* June 22, pp. 25–27.

Jyotsena, Saskena. 1973. *Le Parti Communiste Français et les travailleurs immigrés.* Thèse du Doctorat en Sciences Politiques, Université de Paris–I.

Kastoryano, Riva. 1986. *Etre Turc en France.* Paris: CIEMI/L'Harmattan.

—— 1987. "Définition des frontières de l'identité: Turcs musulmans." *Revue française de science politique* 37, no. 6 (Dec.):833–854.

Katzenstein, Peter J. 1984. *Corporatism and Change: Austria, Switzerland, and the Politics of Industry.* Ithaca: Cornell University Press.

Katznelson, Ira. 1973. *Black Men, White Cities.* London: Oxford University Press.

—— 1981. *City Trenches.* New York: Pantheon Books.

Kepel, Gilles. 1987. *Les banlieues de l'Islam.* Paris: Seuil.

Khammar, Driss el-Yazami. 1985. "Les *Beurs* civiques." In Sans Frontière, *La "Beur" génération.* Paris: Editions Sans Frontière, pp. 11–14.

Kitschelt, Herbert P. 1986. "Political Opportunity Structures and Political Protest: Anti-Nuclear Movements in Four Democracies." *British Journal of Political Science* 16, pt. 1 (Jan.):57–85.

Klandermans, P. Bert. 1990. "Linking 'Old' and 'New' Movement Networks." In Russell J. Dalton and Manfred Kuechler, eds., *Challenging the Political Order.* New York: Oxford University Press, pp. 122–136.

Kohler, Jean-Michel. 1982. *Notes concernant l'appui aux enfants non francophones et étrangers.* Ville de La Chaux-de-Fonds: Direction de l'Ecole Primaire.

Köppel, Urs. 1982. *Immigration musulmane en Suisse.* Stuttgart: Comité Internationale Catholique pour les Migrations.

Kriesi, Hanspeter. 1982. *Die Zürcher Bewegung.* Frankfurt: Campus Verlag.

Ladner, Andreas. 1992. "Switzerland." *European Journal of Political Research* 22:527–536.

Lahalle, Dominique. 1975. "L'insertion des immigrés dans la vie politique." *L'année sociologique* 26:189–200.

Laigre, Patrick. 1987. "Comme un chien." *Regards* (Ville de La Courneuve), Jan. 10, p. 19.

Landes, David S. 1983. *Revolution in Time.* Cambridge, Mass.: Harvard University Press.

Lannes, Xavier. 1953. *L'immigration en France depuis 1945.* The Hague: Martinus Nijhoff.

Lapeyronnie, Didier. 1987. "Assimilation, mobilisation et action collective chez les jeunes de la seconde génération de l'immigration maghrébine." *Revue française de sociologie* 28:287–318.

Lawrence, Daniel. 1974. *Black Migrants, White Natives.* Cambridge: Cambridge University Press.

Layton-Henry, Zig, ed. 1990. *The Political Rights of Migrant Workers in Western Europe.* London: Sage.

Lazzarato, Maurizio. 1989–90. "Peugeot 89." *L'Europe multicommunautaire*, special issue of *Plein droit*, p. 119.

Lebon, André. 1977. *Immigration et le VIIème Plan*. Paris: La Documentation Française.

————— 1979. "L'aide au retour des travailleurs étrangers." *Economie et statistiques* 113 (July–Aug.):37–46.

————— 1981. "Les jeunes migrants dans la vie active en Europe occidentale." *Studi emigrazione*, no. 61 (March).

————— 1991. "Recensement de 1990." *Migrations-société* 3, no. 16–17 (July–Oct.):7–13.

Leca, Jean. 1985. "Une capacité d'intégration défaillante?" *Esprit*, no. 6 (June):9–23, 102–106.

Leclercq, Robert-Jean. 1985. "Génération des cités: Conditions de vie et revendications collectives." *Revue européenne des migrations internationales* 1, no. 2 (Dec.):161–168.

Legrain, Jean-François. 1985. "Islam en France, islam de France." *Esprit*, no. 10 (Oct.):1–30.

Lempen, Blaise. 1985. *Un modèle en crise: La Suisse*. Lausanne: Editions Payot.

Le Pen, Jean-Marie. 1985. *La France est de retour*. Paris: Editions Carrere/Michel Lafon.

Leveau, Rémy. 1989. "Les conséquences de l'affaire Rushdie," *Migrations-société* 1, no. 3 (June):17–23.

————— 1992. "Maghrebi Immigration to Europe: Double Insertion or Double Exclusion?" *Annals* 524 (Nov.):170–180.

Leveau, Rémy, and Dominique Schnapper. 1987. "Religion et politique: Juifs et musulmans maghrébins en France." Paper presented at the Round Table on Les musulmans dans la Société Française, Institut d'Etudes Politiques, Paris, Jan. 29–30.

Leveau, Rémy, and Catherine Wihtol de Wenden. 1985. "Evolution des attitudes politiques des immigrés maghrébins." *Vingtième siècle* 7 (July–Sept.):71–83.

————— 1988. "La deuxième génération." *Pouvoirs* 47:61–73.

Liger, Didier. 1972. "L'immigration turque en France." Mémoire, Institut d'Etudes Politiques, Paris.

Ligue Marxiste Révolutionnaire. 1974. *L'immigration en Suisse*. Lausanne.

Lijphart, Arend. 1971. "Comparative Politics and the Comparative Method." *American Political Science Review* 65:682–693.

————— 1984. *Democracies*. New Haven: Yale University Press.

Linz, Juan J., and Amando de Miguel. 1970. "Within-Nation Differences and Comparisons: The Eight Spains." In Stein Rokkan and Richard L. Merritt, eds., *Comparing Nations*. New Haven: Yale University Press.

Livian, Marcel. 1982. *Le Parti Socialiste et l'immigration*. Paris: Anthropos.

Lochon, Christian. 1990. "Vers la création d'instances supérieures de l'Islam en France." *L'Afrique et l'Asie modernes*, no. 165 (Summer):43–67.

Lohneis, Hans. 1984. "The Swiss Election of 1983: A Glacier on the Move?" *West European Politics* 7, no. 3 (July):117–119.

Lorenzi-Cioldi, Fabio, and Gil Meyer. 1986. *Semblables ou différents: Identité sociale et représentations collectives des jeunes immigrés.* Geneva: International Labour Organization.

Lowi, Theodore J. 1964. *At the Pleasure of the Mayor.* New York: Free Press of Glencoe.

MAAA–Yuro Théâtro. 1982. "A La Courneuve, le Yuro Théâtro." *Migrants-information,* Oct., pp. 123–126.

"Mach meinen Kumpel nicht an!" 1985. *Piazza,* no. 9 (Dec.):10–11.

Maffesoli, Michel. 1978. *La violence fondatrice.* Paris: Editions du Champ Urbain.

Maillard, Alain. 1991. "Le printemps communiste." *L'Hebdo,* April 18, pp. 24–25.

Malaurie, Guillaume. 1990. "France: Le risque de la contagion." *L'Express,* Feb. 9, pp. 30–31.

Malik, Serge. 1984. "La carte de France de SOS-racisme." *Murs, murs, le journal des villes* 3, no. 4:28–29.

"Manifeste de soutien à la marche Marseille-Paris." 1983. *Presse et immigrés en France,* no. 111 (Oct.):14–15.

March, James G., and Johan P. Olsen. 1989. *Rediscovering Institutions.* New York: Free Press.

Marrucho, Antonio. 1982a. "Roubaix: Um exemplo da vida associativa portuguesa em França." *Jornal do Fundão,* Jan. 22.

——— 1982b. "L'immigration portugaise dans la ville de Roubaix." Mémoire de maîtrise, Université des Sciences Techniques de Lille.

Marshall, T. H., ed. 1973. *Class, Citizenship, and Social Development.* Westport, Conn.: Greenwood Press.

Martin, Philip L., and Mark J. Miller. 1982. *Administering Foreign-Worker Programs.* Lexington, Mass.: D. C. Heath.

Marty, Laurent. 1982. *Chanter pour survivre.* Lille: Fédération Léo Lagrange.

Marx, Gary T., and James L. Wood. 1975. "Strands of Theory and Research in Collective Behavior." *Annual Review of Sociology* 1:363–428.

Mauco, Georges. 1932. *Les étrangers en France.* Paris: Armand Colin.

Mauroux, J.-B. 1968. *Du bonheur d'être suisse sous Hitler.* Paris: Pauvert.

McAdam, Doug. 1982. *Political Process and the Development of Black Insurgency, 1930–1970.* Chicago: University of Chicago Press.

McCarthy, John D., and Mayer N. Zald. 1977. "Resource Mobilization and Social Movements: A Partial Theory." *American Journal of Sociology* 82:1212–41.

Mehideb, J. 1973. "Usines Renault-Billancourt: Le Tiers monde à l'usine." *Croissance des jeunes nations,* June, pp. 19–26.

Mellouk, Mohamed. 1985. "Histoire du mouvement associatif immigré." *Forum des associations* (CAIF), May, pp. 9–13.

Menghini, Vitaliano. 1982. "Una valutazione errata." *Essere solidali—bulletin,* no. 23 (May):6.

——— 1984a. "Collaborazione con la Missione di La Chaux-de-Fonds." *L'Amico,* no. 155 (May):39.

——— 1984b. "Dal Co.Co.Co." *L'Amico,* no. 155 (May):15.

———— 1988. "Bald passives Wahlrecht im Kanton Neuenburg?" *Piazza,* no. 20 (Sept.):14–15.

"Merhaba." 1985. *Piazza,* no. 8 (Sept.):10.

Messina, Anthony M. 1987. "Postwar Protest Movements in Britain: A Challenge to Parties." *Review of Politics* 49, no. 3 (Summer):410–428.

———— 1990. "Political Impediments to the Resumption of Labour Migration to Western Europe." *West European Politics* 13, no. 1 (Jan.):31–46.

Meyer, Jürg. 1991. "Switzerland: Between Xenophobia and Equity." *Race and Class* 32, no. 3 (Jan. 1):97–103.

Miles, Robert. 1982. *Racism and Migrant Labour.* London: Routledge & Kegan Paul.

Miles, Robert, and Annie Phizacklea. 1977. "Class, Race, Ethnicity and Political Action." *Political Studies* 25 (Dec.):491–507.

———— 1980. *Labour and Racism.* London: Routledge & Kegan Paul.

———— 1984. *White Man's Country.* London: Pluto Press.

Miller, Mark J. 1981. *Foreign Workers in Western Europe: An Emerging Political Force?* New York: Praeger.

———— 1982. "The Political Impact of Foreign Labour." *International Migration Review* 16, no. 1 (Winter):27–60.

———— 1986. "Policy Ad-Hocracy: The Paucity of Coordinated Perspectives and Policies." *Annals* 485 (May):65–75.

Millet, Raymond. 1938. *Trois millions d'étrangers en France. Les indésirables, les bienvenus.* Paris: Librairie de Médicis.

Milza, Olivier. 1985. "La gauche, la crise et l'immigration." *Vingtième siècle* 7 (July–Sept.):127–140.

Milza, Pierre. 1987. *Fascisme français: Passé et présent.* Paris: Flammarion.

Minces, Juliette. 1973. *Les travailleurs étrangers en France.* Paris: Seuil.

Minet, Georges. 1978. "Marginalité ou participation? Migrations et relations professionnelles en Europe." *Revue internationale du travail* 17, no. 1 (Jan.–Feb.).

———— 1984. *La participation des migrants aux associations syndicales, aux activités syndicales et à la vie de l'entreprise.* Strasbourg: Council of Europe/Migrations.

Mitenand-Initiative. 1980. *'Mitenand' Statt Diskriminierung: 1. Kongress der Emigrantenorganisationen.* Flyer, Jan. 12.

Monnier, Laurent, Gérard de Rham, and Sophie Martin, eds. 1976. *Pour une recherche sur l'immigration—bilan d'un séminaire.* Lausanne: Institut de Science Politique, Université de Lausanne.

Montaldo, Jean. 1978. *La France communiste.* Paris: Albin Michel.

Montville, Joseph V. 1990. *Conflict and Peacemaking in Multiethnic Societies.* Lexington, Mass.: D. C. Heath.

Moore, Robert. 1975. *Racism and Black Resistance in Britain.* London: Pluto Press.

Morange, Jean. 1981. "Les étrangers et la liberté d'association." *Hommes et migrations,* no. 1015 (July 1):12–18.

Moreau, Gérard. 1986. "Et l'état?" *FONDA lettre d'information,* no. 37 (Feb.):44–46.

Morin, Edgar. 1975. *L'esprit du temps.* Vol. 2 Paris: Nécrose.

Moulin, J.-P. 1985. *Enquête sur la France multiraciale.* Paris: Calmann-Lévy.

Mouriaux, René. 1982. *La CGT.* Paris: Seuil.

Mouriaux, René, and Catherine Wihtol de Wenden. 1987. "Syndicalisme français et islam." *Revue française de science politique* 37, no. 6 (Dec.):794–819.

"MTA: A quand un syndicat arabe?" 1973. *Frontière,* Oct., pp. 33–34.

Mulette, Brigitte. 1981. "Des Maghrébins parmi nous." *Revue du Nord* 63 (July–Sept.):801–824.

Müller, Edward N. 1979. *Aggressive Political Participation.* Princeton: Princeton University Press.

Müller, Kurt. 1992. "Die 'multikulturelle Gesellschaft'—eine valable Zukunftsvision?" *Neue Zürcher Zeitung,* July 17.

Müller von Blumencron, Mathias. 1991. "Perestroika in Bern." *Wirtschafts Woche* 29 (July 12):38–46.

"Les musulmans de Joxe." 1990. *L'Express,* March 16, p. 12.

Muxiel, Anne. 1988. "Les attitudes socio-politiques des jeunes issus de l'immigration en région parisienne." *Revue française de science politique* 38, no. 6 (Dec.):925–939.

Nicod, Rüçhan. 1983. *Aspects d'une migration: De la Turquie à la Suisse romande.* Diss. Diplôme d'Assistante Sociale, Ecole d'Etudes Sociales et Pédagogiques, Lausanne.

Noiriel, Gérard. 1980. *Longwy, immigrés et prolétaires.* Paris: Presses Universitaires de France.

———— 1988. *Le creuset français.* Paris: Seuil.

"Nouvelle politique de l'immigration: Le logement des isolés." 1977. *Hommes et migrations,* no. 927 (May 15):11–14.

Oberschall, Anthony. 1973. *Social Conflict and Social Movements.* Englewood Cliffs, N.J.: Prentice-Hall.

Offe, Claus. 1985. "New Social Movements: Changing Boundaries of the Political." *Social Research* 52:817–868.

Olmos, Arlette. 1983. *Etude de cas sur les communautés de travail suisses-étrangers.* Strasbourg: Conseil de l'Europe.

Oppliger, Simone. 1980. *Quand nous étions horlogers.* Lausanne: Editions Payot.

Organization of Economic Cooperation and Development. 1981. *Young Foreigners and the World of Work.* Paris.

Osterwald, F. S. 1913. *Description des montagnes (1766).* La Chaux-de-Fonds.

Panorama de la presse. 1991. Paris: ADRI, May 27–June 17.

Papadopoulos, Ioannis. 1988. "The Swiss Election of 1987: A 'Silent Revolution' behind Stability?" *West European Politics* 11, no. 3 (July):146–149.

Park, Robert E. 1925. *The City.* Chicago: University of Chicago Press.

Parra Luna, Francisco. 1978. *La emigración española en Francia.* Madrid: Instituto Español de Emigración.

Parti du Travail. 1974. *De l'émigration des Suisses à la "surpopulation étrangère."* Geneva: Voix Ouvrière.

Passamonte, Mariano. 1984. "Le Comitato Nazionale d'Intesa." *Piazza,* no. 2 (March):7.

Pauchard, Pierre. 1988. "Le droit d'être élu." *L'Hebdo,* Aug. 18, p. 24.

PCF. 1977. *Un nouveau contrat municipal.* Paris.

Pekin, Huseyin. 1979. "Participation of Migrants in the Political Life of Their Country of Origin in the Context of Their Adaptation." *International Migration* 17, no. 1/2:226–229.

Perotti, Antonio. 1988. "Le mouvement associatif immigré face à l'Europe sans frontières." *Presse et immigrés en France,* no. 167–168 (July–Aug.):1–4.

―――― 1991. "Immigration et télévision." *Migrations-société* 3, no. 18 (Nov.–Dec.):39–55.

Perotti, Antonio, and France Thépaut. 1990. "L'affaire du foulard islamique." *Migrations-société* 2, no. 8 (March–April):61–82.

"La perturbation Le Pen." 1984. *L'Express,* Sept. 24–30, pp. 73–81.

Peters, B. Guy, and Martin O. Heisler. 1983. "Scarcity and the Management of Conflict in Multicultural Polities." *International Political Science Review* 4, no. 3 (Sept.):327–344.

Phizacklea, Annie. 1980. *Labour and Racism.* London: Routledge & Kegan Paul.

Piat, Jean. 1981. *Roubaix: Histoire d'une ville socialiste—période 1819–1945.* Roubaix: Ville de Roubaix.

Pichard, Alain. 1978. *La Romandie n'existe pas.* Lausanne: Editions 24 Heures.

Pierrot, Alain. 1985. "L'école française et ses étrangers." *Esprit,* no. 6 (June):143–154.

Pike, David W. 1984. *Jours de gloire, jours de honte.* Paris: Société d'Edition d'Enseignement Supérieur.

Pinero, Maïté. 1983. "Une gerbe pour Toufik." *Huma-dimanche,* Dec. 4, p. 1.

Piñero, Félix. 1982. "El congreso democrático de las asociaciones de emigrantes españoles en Suiza." *Etre solidaires bulletin,* no. 23 (May):6.

Pinto, Diana. 1988. "Immigration: L'ambiguïté de la référence américaine." *Pouvoirs* 47:93–101.

Piore, Michael J. 1979. *Birds of Passage.* London: Cambridge University Press.

Pittau, Franco, and Giuseppe Ulivi. 1986. *L'altra Italia.* Padova: Edizioni Messaggero.

Piven, Frances Fox, and Richard A. Cloward. 1979. *Poor People's Movements: Why They Succeed, How They Fail.* New York: Vintage Books.

Planchais, Jean. 1986. "Le milliard perdu des associations." *Le Monde,* Oct. 25, p. 8.

Plenel, E., and A. Rollat. 1984. *L'effet Le Pen.* Paris: La Découverte.

"Le poids des immigrés." 1984. *Piazza,* no. 4 (Sept.):13.

Poinard, Michel. 1979. *Le retour des travailleurs portugais.* Paris: La Documentation Française.

"Le point en Belgique." 1979. *Hommes et migrations,* no. 980 (Dec. 1).

"La politique sociale en Suisse, 1975–85: Un modèle vulnérable?" 1985. *Revue française des affaires sociales* 39, no. 4 (Oct.–Dec.):1–132.

Polsby, Nelson W. 1963. *Community Power and Political Theory.* New Haven: Yale University Press.

"Presa di posizione della CLI di Ginevra sulla assicurazione per gli stagionali." 1976. *Emigrazione italiana,* March 1, p. 1.

PS. 1977. "La commune et les travailleurs immigrés." *Le poing et la rose.* Paris.

———— 1979. "Spécial immigrés." Special supplement to *Le poing et la rose*, Oct.

PSU. 1983. "Les immigrés dans la cité." *PSU documentation*, no. 154 (Jan.):7.

Puyol Antolín, Rafael. 1979. *Emigración y desigualdades regionales en España*. Madrid: EMESA.

"Qu'attendez-vous de l'Eglise?" 1986. *Communio: Revue catholique internationale* 11, no. 2 (March–April):113–119.

"Radioscopie d'une communauté." 1986. *Actualités de l'émigration de l'AEE*, no. 62 (Nov. 5):6–7.

Rakotoson, Michèle. 1986. "Mars '86: Le vote à la marge." *Baraka* 1 (March 13):8–9.

Ralle, Bianka. 1981. *Modernisierung und Migration am Beispiel der Türkei*. Saarbrücken: Verlag Breitenbach.

"Rappresentatività e partecipazione negli organismi di tutela degli emigrati: Il case del CCIE." 1974. In *Conferenza Nazionale dell'Emigrazione*. Rome, pp. 79–80.

Rath, Jan. 1988. "Political Action of Immigrants in the Netherlands: Class or Ethnicity?" *European Journal of Political Research* 16, no. 6:623–644.

———— 1991. "Minorisering: De Sociale Constuctie van 'Etnische Minderheden.' " Diss. Rijksuniversiteit te Utrecht.

Rath, Jan, and Shamit Saggar. 1987. "Ethnicity as a Political Tool: The British and Dutch Cases." Paper presented at the Conference on Ethnic and Racial Minorities in Advanced Industrial Societies, University of Notre Dame, Ind., Dec. 3–5.

Rebeaud, Laurent. 1978. *La Suisse, une démocratie en panne*. Lausanne: Editions l'Age d'Homme.

Rébérioux, Madeleine. 1986. "Citoyens et prolétaires." *Après-demain*, no. 286 (July–Sept.):4–7.

Reich, Richard. 1991. "Der Geist von Bellinzona und die schweizerischen Identitätsprobleme." *Schweizer Monatshefte* 71, no. 2 (Feb.):83–84.

Reverier, Jean-Loup. 1989. "Islam: La deuxième religion de France." *Le Point*, March 12: 26–27.

Revolutionäre Marxistische Liga. 1974. *Gegen die Fremdenfeindlichen Bewegungen*. Zurich: Veritas Verlag.

Reynaud, J. D. 1971. *Les conflits sociaux en Europe*. Brussels: Verviers, Gérard.

Rex, John. 1979. "Black Militancy and Class Conflict." In Robert Miles and Annie Phizacklea, eds., *Racism and Political Action in Britain*. London: Routledge & Kegan Paul.

Rex, John, and Robert Moore. 1967. *Race, Community, and Conflict: A Study of Sparkbrook*. Oxford: Oxford University Press.

Rex, John, and Sally Tomlinson. 1979. *Colonial Immigrants in a British City: A Class Analysis*. London: Routledge & Kegan Paul.

Richmond, Anthony H. 1988. *Immigration and Ethnic Conflict*. New York: St. Martin's Press.

Riedo, René. 1976. *Das Problem der ausländischen Arbeitskräfte in der schweizerischen Gewerkschaftspolitik*. Bern: Herbert Lang.

Robatel, Nathalie. 1988. "Les élus locaux de la région parisienne et l'immigration." In Nadir Boumaza, ed., *Actes du séminaire: Banlieues, immigration, gestion urbaine.* Grenoble: Université Joseph Fourier–Grenoble I, pp. 427–440.

Rocha Trindade, Maria Beatriz. 1981. *Estudos sobre a emigração portuguesa.* Lisbon: Sá da Costa Editoria.

Rochefort, Madeleine. 1963. "Sardes et Siciliens dans les grands ensembles de charbonnages de Lorraine." *Annales de géographie,* no. 391 (May–June).

Rodrigues, Nelson. 1985. *La ruée vers l'égalité.* Paris: Mélanges.

Rogers, Rosemarie. 1985. *Guests Come to Stay.* Boulder: Westview Press.

——— 1986. "The Transnational Nexus of Migration." *Annals* 485, (May):34–50.

Rokkan, Stein. 1966. "Norway: Numerical Democracy and Corporate Pluralism." In Robert A. Dahl, ed., *Political Opposition in Western Democracies.* New Haven: Yale University Press, pp. 70–115.

——— 1970. *Citizens, Elections, Parties.* Oslo: Universitetsforlaget.

Rokkan, Stein, and Richard L. Merritt. *Comparing Nations.* New Haven: Yale University Press.

Rose, Arnold. 1969. *Migrants in Europe.* Minneapolis: University of Minnesota Press.

Ross, Marc Howard. 1988. "Political Organization and Political Participation." *Comparative Politics* 21, no. 1 (Oct.):73–89.

Rossi, Martino. 1985. "Toujours moins différents, toujours plus incertains." *Piazza,* special supplement.

"Roubaix: Une démonstration sans équivoque." 1987. *CAIF infos,* May, p. 3.

Roux, Michel. 1992. "A propos des évènements de l'été 1991." *Migrations-société* 4, no. 2 (March–April):17–27.

Royce, A. P. 1982. *Ethnic Identity: Strategies of Diversity.* Bloomington: Indiana University Press.

Sabel, Charles. 1982. *Work and Politics.* Cambridge: Cambridge University Press.

Safran, William. 1985. "The Mitterrand Regime and its Policies of Ethnocultural Accommodation." *Comparative Politics* 18, no. 1 (Oct.):41–63.

——— 1986. "Islamization in Western Europe: Political Consequences and Historical Parallels." *Annals* 485 (May):99–112.

——— 1990. "The French and Their National Identity: The Quest for an Elusive Substance?" *French Politics and Society* 8, no. 1 (Winter):56–67.

——— 1991. "State, Nation, National Identity, and Citizenship: France as a Test Case." *International Political Science Review* 12, no. 3:219–238.

Salah, Ali. 1973. *La communauté algérienne dans le département du Nord, 1945–72.* Paris: Université de Lille III.

Sammali, Jacqueline. 1978. *Les enfants des travailleurs immigrés.* La Chaux-de-Fonds: CASS.

Sanchez, Pedro. 1981. "De que ha servido la mitenand." *Juventud obrera,* no. 61 (May):1–2.

Sans Frontière. 1985. *La "Beur" génération.* Paris: Editions Sans Frontière.

Sayad, Abdelmalek. 1979. "Immigration et conventions internationales." *Peuples méditerranéens,* Oct.–Dec., pp. 29–43.

——— 1981. "La naturalisation, ses conditions sociales et sa signification chez les immigrés algériens." *Recherches sur les migrations internationales* (CNRS/ GRECO 13) 3:23–47.

——— 1985. "Exister, c'est exister politiquement." *Presse et immigrés en France*, no. 135 (Nov.):1–11.

Schain, Martin A., 1982. "Local Politics and Immigration Policy in France." Paper presented at the annual meeting of the American Political Science Association, Denver, Sept. 2–5.

——— 1985. *French Communism and Local Power*. New York: St. Martin's Press.

——— 1987. "The National Front in France and the Construction of Political Legitimacy." *West European Politics* 10, no. 2 (April):229–252.

——— 1988. "Immigration and Changes in the French Party System." *European Journal of Political Research* 16, no. 6 (Nov.):597–621.

Schaller, Veronica. 1984. "Die CACEES." *Piazza*, no. 3 (June):8.

Schattschneider, E. E. 1960. *The Semisovereign People*. New York: Holt, Rinehart and Winston.

Schlaepfer, Robert. 1969. *Die Ausländerfrage in der Schweiz vor dem ersten Weltkrieg*. Zurich: Juris Druck und Verlag.

Schlegel, Jean-Louis. 1985a. "Comment parler de l'immigration?" *L'Esprit*, no. 6 (June):82–88.

——— 1985b. "Le Pen dans sa presse." *Projet*, no. 191 (Jan.–Feb.):33–46.

"Schlieren: A votazione 'salviamo la Wagi.' " 1984. *Emigrazione italiana*, May 16, p. 8.

"Schlieren—I corsi di lingua e cultura integrati nelle classi." 1982. *Emigrazione italiana*, June 9, p. 10.

"Schlieren—Sulla casa." 1984. *Emigrazione italiana*, March 28, p. 8.

Schmid, Carol. 1981. *Conflict and Consensus in Switzerland*. Berkeley: University of California Press.

Schmitter Heisler, Barbara. 1980. "Immigrants and Their Associations: Their Role in the Socio-Political Process of Immigrant Worker Integration in West Germany and Switzerland." *International Migration Review* 14, no. 2 (Summer):179–192.

——— 1981. "Trade Unions and Immigration Politics in West Germany and Switzerland." *Politics and Society* 10:317–334.

——— 1983. "Immigrant Minorities in West Germany: Some Theoretical Concerns." *Ethnic and Racial Studies* 6, no. 3 (July):308–319.

——— 1985. "Sending Countries and the Politics of Emigration and Destination." *International Migration Review* 6, no. 3 (Fall):469–484.

——— 1986. "Immigrant Settlement and the Structure of Emergent Immigrant Communities in Western Europe." *Annals* 485 (May):76–86.

——— 1988. "From Conflict to Accommodation." *European Journal of Political Research* 16, no. 6:683–700.

Schnapper, Dominique. 1974. "Centralisme et fédéralisme culturels: les émigrés italiens en France et aux Etats-Unis." *Annales*, Sept.–Oct., pp. 1141–59.

——— 1987–88. "La 'France plurielle'?" *Commentaire* 61 (Winter):220–227.

Schor, Ralph. 1985a. *L'opinion publique en France et les étrangers, 1919–1939*. Paris: Publications de la Sorbonne.

————— 1985b. "Le facteur religieux et l'intégration des étrangers en France, 1919–1939." *Vingtième siècle* no. 7 (July–Sept.):103–115.

Schuck, Peter H., and Rogers M. Smith. 1989. *Citizenship without Consent.* New Haven: Yale University Press.

Schumann, Maurice. 1969. "La politique française d'immigration." *Revue de défense nationale,* June, pp. 933–935.

Schumpeter, J. A. 1954. *Capitalism, Socialism and Democracy.* London: Allen & Unwin.

Schwartz, Michael. 1976. *Radical Protest and Social Structure.* Chicago: University of Chicago Press.

Schwarzenbach, James. 1974. *Die Überfremdung der Schweiz wie ich sie sehe.* Zurich: Verlag der Republikaner A. G.

Schworck, Andreas. 1991. "Helvetias Götterdämmerung." *Neue Gesellschaft/ Frankfurter Hefte* 8:745–750.

Scott, James C. 1985. *Weapons of the Weak.* New Haven: Yale University Press.

Sebbar, Leila. 1991. *Le fou de Shéhérazade.* Paris: Editions Stock.

Segalman, Ralph. 1986. *The Swiss Way of Welfare.* New York: Praeger.

Servet, Michel. 1985. "La politique de la main tendue." *Jeune Afrique,* June 6, p. 40.

Shingles, Richard D. 1987. "Minority Consciousness and Political Action." Paper presented at the Conference on Ethnic and Racial Minorities in Advanced Industrial Societies, University of Notre Dame, Ind., Dec. 3–5.

Sigg, Oswald. 1985. *Les institutions politiques en Suisse.* Zurich: Fondation Pro-Helvetia.

Simon, Patrick. 1992. "Belleville, un quartier d'intégration." *Migrations-société* 4, no. 19 (Jan.–Feb.):45–68.

SONACOTRA. 1978. *"Grève des loyers": Mise au point.* Paris.

————— 1979. *Nous, les gérants racistes.* Paris: Les Editions Cerf.

Sorel, Andrés. 1974. *4° Mundo.* Madrid: Edita ZERO.

SOS-Racisme. 1988. "The Right Man in the Right Place." *Piazza,* no. 20 (Sept.):15.

Sowell, Thomas. 1978. "Ethnicity in a Changing America." *Daedalus* 107, no. 1 (Winter):213–237.

————— 1981. *Ethnic America: A History.* New York: Basic Books.

Soysal, Yasmin. 1994. *Limits of Citizenship.* Chicago: University of Chicago Press.

Spicer, E. H. 1971. "Persistent Cultural Systems." *Science,* Nov. 19, pp. 795–800.

"Statistiques relatives aux associations étrangères." 1981. *Presse et immigrés en France,* no. 20 (Nov.):4.

Statistische Mitteilungen des Kantons Zürich. 1978. *Statistisches Handbuch des Kantons Zürich.* Zurich.

————— 1985. *Siedlungen und Gemeinden des Kantons Zürich.* Zurich.

Steiner, Jürg. 1974. *Amicable Agreement versus Majority Rule.* Chapel Hill: University of North Carolina Press.

Subhi, Toma. 1985. "Musulmans dans l'entreprise." *Esprit,* no. 6 (June):216–221.

Taboada-Leonetti, Isabelle. 1987. *Les immigrés des beaux quartiers*. Paris: Editions CIEMI/L'Harmattan.

Talha, Larbi. 1974. "L'évolution du mouvement migratoire entre le Maghreb et la France." *Maghreb-Machrek* 61:25–27.

Tapinos, Georges. 1975. *L'immigration étrangère en France*. Paris: Presses Universitaires de France.

Tarrow, Sidney. 1977. *Between Center and Periphery*. New Haven: Yale University Press.

——— 1982. *Social Movements: Resource Mobilization and Reform during Cycles of Protest*. Western Societies Program, Occasional Paper No. 15. Ithaca: Center for International Studies, Cornell University.

——— 1989. *Democracy and Disorder*. Oxford: Clarendon Press.

Thépaut, France. 1985. "Antiracisme: Urgence." *Presse et immigrés en France*, no. 128 (Mar.):1–7.

Thévenaz, Jean-Pierre. 1989. "Quelques réflexions critiques." *Piazza*, no. 23 (June):14.

Thomas, Eric-Jean. 1982. *Immigrant Workers in Europe: Their Legal Status*. Paris: UNESCO Press.

Thomas, Eric-Jean, and Catherine Wihtol de Wenden. 1985. "Le chemin difficile du retour." *Le courrier de l'Unesco*, Sept., pp. 33–34.

Thompson, John L. P. 1983. "The Plural Society Approach to Class and Ethnic Political Mobilization." *Ethnic and Racial Studies* 6, no. 2 (April):127–153.

Thürer, Daniel. 1990. "Der politische Status der Ausländer in der Schweiz." *Zeitschrift für Ausländerrecht und Ausländerpolitik*, no. 1 (Jan.):26–36.

Tilly, Charles. 1978. *From Mobilization to Revolution*. Reading, Mass.: Addison-Wesley.

Todd, Emmanuel. 1988. "La carte électorale de Le Pen." *Le Point*, April 11, pp. 28–29.

Tosato, Oscar. 1985. "Les communautés portugaises se manifestent." *Piazza*, no. 9 (Dec.):8.

Toulat, Pierre. 1992. "Les associations d'étrangers, structures de la société française." *Migrations-société* 4, no. 19 (Jan.–Feb.):23–34.

Touraine, Alain. 1990. "Pour une France multiculturelle." *Libération*, Oct. 15, p. 8.

Tschudi, Hans Peter. 1978. "Social Security." In J. Murray Luck et al., *Modern Switzerland*. Palo Alto: Society for the Promotion of Science and Scholarship, pp. 199–212.

Tung, Ko-Chih R. 1981. *Exit-Voice Catastrophes*. Stockholm: Department of Political Science, University of Stockholm.

Turner, Bryan S. 1986. *Citizenship and Capitalism*. London: Allen & Unwin.

Unión General de Trabajadores–Federación Suiza. 1977. "La actividad política de los extranjeros en Suiza." *Boletín informativo*, no. 112 (Oct.):3–9.

Urio, Paolo, and Nedjalka Markov. 1986. "Les administrations cantonales." In Raimund E. Germann and Ernest Weibel, eds., *Handbuch Politisches System der Schweiz*. Vol. 3: *Föderalismus*. Bern: Verlag Paul Haupt, pp. 107–136.

"L'USS et l'obligation absolue de la paix du travail." 1973. *Schweizerische Handelszeitung*, May 17, p. 1.

USS/SGB. 1974. *Rapport concernant la votation sur la troisième initiative contre l'emprise étrangère.* Bern.

Valentin, Claude-Marie. 1983. "L'immigration clandestine en France." *Travail et emploi* 17 (July–Sept.):27–39.

Vaulont, Isabelle. 1977. "Institutions municipales et gestion des contradictions sociales." *Pour,* no. 52/53 (Jan.–Feb.):5–11.

Verba, Sidney. 1967. "Some Dilemmas in Comparative Research." *World Politics* 20 (Oct.):111–127.

Verba, Sidney, Jae-On Kim, and Norman Nie. 1978. *Participation and Political Equality.* Cambridge: Cambridge University Press, pp. 127–164.

Verbunt, Gilles. 1980. *L'intégration par l'autonomie.* Paris: CIEMI.

———— 1982. "Quelle reconnaissance des associations d'immigrés?" *Les droits politiques des immigrés: Compte rendu du colloque des 5 et 6 décembre 1981.* Paris: Etudes, pp. 37–38.

———— 1985a. "France." In Tomas Hammar, ed., *European Immigration Policy: A Comparative Study.* Cambridge: Cambridge University Press.

———— 1985b. "Relations associations immigrées/associations de solidarité." *Forum des associations* (CAIF), May, pp. 23–25.

———— 1985c. "Les immigrés d'aujourd'hui dans la vie locale." *Presse et immigrés en France,* no. 134 (Oct.):6–7.

Vercellino, Enrico. 1971. "I sindicati e gli emigrati." *L'Unità,* Jan. 22.

Vieuguet, André. 1975. *Français et immigrés.* Paris: Editions Sociales.

Ville de Roubaix. 1985. *Constat et réflexions sur l'immigration à Roubaix.*

Vinatier, Jean. 1984. *Les prêtres ouvriers.* Paris: Les Editions Ouvrières.

Vuillomenet, Henri. 1986. "Les mouvements xénophobes en Suisse romande." *Piazza,* no. 11 (June):8.

Walzer, Michael. 1983. *Spheres of Justice.* New York: Basic Books.

Warner, W. Lloyd, and Leo Srole. 1945. *The Social System of American Ethnic Groups.* New Haven: Yale University Press.

Weber, Eugen. 1976. *Peasants into Frenchmen.* Stanford: Stanford University Press.

Weil, Patrick. 1991a. *La France et ses étrangers.* Paris: Editions Calmann-Lévy.

———— 1991b. "Immigration and the Rise of Racism in France: The Contradictions in Mitterrand's Policies." *French Politics and Society* 9, no. 3–4 (Summer–Fall):82–100.

Welch, Susan, and D. T. Studlar. 1985. "The Impact of Race on Political Behaviour in Britain." *British Journal of Political Science* 15, pt. 4 (Oct.):528–539.

Wertenschlag, Rudolf. 1980. *Grundrechte der Ausländer in der Schweiz.* Basel: Universität Basel.

Whelan, Frederick G. 1983. "Prologue: Democratic Theory and the Boundary Problem." In J. Roland Pennock and John W. Chapman, eds., *Liberal Democracy, NOMOS XXV.* New York: New York University Press, pp. 13–47.

Wihtol de Wenden, Catherine. 1977. "La représentation des immigrés en Europe." *Recherches sur les migrations,* no. 5–6:1–23.

———— 1978. *Les immigrés dans la cité.* Paris: La Documentation Française.

———— 1979. "Face à la loi." *Informations sociales,* special issue: 26–37.

———— 1982. "Droits politiques des immigrés." In *Les droits politiques des immi-*

grés: Compte rendu du colloque des 5 et 6 décembre 1981. Paris: Etudes, pp. 53–58.

———— 1984. "The Evolution of French Immigration Policy after May 1981." International Migration 22, no. 3:199–213.

———— 1985. "L'émergence d'une force politique? Les conflits des immigrés musulmans dans l'entreprise." Esprit, no. 6 (June):222–231.

———— 1986a. "Les collectivités locales et le cadre juridique relatif aux immigrés." In Le droit et les immigrés. Vol. 2. Aix-en-Provence: Edisud, pp. 137–157.

———— 1986b. "Les immigrés et la politique: Insertion et participation." Les cahiers de l'orient 3:73–94.

———— 1988. Les immigrés et la politique. Paris: Presses de la Fondation Nationale des Sciences Politiques.

———— 1990. "La naissance d'une 'beurgeoisie.'" Migrations-société 2, no. 8 (March–April):9–16.

Wihtol de Wenden, Catherine, and Claude-Valentin Marie. 1989. "Droits civiques et action politique." Migrations-société 1, no. 1 (Feb.):5–14.

Willard, Claude. 1981. La naissance du Parti Ouvrier Français. Paris: Editions Sociales.

Willi, Victor J. 1977. "Zu einer neuen Ausländerpolitik." In Victor Willi, ed., Denkanstösse zur Ausländerfrage. Zurich: Orell Füssli Verlag, pp. 135–190.

Wilpert, Czarina, ed. 1988. Entering the Working World. Aldershot: Gower.

Windisch, Uli, Jean-Marc Jaeggi, and Gérard de Rham. 1978. Xénophobie? Logique de la pensée populaire? Lausanne: L'Age d'Homme.

Zehraoui, Ahsène. 1985. "De l'objet parle au sujet parlant: Le mouvement social des jeunes d'origine maghrébine." Migrations et méditerranée, no. 31–32 (April–Sept.):97–110.

Zeller, Dieter. 1974. Ausländische Arbeitnehmer. Basel: Z-Verlag.

Zimmermann, Ekkart. 1989. "Political Unrest in Western Europe: Trends and Prospects." West European Politics 12, no. 3 (July):179–196.

Zolberg, Aristide. 1978. "Migration Policies in a World System." In William H. MacNeill and Ruth S. Adams, eds., Human Migration: Patterns and Policies. Bloomington: Indiana University Press, pp. 241–286.

Zuppinger, Urs. 1981. "Nationales Mitenand–Forum Schweizer–Ausländer." Mitenand Bulletin 21 (Oct.):4.

"Die Zürcher Kontaktstelle und die 'Mitenand-Initiative.'" 1980. Bulletin der Zürcher Kontaktstelle für Ausländer und Schweizer 10 (Feb.).

Zysman, John. 1977. Political Strategies for Industrial Order: Market, State, and Industry in France. Berkeley: University of California Press.

Index

Abbas, Cheikh, 71, 143
Abdel Benyahia Justice Committee, 121
Action for Independent and Neutral Switzerland, 193
Action-Research-Culture group, 142
Africa, 39, 49, 69. *See also Beurs;* North Africa
Aide au retour, 49. *See also* Deportation
AIDS, 84, 190, 198
Algeria: immigration of workers to France, 15, 16, 36–38, 51–52, 67, 69, 89, 111–112, 121, 125; worker organizations in France, 65, 130–131; worker strikes, 71–72; Islamic Salvation Front, 95. *See also* Fraternal Association of Algerians in Europe; *Harkis*
Algerian People's Party, 134
Allarde Law, 33
Angola, 111
Anticlericalism, 123
Antifascism, 157
Anti-immigrant sentiment, 65, 68, 269, 270; in France, 78–86, 97, 99, 114, 134–135, 137, 143; in Switzerland, 174, 194, 197, 207–208, 222, 230
Antixenophobic movement, 180, 233
Arab Workers' Movement (MTA), 43, 44
Arab Youth of Lyons and Its Suburbs, 86
Armenia, 32, 33–34, 67, 71
Asia, 193
Association Law (France), 63–64, 113
Association of Algerian Workers in France (ATAF), 65

Association of Emigrant Spanish Workers in Switzerland (ATEES), 177, 179, 180, 184, 194; in Schlieren, 219; in La Chaux-de-Fonds, 232, 234, 236
Association of Parents of Emigrated Spanish Families in France (APFEEF), 66
Association of Portuguese Natives (AOP), 59, 111, 126
Association of Portuguese Workers (ATP), 232, 234, 236
Association of Young Moslems, 142
Association Texture, 142
Auroux, Jean, 72
Auroux Laws, 62
Australia, 5
Austria, 213
Autain, François, 61
Automotive workers, in France, 59, 60, 62, 71–72

Badinter Law, 73
Barre-Bonnet laws, 57
Barth, Fredrik, 8
Baudry, Michel, 137
Bavaria, 213
Belgium, 1, 60, 124, 125, 129, 135, 179
Bérégovoy, Pierre, 95
Berger, Suzanne, 249
Beurs, 77, 80, 82, 85, 86, 88, 97, 143, 185, 260, 261; in political office, 89, 144; protests, 92, 93; culture, 116,